SO-ADH-678

Fernald Library
Colby-Sawyer College
New London, New Hampshire

Presented By

Harold Perkins

THE STORY OF MODERN FRANCE

The Story
of Modern France

1610-1914
FRONTIER OF LIBERTY

By JOHN G. COULTER

Author of *Old France*

THE BOBBS-MERRILL COMPANY
PUBLISHERS
INDIANAPOLIS · NEW YORK

LIBRARY
COLBY-SAWYER COLLEGE
NEW LONDON, N.H. 03257

DC
110
.C6

Copyright, 1939, by The Bobbs-Merrill Company
Printed in the United States of America

2/85

96130

PREFACE

THE history of France is a history of man's resistance to oppression, of his long fight for rightful opportunity. It is a history that touches all of us. It has affected the shape of life in America as well as in Europe. The form of our institutions came from England; the spirit that gave them life, the spirit that has increasingly liberalized them, came from France. We are the beneficiaries of an heroic and sacrificial past in which the liberties we now enjoy were dearly won.

The value of liberty is not easily appreciated by those who have never known its opposite, by those who have never known oppression, by those who do not know how surely their happiness will cease if liberty is lost. Still more difficult to appreciate is the necessity for effort if the rights we now enjoy are to be preserved. Concepts of those rights came to America from France nearly two centuries ago. Based upon those concepts, a new nation of free people came into existence. The contagion of ideas more than the force of arms gave us our liberty, and therewith our opportunity to experiment with that by-product of liberty which is called democracy.

In some respects our democracy has not been successful. It has not made all of our citizens immune to the contagion of ideas that are very different from those which came from France two centuries ago. From other quarters comes the idea that, because of economic distress, we should surrender liberty itself in order to attain greater prosperity, that we should do well to sell our souls in order that we may fatten our bodies.

In certain European countries there has been an abrupt return toward conditions like those from which the French fought to be free, and against which they now prepare to fight again if fight they must. Frightened by the pinch of hunger, the people of two great nations have sold their freedom for a mess of pottage. They have accepted dictatorship, and they have enabled that dictatorship to impose its will upon the tolerance of the free nations. The world has been astounded by the swift successes achieved through threat of war. We did not realize the extent of the sacrifices free nations would make rather than return to the slaughter of women and children. We do not realize how much our own freedom is threatened. Many of us are blind to the fact that civilization cannot continue to exist half slave and half free. It must become one or the other. The ideas that threaten human liberty are more dangerous than the guns. The ties that bind humanity have grown stronger with the years, and ideas move today with the speed of light.

The question whether freedom is still worth fighting for now confronts us. In the conflict between autocratic and democratic states, the question of American duty and interest perplexes us. The facts of French history throw light upon these questions. We may not expect rightly to judge the present situation unless we know something of the past out of which that situation has evolved. The causes of the great dilemma in which the world now finds itself are more than a century old. The critical situation that confronts us is bewildering unless we understand its origins.

The book stops at 1914, when France was on the brink of war. Any adequate account of France from then until now would require another book. It seems impossible as yet to write quite objectively about the war and about developments since the war. Books that have been written indicate that this is true. But let no one believe that the history of the war began in 1914. He who is interested in its fundamental causes will find a record of them here. The effects of those causes have not ceased; they continue to threaten the peace of the world.

Divergence in political and philosophical thought had to do with the appeal to arms. That divergence began to be significant when the all-German parliament at Frankfort failed in 1849; it became paramount after Germany seized Alsace-Lorraine in 1871. Economic ambition appeared to be the cause of the war, but the effort to fulfill that ambition through the use of force had a deeper and more remote raison d'être.

This book has been written by one who is not a professional historian. Its existence is due to the discovery that the formal histories of France are not widely read; the technique of scholarship appears to limit the audience of the scholar. An effort has been made to present accurately the story of modern France in easily readable form. Generalizations are minimized and excursions into the philosophy of history are not made. It is largely left to the reader to draw his own conclusions.

Ten years ago, while resident near Paris, I wrote a book called *Old France*. It was written because friends whom I accompanied on motor tours rarely read beyond the first chapter of books laid on their laps. They appreciated the beauty of the French countryside, and the excellence of the food and the wines, but most of them lacked a basis for sustained enjoyment of the cathedrals, the châteaux, and the castles. I too felt the need to know more about them. So I read about them, and then wrote, quite informally, an account of France that ran from Julius Caesar's conquest of Gaul to the threshold of the Sixteenth Century. The informality of the language appeared to have something to do with the fact that people read the book.

I had hoped to carry the story forward, but there came a period of coolness in American interest in France. I did go forward, however, to 1610, striving to write an account of the momentous Sixteenth Century that might be popular. But, when that was done, I encountered a publisher who asked for a similar account of France from 1610 to 1914. He believes that people are more interested in modern France than in old France. He must be right. The Sixteenth Century will have to wait.

The French are masters of an art which they call *vulgarisation*. It is the art of presenting knowledge in simple language. Because of that art, the French people are superior to others in their knowledge of history and philosophy; that knowledge has served them well in times of crisis. *The Story of Modern France* has been written in imitation of that art, in imitation of the *vulgarisateur* rather than of the scholar. It attempts no contribution to scholarship; its seeks to contribute only to enlargement of that understanding of France which has become essential to an understanding of the world situation. It is a book for those who do not know French history rather than for those who do.

The sources which have been used are largely histories which have been for years subjected to the acid test of use in French schools and colleges. These books, written by eminent scholars, reveal the departure of modern French thought from the dreams of glory that once prevailed. They are realistic and objective. Napoleon has long since ceased to be a hero to the French; in a popular vote for the "greatest Frenchman of all time," held nearly thirty years ago, Napoleon was far down on the list; the name at the head of it was Louis Pasteur; he had done "the most for humanity."

The books that have been used are more critical of France than many written by English and American historians. They offer no excuses to comfort national pride. They examine the record in the spirit of science. They quote German material as well as their own in order to present both sides of a case. Their authors evidently believe that France can be served best by presenting to its youth the facts undraped by prejudice. There is no effort in their books to stimulate emotion, but there is constant effort to make evident the truth that, in the modern world, no nation can be sufficient unto itself, that enduring peace and prosperity can be achieved only by international cooperation, and that national destiny can be fortunate only as it emerges from injustice.

He who yields to sentiment when writing about France may render a disservice. Modern France does not ask for that. To her own youth she seeks to present only facts which are beyond dispute. She has become critical of herself. This is apparent in the official syllabus for history study. For the proportion and organization of the material I am indebted to that syllabus.

France, a pioneer in the long struggle for liberty, is now in the forefront of the struggle to preserve those conditions in which free men may yet justify their freedom. She has lost her power to impose those conditions, but she has not lost her zeal for their defense. France remains a Verdun of human rights.

CONTENTS

ix

LIST OF MAPS

THE STORY OF MODERN FRANCE

A SKETCH OF FOUR CENTURIES

IN the Thirteenth Century France touched the height of her medieval glory. In that century her Gothic cathedrals were built. Louis IX, her saintly king, the hero of all Christendom, dispensed justice as he sat under an oak in the forest of Vincennes. That which was spiritual prevailed over that which was material. Men left all behind to go on perilous crusades to the Holy Land. It was a century of faith in things of the spirit.

Knighthood and chivalry were in flower. Men willingly submitted to a social order in which each served loyally the liege lord who protected him. The pyramidal hierarchy of feudalism led up to the king whose divine authority in temporal matters was as uncontested as that of the Pope in the spiritual realm.

In 1200, under Philip-Augustus, there had been formed a corporation of colleges called the University of Paris. The most famous of this group was the Sorbonne, a theological seminary founded by Robert Sorbon, chaplain of Saint Louis. All instruction was given in Latin. Students thronged to Paris from all quarters of Europe, there to live in Spartan simplicity and to submit themselves to the rigors of an adult curriculum based on the syllogistic method of Aristotle. The most illustrious of the early teachers in Paris was Abelard. His brilliant argumentation and eloquence attracted thousands of scholars. When his liberalism led to banishment, they followed him and, to be near him, slept in the fields.

The records in words of the life of the Thirteenth Century are meager and few, but the records in monuments are many. Miracles wrought with stone and glass reflect the life of those ancient days as no writing does. The churches and cathedrals, with what remains of

17

their rich sculpture and of portrayal in their superbly colored windows, throw more light upon the life of the Middle Ages than all that may be found in the archives. The world still marvels at the beauty of these things, and envies the skill of workmen whose like may not be found today.

A new kind of architecture appeared in the Ile-de-France. Gradually it replaced the Roman style. Stone arches became pointed instead of rounded. This new style was called Gothic, but it had nothing to do with the Goths; they were long since gone; the word was used at first in the sense of outlandish or barbaric.

The massiveness of the Roman style was replaced by an upspringing lightness which reflected the religious thought of the time. The naves of the new cathedrals were like groves of tall and slender trees. Pious thoughts followed the long gray columns heavenward. The beauty and serenity of the places of prayer helped men's souls to gain mastery over their bodies. Thousands labored at the work of building and embellishing the churches and cathedrals without thought of pay.

In 1302, King Philip the Fair, Saint Louis's grandson, summoned representatives of his subjects to an assembly in Notre Dame cathedral in Paris. He was in conflict with the Pope and needed an endorsement by his people of the policy he was pursuing. The assembly was composed of representatives of the nobles, of the clergy, and of the *bourgeoisie*. To this last group the name Third Estate was given; the assembly as a whole was called the States-General. The States-General became an emergency feature of royal government in France. It could meet only at the king's call and it was summoned only in times of crisis. It became an instrument whereby the people were able to resist royal authority, and ultimately to overcome it.

In the period that followed, the fateful pendulum of history swung to the darker side. All the brightness of the Thirteenth Century seemed extinguished in the gloom of many tragic years. The Hundred Years' War with England ran from 1337 to 1453. Civil war accompanied it. The country was ravaged and made desolate by bandit soldiery. There was no authority to control them. Anarchy prevailed.

At last the long-suffering peasants revolted. Jacques Bonhomme, armed only with a scythe or club, rose against the men in mail who had burned his house, tortured his parents, and ravished his wife and sisters. He did not stop to find who might be French and who English. He lost all sense of loyalty save to his own great need. Driven to despair, he fought blindly, like a cornered beast. A hundred thousand peasants marched to avenge their wrongs. Nobles were hunted down, massacred, burned in their castles. A lord was burned alive and his wife and daughter forced to eat his roasted flesh. Such was the *Jacquerie.* But the bare-shanked peasantry could not stand against the armored knights with lances who came to ride them down. The men in mail prevailed again, hunted down Jacques Bonhomme like a wild beast, and drowned the *Jacquerie* in blood.

For more than forty years the crown of France was worn by pathetic King Charles VI who was called the Well-loved. His periodic insanity permitted others to control him. He was induced to outlaw his own son and to sign a treaty which made the King of England his successor. When he died in 1422, Henry VI, then an infant at Windsor, was proclaimed to be King of France as well as of England. Little thought was given to the rightful heir, a timid prince who had fled beyond the Loire, and no thought at all was given to a thirteen-year-old shepherd girl, then tending her flocks on the hills behind Domremy, in Lorraine.

Joan of Arc saved France. The French peasantry believed that she had been sent by God to deliver them. The English believed that she was a sorceress sent by the devil; when finally she fell into their hands, they burned her at the stake, at Rouen, May 30, 1431. But her great work had been accomplished. The Dauphin, whom she had led to his coronation at Reims, ruled until 1461. He was Charles VII, the Well-served. In his reign the devastation of the Hundred Years' War began to be repaired. His son, crafty Louis XI, suppressed rebellious nobles, put France on her feet again, enlarged her territory, and made her frontiers sure. He died in 1483.

The Sixteenth was one of the great transitional centuries in human history. Like the one in which we live, it was marked by new ideas, new discoveries, new standards of living, new desires, and a strong impulse toward a reorganization of society. But the reformers were unable to make their new ideas prevail without fighting for them, and the forces of reaction often won. There was much warfare and senseless slaughter in the Sixteenth Century, but there has been no less in our own. The struggle between those who seek to maintain the existing order and those who seek to change it is no less bitter in our day than it was four hundred years ago.

The Sixteenth Century witnessed the fruition of great achievements previously accomplished. In 1453 the Greeks were driven out of Constantinople by the Turks. About the same time, Gutenberg in Strasbourg began to print books from movable type. In 1479 Aragon and Castille were united under Ferdinand and Isabella. In 1492 Columbus discovered America. There was the Renaissance in Italy. These things had a profound influence upon the century that followed.

The roots of the Renaissance lie in the Fourteenth Century. The Italian scholars, Petrarch and Boccaccio, did pioneer work in unearthing manuscripts of the Latin classics which, neglected and half-decayed, had been long forgotten. They gave the initial impetus to the intellectual awakening that followed. Later, Greek scholars, fleeing from the Turks, found refuge in Italy and brought with them precious records of the ancient culture of Athens.

The Renaissance continued its development in Italy in the Fifteenth Century and attained its full flowering early in the Sixteenth, about the time of the French invasions. The uncultured invaders found in Italy works of art that have never been surpassed. They found a grace and urbanity in living of which they had never dreamed. New and far better possibilities for life were revealed. Delighted with their discoveries, they sought to transplant to their native soil both the spirit and the flesh of the Renaissance.

France, in 1500, was a rude and almost barbarous country to which culture and refinement were yet to come. While Italy had been growing rich and artistic, France had been devastated by the Hundred Years' War. Under Charles VII and Louis XI the physical devastation was repaired, but there was little intellectual progress. The ignorant and superstitious people still believed in witchcraft, hell-fire, the divine right of kings, and the unalterable nature of their fate. They had no opportunity to learn anything different. However, after the death of Louis XI in 1483, France was without invasions or civil wars for nearly a century. The royal authority increased and prosperity with it. The power of the old nobility had been hostile to progress; that power was greatly diminished. More people learned to read.

In the period of the Renaissance there developed a philosophy based on devotion to the welfare of mankind as a whole. It questioned the justification of the existing order. It was called humanism. The Dutch scholar Erasmus was its most illustrious exponent. Passing through Paris in 1500, he published there, in the form of proverbs, a brief summary of humanistic ideas. His little book had a huge success. It revealed ancient truth which made men realize the eternal identity of human nature. It led them to believe that all the Greeks possessed of beauty and serenity was theirs too by right. It sowed broadcast the germs of thought from which the Reformation rose.

Conjure up, if you can, a world without books and try to imagine what the first books meant to hungry minds. In Germany, France, and Italy hundreds of printers worked night and day, making the work of the scholars and philosophers available to all who could read. The authority of a great past came, like a joyous miracle, to justify and to strengthen gropings toward better things that had hitherto been fruitless. Man's conception of the meaning of life was remodeled. His weak faith in his own dignity and right to happiness was strengthened. There was a sudden discovery that accepted ideas and customs were of doubtful validity, a discovery that submissiveness might not be a virtue, discovery that life, if lived without greed or intolerance, may bring beauty and joy within the reach of all. Mankind, having now been in possession of this discovery for more than four hundred years, appears to have profited by it in the Twentieth Century little more than in the Sixteenth.

Men began to think as they had not thought before. There were new things to think about. Mental horizons were lightening and brightening, and few could see the threat of storm. Ideas spread as spring spreads and broke the winter of men's minds. Who could believe that to talk of beauty would lead to bloodshed, or that a new conception of man's dignity might lead to death?

The philosophy of humanism contradicted the principles upon which the social order of its time was based. It asserted the right of the individual to challenge and to examine before acceptance. The Church and the State acknowledged no such right; according to their philosophy the individual should submit to established authority without challenge or examination. The feudal system had broken down with respect to its outward forms, but the relationships of the individual to Church and State had been modified little if at all. Serfdom had ceased. Men were no longer bound body and soul to serve lords and masters, but that did not mean that they were free. They were not free to do anything that ran counter to the will of their king or to the authority of the Church. Since humanism ran counter to both of these, its devotees were headed for disaster.

For centuries Church and State had had a common policy of subordinating the individual to the group, the citizen to the city, the city to its suzerain, the workman to his guild, the guild to the commune, the churchman to his parish, the parish to the bishop, the monk to the rule of his order, and the teacher to the rule of his school. Individual rights were practically nonexistent. In medieval society the individual was compelled to be submissive to the regime that had been established "for the glory of God and the good of his children." This was the ancient collectivism.

The Renaissance made a conflict between individualism and collectivism inevitable, a conflict in which individualism was largely victorious. In our time the pendulum appears to be swinging back again; individualism now is on the defensive against a new kind of collectivism.

Crafty King Louis XI, who reigned from 1461 to 1483, left France in excellent condition. His son, Charles VIII, 1483 to 1498, did less well. His expedition into Italy was physically disastrous, but it brought new ideas back to France.

Charles, whose children died before their father, was succeeded by his cousin, Louis of Orléans. He reigned as Louis XII from 1498 to 1515 and married Anne of Brittany, his predecessor's widow. His expeditions to Italy were no more fortunate than Charles's. Twenty-one year old François of Angoulême married Louis's daughter and succeeded him.

The reign of robust and vainglorious François I, 1515 to 1547, was marked by campaigns in Italy, by the coming of the Renaissance to France, by the building of many beautiful châteaux, by the beginning of the Reformation, by the development of court life in which fair women played leading roles, and by the capture in Italy of King François by soldiers of his great rival, Emperor Charles V, head of the House of Hapsburg. Charles, through marriage, inheritance, and election as Emperor of the Holy Roman Empire, had become the ruler of most of western Europe outside of France. King François spent nearly a year (1525) in Madrid as Charles's prisoner. The famous meeting between François and King Henry VIII of England on the Field of the Cloth of Gold occurred in June, 1520.

In 1517 Luther, at Wittenberg in Germany, began his attack on the Church that led to the Reformation. In 1541 John Calvin, a Frenchman, became head of the Protestants at Geneva; from there he directed the development of Protestantism in France which led to the religious wars. His followers in France were called Huguenots.

King François's son, Henri II, reigned from 1547 to 1559. He was better endowed physically than mentally. His wife, Catherine de Medici, and his mistress, Diane de Poitiers, are both more famous than he. In his reign the persecution of the Huguenots began. He was killed in a tourney by an accidental lance thrust.

The next three kings were all sons of Henri II; François II, 1559-1560; Charles IX, 1560-1574; Henri III, 1574-1589. In this period the Queen-Mother, Catherine de Medici, was the dominant figure. She belonged to a very wealthy family of Florence; three of her relatives became popes; other members of this illustrious family were rulers of Florence; Lorenzo the Magnificent was the best known.

François II, to whom sixteen-year-old Mary of Scotland had been married the year before his father died, was only fifteen when he became king. The Guises of Lorraine were his wife's uncles; during his brief reign they took charge of the government. They sought to exterminate the Huguenots. Executions at Amboise made them hated.

With the death of her first-born, the historic career of Catherine de Medici began. Throughout the troubled reign of her son Charles, she sought by devious ways to preserve peace in a country that was torn by the civil wars of religion. She favored in turn the Huguenots led by Condé and Coligny and the Catholics led by the Guises. She finally became convinced that the Huguenots had to be suppressed. The Massacre of Saint Bartholomew occurred on August 24, 1572.

Henri III, the last of the Valois dynasty which had reigned since 1328, was king from 1574 to 1589. He took life lightly. Henri de Guise, head of the Catholic League, held him in contempt and planned to succeed him. The King was compelled to flee from Paris to Blois. There, in December, 1588, he had Henri de Guise assassinated. The Catholics were furious over the death of their powerful leader; their League was in control of most of France. Henri III was compelled to turn for aid to his Protestant brother-in-law, vigorous and fearless Henri de Béarn, who had married Marguerite de Valois.

The two Henris marched on Paris. Charles de Guise, Duke of Mayenne, had succeeded his brother as leader of the League. Paris prepared to resist the entrance of the King. On August 2, 1589, Henri III was assassinated at Saint Cloud by Jacques Clément, a monk.

Henri de Béarn (Henry of Navarre) was the legal successor to the throne, but, since he was a Protestant, Catholic France would not accept him as king. He was compelled to win his kingdom a town at a time. For nearly five years, at the head of a motley army, he fought the forces of the League and Spanish forces that helped them. He won brilliant victories at Arques and at Ivry, but it remained evident that France could have peace only if her "vagabond king" became a Catholic; if he did not, Catholic Spain might place her candidate upon the throne. In July, 1593, Henri, for the sake of his country, became a Catholic. In February, 1594, he was crowned at Chartres as Henri IV. In the following month Paris opened its gates to him and he entered into possession of his kingdom.

Sully, Baron of Rosny, the King's right-hand man, remained a Huguenot. He took charge of the finances, and, by rigid economies and strict administration, brought order out of chaos. The great problem was to bring about peace between the Catholics and the Huguenots. The King was tactful and generous in treatment of his former enemies. After he had made sure of Catholic support, he sought to appease the Huguenots who had turned against him.

In April, 1598, the Edict of Nantes was issued. This historic document assured safety, civil equality, and liberty of worship to the Protestants; it changed the traditional relationship of the State to the Catholic Church; it broke the fetters of religious intolerance; it was the act of a very humane king who was also a practical politician.

In 1600, having obtained a divorce from Marguerite de Valois, the King married Marie de Medici of Florence. There were important financial and political reasons for this marriage.

King Henri encountered constant opposition. He became depressed. In 1610 he planned a campaign against Spain. On the fourteenth of May, when all was ready for departure, he went to see Sully who was ill. On his way, when his carriage was stopped in a crowded street, he was fatally stabbed by a religious fanatic.

Chapter One

CHAPTER ONE

FROM HENRI IV TO RICHELIEU

FRANCE FELL INTO STRANGE HANDS. THE LAWYERS BECAME MORE
INFLUENTIAL. SULLY RESIGNED. CONDÉ AND CONCINI COMPETED FOR
CONTROL. HIS CONTROL OF AN ECCENTRIC WOMAN GAVE CONCINI THE
UPPER HAND UNTIL LITTLE LOUIS XIII HAD HIM MURDERED. LUYNES, THE
NEW FAVORITE, FORTUNATELY DIED. THEN CAME RICHELIEU.

MID-MAY, 1610. For twelve years France had had peace within her
borders. A wise and tolerant king had done much to repair the devastation and confusion that thirty years of civil war had wrought. His
son and heir was nine years old. Suddenly the hand of an assassin
threw all into confusion again. Henri IV was stabbed to death by
Ravaillac, May 14, 1610.

When they brought the news to Sully, the King's great minister,
"God have compassion on us and on the state," he cried. "France
will fall into strange hands." Sully knew well whereof he spoke.

The Queen, Marie de Medici, was fat, indolent and selfish. It was inescapable that she should be regent during the minority of her son.
She knew nothing of statecraft and those who had most influence
with her were interested primarily in their personal fortunes. All that
King Henri and Sully had labored for years to accomplish was placed
at the mercy of an unintelligent woman and her greedy friends.

The territory of France was about four-fifths of what it is today.
The difference lay to the north and east. There uncertain and unnatural frontiers were a constant threat to peace. Lille, Arras, and Maubeuge were possessed by Spain. Nancy and Strasbourg belonged to the
German empire. Franche-Comté with Besançon was Spanish. Savoy
and Nice were outside the kingdom. A new feeling of nationalism
had grown in King Henri's reign, and, with it, an awareness that

26

France could not be secure from invasion until her frontiers lay on the Alps, the Pyrenees, and the Rhine—the limits of ancient Gaul.

There were about sixteen million people in France, and about four hundred thousand in Paris. France was the most populous state in Europe and the richest. Her production was far in excess of that of neighboring states; the balance of trade was steadily in her favor. Her governmental organization, both civil and military, was, for those days, in excellent condition. A Venetian ambassador reported that "France could be conquered only by the French." It was there that danger lay.

Monarchy was the only form of government that could be successful. The people had neither confidence nor interest in any other form. A wise and courageous king was all that was needed, a king who could control the elements that were a danger to the state and permit her people to work in peace. But no such king was there. There was instead a regrettable regent who knew how to preserve peace only by paying for it.

Three elements were certain to make difficulty for the royal authority unless that authority was held in firm hands. These elements were the Protestants, the high court of law called the *Parlement,* and the few nobles rich and influential enough to raise armies of their own.

The old feudal nobility had become less influential than the new nobility, the *noblesse de robe,* that large class of hereditary magistrates and other officeholders, bourgeois in origin, that, since King François's day, had bought its way into rank and power. By 1610 the *gens de robe* had become very important. They had risen from the people and they had opposed increases in taxation. No wonder they were popular. They had both money and official positions.

It had taken all the courage of a Henri IV to compel the magistrates who composed the *Parlement* of Paris to register edicts of which they disapproved. The "first president" of the *Parlement* stood at the apex of his caste; by virtue of his office he preceded even the princes of the blood. The costumes and manners of the *gens de robe* added to their impressiveness. The members of the *Parlement,* the *conseillers,* wore long red robes and impressive beards, preferably white. They were very dignified. They created the popular impression that they were a sort of Supreme Court whose function it was to protect the ancient rights and privileges of the people. They had the right to pass legal judgment on royal decrees, but no right to annul them. Their influence, nonetheless, was something to be reckoned with. They could quickly rally all Paris to their support. The Queen-Mother recognized the importance of *Parlement* by soliciting its endorsement of her regency.

Marie de Medici was not interested in governing the state, but she was interested in governing the treasury. She knew about the reserve that Sully had built up for war expenses. She wished to make peace with Spain and then to spend that money as she saw fit.

Sully, growling watchdog of the treasure that Marie coveted, was loved by no one after King Henri was dead. In January, 1611, he saw that it was time for him to go. If he waited longer, still greater misfortune might befall him. No sooner had the watchdog left than the Queen-Mother laid heavy hands upon the millions that had been stored under triple locks in the Bastille. Marie had found that only through liberal gifts and pensions could she maintain a semblance of respect for her authority. The principal flouter of her authority was the Prince de Condé, head of a collateral branch of the House of Bourbon and "first Prince of the Blood." His support of the government had to be liberally paid for. Marie was afraid of him.

Sully's retirement added to the discontent of the Huguenots. They no longer had an influential representative at court. They were also disturbed by the Queen's policy of reconciliation with Catholic Spain. In a General Assembly at Saumur they made demands that were inacceptable to the government and declined to obey a royal order to disperse. The Queen, alarmed, bribed the Duke of Bouillon, one of their leaders. When that double-dealer had persuaded his co-religionists to adjourn, Marie made public the treaty she had signed with Spain, a treaty that involved the marriage a few years later of Louis XIII, then ten, with Anne of Austria, granddaughter of Philip II, and also the marriage of Louis's younger sister Elizabeth with Philip IV, King of Spain after 1621. The Spanish policy of Henri IV was thus reversed.

A strange Italian woman controlled the Queen. To Leonora Galigaï, daughter of her nurse, *sa sœur de lait,* Marie had been devoted since

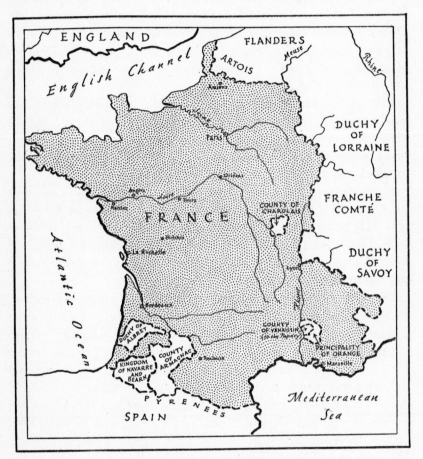

A sketch of the limits of France in 1610.

childhood. Leonora was a swarthy, skinny little woman with a nervous disease. King Henri took a strong dislike to her the moment he saw her. It was easier, however, for Henri to be indulgent than it was for him to be faithful. Marie was allowed to keep her abnormally beloved Leonora. Some other Florentines who had followed the Queen to France were also allowed to hang around the Court. One of them, Concino Concini, a handsome devil, conceived the idea of seducing the Queen's jittery *femme de chambre,* and then marrying her. It was a smart trick.

Leonora was a mild maniac. She was subject to hallucinations. She would not leave her tiny apartment for fear of the "evil eye," but she held the Queen of France in her power. It was a preposterous situation made possible only by the feeling that to change it might make for worse. But it could not endure.

Concini's control of Leonora was no less than Leonora's control of the Queen. He had a way of brandishing a dagger under his wife's nose. He became the Marquis d'Ancre, marshal of France although he had never been near a battle, the governor of Roye, Péronne, and Montdidier, and the Queen's chief counselor. The government drifted steadily toward crisis.

Condé would not stay bought. This peculiar prince was brutal, rapacious, and smelly. Even in those days when baths were rare, he was notably *crasseux.* He formed a coalition of the *grands* to restrain the power of the regent. The *grands* were certain princes, certain royal bastards, and some noble provincial governors whose personal following was reminiscent of feudal days; the civil wars had permitted them to achieve semi-independence in their domains. This group was in no sense representative of the nation; it constituted a danger only because the King lacked in years and the regent lacked in courage. The argument of the *grands* was always that they were acting in the best interest of king and country. As a matter of fact they were out for loot.

In 1614, Condé, who had been chief beneficiary of Queen Marie's looting of the treasury, issued a manifesto against the extravagances of the government! With Bouillon, Mayenne, and the Duke of Vendôme, King Henri's favorite natural child, he took possession of Mézières and threatened war. Marie could think of nothing better to do than to buy off these noble rebels. Condé got 450,000 *livres* and the others accordingly. By that time the treasure stored in the Bastille was nearly exhausted.

In October of that same year the States-General met in Paris; this was the last time they met until 1789. The *grands* had flattered themselves that the deputies would favor them, but it turned out otherwise. Little as they liked the ascendancy of Concini, the majority of the deputies like the Condé group even less. It was not, however, a truly representative assembly. It was dominated by the *gens de robe.*

The nation had not forgotten its bitter lesson of the civil wars. It remembered that the tragedy of those years was associated with the weakening of royal authority, and that the restoration of that authority had given twelve years of peace. Despite the preposterous greed of Concini and the timidity of the Regent, there was no disposition on the part of the States to weaken the government that Henri IV had left. It was a sorry heritage, but preferable, the deputies believed, to any increase in the power of Condé.

The States-General failed to agree about any reforms, but some notable speeches were made. These speeches brought into the open the issues that were troubling men's minds, and made it evident that there were men of the *bourgeoisie* whose understanding of the needs of the country was far in advance of that of the nobles. The leaders of the Third Estate proved their superiority in intelligence and in patriotism. They believed that absolute monarchy was legitimate, not because of divine right, but because it was necessary for peace and order. They were not blind to its shortcomings, but they knew that, conditions being what they were, any other form of government might be worse.

Robert Miron, representing the merchants of Paris, gave fair and fearless warning. "If royal government fails in justice," he said, "despair will inform the people that a soldier is merely a peasant who bears arms, and when the vine-dresser has assumed the musket, that which is today the anvil will become the hammer." Prophetic words!

The nobles of the old order demanded the abolition of the *Paulette,* the system whereby, through annual payments, governmental offices had become hereditary. This would have struck a vital blow at the

power of the bourgeois *gens de robe*. The Third Estate countered with
the suggestion that, since the Condé group criticized the extravagance
of the government, it might be reasonable to reduce the pensions paid
to the nobles. These pensions, these bribes for loyalty, amounted to
more than five million *livres* per annum; they had been doubled since
King Henri died. To this proposal the only answer the nobles could
find was to say that they had been insulted.

On another issue the clergy was involved. The Third Estate proposed a measure that would eliminate interference by the Church in
the temporal affairs of France; the legislation of the Council of Trent
was to be declared ineffective on French territory. The clergy, wiser
than the nobility, did not declare itself insulted. Instead of arguing,
they poured oil on the troubled waters. They persuaded a majority
of the deputies that the end they sought was already effectively attained and that it would be better not to bring this issue into the open
again. One of the most effective talkers for the clergy was a young
bishop named Armand Du Plessis de Richelieu.

The States continued to meet until February 24, 1615. On that day
the hall in which they met was locked on the pretext that it was needed
for a ballet. The deputies had had their say, and they were not yet in
a mood to adjourn to a tennis court as they did in 1789. They peacefully dispersed.

The Third Estate had voted certain reforms that the Court ignored.
This gave Condé excuse for another rebellion. He took up arms again,
again in the role of the friend of the people! It was, the Queen
thought, a very inconvenient time for a rebellion. The Court was due
to go to the Spanish frontier, there to meet Boy-King Louis's bride,
blonde Anne of Austria, who had already started from Madrid. The
Princess Elizabeth was to be handed over to the envoys of the King
of Spain. Louis and Anne were married at Bordeaux, November 28,
1615. They were both fifteen.

In his second rebellion Condé had the co-operation of some of the
Protestants of the south who were alarmed by the increasing intimacy
of their government with that of Spain, their ancient and unforgiven
enemy. When the Court moved on its southern journey, a royal army
was required to protect it from Condé and the Huguenots. Resolute

action might have quickly suppressed this second irresolute rebellion, but a timid Queen and her timid counselors preferred again to purchase peace. This time it cost more than twice as much as before. The friend of the people and his fellow racketeers were paid six million *livres* for signing the Treaty of Loudun, May, 1616.

The *grands* declared that they had had only the best interests of the country at heart. They called attention to a provision in the treaty that limited the power of the Church, and to another that deprived hated Concini of the government of Amiens. They said nothing, however, about the secret clauses that gave them six million *livres*.

Condé, "defender of the people," more arrogant than ever, returned to Paris where he was acclaimed by the fickle populace. His brief popularity was chiefly due to the great unpopularity of Concini, whose irreconcilable enemy Condé had declared himself to be. But, of these two magnificent grafters, it would be difficult to say which was worse.

At this time, 1616, Queen Marie had managed to rid herself of the last of the bewhiskered old counselors whom she had inherited from her husband. They went the way of Sully and were replaced by four others. Of these others it was believed that they would be less interested than their predecessors in interfering with the many profitable rackets that Concini was operating; that crafty Italian was amassing a colossal fortune at the expense of France. One of the new counselors was the young Bishop of Luçon, M. de Richelieu.

Co-operation between Concini and Condé was impossible. One or, preferably, both of them would have to be suppressed. Condé's momentary popularity turned his head. He imagined himself to be more powerful than anybody else; his palace in Paris was called the "new Louvre"; those who had favors to ask of the government went to him first; the government did not dare to oppose him openly. But Concini, frequently half-choking her, still controlled Leonora, and Leonora still controlled the Regent Marie. In September, 1616, an order was issued for Condé's arrest. The Prince, who imagined himself to be nearly King of France, suddenly found himself a prisoner in the Bastille. His mother, escorted by a group of gentlemen riders, tried to arouse the Parisians to an attack on Concini. They went clattering through the streets, the venerable Princess crying out from

96130

LIBRARY
COLBY-SAWYER COLLEGE
NEW LONDON, N.H. 03257

her carriage, "To arms, you men of Paris! The *Maréchal* has killed the Prince!" The men of Paris received this news without emotion. All they did was to pillage Concini's palace. The cause of the Prince left them cold.

Concini lost some valuable furniture, but he remained more powerful than ever. He had an army at his bidding and plenty of *livres* wherewith to pay his soldiers. There was only one who might successfully move against him—an eccentric boy of sixteen who was still busy with his playthings. Him Concini held in contempt.

King Henri's children, legitimates and illegitimates together, had been brought up "pell-mell" at the château of Saint Germain. Of the legitimates there were five: Louis, nine years old when his father died, Elizabeth eight, Christine four, Gaston two, and Henriette-Marie one. Elizabeth, as we have seen, married Philip IV of Spain, Christine married the Duke of Savoy, and Henriette-Marie, in 1625, married Charles I of England. Gaston, Duke of Orléans, his mother's favorite, a bastard in behavior if not by birth, was a disgrace to his family as long as he lived.

At sixteen Louis seemed to be no more mature than when his father died. Nothing had been done to mature him. His mother treated him as though he were an imbecile. His favorite sport was to play soldier; he liked to hitch little cannon to his dogs and to beat a drum. He was allowed to play all day. He was not interested in his wife. There was no idea that he would ever be capable of taking charge of the government. The gentlemen of the Court paid no attention to him for fear of giving offense to Concini. The Boy-King led an abnormal life. His only close companion was a poor but handsome gentleman of Provençe, a M. de Luynes, whose principal occupation was the training of birds. He trained the King's falcons and took him hunting.

But Louis was not such a fool as his mother and Concini thought him to be. He bitterly resented his treatment by the arrogant *Maréchal* and hated that foreigner's control of the Queen-Mother. Luynes, a timid gentleman, advised the King to escape from the Louvre and join the Condé group, but Louis was less timid than his falcon trainer. He decided to order Concini's arrest. The Marquis de Vitry, a fearless soldier, was captain of the palace guards. There was no love lost between him and the Italian upstart. When the King told Vitry to arrest Concini, that soldier asked but one question: "What shall I do, Sire, if the *Maréchal* resists?" The King did not reply, but another said, "Kill." The King remained silent. "Sire," replied Vitry, "I shall execute your order."

On the morning of April 24, 1617, Concini, then at the height of his power, entered the Court of the Louvre. Reading a letter and carrying a bouquet, he was followed by a group of courtiers. Vitry pushed his way through the crowd and stopped the *Maréchal* with the words, *"De par le Roi, je vous arrête."* Concini, utterly astounded, dropped his flowers and seized his sword. That was the end. He was shot down where he stood, and no one raised a hand against those who killed him. The curtain had fallen with a crash; a seven-year farce was ended. A new one was about to begin.

The Boy-King had found a new and more exciting game. And he had found his tongue. He witnessed the assassination. He scrambled onto a billiard table and there, flushed and loquacious, received the felicitations of those who, to give them, strode over the corpse of him who had been their master the day before. Louis sent word to his mother to pack up and get ready to go to Blois. He would now run the kingdom and he had no need of her. All this was a tremendous shock to large and indolent Marie.

The Parisians, delighted with the turn of events, took possession of the distinguished corpse and dragged it through the streets. Leonora Galigaï was tried and unjustly condemned to death. Vitry became *Maréchal*. The only catch was that Luynes became a new and less intelligent Concini. But at least he was French. It was soon said, "The tavern is the same. Only the sign has been changed."

There had been seven years of too much Concini. Now there were to be five years of too much Luynes. The Boy-King had good stuff in him, but he had not been prepared for kingship. He was too young and too inexperienced to be able to refuse anything to the amiable gentleman who had been the one devoted friend and confidant of his boyhood. The influence that Luynes had upon Louis was, for some

years, almost as great as that of Leonora upon Marie. Nearly all that
Concini had of positions and emoluments Louis gladly gave to
Luynes and his relatives.

The King recalled the old counselors of his father whom his mother
had dismissed. Although he heaped great honors upon Luynes, in
matters of state it was the advice of the *barbons* (graybeards) that
was respected. In matters of state Luynes had no advice to give that
was worthy of attention. Once when he put forward his views, Louis
said to him, "Keep still; you don't know what you are talking about."

The Council believed that Queen Marie had gone too far in favor
of Spain. To counterbalance the two Franco-Spanish royal weddings,
it was decided that the Princess Christine should marry the son and
heir of Charles Emmanuel, Duke of Savoy. Mother Marie was not
even invited to attend the wedding.

The ex-Regent, confined at Blois, showed more energy in her confinement than she had displayed when free in the Louvre. She was
determined not to give up without a struggle. One of those who
strengthened her determination to struggle was the Bishop of Luçon.
He too had lost his place at court and was determined to get it back.
He wrote to her. He even came in disguise to see her.

On a dark night some who thought it to their interest to do so eased
heavy Marie out of a high window in the château of Blois. She was
escorted to Angoulême. There she had the protection and support of
the governor, old Epernon, favorite of Henri III. Since Epernon,
general of infantry, controlled the major strength of the army, the
situation was delicate. The Council decided to make concessions.
Richelieu, who could control Marie, was authorized to negotiate an
agreement. The Queen-Mother was given the government of the
province of Anjou, and certain other considerations. She installed
herself at Angers.

Marie, and others who could use her as means for their own advancement, were not willing to accept the new arrangement as final.
Plots were hatched at Angers. Some of the dissatisfied *grands* agreed
to co-operate with Epernon, ostensibly in the cause of Marie, and the
dissatisfied Protestants showed inclination to join with them in rebellion. The Council favored making new concessions, but young Louis
showed a flash of his father's courage and resolution. He said that he

would march *tout droit* against the rebels. He did so, and the rebels, encountered near Angers, dispersed without a fight.

Flushed with that success, Louis, then nineteen, went on to Béarn where the Protestants had not permitted the reopening of Catholic churches as ordered by royal edict. The King reopened them, and the Protestants became more dissatisfied than ever. In May, 1621, they held a General Assembly at La Rochelle in defiance of royal orders. There they made what was in effect a declaration of independence; they proposed to organize an ecclesiastical republic within the confines of the kingdom. In view of the act of *lèse majesté* (high treason), the King led an army into Huguenot territory. He captured many cities without difficulty. Finally the army besieged Montauban, one of the Protestant strongholds. The others were Montpellier and La Rochelle.

Louis made the mistake of giving the command to Luynes. That hunter and bird-trainer had never fought against men. He was timid as a soldier and ridiculous as a general. The siege of Montauban was unsuccessful. After three months of loss and failure, the royal troops, at the approach of winter, withdrew. The King became very cool to his favorite. Luynes was in a fair way to be disgraced when, in December, 1621, he died.

King Louis, then twenty, decided to act on his own. Against the advice of all his counselors except Condé, who had been released from the Bastille after Concini's death, he led his army south again and won some minor victories. But Montpellier, like Montauban, proved too tough a nut to crack. In October, 1622, a new treaty was signed with the Protestants. They retained the rights granted by the Edict of Nantes. Condé, who had opposed the making of this treaty, went to sulk in Italy.

The loss of Condé's support made it the more advisable to make peace with the Queen-Mother, whose astute adviser Richelieu continued to be. One condition of the reconciliation was that the Bishop of Luçon should become a cardinal. In 1622 he received from Rome the scarlet hat he had long coveted. At this time Louis hated the influence of Richelieu upon his mother nearly as much as he had hated the previous influence of Concini.

Marie, admitted to the Council, was the mouthpiece of Richelieu, and, though the King was extremely loathe to admit it, it became obvious that the Cardinal's ideas were far better than those of the actual counselors. Under their vacillating guidance, foreign relations went from bad to worse. The Cardinal was the first to realize that he was indispensable. When the chairmanship of a secondary council was offered to him, he declined it. Louis, fortunately, was man enough to overcome his prejudice in the interest of the state. In April of 1624, at Compiègne, he presented his new counselor, Monsieur le Cardinal de Richelieu. Four months later, through sheer force of ability reluctantly recognized, the Cardinal, whom no one loved, became prime minister. For the first time since the death of King Henri, the government of France was in wise and capable hands. The losses of fourteen years were to be regained.

CHAPTER TWO

THE RECORD OF RICHELIEU

AN IRREPRESSIBLE YOUNG MAN BECAME FRANCE'S GREATEST DIPLOMAT.
HE SOLVED THE PROBLEM OF THE HUGUENOTS AND MADE FRANCE THE
STRONGEST STATE IN EUROPE, BUT NEARLY EVERYBODY HATED HIM. THE
FAVORITE SPORT AT COURT WAS TO PLAN TO KILL THE CARDINAL.

ARMAND-JEAN DU PLESSIS DE RICHELIEU, born in Paris in 1585, was the third son of a gentleman of Poitou and of Suzanne de la Porte, daughter of an influential lawyer of the *Parlement*. It was planned for him to become a soldier, but when one of his older brothers resigned the bishopric of Luçon in Vendée, Armand had to become a priest in order to keep that poor bishopric in the family. At the Sorbonne he made a record of excellence in theological studies. He became a bishop when only twenty. The influence of his lawyer-grandfather was helpful. Bishops, according to the rules of the Council of Trent, had to be at least twenty-five, but Luçon was the dirtiest and most disagreeable bishopric in all France. There were no rival candidates for it.

The precocious new bishop was one of those rare young men whom nothing can restrain. He planned to make his sojourn in his dirty diocese as brief as possible; his ambition, his self-confidence, his ability, his suavity, his tenacity, and his amazing capacity for work made a combination that could not be denied. He was alert for every chance. He thought he might win a place at court when King Henri died. He went to Paris and pulled every string he could, but nothing came of it at that time. That was his only failure.

Undaunted, ambitious Armand went back to the country, and, by letters and by speeches, he so effectively advertised his ability that he was chosen to be a delegate to the States-General of 1614. There he was a successful spokesman for the clergy. That, and some discreet wire-pulling, led to the foothold at court that he coveted; he was appointed chaplain to the Boy-King's bride, young Anne of Austria. Adroitly he courted the favor of Concini and of Leonora. He became a member of the royal council. Five months later Concini was killed, and the irrepressible young bishop had to return for a time to rural life. But not for long. We have seen that, through clever insinuation, he made his way back to a place of power. It was Marie de Medici, the banished Queen-Mother, who at this time served the purposes of his ambition.

One of Richelieu's first acts after he came to power was to accomplish, in 1625, the marriage of Henriette-Marie, King Louis's youngest sister, with Charles I of England, whose reign began in that year. That was a first achievement in the new minister's long record of success in foreign relations, but there was a domestic difficulty to be overcome before he could act effectively outside the frontiers of France. That difficulty was the Huguenots.

Richelieu, whose religion was the good of the state as he saw it, never let his Catholicism interfere with his statecraft. The Thirty Years' War in Germany had begun in 1618. In 1624 it looked as though Catholic Austria might exterminate her Protestants and renew her old threat to France. Richelieu delayed that threat by aiding both Dutch and German Protestants. Catholic Spain, linked to Austria, retaliated by giving financial aid to the Protestant rebels of France. It became obvious that France could have but small effect upon the House of Hapsburg until she put her own house in order.

It required two years of cautious preparation and of temporary concessions before Richelieu felt strong enough to fight the Huguenots to a finish. Then he moved directly against La Rochelle, their chief city. By that time Charles of England, despite his French bride, had decided to support the Huguenots against his brother-in-law's government. He sent a fleet of ninety ships to aid them; the handsome and incapable Buckingham was in command.

The English installed themselves on the *Ile de Ré,* just off the port of La Rochelle. Richelieu, able general and engineer as well as cardinal and minister, directed the French operations. He compelled Buckingham's badly organized forces to withdraw, and then blockaded La Rochelle from the sea by constructing a dike more than a mile long. He left nothing to chance. The English tried twice again to come to the aid of La Rochelle, but Richelieu's engineering was too much for them. They never got past the dike.

The Huguenot defense was heroic. It continued for fifteen months and came to an end in 1628 only when starvation was at hand. The siege of La Rochelle was a very expensive business for the government, but it was worth all it cost. It made France a united kingdom. The Huguenot "state within the state" came to an end. Richelieu, like Henri IV, treated his conquered compatriots with fairness. He made no discriminations against them, employing them freely in governmental positions. The Edict of Nantes was modified by the Edict of Alais, 1629, only with respect to those clauses that had permitted successful military resistance of the government. The fortifications of La Rochelle were razed, but no change was made in Huguenot freedom of worship or in their civil rights. Richelieu had proved his right to rule.

In the fourteen years between his success at La Rochelle and his death in 1642 Richelieu made a record in statecraft that no one has surpassed. His ambition for personal advancement, once realized, evolved into a still more passionate ambition to fulfill his dream for France. That was not a dream of democracy; he had no confidence in the ability of the people to rule. He believed that he served France best in seeking to remove all threat, both at home and abroad, to the authority of her monarchy. This great task he successfully accomplished. He laid the foundation for the supremacy of France and for the absolute authority of her kings for a hundred and fifty years. It was he who made the "glory" of those years possible.

Like Henri IV, Richelieu realized that peace and security could be obtained for France only by attainment of her natural frontiers, those of ancient Gaul. He knew, however, that those frontiers would never be attained if Spain and Austria could prevent it. Within the "natural" domain of France there lay important territory and rich cities that the Emperor Charles V, when he retired in 1556, had divided between the Spanish and the Austrian branches of his family, the powerful Hapsburgs. His son Philip had then become

King of Spain, and his brother the German Emperor as Ferdinand I.
The early phases of the Thirty Years' War (1618-1648) had greatly
increased the power of Emperor Ferdinand II, grandson of Ferdinand I. Spain, having never recovered from her disastrous war
with England, was less dangerous than Austria, but no less hostile
to the fulfillment of Richelieu's designs. King Philip IV, a great-
grandson of Charles V, had married Elizabeth of France, and King
Louis had married King Philip's sister, but all this intermarrying
would not lessen resistance to readjustment of the French frontiers
at the expense of Spain. Richelieu foresaw that need might presently arise for swift and effective military action. So, even though
tremendously occupied with affairs that were more immediately
urgent, he gave unremitting attention to army organization. He
prepared to move without delay in more than one direction when
the time became ripe.

Richelieu had a sort of feline grace. He was delicate in health,
dignified in bearing, and restrained in gesture. The long red robe,
the pale and finely-cut features, the air of a cool intelligence that
could not be deceived—the impression of authority that the combination of these things made was irresistible. To this true prince of
Church and State even those who hated him felt impelled to bow in
deep respect.

The "terrible Cardinal" had every mental talent except the talent
for making himself popular. He craved popularity, but he never could
attain it; he was the most hated man of his time. Anne of Austria,
the King's wife, Gaston his brother, Marie his mother, and many
others of influence and high position made desperate attempts to
bring about the Cardinal's downfall. Only constant vigilance and
rare intelligence permitted him to continue to serve France. Despite
persistent ill health, "the ambition of the Cardinal was served by a
sublime energy." He had no weakness and he had no pity. He did
the work of an entire cabinet, four ministers in one.

Political plots became the fashion. The great sport at court was
to cook up new schemes to destroy the man who made that court
possible. Most active among the plotters was Queen Anne's closest

friend, Madame de Chevreuse, of whom Dumas in his *Three Musketeers* has made a dubious heroine. At seventeen this incorrigible mischief-maker, then Marie de Rohan, had married the King's favorite, Luynes the bird-trainer. She was notoriously unfaithful to that handsome fathead. When he died she married the Duke of Chevreuse, of whom the King was very fond. Louis, for good cause, banished her from the Court, but her second marriage brought her back again. She then got herself an English lord for a lover and, the King being very inadequate in that capacity, she undertook to get another English lord as lover for neglected Anne.

Magnificent Buckingham came to court as an ambassador of England. It appealed to him to play the part that Madame de Chevreuse suggested. Once he was discovered on his knees at the Queen's bedside. All this made the King cooler than ever to his Spanish bride. There was no divorce, but the birth of Louis XIV in 1638 was the result of duty done rather than of love fulfilled.

Madame de Chevreuse had another fantastic idea—to have Richelieu stabbed, the King suppressed, his whistling and pirouetting brother Gaston crowned, and Anne then to marry Gaston, whose life had been as full of amorous escapades as Louis's had been empty. An amazing thing was the number of prominent people who gave ear to this mad scheme. The two Vendôme bastards of Henri IV were in it, Condé was in the background, and the Duke of Savoy had agreed to help. It was 1626. Richelieu was busy with preparations to move against La Rochelle and up to his ears in complicated foreign negotiations. Nonetheless, he got wind of the plot. He told the King of it and offered his resignation. Louis's instant response was, "Whoever attacks you, attacks me." The Vendôme illegitimates were confined in jail where one of them died, a young noble named Chalais who had been bewitched by Madame de Chevreuse was beheaded, and Gaston got off by telling on everybody and then signing an apology and a promise to plot no more. The Chevreuse witch fled to Lorraine.

In 1627 the Cardinal again proved to the nobility that he had no fear of them. He was determined to put a stop to dueling. That insensate business had become a mania. It had put dishonor upon honor by using it for an alibi for what were often cold-blooded assassinations. In eighteen years, more than four thousand had been killed.

An edict was issued that forbade dueling under pain of death. To show their contempt for it, two counts fought in broad daylight in the middle of the *Place Royal,* now *Place de la Concorde.* Richelieu showed neither pity nor hesitation. He had both of the contemptuous counts beheaded. Dueling became a little less popular, and many idle nobles wondered what else they could use for excitement.

Marie de Medici became bitter against Richelieu because in serving the state he ceased to serve her personal interests. The King fell ill and thought he was going to die. Marie took advantage of that. She extorted from her son on what he thought to be his deathbed a promise to dismiss the Cardinal. On November 10, 1630, the King, then convalescent, went to visit his mother at her new Luxembourg palace; there, in these days, the Senate meets. Marie thought the time had come to make Louis fulfill his promise. She staged an hysterical scene, demanding that he "choose between his mother and a valet." The situation was extremely distressful for Louis. The discussion became bitter. Suddenly Richelieu appeared. Marie had forgotten to lock the door. The interview became more hysterical than ever. Marie screamed and Richelieu wept. He asked for his dismissal, which the King appeared to grant. Louis, sick of the whole business, ordered his carriage and left for the little "hunting château" that he had built at Versailles. Marie made the mistake of not going with him, but others went, and on the long ride to Versailles they made it clear to the King that it would be a grave mistake to dismiss his prime minister.

News of Richelieu's alleged dismissal spread like wildfire. On that evening Marie's palace was thronged with those who came to congratulate her, and Richelieu, in his new *Palais Cardinal,* now the *Palais Royal,* sat alone in a great empty room. For once he felt defeated. He prepared to go. And then one caller was announced. Saint Simon, father of the famous historian of the reign of Louis XIV, was one of those who had hastened to tell the King what a mistake he was making. He advised the Cardinal to go at once to Versailles. The Cardinal did so. The King, having reflected, spent half the night talking things over with his guest. While they were still celebrating his downfall at the Luxembourg, Richelieu was restored to power. That day became famous as the Day of the Dupes.

Some of the dupes, revealed in their true colors, paid dearly for their quick disloyalty. Mother Marie, who refused to be reconciled, was directed to reside at Compiègne. From there she fled to Brussels and never returned. Richelieu gladly let her flee. She died at Cologne in 1642. Brother Gaston also left France. He went to the court of the Duke of Lorraine, whose wealthy sister, Mlle. de Montpensier, he had married. The Duke was friendly to Austria. At his court at Nancy a new plot was hatched.

This new conspiracy, in which Gaston was a leading spirit, was a serious business because Henri II de Montmorency, the governor of Languedoc, was involved in it. He was a grandson of old Anne de Montmorency, who had been all-powerful in the reigns of François I and Henry II. For centuries the noble Montmorencies had stood next to the princes of the blood.

Giddy Gaston entered Languedoc at the head of a band of fortune-seekers. He joined the forces that Montmorency had raised in the dissatisfied south; the south resented Richelieu's establishment of royal control of their affairs. In September, 1632, the rebels encountered an army that Richelieu had sent to Castelnaudary, near Carcassonne. "At the first onslaught the Duke of Orléans fled, throwing his arms on the ground and saying that he would play no more." (Duruy) That was the sort of hero Prince Gaston was. Since the Duke of Lorraine was a party to this conspiracy, *Lorraine was occupied by France*.

All the nobility petitioned that Montmorency be pardoned, but he was not. He was beheaded. That was the harsh discipline the situation called for and Richelieu was the man to impose it. It took vision and it took courage. Gaston merited the same fate, but there was too strong a tradition against shedding the blood royal. That tradition had its advantages, but they are hardly perceptible in a case like Gaston's. He was allowed to join his mother in Brussels and to continue his efforts to destroy Richelieu and to overturn the government. He was finally pardoned again, but banished to Blois. There his effeminate face still ornaments the façade of the château that he built. Fortunately he died when he had destroyed only a part of the more beautiful one built by François I.

In 1636, at a time when Spanish troops had occupied Corbie and were threatening Paris, the Comte de Soissons, one of the Condé family, turned traitor. He assembled a force of Richelieu-haters near Sedan, and Spain sent seven thousand men to help him in an effort to revive civil war. Fortunately the traitor count was killed before his war became serious. Gaston, true to form, was a party to this new fiasco. One of its features was an elaborate plan to assassinate Richelieu. All that saved him was that Gaston lost his nerve. He was to give the signal to the assassin at the moment that Richelieu emerged from a war council held at Amiens but, when, imposing in his majestic robes, the Cardinal emerged, Gaston did not give the signal. Terror-stricken, he fled and his fellow plotters could not stop him. That was one plot of which the Cardinal was unaware, but he was aware that his life never ceased to be in danger.

Some years later a charming young marquis named Cinq-Mars became the King's closest companion. His social success went to this young man's head. He believed that, if only hated Richelieu could be put out of the way, he might become a second and a better Luynes. He, with Gaston's backing, solicited Spanish aid in a new attempt to destroy the man who was saving France. He did all he could to poison the King's mind against the Cardinal and believed that he had succeeded in doing so; he believed that the King was secretly sympathetic with the plan that was afoot. Queen Anne was, but the King was getting fed up with the overambitious young marquis.

Cinq-Mars, Prince Gaston, and the Duke of Bouillon signed a secret agreement with Spain. One of Richelieu's clever agents secured a copy of it. The Cardinal forwarded the copy to the King. Both King and Cardinal were ill. Louis had himself carried to his minister's bedside. There he wept and humbly apologized for having failed to make clear to all that he appreciated the great services of Richelieu to France, and that he would loyally support him. Richelieu also wept. Pure drama! This pitiless servant of the state proved on more than one occasion that he could shed tears when tears served his purpose, but histrionic show of emotion never deflected his mind from its fixed purpose. The royal and the ministerial tears did not keep those who shed them from agreeing that Cinq-Mars and his loyal friend De Thou should be beheaded. Again it became a pity that Gaston had to be spared. Cinq-Mars and De Thou, whose only fault was that he had not betrayed his friend, met death bravely together. That was in September, 1642.

The somber background of Richelieu's greatest achievements was the terrible Thirty Years' War, which came near to making Austria and Spain stronger than before and France weaker. This would have happened except for Richelieu's superb diplomacy and his swift intervention by arms when the chance came to make intervention effective. Richelieu did not live to see the war ended by the Treaty of Westphalia in 1648, but his wise precautions made it fairly easy for Mazarin, his able successor, to complete his work. The Treaty of Westphalia opened a long era in which France was preponderant in Europe.

Beginning as a civil war in Germany, the Thirty Years' War became a general European conflict. Denmark was drawn into it in 1625, Sweden in 1630, and France in 1635, all with the purpose of arresting the menacing progress of Austria. The figures of Luther and Calvin loom in the background. The Peace of Augsburg, 1555, had been, like the later Edict of Nantes, an effort to end the religious difficulties. It granted rights to the Lutherans, but it ignored the Calvinists. Calvinism later made great progress in western Germany, but the Lutherans were nearly as hostile to the Calvinists as they were to the Catholics. Meanwhile the Jesuits, those indefatigable agents of the Counter-Reformation, made Catholicism stronger and more intolerant than ever in Bavaria and in other parts of Germany. Politico-religious leagues were formed and armed forces organized to defend their interests. Peace could not continue.

Ferdinand II, devoted to the ideals of the Jesuits, was elected emperor in 1619. He was no less ardent in his Catholicism than his cousin, Philip II of Spain, whose reign ended in 1621. He believed that Protestantism and rebellion were the same thing; to him it seemed indispensable to re-establish uniformity of religion. His policies pushed his Protestant subjects into open rebellion. More than the religious question became involved. In Bohemia, Protestant nobles inflamed the antagonism of the Czechs for the Germans.

A few months before Ferdinand became emperor, a picturesque incident occurred at Prague, Ferdinand being then King of Bohemia and Prague his capital. On the twenty-third of May, 1618, a group of his unpopular officials were in conference at the palace in a great high-windowed room. Some Protestant gentlemen rushed in and broke up the conference. They called Ferdinand's officials "Jesuit dogs" and other hard names. Those who were particularly hated were pitched heels over head out of the high windows. They took a sixty-foot drop into a muddy moat, but were not killed. This "Defenestration of Prague" was the historic prelude to one of the world's worst wars. The Czechs, a few days before Ferdinand was elected emperor, declared him unseated as King of Bohemia. To succeed him they chose the Palatinate elector, Frederick V, chief of the Protestant League. That made war certain.

When the fighting began, Catholic Bavaria, whose King was Maximilian, had the only well-organized army. It was commanded by Count Tilly, a redoubtable and extremely hard-boiled soldier of fortune whose record as a beer-drinker has never been surpassed. Mansfeld was the most important of the various Protestant commanders. Utter ruthlessness was the order of the day. Soldiers were recruited by giving peasants and villagers their choice between a musket and a rope; if they did not shoulder the musket they were left hanging at the end of the rope. Many were hanged. An amazing Czech noble named Wallenstein became the Emperor's general. He was very able, very cruel, and very ambitious. It was a terrific war in which noncombatants suffered more than the soldiers. Wherever the armies passed, they left desolation, ruin, and torture in their wake. Attila and his Huns could have done no worse.

Tilly's Bavarian army defeated the Czechs near Prague in 1620. King Frederick barely escaped with his life. More than a million Czechs were murdered; this people practically disappeared from history for nearly three centuries. Tilly invaded and mastered the Palatinate. Emperor Ferdinand, in violation of the sacrosanct stipulations of the Golden Bull, declared Catholic Maximilian of Bavaria successor to all the rights and possessions of Protestant Frederick. The Lutherans and the Calvinists, finding themselves in equal peril, made common cause against the Emperor. A Protestant prince, Christian IV of Denmark, came to the aid of his co-religionists, but Christian was defeated by Tilly and Mansfeld by Wallenstein. After these victories, Wallenstein and the Emperor planned to make a unified monarchy out of the loosely federated Empire, with a kingdom on the western side of it for the Emperor's ambitious general.

Richelieu saw that it was high time for him to take a hand in the game. He negotiated with all the powers to whose interest it might be to oppose the fufillment of Ferdinand's and Wallenstein's ambitions. He found a magnificent ally in Protestant Gustavus Adolphus of Sweden. In July of 1630 Gustavus led into Germany a splendidly disciplined army trained in new and very effective tactics.

In August of that same year the Imperial Diet met at Ratisbon. Ferdinand counted on securing the co-operation of his ally, Maximilian of Bavaria, and of other Catholic princes, against the Swedish invader. But Richelieu had sent to Ratisbon his most able agent, a Capuchin monk, Father Joseph, the famous *"Eminence grise."* Father Joseph persuaded the Catholic princes that the ambitions of Ferdinand and of Wallenstein were a greater danger to them than the Swedish invasion. The princes declined to co-operate with Ferdinand unless he dismissed Wallenstein and reduced his army. Wallenstein was dismissed and command of the reduced army passed to Tilly. Tilly sacked Magdeburg, a rich Protestant city. That aroused the Protestant princes to active co-operation with Gustavus Adolphus, who, his army reinforced by German troops, crushingly defeated Tilly at Breitenfeld, near Leipzig, in September, 1631. In the following spring Gustavus became master of Bavaria, Tilly having been defeated and mortally wounded in the battle of Lech. The Protestant army occupied Munich. The way to Vienna lay open. To defend his threatened capital, Emperor Ferdinand hastily recalled Wallenstein, who had raised a new army, sixty thousand strong. After two months of masterly maneuvers, Gustavus and Wallenstein fought at Lützen, November 16, 1632. Gustavus won the battle, but lost his life. He was only thirty-eight. His death saved the Emperor. The successes of the Protestant army ceased when its great leader fell. Then Wallenstein became a menace; his ambition was vast and his loyalty was dubious; in 1634 Ferdinand had him assassinated.

Richelieu, having by that time put his own house in order, took a more active part in the urgent business of holding down the Hapsburgs. He had five armies at frontier points and he had made useful alliances. In 1635 he declared war on Spain, Austria's strongest ally. The Spaniards made a quick invasion of France and came to Corbie, near Amiens. Their outriders came even to Pontoise. There was a great flight from Paris and much cursing of Richelieu. But the Cardinal, Father Joseph, and the admirable old Maréchal de la Force succeeded in turning the Parisian panic into a passion to fight the Spaniards. The King, at the head of a quickly assembled army of forty-five thousand, marched against the invaders and they withdrew.

In 1639 Richelieu bought off the German army that occupied Alsace, and so *France gained Alsace.* In 1640 Arras was won from Spain, and in 1642 Roussillon with Perpignan. Lorraine had been occupied in 1632. France was moving rapidly toward the goal of her natural frontiers.

In 1637 Ferdinand II was succeeded by his son as Ferdinand III. The new Emperor agreed to the opening of negotiations looking to a general peace. When Richelieu died in 1642 peace seemed near, but it was only a lull. In the years that immediately followed there were new French victories by new and brilliant generals, but it was Richelieu's spade work that had made those victories possible.

In the year of his death Richelieu went to the south to supervise the operations in Roussillon against Spain; he was determined to carry the frontier to the Pyrenees. When the Cinq-Mars conspiracy was unmasked he lay ill at Narbonne. It was at Tarascon, on his way home, that he and the King, both sick men, determined the fate of the conspirators. The Cardinal was carried in his bed aboard a barge that made the slow journey up the Rhône from Tarascon to

Lyon. His bed was wide and high and hung all round with light-purple draperies. Close beside it one of his secretaries was always installed at a small writing table. At Lyon the minister in his bed and the secretary at his table were placed together on a great draped litter. Twenty-four stalwart guards, their wide-brimmed hats held respectfully in their hands, carried the Cardinal and his bedroom along the road to Paris. Where they stopped at night, breaches were made in the walls of houses so that His Eminence might be moved in without disturbance.

Richelieu knew that he had but little time to live, but until the very last he gave all his energy to affairs of state. On the first of December he concerned himself with an important Declaration, and on the next day "entered into agony." He asked forgiveness for all his enemies, of whom he said he had had none except those who were enemies of the state. He met death bravely on the fourth of December, 1642. He was fifty-seven. His magnificent tomb is in the chapel of the Sorbonne, which was one of the few educational institutions he befriended.

CHAPTER THREE

MAZARIN, THE GREAT CONDÉ, AND THE FIRST FRONDE

LOUIS XIII HAD HIS GOOD POINTS. A SNOW STORM HELPED HIM TO DO HIS DUTY. A HANDSOME ITALIAN REPLACED RICHELIEU. EAGLE-BEAKED ENGHIEN DEFEATED THE SPANIARDS AND THE PARLEMENT ATTEMPTED TO REFORM THE KINGDOM.

FRANCE reaped more benefits from Richelieu's statesmanship after his death than during his life. Cold and calculating, he was more concerned with making the future secure than with making the present enjoyable. He made the present extremely disagreeable for many people. He had the political aims of Henri IV, but nothing of Henri's social vision and understanding. His sole objective was to strengthen and to expand the royal government. He believed that absolutism in government was best for France. He believed that the more submissive the people were the better off they would be. He was troubled by no thought of political rights for the low-born. Very few of the low-born were, in his time, politically-minded.

The Cardinal was not interested in justice for the sake of justice. He disregarded it when he wished to eliminate those who were obstructive of his policies. Nor was he interested in improvement of the common life save as that life might be improved through obedience to a strong government. Judged by modern ideals of democracy, Richelieu was wrong. Judged by the ideals and the conditions of his time, he was right. The century that followed his death justified his accomplishments.

The great minister was a prolific writer. Some of his writings indicate the harsh certainty of his beliefs. "If the people lived too much at ease it would be impossible to keep them within the bounds of their duty; if freed from taxation they would aspire to be released from obedience; like mules, they would be more spoiled by rest than by hard work. . . . It is absolutely needful to suppress the growth of such [democratic] ideas since otherwise France will never be that which she ought to be, but will become a monstrous body without substance or durability." He suppressed most of the colleges, "In order to prevent the mania of the poor for educating their children which distracts them from the pursuit of trade and war."

The nobles hated Richelieu because he deprived them of many of their perquisites and privileges, and ruthlessly suppressed all who interfered with the carrying forward of his plans. The people hated him because of the heavy taxes that were necessary in order to fulfill his policy of pushing forward to the natural frontiers. Tax collectors were murdered in Guyenne and in Normandy, and the peasant revolts that followed were brutally suppressed.

Richelieu believed in paying for the future out of the present. But no one else did. Then, as today, there was lack of constructive imagination. Planners for a better future may still count on unpopularity if their plans diminish present profits. They may even count on the murderous hatred that Richelieu knew.

The terrible Cardinal ordered the dismantling of all feudal castles that might serve to aid rebellious nobles. He created new officials called *intendants* who were sent into the provinces as direct representatives of the government. The *intendants* assumed charge of all civil administration, leaving to the noble governors only a shadow of their former power—their military rank.

After the siege of La Rochelle a navy was developed. During the latter part of the Thirty Years' War, France dominated the Atlantic and the Mediterranean. Seven armies were maintained on different fronts and heavy subsidies were paid to the Dutch, to Gustavus Adolphus, to the Duke of Savoy, and to various German princes. This expensive business made for much discontent among the taxpayers, but it made France stronger and more secure than she had been before; had it not been undertaken and skillfully brought to successful conclusion, she would have found herself at the mercy of Spain and Austria.

History has been unfair to Louis XIII. He has been presented as a nincompoop; a handicap rather than a help to Richelieu. Socially

he was a failure and in politics he was overshadowed by his great
minister, but there could have been no Richelieu had not the King
possessed courage, imagination, and a strong sense of duty. He
maintained in power one whom he admired but never liked, one
whom his family, his friends, and all the nobles detested, one against
whose government the people revolted. That took courage. Louis
was willing to let his reign be marked by discontent so that future
reigns might be more fortunate. That took unselfishness and clear
vision. Fortunately for France, Louis was not an immediatist. It
is recorded that "he always preferred his duty to his personal
convenience."

The King dressed drably when all the Court wore bright colors
and gilded fringes. He danced badly when everybody else danced
well. He was shocked by the loose behavior of the Court that his
father had tolerated. He was prudish. He was very thin, he had a
big nose, his mouth was always half-open, and he was ill at ease
with the fair sex. No true son of his gallant father! He neglected
his wife and his "mistresses" were merely his platonic friends.

Louis insisted upon being thoroughly informed by Richelieu
about all new plans. The Cardinal prepared admirable documents,
setting forth both the advantages and the disadvantages of whatever
he proposed. To these the King gave careful attention. He sometimes overruled his minister, especially in military matters, about
which he was well informed. Richelieu once said that "the few square
feet of the King's cabinet are more difficult to win than all the
battlefields of Europe."

Louis's coolness toward his wife became mental as well as
physical. It was increased by the unfortunate influence that Madame
de Chevreuse had upon her. There was very slight conception of
patriotic duty in those days, and Anne had as little of it as anyone.
She seemed to believe that she was doing no wrong in aiding Chevreuse in that devilish woman's constant plotting. Chevreuse, who
had only to look at a man to make a fool of him, was said to possess
lovers in all the important courts in Europe. Even Richelieu tried
to make love to her. After her flight from Paris to Lorraine and
other places, she made headquarters at Tours, and for years carried
on a secret correspondence with Queen Anne. Her colossal objective

was to unite the Empire, Savoy, Lorraine, and Spain against France, and especially against Richelieu. Anne helped by sending all the useful information she could to her brother, the Cardinal-Infant (Crown Prince) of Spain. One of her letters to Chevreuse was intercepted. There was a harrowing scene. Anne tearfully apologized both to Richelieu and to her husband, and was formally forgiven, but Louis did not forget. He put a strict censorship on Anne's correspondence and saw as little of her as he could. Others involved in this business went to the Bastille.

Richelieu, well aware of Chevreuse's influence in foreign courts, and hoping to turn it to advantage, had tried to win that dangerous lady's favor, but his friendliness did not appeal to her. In September, 1637, disguised as a cavalier, she fled across France and took refuge in Spain.

There was the serious question of an heir to the throne. Louis had been married for twenty years without offspring. What a calamity if Brother Gaston should succeed him! Louis had this matter on his conscience, but he was not amorous—least of all was he amorous of Queen Anne. Fate seemed to take a hand. On a December afternoon of 1637 the King was driven in from his little château at Versailles to visit Mademoiselle de La Fayette, one of his platonic mistresses, who lived in a convent and was about to take the veil. Louis was much taken with this young lady's simplicity and good behavior. At dusk such a heavy snow storm raged that return to Versailles was out of the question. There was nothing to do but to take refuge in the Louvre, where Anne was living. But the King's bed had been taken to Versailles. The only one fit for him left at the Louvre was Anne's. Louis, resigned to fate, decided that the time had come to do his duty. Louis XIV was born September 5, 1638. His brother, Philippe d'Orléans, was born in 1640.

Despite constant ill health, the King often rode with his armies. He delighted to fraternize with his soldiers. He was at the siege of La Rochelle, and he led expeditions into Lorraine and into Italy. He must have had something of his father's remarkable vitality. It is recorded that, on account of persistent intestinal trouble, forty-seven bleedings, two hundred and twelve purges, and two hundred and fifteen enemas were given to him in one year of his youth. He had to suffer this sort of medical treatment all his life.

The King lived only a few months after Richelieu died. He directed the Cardinal's subordinates to make no change in policy; the Council was composed of four ministers of whom Mazarin, Richelieu's chief lieutenant, was one. The only difference was that some undesirable gentlemen who had been exiled or imprisoned made their appearance again at court. Richelieu never would have permitted that.

At Saint Germain, where his heir was born, Louis XIII died, May 14, 1643. He was forty-two. His successor, who was to reign for seventy-two years, was then only five.

The reign of Louis XIII after the death of Luynes and the minority of Louis XIV are of one historic piece; together they constitute that formative and victorious period that Richelieu inaugurated and that Mazarin continued.

Giulio Mazarin was a strikingly handsome Italian whose lively eye, quick wit, keen intelligence, and wavy chestnut hair made his social success certain. He was a model student in a Jesuit college in Rome, but less so at the University of Alcalá in Spain. There his gambling debts nearly necessitated his marriage to a prosperous lawyer's daughter. Escaping that fate, he became an officer in the Pope's army, and then a minor member of the diplomatic staff of the Vatican. His great chance came in 1630. French and Spanish forces were about to renew hostilities in one of their frequent encounters on Italian soil when Mazarin, then twenty-eight, dashed across the battle front. He waved a document that the Pope had signed and cried out, *"La paix! La paix!"* Since he had done much to persuade the Pope to sign this treaty, and since it was favorable to France, Richelieu, who was there, took a great liking to this young man. He solicited his appointment as the Pope's representative in France and, in 1641, secured a cardinal's hat for him. Mazarin had then become Richelieu's chief assistant.

One of the last acts of Louis XIII was to issue a Declaration that subordinated Anne, as regent, to the Council of which Mazarin was a member. One of the first acts of Anne, as a widow, was to induce *Parlement,* acting under the theoretical order of her son, aged five, to invalidate that Declaration and to invest her with full powers. The infant King sat on a pile of five embroidered cushions during this solemn procedure, and the Chancellor declared that "the King, sitting on his bed of justice, declares". . . etc. Due form and etiquette were observed and it is not recorded that anyone laughed out loud.

One might have thought that the first counselor Anne would dismiss would be the chief lieutenant of the man whom she had so much hated. But not at all. Three days after *Parlement* had broken the late King's will, Regent Anne named Mazarin her prime minister. The wavy chestnut locks may have had something to do with that selection. Lonely Anne was falling in love with her new minister, and that turned out to be well for France.

Dirty old Henri de Condé, first Prince of the Blood, whom Concini imprisoned and whom Richelieu required to take a bath before coming to see the King, had a son named Louis. This Louis de Condé, then Duke of Enghien, was twenty-two when Louis XIII died. Like his father, he was negligent about his toilet, and he was ferociously ugly. He had the face of a bird of prey. But what a soldier! He was to become "the Great Condé," of whom even the King was jealous.

In the winter before he died, Louis XIII was occupied with plans to march in the spring against Spanish forces that, encouraged by Richelieu's death, were preparing to invade Champagne from Flanders. When he realized that it would be impossible for him to lead his army in person, he appointed Enghien, his cousin, to command in his place.

Spain opened its campaign of 1643 by besieging Rocroi, a frontier town in the hilly and heavily wooded Ardennes. On May 17 Enghien and his army reached the edge of the dense woods and swamps that had to be traversed to reach Rocroi. A dusty courier came galloping into camp with news that the King had died three days before. That made for hesitation. The King was dead and his orders died with him. In a council of war, all the old-timers were for awaiting new orders; they were opposed to a direct attack. The

famous Spanish battalions were held in great respect; they still
enjoyed a reputation for invincibility. But eagle-beaked young Enghien, eager for glory, commanded battle. Refusing a helmet, he
rode into action under a wide-brimmed hat adorned with white
plumes. He wished to be another Henry of Navarre.

The battle of Rocroi, for those who like battles, was magnificent.
Enghien led the right wing. His center and his left gave way. He
did not hesitate. Risking everything, he led his cavalry on a dash
around and behind the Spanish lines. He fell upon them from the
rear. It was a brilliant, dare-devilish maneuver that should have
failed, but it succeeded. The proud *tercios,* taken unawares, were
compelled to yield. The battle, begun at three in the morning, ended
at ten. Nearly eight thousand of the enemy lay dead and all their
cannon were captured.

Enghien continued his victorious campaign until September. He
hastened then to Paris and insisted upon liberal payment for his
services. A true Condé!

Another great captain for France, less greedy and vainglorious,
appeared at this time. The Vicomte de Turenne, who had shown his
worth in Italy, was appointed *maréchal* and sent to command the
forces on the Rhine. Enghien was soon to become Prince de Condé
because of the death of his father. Turenne, ten years older than the
new Condé, was a heavy man who rode badly and spoke poorly,
but he was a thinker. He was as prudent as Condé was impetuous,
and he steadily improved. He became the most skillful tactician
of his time. Condé's brilliance and Turenne's thoroughness combined to make a glorious chapter in military history.

Turenne's first problem was to dislodge strong forces of the enemy
that occupied Fribourg. His army was chiefly composed of German
Protestants; the enemy's, of Bavarian Catholics. It was still the Thirty
Years' War. Turenne needed more troops. In August, 1644, Condé,
leading ten thousand, joined Turenne. The Bavarian army established itself in strong positions on a wild rough hill. It could not
be dislodged. The French attacked in terrific midsummer heat in
uphill fighting that had no result except carnage. They decided to
withdraw, knowing that the enemy would soon run out of food and
forage. Mercy, the Bavarian general, made a masterly retreat, but

he had to abandon his artillery and he lost many men. The Bavarian army ceased to be a threat that year.

Condé ended his campaign with a victorious march down the Rhine, and then returned to Paris to enjoy his glory and to make sure that he was again suitably rewarded. Turenne remained at the front. He resumed hostilities in March, 1645. He might have done better to wait a month or two. The German tradition was all against fighting until the weather became warm. The Protestant soldiers, seriously discontented with being routed out of comfortable quarters into bad weather, fought badly. At Marienthal they were repulsed by General Mercy's new army.

It was spring by that time. Condé came to the front with reinforcements. He led an attack on Mercy near Nördlingen. His audacity and Turenne's tactics brought victory. Mercy was killed and his army retreated, having lost more than four thousand. That victory made the French foothold on the Rhine secure. The campaign of the following year was to take a new direction. To Mazarin, as to Richelieu, it seemed of the utmost importance to strengthen the vulnerable northern frontier. There lay the greatest threat to Paris.

The glory of Condé was like poison to his cousin, Gaston d'Orléans. Richelieu's death had permitted the return to favor of this ignoble uncle of the new king. He wished to be glorious too. He was allowed to have titular command of the Army of Flanders, already provided with capable generals. That army, no thanks to Gaston, captured Gravelines from the Spaniards in 1644 and Cassel in 1645. In 1646 it won Courtrai, Condé being there to help. Gaston, feeling "saturated with glory," returned to court, but Condé went on and captured Dunkirk which had never been French before.

Condé, yet to meet his first defeat, met it the following year on Spanish soil. French troops had been repulsed in attempts to capture Lerida in Catalonia. The glorious hero of Rocroi went to the south, easily to repair this error. He took the affair lightly. An orchestra of twenty-four violins marched at the head of his regiment! In the trenches before the walls of Lerida the orchestra gave an evening concert while Condé and his officers made merry. The Spaniards did not care for the concert. Their artillery opened fire in that direction. Their musketeers charged the musical trench and the concert ended in a French retreat with heavy losses.

Gregorio de Brito, the Spanish commander, sent next morning a present of ices and fruits, and an apology for not having violins of his own to return the serenade of the night before. "However," his emissary added, "if you enjoyed the kind of music that we did furnish last night, we promise to furnish the same sort as long as you honor us by your presence." De Brito kept his word so well that Condé soon had enough of it. He went back to France.

While Condé was losing at Lerida, Turenne beat the Bavarians, and that was more important. Co-operating with Swedish General Wrangel, he defeated the forces of the Empire at Lavingen in 1647 and at Zusmarshausen in 1648. Bavaria was at his mercy, and again, as in the time of Gustavus Adolphus, the way to Vienna lay open. Emperor Ferdinand III considered flight.

Condé's departure for Spain and his musical misadventure there encouraged the Spaniards to become aggressive in the north. They invaded the province of Artois and captured Lens. Condé was sent against them. He was eager to re-embellish his slightly tarnished reputation, and he had learned something about strategy. At Lens he deployed his army and then feigned a retreat. This maneuver came near to disaster because the enemy pursued so vigorously that Condé was nearly captured. He had amazing luck. His army made the planned about-face in the nick of time and their counter-attack succeeded. Three thousand Spaniards were killed and five thousand made prisoners. The victories of Condé and Turenne made Emperor Ferdinand yearn for peace.

Peace had been discussed for years, but neither side had been willing to admit defeat. In 1648, however, the Emperor gave in; otherwise Turenne would have occupied Vienna. In October the Treaty of Westphalia was signed, and thereby Ferdinand became little more than one of a number of German princes. The princes who had been allies of France gained more than their former powers and privileges. The Empire became even more disunited than it had been before. *Alsace was ambiguously conceded to France and her rights to Metz, Toul, and Verdun were definitely recognized.* The ruinous Thirty Years' War brought profit only to France.

Spain was not a party to the Treaty of Westphalia. She made a separate peace with the Dutch Protestants and withdrew from the conference. She preferred to continue at war with France because a strange revolt had broken out in the streets of Paris. Spain hoped to profit by that revolt. The Treaty of 1648 removed the threat of a unified Austro-Germany, but an advantageous peace with Spain was not attained until ten years later.

After the Treaty of Westphalia came the Fronde. A *fronde* is a slingshot. A popular game with the gamins of Paris three centuries ago was to sling pebbles at the police with their *frondes* and then to run away. The civil war that postponed peace with Spain was called the Fronde because it too was a boyish business, and there was much running away. It lasted for five years, 1648 to 1653, and it served no useful purpose.

Richelieu was unpopular on account of the heavy taxes and Mazarin had to make them still heavier. He was also unpopular because he was an Italian. Concini had not been forgotten.

A mounting deficit had to be met and the war expenses did not grow less. Mazarin and Richelieu were not adroit in government finance. Many devices that they used for raising urgently needed funds were ill-judged. In 1648, when it came time for those who held hereditary offices to make their annual payment for that privilege (*la Paulette*), an order was issued that, in lieu of the annual payment, the government would retain the revenue of those offices for the next four years! The *Parlement,* exempted from this order, opposed it nonetheless. Besides, there was a tax on fruit and wine coming into Paris that greatly annoyed the *conseillers* who had country estates.

The *Parlement,* and its capacity to make difficulties for the government, were described in Chapter One. Richelieu was able to keep it submissive, but Mazarin was not so fortunate. Two things contributed to the *Parlement's* new assumption of authority. One was that Queen Anne had vastly increased its prestige when she asked it to break the King's will; *Parlement,* having legalized the powers of the Regent, felt entitled to oppose what it held to be illegal use of those powers. The other factor was the news from England. The

English Parliament had overruled its king, Charles I. Might not the *Parlement* of Paris do likewise? But there was an important difference between these two bodies. The English Parliament was a legislative body, representative of the nation. The *Parlement* of Paris was a judicial body, created by the crown and representative only of its own class. It had neither right nor mandate to change the form of government, but it undertook to do so. It tried to usurp powers that belonged only to the States-General.

In May of 1648 the *conseillers* invited the magistrates of other courts to meet with them and "to deliberate upon the reform of the kingdom." The Regent forbade this meeting, but it was held in defiance of her order. A Declaration resulted which, if fulfilled, would have greatly reduced the authority of the crown. The unpopularity of Mazarin contributed to the popularity of this Declaration. The Parisians hailed the *conseillers* as "*pères de la patrie.*"

Mazarin advised Anne to appear to yield, and she took his advice. A few weeks later Condé's victory at Lens occurred. Paris rejoiced. Confident that this victory would swing popular favor to the side of the government, the Regent issued an order for the arrest of the venerable *conseiller* Broussel and some others who had been prominent in the forbidden attempt "to reform the kingdom." Broussel's arrest was a blunder. He was very popular because he was poor and honest and had resisted the taxes and had a long white beard. The Parisians poured into the streets and threw up many barricades so that troops could not pass. The rusty old arms of the League reappeared. Shots were fired at the palace guards. That was on August 26, 1648. For two days the Court was blockaded in the *Palais Royal.*

The *Parlement* went in a body to ask Regent Anne to release the prisoners. She curtly refused. Then the Parisians turned on the *conseillers* and, demanding Broussel or blood, sent them back to the *Palais Royal.* Mazarin, an expert at ducking danger, persuaded Anne to yield. Broussel was released. But that was not the end of the business. Paris, unconvinced, remained hostile. A few months later, January 6, 1649, Anne led the Court in a flight by night to Saint Germain where Condé's returning troops could afford protection. There was little furniture at Saint Germain. Most of the accompanying nobility shivered on straw that night.

The Fronde began. The ostensible point at issue was the government's refusal to accept the *Parlement's* Declaration. But the assembled magistrates had had no authority to make that Declaration, and they had no convincing support. They were supported only by a Paris mob eager for pillage, and by some of the *grands* who either had axes to grind or to whose romantic tastes the adventure appealed. Romance was more the fashion than reason, and there was less fear of Mazarin than there had been of Richelieu. To fight even in a foolish cause was more esteemed than not to fight at all. An ambassador wrote that "the French fought as though they believed that, if killed, they would come to life again the next morning."

There were fantastic episodes. Certain *grands* took the side of the magistrates merely for the sake of excitement. Among these there were beautiful Madame de Longueville, a sister of Condé, and a long-legged daughter of Gaston d'Orléans known as *la Grande Mademoiselle*. Longueville was incurably romantic and adventurous. She said, "I do not like innocent pleasures." Chevreuse had set a style; the Fronde became the fashion. When the *frondeurs* attacked the Bastille, lovely ladies had chairs brought and sat behind the battery that fired a few rounds at the grim old fortress. The old fortress gallantly surrendered to the lovely ladies. The event was more social than military.

Condé's troops had little difficulty in bringing Paris to terms. They made no direct attack; they merely cut off supplies from the country. *Parlement* authorized a motley army of twelve thousand. This army, adorned with plumes and ribbons, made several sorties from Paris, but "they fled as soon as they met two hundred of the royal troops; they always returned beaten and were received with roars of laughter." (Duruy)

The *conseillers* saw the folly of keeping up the farce. Paul de Gondi, Coadjutor of the Archbishop of Paris and later Cardinal de Retz, was the aggressive leader of this phase of the Fronde; he hated Mazarin and he had an ambition to become a second Richelieu. It became clear to *Parlement* that the Coadjutor was serving his personal ambition rather than the good of the country, and that most of the *grands* who were with them had even less desirable objectives. It was proposed that the proffered help of Spain be accepted. Matthieu Molé, heroic first president of the *Parlement,* rejected this treasonable proposal with the scorn that it deserved. His fellow magistrates authorized him to treat with Mazarin. They met at Rueil, a village on the road to Saint Germain, and came to terms. Some taxes were reduced and it was agreed that some of the reforms proposed by the magistrates should be put into effect. The Court returned to Paris in April, 1649. That ended the *Parlement* vs. Government phase of this civil war, but a more serious phase of it was soon to develop.

CHAPTER FOUR

A KING'S TUMULTUOUS BOYHOOD

CONDÉ AND THE CARDINAL DE RETZ LED A SECOND FRONDE THAT FAILED. TURENNE TURNED THE TIDE AGAINST THE SPANIARDS. THE NOBILITY TOOK UP WITH REFINEMENT. DESCARTES, PASCAL, AND CORNEILLE. AFTER MAZARIN DIED LOUIS TOOK COMPLETE CHARGE. COLBERT WAS HIS RIGHT-HAND MAN. REVOCATION OF THE EDICT OF NANTES.

THE second phase of the Fronde was more formidable than the first, but no less fantastic. The suggestion of comic opera remained. It was the "Fronde of the Princes," the other one having been the Fronde of the *Parlement*. Turenne and Condé, at different times, led Spaniards against the French and ended by fighting each other. Gaston d'Orléans, terrified when he found himself momentarily in command, took to his bed; whenever he was asked for orders he said that he was about to die. When Condé attacked Paris and Turenne thought he was defending it, Gaston's daughter, *la Grande Mademoiselle,* let the attackers in and had the guns of the Bastille turned on the defenders. Condé spent two years in jail and Mazarin went twice into exile. The bewildered populace, uncertain which side to favor, ended by favoring neither. Anything for peace. The Queen and the Boy-King were urged to come back to the Paris from which they had fled, Mazarin returned from exile, and, after its bad dream was over, France found herself almost precisely where she had been before.

The new trouble began with Condé. To a greed rivaling that of his father, he added an arrogance that was intolerable. He insulted Mazarin, he insulted *Parlement,* he even insulted Queen Anne. In 1650 she had him arrested. His brother, the Prince of Conti, and his brother-in-law, the Duke of Longueville, went to jail with him.

Condé's arrest delighted the Parisians, but it started the Fronde of the Princes. Condé's wife and his sister, Madame de Longueville, were

65

active in this second Fronde. Even wise Turenne was in it at the beginning; his weakness for beautiful Longueville had much to do with
his temporary defection. It should be remembered in his favor that
this was a revolt against Mazarin, not against the monarchy; whenever
the king was a minor, princely revolters made themselves semi-
respectable by claiming to be acting in the true interests of the king as
well as of the country.

Turenne invaded Champagne with a small Spanish force, but was
defeated at Rethel by royal troops. The new Fronde might have ended
there except for Gondi, the Coadjutor. To win him over, Mazarin had
promised Gondi a cardinal's hat, but the hat had not been delivered
and the Coadjutor was extremely annoyed about that. Amazingly
adroit and energetic, he succeeded in making the *Parlement* and the
people actively anti-Mazarin again. Mazarin, fearing for his life,
prudently departed. Condé and his relatives were released and the
Coadjutor got his hat. After that he was the Cardinal de Retz, but it
was Mazarin at Cologne who continued to control Anne. She loved
him.

Hundreds of the dissatisfied nobles flocked to Paris and there was
talk of a States-General, again "to reform the kingdom." But the
program of the nobles and the clergy was not acceptable to the magistrates. Soon *Parlement* and its host of followers ceased to be allies of
the princes.

Condé, whose release had been coincident with Mazarin's flight,
counted on taking the Prime Minister's place. When he discovered
that an Italian, absent, had more influence than the first Prince of the
Blood, present, he left Paris in disgust. He went to the south, determined to win his way to power by force of arms, and with the ever-
ready aid of Spain. One of the companions of Condé's revolt recorded
that the Prince had designs on the throne itself.

Mazarin, returning to court in December, 1651, gave command of
the army to Turenne, who had recovered from his temporary defection. In April of the following year, Condé's army of twelve thousand
dispersed royal forces in the valley of the Loire. Turenne came to
Briare with four thousand and, by skillful maneuvers, delayed the advance of the army of the princes. Finally the two armies met under
the walls of Paris which had closed its gates to both of them. Gaston,

who had been named lieutenant-general of the kingdom, quaked with fear and took to his bed.

Parlement awaited the issue of the battle before committing itself, but the battle was indecisive. Condé fought more brilliantly than ever, but his army might have been destroyed except that Gaston's long-legged daughter had the courage that her father lacked. *La Grande Mademoiselle* had planned for a long time to marry the young King, but when she thought that Condé's star was in the ascendant she shifted her interest to him. Thanks to her, gates were opened to the Prince when he had his back to the wall, and the cannon of the Bastille opened fire on the royal troops. Amazed Turenne withdrew.

Condé found himself no more popular in Paris than he had been before and no more influential with Anne of Austria. A small massacre of some of his opponents did not add to his popularity. He turned again to the Spaniards, this time toward Flanders, and a crowd of the nobles went with him, leading ten thousand of their retainers.

This treachery of the nobility swung popular favor back to the crown. Mazarin had returned because Anne asked him to, but he knew that his presence made reconciliation more difficult. He went into voluntary exile again in August, 1652. *Parlement* and the Parisians were eager for restoration of normal order; they "prayed" the Regent to return from Compiègne where she had taken shelter from the latest storm. In October King Louis, fourteen the month before, returned with his mother to Paris—a Paris that had had its fill of rebellion and was eager to be submissive again to royal authority. The experiment in reform had not been a success.

From Saint-Cloud to the Louvre crowds lined the way to cheer the royal carriage as it passed. The Cardinal de Retz, arch-fomenter of trouble, was imprisoned, Condé, in his absence, was tried and condemned to death, and Gaston was banished to Blois. Mazarin, when he returned in February, 1653, found himself less unpopular and more powerful than ever. The Fronde was over.

For nearly four years the royal family had led a semi-fugitive life that was filled with uncertainty and alarm. They had undergone hardships. Those years produced a permanent effect upon Louis's mind. They convinced him that the security of the state and of its sovereign required the exercise of absolute authority. Fortunately for him, most of his subjects had arrived at the same conclusion. Technically, Louis had attained his majority in September, 1651, at the age of thirteen. He had appeared before *Parlement* at that time and had announced his intention to take charge of the government. As a matter of fact, it was Mazarin who had charge of it until his death in 1661.

One of the first acts of the re-established authority was the issuance of a decree forbidding *Parlement* to concern itself with anything beyond its legal jurisdiction; there was to be no new assumption by the *gens de robe* of the functions of the States-General—and there was no States-General until 1789. The royal *intendants,* suppressed during the Fronde, were re-established and their powers were increased. They supervised provincial administration and were authorized to annul court decisions. The magistrates made no serious effort to resist this great curtailment of their former importance.

Mazarin's first problem was to conclude the war with Spain, a Spain reinforced by Condé and his following. Fortunately for France, Condé's arrogance was no more acceptable to the proud Spaniards than it had been to the French. They did not readily co-operate with him. Turenne was able to hold him in check north of the Somme while Mazarin was negotiating with Oliver Cromwell who had become master of England. When satisfactory terms had been agreed upon, England joined in fighting Spain. The Spaniards had re-captured Dunkirk, the key to Flanders. Turenne, aided by six thousand English, went to besiege it. An English fleet prevented the approach of Spanish ships. A Spanish army, led by two princes, one of Spain and one of France, advanced along the shore. The Battle of the Dunes occurred on the fourteenth of June, 1658. It was one of Turenne's greatest victories. Condé had predicted defeat before the battle began. The only drawback was that, in accordance with the hard bargain Cromwell had made, Dunkirk was turned over to the English.

Spain asked for peace. Mazarin and the Spanish Minister, Don Luis de Haro, met on an island in the Bidassoa, that historic little river at the foot of the Pyrenees where, more than a century before, François I had regained his liberty at the price of a disastrous treaty. Now the roles were reversed. It was France that was in a position to drive a hard bargain.

The negotiations continued for months. Don Luis delayed them as much as he could and won important concessions thereby. The Treaty of the Pyrenees was signed November 7, 1658. *France retained Artois, Roussillon and Lorraine,* but the clause which interested Mazarin most was the clause whereby Maria-Theresa, heiress to the crown of Spain, was pledged to marry the young King of France. Mazarin's dream for France went far beyond her natural frontiers. He provided for her a technical claim to the throne of Spain. He even considered at this time the possibility that his young master might be elected emperor. One of the concessions made by Mazarin in the Treaty of the Pyrenees was the pardon of the traitor Condé. Spain was glad to be rid of him.

Upon the death of Ferdinand III in 1657, Mazarin did not succeed in having Louis XIV elected emperor; Leopold I was elected. But he did succeed in forming the League of the Rhine which committed certain German princes, including the Duke of Bavaria, to co-operate with France in maintenance of the Treaty of Westphalia. Sweden and Denmark were similarly committed. Mazarin concluded and extended that notable chapter in diplomatic history that Richelieu had not lived to finish.

The Prime Minister had a number of nieces who came to France from Italy. Their Uncle Giulio arranged splendid matches for them with prominent members of the nobility and charged their dowries to state expenses, but he drew the line when one of them wanted to marry the King. That was in 1658. Louis, nearly twenty, became amorous of niece Marie, a slim, seventeen-year-old brunette who gave him encouragement. But Mazarin would have none of it. He considered Louis's engagement to the Infanta of Spain the *chef d'oeuvre* of his diplomacy, not to be sacrificed even in the interest of his own family. He sent Marie away. In the following year Louis married Maria-Theresa.

Mazarin, great in diplomacy, was not good in government. He was more interested in his personal profit than in public prosperity. He ran up a public debt of over four hundred million, and made a hundred million for himself. He did nothing to encourage industry and agriculture, but he accumulated the finest library in France and he endowed the College of the Four Nations, open to students from Spain, Italy, Germany, and Flanders. He bought many fine paintings and statues and pensioned the great philosopher Descartes. He liked to think of himself as an artist of politics, and that he was. He "made a brave death" on the ninth of March, 1661. He was fifty-nine.

In the Richelieu-Mazarin period a profound change occurred in the French nobility. Their leaders in the time of Henri IV had been rude gentlemen. Refinement was held in slight esteem. But after Richelieu took charge of the government and successfully resisted all efforts to overthrow him, the gentry, finding time hanging heavily on their hands, took up with refinement. Nobles, when the rough traditions of feudalism no longer served, became courtiers. When they discovered that preferment could be best attained through suavity and diplomacy, they tried to become suave and diplomatic. An exaggeration of politeness and of elegance in expression became the fashion. This laid the foundation for that magnificent flowering of artificiality that attained, in the reign of Louis XIV, a preposterousness that has never been surpassed.

There was a tendency to go from one extreme to the other. Rough feudal gentlemen sought to polish their manners in the literary *salons* that became the vogue. A pioneer in this *salon* movement was Madame la Marquise de Rambouillet. She received her friends in a blue bedroom that was a novelty and her receptions had great success. After the Marquise had had herself nicely fixed up in bed, her guests were admitted. It was no rough party; precisely the opposite. Refinements in behavior and in the use of language were discussed. Artists and men of letters took rank over renowned duelists; they were allowed to sit nearer to their horizontal hostess. Those whose grammar was uncertain sat farthest away. The poker players hated it at first, but they ended by learning contract. Madame la Marquise had many imitators. It was a triumph for femininity.

There lived in this period two Frenchmen whose work has made them immortal. The minds of René Descartes and of Blaise Pascal were two of the greatest the world has ever known.

Descartes, son of a *conseiller* of the *Parlement* of Brittany, was born in Touraine in 1596 and died in Sweden in 1650. A soldier in the Thirty Years' War, he saw much of Europe. In 1630, "in order to be tranquil," he left France for Holland and remained there until a few months before his death. In his *Discours de la Méthode,* published in 1637, Descartes laid the foundation of modern philosophy. Great apostle of reason, he recognized its limitations. Placing religion above philosophy, he acknowledged the large significance of ideas whose critical examination lies beyond the powers of the human mind.

Blaise Pascal, born at Clermont-Ferrand in 1623, died in Paris when thirty-nine. Like Descartes, he was of a family of the *noblesse de robe.* His amazing mind dwelt in a fragile body. He was ill all his life. When twelve, without the use of any book, he reproduced the geometry of Euclid. At sixteen he wrote a treatise on conic sections. At twenty-four he made the pioneer measurements of atmospheric pressure. Pascal's genius was not limited to mathematics. In his *Lettres provinciales,* 1656, he discussed theological questions with a clarity that such discussion had not known before. Though devout, he brought confusion to the Jesuits. His *Lettres* had a great success. His sensitiveness to the drama of human life was as perfect as his mathematical intelligence. His greatest work is his unfinished *Pensées,* fragments that were written in his last cruel illness, unfinished paragraphs, "beautiful as a ruin at sunset." Madame de Sévigné said of the *Pensées* that they deprived her of interest in all other books. Sainte-Beuve wrote that Pascal, "admirable when he finished, was even better when he was interrupted." It was death that interrupted the completion of what, even incomplete, is one of the world's Great Books.

Pierre Corneille, born near Rouen in 1606, died in Paris in 1684. He had no elegance; he looked and talked like a provincial bourgeois. Voltaire's father called him the biggest bore he had ever met. He was more interested in his income than in his art and his conversation was deplorable. But within this unattractive son of a magistrate there burned a divine fire. His inspiration pushed him out of the law into the writing of drama. He became the true creator of dramatic art in France.

Corneille's genius compelled him, even against his will, to break with established dramatic standards. *Le Cid,* produced in 1636, pleased the public, but displeased the pundits. Richelieu, who had granted Corneille a pension, ordered a revision of *Le Cid* by the French Academy that he had founded. Corneille conceded his mistakes, but continued to write in the same manner. *C'était plus fort que lui.* His pension was withdrawn. He died in poverty.

Corneille reflected the philosophy of Descartes. His dramas were based on the interpretation of human character, on the conflict between passion and duty, between liberty and tyranny. Without the courage of a pioneer, he was one nonetheless. "He was the more to be admired," wrote Voltaire, "because he was surrounded only by bad models," and these bad models were approved by Richelieu and his Academy. Corneille advertised to his public the nobility of character. In superbly poetic lines he broke with the classical tradition and extolled man as master rather than slave of his passions and of his environment. He was, unconsciously perhaps, a great liberator of the mind. He bore the brunt of a revolution in literary taste that facilitated the successes of Racine and Molière.

The personal reign of Louis XIV was from the death of Mazarin in 1661 to his own death in 1715. It was extremely personal. He had no prime minister. Louis's most famous saying was, *"l'État, c'est moi."* There is doubt whether he said just that, but there is no doubt that he lived up to that idea.

One gets the impression that Louis set for himself a role to play, a role that served at first a useful purpose. But, after a while, the role mastered the actor who played it. He could not become normal again. His conception of absolutism ended in a conception of himself as God-on-earth. He developed a mania for a glory through whose clouds he could discern but dimly the facts of life, the needs of his people. His reign began with magnificence and ended close to disaster.

Louis very rarely let his behavior depart from his conception of what a great king's behavior should be. He allowed himself to lose his temper only two or three times. His calm and stately speech was as measured as the elaborate etiquette that he imposed upon himself and upon the Court. There was nothing natural; all artificial. The Court mistook the world that the Sun-King created for a real world; that inescapable obtuseness which privilege engenders permitted the nobles to believe that their unnatural prosperity was natural and could endure. It took a Voltaire to tell the truth that no one heeded. There occurred one of those long flights from reality that mankind's imperfect reasoning impels from time to time, a flight that reality, unheeded, brings to an end with a crash, a disaster, perhaps a revolution.

Louis did not spare himself the rigidity that he imposed on others. He was faithful to a schedule for each hour of the day. His education had been neglected. He repaired it by long hours of diligent study. He was handsome, tall, and strong. His chestnut hair suggested Mazarin, but he had a Bourbon nose. To natural majesty he added a courtesy that could not be surpassed. He doffed his hat even to chambermaids. He "radiated glory and authority," and he ate twice as much as anybody else. "Four bowls of soup, a pheasant, a partridge, a great dish of salad, two large slices of ham, mutton with garlic, pastry, and a dessert of fruit and hard-boiled eggs"—that is reported to have been an ordinary meal for Louis. Autopsy revealed that his digestive tract was phenomenally developed. The King's endurance was also phenomenal. The Court often panted and perspired in its efforts to keep up with him. *Grandes dames,* ill or well, had to follow His Royal Highness in all weathers on long rides over rough roads, even to Flanders and beyond, and all in their tight court dresses; never a complaint, never a delay, always gay and ready to dance if they wished to be well with their king.

Louis outshone even magnificent François. King François took a salamander for his symbol. Louis took the sun. In his later years, Saint-Simon reports, it was only fear of the devil that kept him from being worshiped like God. When his room was empty, the courtiers saluted its emptiness, and when they passed in front of the casket that contained the royal undershirts they made reverence as if before the altar of a church. The royal emergence from bed, regularly at eight, called for fantastic ceremony. It called for everything except a bath, of which the King is known to have taken but one in his life. Only a

Prince of the Royal Blood could hand Louis his shirt. One duke helped him into the right sleeve and there was another to help him into the left. The whole show included a hundred "domesticated" nobles. Dressed at last, the King wiped his hands on a perfume-moistened napkin—that was his bath—and then went to his office for a hard day's work. When he ate, five nobles had the honor to stand at attention behind his chair while others competed for the distinction of passing the gravy.

Despite his mania for magnificence, Louis was a diligent worker. He gave painstaking attention to all matters about which he had to make decisions. He held himself firmly to the performance of his duty as he saw it. He improved the organization and efficiency of the royal cabinet, chosing his ministers, as a matter of policy, from the *bourgeoisie* rather than from the nobility. The best of them was Colbert, who devoted prodigious energy to the material improvement of the state. Louvois was his minister of war. There was a cabinet meeting every other day. The *intendants,* who represented the King in the provinces, became more powerful than ever and the nobility became a leisure class. Titles gave social distinction only.

Under Mazarin, Nicolas Fouquet was superintendent of finance. Like Mazarin he accumulated an enormous fortune and was a patron of the arts. At Vaux-le-Vicomte near Melun he built a magnificent château that is still a show place. There he gave "marvellous fêtes" at which young Louis was an uncomfortable guest. He felt himself outshone. When he took charge of his government, and Colbert brought to his attention serious irregularities in Fouquet's accounts, he had him arrested. After a long trial the magnificent superintendent of finance was condemned to life imprisonment.

Jean-Baptiste Colbert, son of a cloth merchant of Reims, also served under Mazarin. He succeeded Fouquet as superintendent of finance. He ended by being superintendent of everything except war and foreign affairs. He surpassed even Sully's record for hard work; he usually spent sixteen hours each day in his office, starting at five in the morning. He was a marvel for thoroughness and, also like Sully, he was frigid to all who sought favors. Colbert's passion was to make

France prosperous and to keep the budget balanced. For ten years he succeeded in doing so. After that Louis was too much for him. Court and war expenses put the budget in the red. Colbert could not curb Louis as Sully had curbed King Henri. Extravagant expenditure, more than anything else, brought about the downfall of absolutism.

Colbert was the creator of organized industry in France. Thousands were employed in the cloth, tapestry, and other industries that were established with governmental support. Colbert insisted upon quality rather than quantity; the French tradition of excellent workmanship owes much to him. In his time the *articles de luxe* made in France became the most highly esteemed in Europe and her export trade was greatly increased thereby. He developed a merchant marine and established a protective tariff which helped the infant industries, but led to trouble with Holland. He believed in colonization. Between 1660 and 1672 four thousand peasants of Normandy and Brittany emigrated to Canada. The hardy and industrious French-Canadians of the Province of Quebec are descendants of those pioneers. The explorations of Joliet, Marquette, and La Salle had his support. When Marquette and Joliet explored the Mississippi they named it *le fleuve Colbert*.

This great minister has been justly called "the artisan of the glory of Louis XIV," but Louis, finally blinded by that glory, ceased to give heed to the prudent counsels of his best adviser. He preferred to listen to Louvois, who talked of war and who hated Colbert. He preferred to pour out millions at Versailles and to disregard the budget. Colbert, profoundly discouraged, died in 1683.

Louis's most serious blunders were committed after the death of Colbert. One of them was the Revocation of the Edict of Nantes in 1685. The Huguenots, after Richelieu's defeat of them in 1629, had ceased their persecution of Catholics and had become submissive subjects. They could no longer be charged with rebellion or disobedience; the only charge against them was that they differed from the King about religion. Louis, like Emperor Ferdinand, believed that the good of the state required that there should be but one religion. Rigorous measures were taken to compel the Huguenots to give up their

Protestantism. Many of them appeared to do so, hoping that the storm would pass. Louis was led to believe that there were only a few hundred intractables left. He signed the Revocation. Then it became evident that those who had abjured their faith had done so only to escape persecution. When all hope of regaining religious liberty was lost, two or three hundred thousand left their property behind and fled at the risk of their lives to England, Holland, and Germany. Many went to Berlin. They and their descendants have been an important source of strength to Germany. There were no better workers or soldiers than the Huguenots. The army lost six hundred officers and more than ten thousand soldiers; the navy and the merchant marine lost nine thousand of their best sailors. The industries that depended on Huguenot workers were ruined. The effect on foreign relations was also disastrous. Protestant states that had formerly been allies of France became allied against her. The Revocation was a capital blunder.

Another notable sect was suppressed. The Jansenists were not Protestants in the sense of hostility to Catholicism. However, they did not accept the supremacy of the Pope in all spiritual matters and they inclined toward Calvinism in some of their beliefs. That put them under the ban of Rome. Jansenism owed its doctrines to a bishop of Ypres, Jansénius, who died in 1638. What gave it a great reputation in France was the monastic colony established at Port-Royal des Champs, not far from Versailles. Some of the most illustrious scholars and thinkers of the day lived there "as puritans of Catholicism, setting an example of constant toil of body and mind, of piety and austerity, bordering on asceticism." (Boulenger) These unworldly intellectuals combined teaching and writing with house and garden work. They published books that were widely read and developed an influence that was considered dangerous. Racine was a student at Port-Royal and Pascal lived there when he began his *Lettres provinciales*. In 1709 the King required the destruction of the buildings at Port-Royal, and more than two thousand Jansenists were imprisoned. This persecution did not stop the spread of thought about religious questions that Jansenism had stimulated.

Although the King and the Pope saw eye to eye about Huguenots and Jansenists, they did not agree about some other matters. Louis would brook no interference by the Pope in temporal affairs. He regarded attachment to the crown of the revenues of vacant bishoprics a temporal affair, and he kept as many as thirty-five of them vacant. The Pope held that this infringed upon his "spiritual authority" to fill the vacancies. He objected strenuously to the King's resistance to the installation of new bishops. This led to an eleven-year conflict between Versailles and Rome. A compromise was finally reached in 1693.

CHAPTER FIVE

THE SUN-KING'S PURSUIT OF GLORY

A PREMATURE INVASION OF FLANDERS. LOUIS XIV HATED HOLLAND, BUT
WILLIAM OF ORANGE HELD HIM IN CHECK. TURENNE'S LAST CAMPAIGN.
AN EX-KING OF ENGLAND BECAME A PERMANENT GUEST OF FRANCE. THE
WAR OF THE SPANISH SUCCESSION. LOUIS'S LOVE LIFE.

RICHELIEU-MAZARIN DIPLOMACY and Condé-Turenne victories
brought France near to her natural frontiers and made her king the
most powerful monarch in Europe. Louis XIV had the Richelieu-
Mazarin objectives in mind, but he was less diplomatic than they in
the means he employed to attain them. Their very success had certain
disadvantages. Richelieu had been able to form alliances against the
threat of the House of Hapsburg, its threat to the independence of the
weaker states. The success of his and Mazarin's policies ended in
making France stronger than Austria and Spain. It was no longer the
House of Hapsburg that was feared by the weaker states. It was
France.

It would have been wise for Louis XIV to allay the anxieties of
some of France's former allies, but he did not do so. A conciliatory attitude was not consistent with his conception of glory. He did not wish
to be co-operative; he wished to be supreme. The result was that
France lost her allies and found herself confronting a hostile Europe
alone. Louis, lover of military glory, was at war during thirty of the
fifty-four years of his personal reign, and with steadily diminishing
success.

Holland, once an ally, showed the new trend as early as 1648 when
she withdrew from the Westphalian conference and made a separate
peace with Spain. She made it clear that, as her neighbor in Flanders,
she preferred a weakened Spain to a strengthened France; threat to
her independence was lessened thereby.

. Michel Le Tellier, war minister from 1643 to 1677, and his son François, the Marquis de Louvois, who succeeded him, devoted their great abilities to making France the most formidable military power in Europe. They created a standing army that had an organization and a discipline superior to anything known before. The military favors to nobility ceased; noble young men had to undergo the same discipline as the commoners; they had to learn to obey before they were permitted to command. Louvois was brutal and violent and his political influence was "detestable," but he was admirable in army administration. Turenne, the greatest soldier of his time, was commander-in-chief. Vauban, a master of military engineering, became "General of Fortifications"; he was a genius both at building them and at attacking them. The military strength of France under this superior leadership made King Louis feel that he could carry all before him. It took many years to prove that he was mistaken.

A situation arose in Spain which had a profound effect upon the reign of Louis XIV. Philip IV died in 1665 leaving as heir Charles II, a sickly boy only four years old. Maria-Theresa, Queen of France, was technically next in line for the throne of Spain, but the Austrian Hapsburgs also had to be considered. Emperor Leopold's mother and wife, like Louis's, were both Spanish princesses, and the claim of Austria to the succession was a more natural claim than that of France. Louis, more reasonable at this time than later, was willing to compromise with Leopold. He proposed to take for his part Flanders, Franche-Comté (Besançon), Navarre, and the Kingdom of Naples and Sicily and to leave the rest of the Spanish domain to the Hapsburgs.

Leopold, after two years of negotiations, agreed to this secret arrangement. Then Louis, without waiting for little King Charles to die, sent Turenne into Flanders to take possession of his self-assigned heritage. Turenne with fifty thousand men had little difficulty in taking as much of Flanders as Louis had told him to take. That was in 1667. In the following year Condé invaded Franche-Comté and had similar success. Spain, under the regency of King Philip's widow, was unable to make successful resistance.

England and Holland took alarm at this sudden extension of the Sun-King's domains. They had been at war with each other; it was in

1664 that the English took New Amsterdam and changed its name to New York. They made peace and, with Sweden, formed the Triple Alliance. The ostensible purpose of this alliance was to mediate between France and Spain, but behind that purpose lay a determination to resist further advance of France to the north and to oppose Louis's claim to the Spanish succession. Louis, biding his time, agreed to the mediation; he signed the Peace of Aix-la-Chapelle with Spain in 1668 and withdrew from Franche-Comté, but he retained eleven cities that Turenne had won in Flanders, and he acquired a strong prejudice against Holland. He determined to attack and to crush the little state that had the presumption to be a competitor of France in commerce as well as a successful opponent of her foreign policy. Louis detested Calvinistic and republican Holland, and "its cheese-merchant government." The Dutch led the world at that time in ships and in foreign trade.

Louvois raised an army of 150,000. England, Sweden, and the Emperor Leopold were liberally paid for agreeing not to interfere. In May of 1672 Holland was invaded. The Dutch, short of powder, resisted with water; they cut the dikes and flooded half the country. That stopped the advance of the French, but it did not win the war. The cheese-merchant government signed a disastrous peace, but the government that signed it was soon replaced by another at whose head was the remarkable Prince William of Orange, then twenty-one.

Prince William, lifelong enemy of King Louis, succeeded in persuading Spain and Germany to co-operate with his country in resisting France. Thus the war with Holland led to a general European war.

France withdrew from Holland, but retook Franche-Comté. Then the scene shifted to the Rhine frontier. German forces, violating the guaranteed neutrality of Strasbourg, crossed the river and occupied Alsace. That was in October, 1674. Turenne, sent to resist the invaders, found himself greatly outnumbered. In December he withdrew toward Lorraine by the pass of Saverne in the Vosges. The Germans settled into winter quarters, but sixty-four-year-old Turenne did not. He said that no French soldier should rest so long as a single German remained in Alsace. He led his troops through deep snow on a forced march down the western side of the Vosges and re-entered

Alsace by way of Belfort. The Germans were frightfully surprised. In a brilliant sixteen-day campaign Turenne drove them all back again across the bridge at Strasbourg. Six months later he was killed when attacking on the other side of the Rhine.

Turenne's successes on land were supplemented by victories at sea. The fleet that Colbert had built, commanded by Duquesne, defeated a Dutch fleet in the Mediterranean. In 1678 the Peace of Nimeguen was signed at the expense of Spain. *Thereby France gained Franche-Comté.* She also gained twelve important places in Flanders that, fortified by Vauban, made a strong line of defense for the new frontier.

With the Peace of Nimeguen, Louis XIV reached the zenith of his power. For ten years thereafter he was undisputed master of western Europe. He annexed the free city of Strasbourg and most of Luxembourg and no power dared to oppose these annexations. A Turkish invasion had approached Vienna; that tied the Emperor's hands. Charles II of England, for family and financial reasons, was favorable to France and he was at odds with Parliament; that tied the hands of England.

It was the English revolution of 1688 that turned the tide against France. Following Cromwell and the Commonwealth, the Restoration had occurred in 1660. The Stuart dynasty was restored in the person of Charles, aged thirty, who had spent ten years abroad, for the most part in France. The ideas of absolutism that Charles II brought home with him, and his Catholic sympathies as well, were not acceptable to his Parliament or to his people. Popular rights, lost in France, had gained much ground in England. James II, avowed Catholic, succeeded Charles II in 1685. Protestant England revolted and called to the throne William of Orange who had married Mary, King James's daughter. James fled to France where he was warmly welcomed by King Louis; he and his family were installed as guests of the state in the château of Saint Germain and Louis promised to win back for him his lost throne. The Catholic believers in absolutism had to stand together against the threat of democracy that was lifting its head in Protestant England.

William and Mary, hostile to Louis, began their reign. Other factors that contributed to new strength of the opposition to the Sun-King were his Revocation of the Edict of Nantes and the defeat of the Turks by the armies of the Empire.

In 1686 Emperor Leopold formed the League of Augsburg, ostensibly for defensive purposes only. It was originally composed of Spain, Sweden, and those German princes who had not succumbed to the prestige of Versailles. In 1688 the revolution in England brought both England and Holland into the camp of the League; that made it strong enough to consider offense as well as defense. In the same year Louis, his confidence in the glory of his destiny unshaken, invaded the Palatinate and compelled the installation of his candidate for the vacant Electorate of Cologne. That meant war with the League.

A nine-year war followed. It was fought on all the French frontiers and it ran from 1688 to 1697. Louvois, to protect the northeastern frontier, ordered the devastation of the Palatinate. On the northern frontier the war took the form of a series of sieges in which, thanks to Vauban, the French were victorious at Fleurus, at Steinkirk, and at Neerwinden. On the Alpine frontier the Duke of Savoy was defeated. But the French effort to replace James II on the throne of England failed. Combined English and Dutch forces won an important victory over a French fleet at La Hogue in 1692. Ex-King James watched that engagement from the shore with anxious eyes; when it was over he had to resign himself to being a permanent guest at Saint Germain at the expense of France.

Both sides became weary of a war that ruined commerce and held small promise of further victories. Peace was signed at Ryswick in 1697. Louis reluctantly recognized William of Orange as King of England and withdrew his troops from most of the territory that they had occupied outside the natural frontiers. He insisted only upon recognition of his possession of Strasbourg. The Sun-King had been held in check. The Treaty of Ryswick stopped the spread of the power of France.

The sickly King of Spain, whose death had been momentarily expected in 1665, lived on until 1700. But he was childless, and the question of his successor was the subject of endless diplomatic conversations. Louis took up this subject with England and Holland, wishing to make sure that they would not oppose the plan he had in mind. He proposed that the Archduke Charles, second son of Emperor Leopold, should succeed as King of Spain, and that France, in lieu of her claim to that throne, should have Naples, Sicily, and Milan which Louis wished to trade for recognition of his rights to Lorraine and Savoy. William of Orange approved this plan, but the Spaniards were less tractable. They opposed the parceling out of their domains by foreign powers. They were willing to accept a foreign prince for king since they had no candidate of their own, but they wanted one who would be strong enough to keep for Spain all her far-flung territory. King Charles, about to die at last, wrote, upon the advice of his counselors, a will which designated as his sole heir the second grandson of Louis XIV, the seventeen-year-old Duke of Anjou. It was stipulated in the will that Spain and France should in no case be united.

This historic will, apparently so favorable to France, turned out to be disastrous for her. It put Louis XIV in a tight place. A copy of it was presented to him a few days after Charles's death. Should he hold to the agreement made with William of Orange or should he disregard that agreement and place his grandson on the throne of the world's most extensive kingdom? National interest, the final extension of France to her natural frontiers and the maintenance of peace with England, called for holding to the agreement made in London, but glory called the other way. Glory prevailed.

After several days of discussion with his ministers, Louis pronounced in favor of acceptance of the throne of Spain by his grandson. One alleged reason for this decision was belief that England and Holland might not, in any case, abide by the conditions of the agreement made with William of Orange. William, however, took this decision as a personal affront.

Louis XIV gave no evidence at that time of wishing to unite Spain to France. When he presented his grandson to the Court as King of Spain, he turned to him and said, "My son, it now becomes your first duty to be a good Spaniard, but remember that you were born French and that it is also your duty to preserve union between France and Spain, for only thereby can the peace of Europe be maintained." The young Duke of Anjou became Philip V of Spain and was recognized as such by all the sovereigns of Europe except disappointed Emperor Leopold. A Bourbon had supplanted a Hapsburg.

Ten months later Louis, still in pursuit of glory, made another mistake. He declared that his grandson's occupancy of the throne of Spain would not invalidate his right of succession in France. The threat of Bourbon dominance became equal to the former threat of the Hapsburgs. More than that, Louis irritated the Dutch by placing French troops in Spanish garrisons on their frontier, and he irritated the English when James II died at Saint Germain by declaring his son, James III, to be the rightful King of England.

William of Orange died in 1702, but the effects of his hostility to Louis lived after him. He devoted the last years of his life to the formation of the "Grand Alliance" against France. England, Holland, the Emperor Leopold, and most of the German princes entered into this coalition. The war that they waged against France continued from 1701 to 1714. It was known as the War of the Spanish Succession. France, with nearly all of Europe against her, had to defend Spanish territory as well as her own. Battles were fought in Spain, Italy, Germany, Flanders, France, on the high seas and in the colonies. The best generals for the allies were the Duke of Marlborough of England and Prince Eugene of Savoy. Eugene, born in Paris, was a great-nephew of Mazarin; he had passed to the service of Austria when Louvois had refused him the command of a regiment. On the side of France there was the Duke of Vendôme, natural grandson of Henri IV, and the excellent *Maréchal* de Villars. Condé had died in 1686.

Vendôme in Italy and Villars in Germany won victories in 1702 and 1703, but these victories were without result. In 1704 disasters began. Marlborough and Prince Eugene, in the Battle of Blenheim, defeated the French army that was in Germany, and the English took Gibraltar. In 1706 the Spanish part of Flanders was lost and in 1708 the allies invaded France and captured Lille. In 1709 Louis XIV, "resigned to the abandonment of his glory," sued for peace, but the conditions the allies imposed were so humiliating that the negotiations were broken off. The King appealed to his people to resist to the end "conditions contrary to justice and to the honor of France."

The nation responded with money and men. In September, 1709, the battle of Malplaquet was fought in the north of France. This was the most important battle of the war. A hundred thousand French fought a hundred and twenty thousand of the enemy. When the *Maréchal* Villars was wounded, retreat was ordered, but the enemy had lost more than twice as many as the French. It was a victorious defeat.

In 1710 Vendôme defeated an Anglo-Austrian army in Spain, but what really saved France was that England withdrew from the coalition. The Archduke Charles of Austria, the Hapsburg candidate for the throne of Spain, became Emperor upon the death of his brother Joseph in 1711. Leopold had died in 1705. The English, not interested in helping to win a war that might result in the union of Spain and Austria, recalled her troops. Only the army led by Prince Eugene remained a threat. With a hundred and thirty thousand men he undertook a march on Paris, but Villars, recovered from his wound, outmaneuvered him and compelled his retreat.

Peace was signed at Utrecht in 1713 with all the allies except the Emperor, and he signed at Rastadt in the following year after Villars had successfully campaigned against Prince Eugene along the Rhine. The treaties of Utrecht and Rastadt confirmed the right of Louis's grandson to the throne of Spain, but with the stipulation that he renounce all claim to the succession in France. France lost no home territory, but she lost much in other ways, in blood, in treasure, in colonies, and in prestige. England was the real winner. Spain was compelled to concede to her important commercial privileges in the colonies, as well as possession of Gibraltar and Minorca. France ceded to her Newfoundland and Nova Scotia. Versailles ceased to be dominant in European politics; it became England's turn to have the most influence. "Acceptance of the will of Charles II," wrote Malet, "was one of the great catastrophes of French history." For later catastrophes Louis was not directly responsible; after the Treaty of Rastadt he had only a year left to live.

The record that Louis XIV made in his love-life was intermediate between that of Louis XIII and that of Henri IV. He far surpassed his prudish father in the number of his love affairs, but he did not approach the amazing record of his illustrious grandfather.

He married Maria-Theresa in 1660. Madame Scarron, who was to become his second wife, witnessed their magnificent entrance to Paris. She wrote to a friend, *"La Reine dut se coucher assez contente du mari qu'elle a choisi."* Maria had not chosen her handsome husband, but she loved him with entire devotion. She was a little blue-eyed blonde, virtuous and unintelligent. She was overjoyed when the King deigned to favor her instead of his mistresses and liked to be congratulated about that. She never could learn to speak French correctly nor to dress stylishly nor to carry herself like a queen, but she had a very amiable disposition. When she died in 1683 Louis said that that was the first grief she had ever caused him.

Maria-Theresa had six children all of whom died in infancy except the eldest, Louis the Grand Dauphin. The Grand Dauphin died in 1711; he had married Marie of Bavaria; they had three sons, Louis, Philip, and Charles; Louis, the eldest, died in 1712, Philip became King of Spain, and Charles died in 1714. Louis, the grandson who died in 1712, had the title, Duke of Burgundy. He married Marie of Savoy; they had three sons, but only one of them outlived the King; it was he who, as Louis XV, succeeded his great-grandfather in 1715.

Louise de La Vallière was a maid of honor of Henrietta of England, a sister of Charles I. Henrietta had married Philip of Orléans, King Louis's brother. La Vallière was a charming, delicate blonde with dark eyes and a slight limp. She was only seventeen when she and the King, then twenty-three, found themselves together on a summer day under a tree in the park of the palace of Saint Germain. They had been caught in a rain storm. The King, trying to keep Louise from getting wet, fell in love with her. He gave magnificent fêtes in her honor and showered her with costly gifts. This new devotion did not prevent him, however, from making nocturnal promenades on the flat roof of Saint Germain in order to visit other maids of honor. Modest La Vallière was greatly embarrassed by the favor of His Royal Majesty. When he made her a duchess she is said to have almost died of shame.

Another lovely young lady came into Louis's life long before La Vallière went out of it. She was a blonde, a blonde with azure eyes. She was quick-witted Madame de Montespan, who was always able to be the life of the party. Her vivacity was in striking contrast to the quiet modesty of La Vallière. Louis could not decide which of them he loved better, so he kept them both. They occupied the same apartment and received the King together. They rode together with him in the royal carriage, the King sitting between them. All this did not embarrass azure-eyed Montespan, but dark-eyed La Vallière hated it. Monsieur de Montespan also had objections. He put on mourning for his wife and draped his house and his carriage in black. It was said, however, that this was because he had not obtained the advantages he hoped for on account of the royal favor shown to his wife.

In 1671, La Vallière, tortured by love and shame, having put up with the co-operative mistress arrangement as long as she could, fled to a convent. Colbert, for the good of the kingdom, persuaded her to return and to continue to share the King's affections with shameless Montespan. Three years later La Vallière fled again, and this time for good. She became Sister Louise in a Carmelite convent.

The palace of Versailles, begun in 1676, was not finished until 1695, but Louis established his official residence there in 1682. He began giving very elaborate and expensive fêtes in the park of Versailles in 1674 and Montespan was the *sultane* of all these festivities. Five years later, however, Louis began to be weary of the azure eyes. Montespan's bursts of temper that he had once found charming got on his nerves. One day she had said that "at least she did not smell as bad as he did." Louis never forgave her for that.

The King's next favorite had red hair. "Beautiful as an angel from head to feet," one courtier wrote of her. "Beautiful as an angel," wrote another, "and as stupid as a bread-basket." She was Mademoiselle de Fontanges. The whole Court turned toward this rising star. That was in 1679. In 1680 Fontanges became a duchess and in 1681 she died. Louis was then forty-four. He began to think a little less about love and a little more about religion.

Françoise d'Aubigné, born at Niort in 1635, was the granddaughter of Agrippa d'Aubigné, a Huguenot soldier and poet who was one of Henri de Béarn's close friends when Henri was a Huguenot. Her father, also a Huguenot, was imprisoned by Richelieu. When he was released he took his family to Martinique where they lived on the charity of relatives. Françoise took care of the poultry and expected to enter a convent. When she was sixteen and had returned to France, she was glad to improve her lot by marrying Paul Scarron, a popular poet who was frightfully crippled. He was forty-two. Françoise took good care of him. When he died in 1660, Anne of Austria granted her a small pension.

Madame Scarron, a widow at twenty-five, dressed modestly. She had beauty, dignity, and intelligence. She radiated refinement. Madame de Montespan made her acquaintance in 1670 and engaged her as governess for her children. That is how King Louis met her. Her distinction and her intelligence made an increasing impression upon him. She was a great relief after stormy sessions with Montespan; she was the only woman with whom he could talk simply and seriously; she became his refuge from storms. In 1674 Louis bought the marquisate of Maintenon for her and presented her in Court as Madame la Marquise de Maintenon.

The new favorite concerned herself with the health, religion, and virtue of her royal lover. She held so strongly for virtue that, a few months after Maria-Theresa died, Louis secretly married her. He was then forty-five and she was approaching fifty. She had no ambition to be recognized as queen. Her greatest interest was in the establishment that the King built for her at Saint Cyr, which is near Versailles. There she superintended the education of two hundred and fifty girls. She had a passion for teaching. She was at Saint Cyr when she was summoned to the deathbed of the King, and it was there that she died four years later. Once a Huguenot, Madame de Maintenon became an ardent Catholic. Her one great mistake was that she encouraged Louis to sign the Revocation of the Edict of Nantes.

The long reign of Louis XIV, begun so auspiciously, ended in misery for the nation and in remorse for the King. The lavish expenditures for war and for glory almost ruined France. There were revolts against the terrific taxes. In the bitter winter of 1709 the women of the markets of Paris marched on Versailles to demand bread. They were stopped at the bridge of Sèvres; their granddaughters were more successful in a similar march on the eve of the Revolution. There was suffering even in the palace that winter. The great rooms could not be kept warm. Food ran short. Palace servants begged for bread in the streets. National bankruptcy was imminent. The population shrank from nineteen to seventeen million.

Louis XIV in his practice of absolutism sowed the seeds of its downfall. His policy of preferment of the bourgeois for civil offices contributed to that; it established the principle of promotion for merit and increased popular interest in study of the problems of government. His domestication of the nobility also contributed to that end. Deprived of their former political power, but sustained in their social and financial privileges, the nobility degenerated; their manners became more polished, but their behavior became more deplorable. The gap between the nobles and the commoners became a yawning chasm; living at court rather than in the country, the nobles lost touch with reality; they became hothouse plants, orchids whose aerial existence could not be sustained.

Vauban, the great engineer, was one of the few close to the King who dared to say what he thought. He published a book in which he predicted disaster. He insisted that there should be equality in taxation, no special privileges, and that the nation should have a voice in the administration of its government. King Louis ordered the suppression of this book.

Fénelon, although an aristocrat, shared Vauban's views. He proposed that there should be a hierarchy of assemblies culminating in the States-General, free election of these assemblies, and free expression of their views. There should be no more restraint upon the assemblies than upon the Royal Council of Ministers; like the Council, they should work side by side with the King.

Fénelon was the teacher of the Duke of Burgundy, an intelligent and studious young man who was the father of Louis XV. The Duke came to appreciate the weaknesses of absolutism as practiced by his grandfather and risked his displeasure by telling him that a king should serve his people rather than the people the king. The Duke's death in 1712 destroyed his chance to put his and his teacher's ideas into practice. It was understood that if the Duke became king, Fénelon was to be his prime minister.

In 1715 Louis began to have trouble with circulation in his legs. Gangrene developed. On the last day of August, knowing that the end was near, he summoned his only surviving great-grandson to his bedside. His son was dead and all his grandsons too, except Philip who was a king in Madrid. To his five-year-old successor the dying King confessed his failure. "My child," he said, "do not follow my example either in lavish expenditure or in making war. Try to improve the lot of your people, which I have failed to do."

The King met death with the dignity that had characterized his life. He said to Madame de Maintenon, "I had thought that dying was difficult. I assure you that I find it not difficult at all." He gave orders for his funeral as though it was simply a matter of starting on an ordinary journey. He died on the first of September, 1715, three days before his seventy-seventh birthday.

When Louis XIV began to reign, his people, disillusioned by revolts that had caused only misery, were eager to accept absolutism. When his long reign came to an end, they were equally eager to find some way to eliminate the evils that absolutism had brought. No peaceful way could be found. Royalty and those who enjoyed its favor had departed so far from understanding of the social situation that the government could not adjust itself to reality. More than seventy years were yet to pass before the Revolution came, but the reign of Louis XIV made a revolution almost inevitable.

When the old King died, his people were glad; they had had too much of religious intolerance, of unendurable taxation, of war, and of misery. When they carried his corpse to Saint Denis, crowds made merry as it passed.

CHAPTER SIX

ARTS, SCIENCE, AND FINANCE

THE reign of Louis XIV was favorable to the arts and the sciences. To be a patron of the arts fitted into the Sun-King's scheme of glory, and to regulate art fitted into Colbert's passion for order. In addition to all his other duties, Colbert, as Minister of Fine Arts, controlled the pensions granted to those deemed worthy. The pension list of 1670 makes record of fifteen hundred *livres* paid to Racine, one thousand to Molière, and six hundred to another gentleman now forgotten, who was "distinguished for collecting animals and dissecting them." Biology had not yet attained the social success that physics and mathematics enjoyed, but it was recognized. Pensions were granted to Dutch and to Italian mathematicians; the glory of the King in the role of Maecenas did not stop at the French frontiers; it radiated over western Europe.

France in the Seventeenth Century became the leader in culture that Italy had been in the Sixteenth. To the French Academy that Richelieu had founded, and to the Academy of Painting and Sculpture founded by Mazarin, there were added an Academy of Science, an Academy of Architecture, an Academy of Music, and an Academy of France at Rome. The function of these academies was "to maintain respect for established principles." Departure from precedent was no more welcome in the arts than in politics. Genius was recognized, but it had to watch its step.

Despite the hobbles placed on creative minds, the best-known classics of French literature were produced in the Seventeenth Century. The Sun-King's patronage helped. The successful writers played safe by looking back rather than forward. They familiarized themselves with the literature of Greece and Rome and imitated it. Their work possessed the virtues of order, clarity, and simplicity. Dignity, majesty, and glory were extolled, but life as it really is was less discernible in their writings. There was no realism in the modern sense. Criticism could not be direct; if it occurred at all it had to take the form of restrained satire. The wonder is that under these repressive conditions work of high quality was produced. The great names were Molière, La Fontaine, Boileau, and Racine, four poets who were "linked in close friendship."

Molière was sixteen years younger than Corneille and their successes overlapped. Born in Paris in 1622, he was the son of an upholsterer. His real name was Jean-Baptiste Poquelin. Like Corneille, he was educated for the law, but his passion was the theater. For twenty years he traveled in the provinces as one of a troupe of actors, writing plays as he went. Returning to Paris in 1658, he played with his troupe before the King and was acclaimed. In the following year his *Les Précieuses Ridicules* had a great success. An indefatigable worker, Molière continued to act and to write more than two plays a year until his death in 1673. *Tartufe, Le Bourgeois Gentilhomme,* and *Le Misanthrope* are three of the best known.

Molière's portrayal of human foibles is magnificent. Human suffering interested him less. Many of his characters have become imperishable and many of his happy phrases have become proverbs. Although it was not opened until some years after his death, Molière was the true founder of the *Comédie Française.*

The genius of Jean de La Fontaine, born at Château-Thierry in 1621, was late in flowering. He was forty-three before he produced anything that would make his name survive. Patronized by Fouquet, he came to Paris and spent years there "looking on." He was a great stroller. He walked slowly in city and country, dreaming and observing. Boileau, Racine, Molière, and La Fontaine were often seen together in the *cabarets;* they stimulated one another. Finally La Fontaine found a way to express himself. He used animals to represent men. His classic *Fables,* "a comedy in a hundred acts," came near to realism; in them he expressed his conception of life and his criticism of the human species. La Fontaine has been called "the most delicate, the most spiritual, and the most French" of all the writers of his time. With Homeric simplicity and beauty, he put the universe into his lyric and picturesque writing.

Nicolas Boileau, a Parisian, was born in 1636. He was not so great a writer as some of his contemporaries, but no one had so much influence upon other writers. Like Malherbe in the last days of Henri IV, he had a passion for criticism, and at that he was a master. His sardonic attacks on bad writing did much to improve the public taste. His *Art Poétique* set the standards of style; he was called the *"legislateur du Parnasse."* Louis XIV presented to Boileau a house in Auteuil which became a rendezvous for literary celebrities.

Jean Racine, born at La Ferté-Milon in 1639, "realized to perfection the ideal of classic tragedy." When he was twenty-seven his *Andromaque,* presented by Molière, had a popular success like that of Corneille's *le Cid.* For Racine, love was the great theme. His sensitive nature made him a victim of it; his devotion to an actress who was his best interpreter came to grief. At thirty-seven, after the triumph of his *Phèdre* and at the height of his glory, he gave up the theater, married a homely girl and, as if in penitence, devoted himself to domestic duties and to religion. His early training at Port-Royal may have determined the scruples that he developed against the theater; he had broken with that training only to return again to its precepts. At Madame de Maintenon's urgent request, he wrote, after his retirement, *Esther* and *Athalie,* two biblical tragedies that were presented by the young ladies of Saint Cyr.

Jacques-Bénigne Bossuet, a burly bishop, was a great orator. Born at Dijon in 1627, he went to Paris when he was thirty-two with a reputation for eloquence already established. He was at his best at funerals. He was the orator at the obsequies of Anne of Austria, 1667, of Henrietta of France, widow of Charles I of England, 1669, and of Henrietta of England, wife of the King's brother, 1670. In that last year he was appointed tutor to the Dauphin. For the benefit of that indolent youth he wrote treatises on politics, history, and religion. He found justification in the Holy Scriptures for King Louis's absolutism.

Bossuet was the great spokesman of his time for the Church; he wrote of its force, of its harmony, of its cohesion, and of the importance to avoid the sin of individualism into which Protestants had fallen. In 1681 he became the Bishop of Meaux. Though only a bishop, he was the true head of the Church in France. His abundant writings in its defense and in criticism of the Reformation are more admirable for their literary quality than for the strength of their argument. He came to be called the Eagle of Meaux. His funeral orations for Turenne and for Condé are classics.

We have already met François de Salignac de La Mothe-Fénelon as tutor of the Duke of Burgundy with whom he achieved better results than Bossuet had achieved with the Duke's father. Fénelon, though an aristocrat to his fingertips, was an opponent of absolutism. His *Télémaque,* a book filled with critical allusions to the King's policies, brought an abrupt end to the favor the King had shown him. He retired to his bishopric of Cambrai. Fénelon's keen intelligence prevented his acceptance of the assumptions of Bossuet; he differed from his eloquent colleague in having more respect for human capacity; in his views he was as much a forerunner of Rousseau as a good churchman could be. His many published letters and essays show that he was ahead of his time. His humane philosophy and his deep sympathy are reflected in a concern for social responsibilties of which his contemporaries were hardly aware. The classic grace of his literary style combined with his tall and slender physique earned for Fénelon the nickname *Cygne de Cambrai.* In a theological dispute with the Eagle of Meaux, the Swan came off second best because the Eagle had the support of the Pope. Fénelon submitted to Church discipline, and eloquently defended it, but vindication of his ideas came in the next century when the Revolution's *Convention,* to honor him, awarded a national pension to his descendants.

A woman of extraordinary talent was a keen observer of the French scene through most of the reign of Louis XIV. She was Madame la Marquise de Sévigné, 1626-1696. Happily widowed at twenty-five, she lavished all her affection upon a "dry and pedantic" daughter who married the Count of Grignan. He became lieutenant-general of Provençe. They lived in the château Grignan at the top of a lonely, sun-baked hill. Madame de Sévigné, to comfort her spoiled child, so far away from the Court and so lonely, wrote many letters. Those letters have become famous. Madame la Marquise was not a literary genius, but she was an extraordinarily gifted reporter with a vivid imagination. She wrote about everything that came to her mind, about Paris styles, about the news of the Court, about the theater, about the movements of armies, and about how to preserve plums. Her letters, written through twenty-five years, are unrivaled as a chronicle of seventeenth-century life in France. Her Paris home, *l'Hôtel Carnavalet*, now houses the museum of the city. Many of those who are historically-minded consider Carnavalet the most interesting museum in Paris.

Louis de Rouvroy, Duke of Saint-Simon, lived from 1675 to 1755. His *Mémoires* provide the fullest and most interesting account of the Court of Louis XIV; for the years between 1691 and 1723 he is the best authority. Saint-Simon caustically criticized the follies of the Court, but he did not fail to share them. His prejudices and his torrential style add to the interest if not to the accuracy of his presentation.

Louis XIV had more influence upon architecture, sculpture, and painting than he had upon writing. At the Louvre, the Invalides, Versailles, Trianon, and Marly he kept many artists steadily employed. All their projects had to be submitted for his approval before they were executed. His taste ran to the solemn, the regular, the majestic. In architecture the Gothic and the Italian styles were not admired by Louis; Roman arches and Greek colonnades were what he liked. Unsuitable though they were to the climate of northern France, and over the protest of practical Colbert, the King insisted on flat roofs that became little lakes after every rain storm. Sculpture was similarly held to classic models. The park of Versailles bears witness to that; it is full of imitations of Greek and Roman statuary. Louis had a statue made of himself attired as a Roman emperor; the only thing not Roman about it is the wig. He could not give that up. In the paintings that he approved, Minerva, Venus and other gods and goddesses add the classic note to portrayals of contemporary scenes.

The great architectural monuments of Louis are the east wing of the Louvre, the Invalides, and the château of Versailles. The colonnade of the east façade of the Louvre set a new style that was copied all over Europe. The *Hôtel des Invalides* was built as a home for crippled old soldiers. Mansart, the most famous architect of his time, added to it a chapel which was his masterpiece. The dome of that chapel has been called the most graceful in the world. It was deemed worthy, more than a century later, to be the monument under which lies the tomb of Napoleon.

The King's memory of the Fronde made Paris distasteful to him. Saint Germain also held painful memories, and he did not like the view from the great terrace there. Far across the valley he could see the steeple of the church of Saint Denis in whose crypt the kings of France were buried. He did not like to look at it. He decided to build a new palace, more worthy of his glory.

Three years after Mazarin's death, Louis XIV began the enlargement of the *pavillon de chasse* that his father had built at Versailles. His ideas expanded with the building. In 1676 he placed Mansart in charge of his magnified project. It took nearly twenty years to bring it to completion. The park, far more extensive than it is today, covered twenty thousand acres. The palace and its dependencies could house ten thousand people, but no rooms had baths. The long suite that looks to the west "was lighted by a hundred thousand candles." The furnishings were the most magnificent that had ever been assembled. Le Nôtre, great landscape architect, achieved for the park a perfect symmetry; far vistas run through the woods across canals and fountains, and there are many marble statues. Versailles is the perfect example of the *style Louis Quatorze*. Its magnificence should not obscure the suffering of the people whom he bled white to build it and to maintain it. No palace surpasses Versailles as a monument to man's inhumanity to man.

France has rarely known such misery as it knew in the latter part of the reign of Louis XIV. The root of the evil lay in the taxes. They were frightfully heavy and there were flagrant injustices in their collection. Colbert did much to enrich the kingdom, but, even before his death, the King's extravagance created a mounting deficit. After his death, things went from bad to worse.

The duties of Vauban, fortification builder, took him to all parts of the kingdom. In his book that the King suppressed he wrote, "Things have come to such a pass that peasants who might have one or two cows or a few sheep do not have them on account of the taxes. They find it better to possess as nearly nothing as possible. They go about almost naked and they only half-cultivate the land so that the blood-sucking tax collectors may not double their charges. . . . The common people do not have meat to eat three times a year. Three-fourths of them are clad in ragged and rotten garments of the cheapest kind of cloth. They wear wooden shoes in which their feet are bare the whole year round." The governor at Grenoble wrote, "Most of the peasants have lived through the winter on acorns and roots. Now that spring has come they are eating grass and bark." Desperate peasants who revolted were quickly hanged. Twenty-five thousand of them revolted in Brittany in 1675; the governor of that province reported, "The trees along the high roads are beginning to suffer from the extra weight with which they have been burdened." That was the price the common people had to pay for the magnificence of Versailles and for the glory of their King.

Louis XV, like his predecessor, was only five when his reign began. Louis XIV had had his mother and Mazarin. Louis XV was less fortunate. He was an orphan, and, instead of a Mazarin, he had his uncle, Duke Philip of Orléans. The will of Louis XIV had provided that Orléans, first Prince of the Blood, should have the title of regent, but not the authority. Most of the authority was to be entrusted to the Duke of Maine, a son of the King and of Madame de Montespan. This will brought the long obscured *Parlement* into the limelight again. It had confirmed the regency of Marie de Medici, and civil war followed. It had annulled the will of Louis XIII, and the Fronde followed. Now, at the request of Orléans, it annulled the will of Louis XIV, and the nobility "merely produced memoirs." The policies of Richelieu and of the Sun-King had so enfeebled the nobles that they were unable to take advantage of a regency. There was no recurrence of feudal reaction.

Maine, deprived of authority, became the bitter enemy of Orléans. The infant King had another uncle besides Orléans who was also a bitter enemy of the Regent. He was King Philip of Spain. Philip believed that Orléans might do away with little Louis in order to become king himself. He declared that, in that case, in spite of his renunciation, he would maintain his own claim to the throne of France. The body of Louis XIV was hardly cold before the alliance with Spain that he had built up at such great cost was shattered.

Orléans, regent at forty-one, devoted himself to debauchery for eight years and died of apoplexy at forty-nine. He was a perfect product of the artificiality that Louis XIV had created. He had proved himself a brave soldier, and he was intelligent, but he was not seriously interested in government. He was more interested in departing as far as possible from the ceremony and solemnity that had marked the last years of the previous reign. He and his companions were carried to bed by their lackeys nearly every night.

To the *Parlement* that had served him by breaking the late King's will the Regent restored the "right of remonstrance." Taking their new right seriously, *Parlement* remonstrated against some of the Regent's financial edicts. He then curtailed their new right.

The Regent felt that his fellow nobles should have a greater share in the government. He established six councils, largely made up of nobles who soon demonstrated their inefficiency. After two years of that, there was a return to the previous system.

One of the Regent's favorite advisers was the Abbé Dubois, his former tutor. Dubois, a very crafty and unscrupulous person, advised an alliance with England as the best way to checkmate the designs of Philip of Spain. Philip wished to break the Treaty of Utrecht. The breaking of that treaty would annul his renunciation of claim to the throne of France, and might regain for Spain her former possessions in Italy. Dubois was authorized to negotiate with England and Holland, recent enemies of France.

These negotiations were facilitated by the fact that, in 1714, the

Elector of Hanover had become King of England. As George I he had succeeded Queen Anne, the last of the Stuarts to reign; he was the grandson of a daughter of James I and he was a Protestant. Protestant England preferred him to the Pretender, Catholic James III, then a guest of France. England, her new regime not yet firmly established and threatened by an invasion in favor of the Pretender, had need of the friendship of France. Her government agreed to cooperate in maintenance of the Treaty of Utrecht, and France agreed to expel the Pretender from her soil. A few months later, Holland, closely allied to England, joined in this agreement. Thus another Triple Alliance was formed. It was to endure until 1740.

France had its Dubois, but Spain had its Alberoni. Both were reminiscent of Mazarin in their methods. Alberoni, son of an Italian gardener, educated by the Jesuits, became chief adviser of the Farnese family that ruled over the duchy of Parma. Representing them at Madrid, Alberoni achieved a master-stroke in bringing about the marriage of King Philip, a widower, to Elizabeth Farnese, niece of the Duke of Parma. The new Queen had every confidence in Alberoni and the King had every confidence in the Queen. In 1714 Alberoni, then a cardinal, had become the real head of the Spanish government. His great ambition was to drive the Austrians out of Italy. With all the energy of a Richelieu he aroused Spain out of its lethargy. He created a new army of sixty thousand and a new fleet. In 1717 his troops invaded and conquered Sardinia. France and England protested against this breaking of the treaty. Alberoni's response was to foment rebellion in France and to concoct an invasion of England by the Pretender, supported by Charles XII of Sweden. His plan for rebellion in France had the ardent support of the Duchess of Maine and of certain provincial nobles; the Duchess had never forgiven the Regent for his treatment of her husband. Alberoni felt that there was little to fear from the Emperor who was being kept busy at that time by the Turks.

In 1718 a Spanish army captured Palermo and a Spanish fleet blockaded Messina. Thereupon the Emperor joined the Triple Alliance, and from that time Alberoni's well-laid plans began to go awry. The Emperor defeated the deteriorated Turks and made peace with them.

An English fleet destroyed the Spanish fleet, Charles XII of Sweden was killed in a battle in Norway, and the plotters in France were found out before their rebellion started. Another general European war was thus stopped before it had fairly begun. In December, 1719, King Philip accepted the conditions that were imposed by the Alliance and expelled Alberoni.

France, while on the brink of another great war, was also on the brink of financial collapse. The state debt was in excess of two billion *livres* and the treasury was empty. Many expedients were tried, but none of them produced satisfactory results. Then a persuasive Scotsman came along with a big idea. John Law was a pioneer in high finance and high-pressure salesmanship. He had had successful commercial experience in London, Amsterdam, Genoa, Florence, and Venice. He presented his case convincingly. He believed that prosperity depended upon an abundance of money, and that, to make it abundant, the state should freely issue notes, redeemable in metal money on demand.

In 1716 Law was authorized by the Regent to open a private bank and to issue notes. The government had already issued *titres de créance* (bonds) which were much depreciated. Law agreed to accept these *titres* in three-fourths payment for shares in his bank. Under these conditions he had no difficulty in floating the shares. The bank was a great success; its paper notes were found to be much more convenient than heavy money. In the following year, over the opposition of *Parlement,* Law succeeded in having the notes of his bank made acceptable in the payment of taxes. In 1718 his bank became the bank of the state. Up to that point, all was well, but the next step proved to be fatal. Law proposed to reduce the debt by accepting claims on the government in payment for shares in commercial enterprises. The government thus found itself in the investment business as well as in banking.

Law organized a Company of the West which received a monopoly on the exploitation of Louisiana. There was talk of mines of gold and silver and precious stones. This was the Mississippi Bubble. The company extended its monopoly to far-eastern territories whose fabulous wealth it would exploit, and took the name Company of the

Indies. Its shares rose like a rocket. There was a tremendous bull market, the sort in which people buy for a rise and, blinded by greed, lose sight of real values. Shares rose to forty times their face value and fortunes were made over night. The whole structure ceased to rest on real value; it rested on confidence alone, a confidence soon to be shaken. The bank and the company were so interrelated that they had to stand or fall together.

Early in 1720 certain prudent gentlemen began to convert their paper holdings into metal. The Duke of Bourbon drove up one day and carried off sixty millions in gold in three carriages. By that time the bank, to meet the needs of business, had issued in notes six times as much as there was of metal money in all France. It had to close its windows. There were tragic scenes. In the rush to change notes into metal several people were trampled to death. Their bodies were laid in front of the *Palais Royal* where the Regent lived. Law's residence was raided. He had to flee from France. He died in poverty in Venice.

The prudent gentlemen who had sold their shares before the crash profited greatly; many of them were Hollanders, the best businessmen of their time. There were also lucky little people; waiters, street-sweepers, and lackeys who made fortunes by selling shares for twenty to forty times what they had paid. But for one who had gained there were a hundred who had lost, and that loss could not be measured in money alone. The great loss was the moral loss. The people lost confidence in all financial institutions, in the government, and in themselves. There was loss of confidence in the value of honesty as well as in the value of money. Crime increased. John Law's schemes demonstrated that the easiest way to demoralize people is to give them a chance to make money without working for it; they demonstrated that speculation undermines morality. Since that time there have been more than two centuries of similar demonstrations, but greed remains stronger than morality and speculation continues to flourish. Few of those who profit thereby even suspect that they are contributory to social delinquency.

The state, having reduced its debt by defrauding the people, found its treasury in better shape in 1720 than it had been in 1715. The bankrupt Company of the Indies was reorganized and carried on with overseas business. That helped maritime commerce. From 1720 to 1740 France had peace and regained some of the prosperity that only war or the threat of war could keep her from having.

The regency came automatically to an end on February 22, 1723, because that was the King's thirteenth birthday. The Duke of Orléans and the Cardinal Dubois died in that same year. The one who had the most influence with the King was his old teacher, Bishop Fleury of Fréjus. Louis wanted Fleury to take charge of the government, but the bishop, a modest and venerable gentleman, thought it better to have a Prince of the Blood placed in authority. The Duke of Bourbon, great-grandson of the Grand Condé, was named prime minister; it was he who had hastened the crash of the Law system by carrying off sixty millions in gold in three carriages.

Bourbon's authority lasted only three years; the King exiled him in 1726 for having tried to disgrace Fleury. The principal event during his ministry was the King's marriage to Marie Leczinska, daughter of a dethroned King of Poland. That marriage widened the breach between France and Spain.

Orléans, shortly before his death, had attempted reconciliation with Spain by proposing that one of the little Spanish princesses should marry Louis XV. Louis's Uncle Philip agreed to this and a four-year-old princess was sent to the Court of France to be brought up there as its future queen. Bourbon did not like this arrangement; since England was hostile to Spain, the proposed marriage would weaken the Anglo-French alliance; it also had the disadvantage of making the birth of an heir to the throne impossible for many years. Since no English princess was available, Bourbon looked for one who would be unobjectionable to England and who could be expected to become a mother with the least possible delay. His choice fell upon the Polish Princess Marie, a healthy and homely girl, seven years older than her prospective bridegroom. She and Louis were married when Louis was fifteen. The little Spanish princess was returned to Madrid and King Philip was furious about that. He broke off all relations with France and came to terms with his old enemy, the Emperor Charles VI.

CHAPTER SEVEN

THE REIGN OF LOUIS XV

A SMALL WAR WITH AUSTRIA. FOREIGN TRADE EXPANDED. FREDERICK
THE GREAT AND MARIA-THERESA. THE BRILLIANCE OF MAURICE DE SAXE
AND THE SUCCESS OF MADAME DE POMPADOUR. MONTESQUIEU, VOLTAIRE,
DIDEROT, AND ROUSSEAU. THE PHILOSOPHICAL MOVEMENT PRODUCED
POLITICAL EFFECTS.

THE CARDINAL FLEURY was seventy-three when he became prime minister. His ministry ran from 1726 to 1743. In all that time he strove for peace and, in striving for it, he brought on war. His pacificism was more idealistic than practical. The times were not ripe for such gentleness and sincerity as his.

Walpole, prime minister of England, co-operated for some years with Fleury in pacific effort; England was in no condition at that time to undertake a foreign war. Fleury succeeded in soothing irate King Philip of Spain. Remembering that he was a Bourbon and born French, Philip, in spite of his grievances, renewed the Franco-Spanish alliance.

Peace was maintained until 1733. In that year the King of Poland died. The kingship of Poland was not hereditary; it was elective. Stanislas Leczinska, King Louis's father-in-law and once King of Poland, was re-elected to that difficult position. There was a rival candidate, however, who had the support of Austria and Russia. Austrian and Russian troops dethroned Stanislas for the second time. Louis XV decided to support the cause of his father-in-law, and that led to war with Austria.

Fleury was greatly embarrassed. Austrian Flanders could not be invaded without causing offense to England. So the Austrian possessions in Italy were invaded. An army led by old *Maréchal* Villars, the hero of Malplaquet, conquered Milan. Fleury, more eager for peace than for victory, made easy terms with Emperor Charles VI. The

Emperor's great interest at that time was to secure the succession to his throne for his daughter, a throne that had never been occupied by a woman. His daughter was the remarkable Maria-Theresa. She was very different from her Spanish namesake who had married Louis XIV. The Austrian Maria married the Duke of Lorraine. In view of Fleury's undertaking that France would support the Emperor's daughter as his successor, it was agreed that Austria would not, on account of her marriage, renew its old claim to Lorraine; Stanislas Leczinska was to rule there until his death; Lorraine would then revert to France. These agreements were reached in Vienna in 1738.

In the years between 1720 and 1739 the foreign trade of France expanded greatly. Her merchant marine numbered more than five thousand ships. Spain, too, had had an economic revival, thanks to the impulse given by Alberoni. Overseas competition with these rivals was vexatious to England. English sailors brought home constant complaints of ill-treatment by Spaniards; there were incidents that bordered on warfare. Finally, in October, 1739, England, under George II and Walpole, declared war on Spain. France, in view of her renewed alliance with Spain, was brought into it. Two French squadrons were sent to co-operate with the Spanish navy. A desultory war on water began. It lasted for years.

The Emperor Charles VI died in 1740. Despite the promises of support for his daughter that Charles had secured in many courts, her right to succeed him as emperor was vigorously contested. Fleury, then approaching his ninetieth birthday, was all for keeping the promise of France, but the anti-Austrian sentiment was too strong for the old man. Belle-Isle, a grandson of Fouquet who had taken the name of his grandfather's famous property off the coast of Brittany, led the movement to support the opposition to Maria-Theresa, and thus to wrest the imperial crown from the House of Hapsburg. This plan was consistent with the traditional policy and interests of France. It led to the War of the Austrian Succession.

The chief adversary of Maria-Theresa was the new King of Prussia, Frederick the Great of the House of Hohenzollern. Frederick had inherited from his father a splendidly trained army. The Hohenzollerns had an ancient claim on Silesia which lay to the southeast of Brandenburg; Berlin was the capital of Brandenburg and Frederick was its Elector. This ancient claim had been renounced by treaty, but a mere treaty was never enough to stop a Hohenzollern. Frederick occupied Silesia in December, 1740. He then offered to support Maria if she would concede Silesia to him. Magnificent Maria spurned the offer and sent an army against the invader. Frederick defeated that army.

Belle-Isle went to Germany and strengthened there the coalition against Maria-Theresa by promising the aid of France. France did not declare war against Austria, but two French armies entered Germany as "auxiliaries" of Austria's enemies. The coalition succeeded in having the Elector of Bavaria chosen emperor as Charles VII.

Maria-Theresa did not give up. The Hungarians had never been docile subjects of the Hapsburgs, but Maria succeeded in arousing them to her support. They called a hundred thousand men to arms. By reluctantly ceding Silesia to Frederick, Maria secured his withdrawal from the coalition in spite of promises to the contrary he had made to France. Belle-Isle, in command of the French forces, found himself isolated in Prague and had to make a difficult retreat in winter across the mountains of Bohemia. The Austro-Hungarian army advanced to the Rhine and threatened an invasion of Alsace.

The venerable Cardinal Fleury, in his last pathetic appeal for peace, wrote a letter of apology to Maria-Theresa, explaining how much it had been against his will that France had taken the part of her enemies. Maria unkindly published this letter, thereby making Fleury the laughingstock of all the hard-boiled diplomats of Europe. That was a final blow for the good old peace-lover. He died in January, 1743.

The War of the Austrian Succession became, in its second phase, largely a duel between France and Austria, with England and Holland as allies of Maria-Theresa. Frederick the Great, alarmed by the rapid successes of Austria, took sides momentarily with France. Charles VII, the new emperor, died in 1745 and the Duke of Lorraine, Maria's husband, was elected to succeed him. Frederick, by two brilliant victories, tightened his grip on Silesia, and then again went back on his agreement to remain an ally of France.

Fortunately for France, a great captain came into her service at this time. He was Maurice de Saxe, a son of the King of Poland. Maurice, as a French general, won a brilliant victory over an English-

Dutch army at Fontenoy, near Tournai in Belgium. That was in April, 1745. At Fontenoy the enemy lost more than fifteen thousand men. Maurice de Saxe was presented with the château of Chambord and a pension of forty thousand *livres*.

France was not so fortunate elsewhere. A Franco-Spanish army was driven out of Italy and the English were steadily victorious on the seas. Peace was made by the Treaty of Aix-la-Chapelle in 1748. It was not the sort of peace that Richelieu would have made. France had won Belgium, Savoy, and Nice. Louis XV, eager for peace and greatly bored by the whole business, gave up all the territory that had been won and took nothing in return. The treaty recognized possession of Silesia by Frederick the Great. France, against her own interests, had served Frederick better than she had served herself. However, the Peace of Aix-la-Chapelle was only a truce. War was to break out again a few years later. The Seven-Years' War was to be fought from 1756 to 1763.

Fleury's two objectives were peace and a restoration of financial order. He had more success with the latter than with the former. With the aid of Orry, an excellent administrator, the budget was balanced in 1739 for the first time since the days of Colbert. The nation had become prosperous again. After the Law catastrophe there was a return to dependable currency. Domestic business was improved by improvement of the roads and the volume of foreign trade was doubled. The ports of Bordeaux, La Rochelle, Nantes, and Havre were more active than ever. As long as there was peace, the superior products of France found ready sale abroad, especially in England.

The people, in spite of the improved conditions, had but limited respect for the government. This was particularly true in Paris. The intolerant absolutism of Louis XIV, the heavy taxes, and the great financial fraud had produced a widespread discontent that did not disappear. Paris, passionately Catholic in the days of the League, became refractory about religion, if for no better reason than to be "agin the government." The Jesuits, once popular, became hated. A papal bull had condemned the Jansenism that Louis XIV had tried to suppress; the Archbishop of Paris ordered that communion should not be administered to those who did not respect this injunction, and the government took a similar position. Paris showed its temper by becoming more Jansenist than ever. The *Parlement* also opposed the government on this issue. When some of the leaders of this opposition were arrested, their fellow magistrates resigned; the entire judiciary went on strike. The government banished the striking magistrates from Paris. Two months later, an impossible situation having been created, Fleury called them back, mutual concessions were made, and calm was temporarily restored. It was evident, however, that the people would never again be so submissive as they had been in the past. New ideas were abroad and there was new determination to resist injustice.

Louis XV was thirty-three when Fleury died. The people had great hopes of him. Despite the critical spirit that prevailed, the French were still swayed by their ancient desire for a king deserving of their love. They had no thought as yet of a government without a king; they thought of a king as the real father of his people; if things went wrong, they preferred to believe that the fault lay with the ladies he loved or with his ministers.

Louis was handsome and sometimes gracious. When an Austrian army was on the threshold of Alsace, he went to Metz to direct the defense. He was with Maurice de Saxe at Fontenoy in 1745. At that time he was called Louis the Well-loved.

Some excuse for the King may be found in the way in which he was brought up. The *milieu* that his predecessor had created was no place for a boy who was an orphan at two and a king at five. He was constantly surrounded by courtiers who did everything to flatter his egotism. There was no spur to effort, no discipline. He was told again and again that the people were his to rule as he saw fit. He was assured of his divine right, but not of his responsibility. The business of government bored him. He preferred to go hunting. He felt that when he had named ministers to do the work his responsibility was over. At Council meetings he showed no interest in the proceedings. He had an inferiority complex from which he never escaped.

Married at fifteen, Louis was for some years "a good husband" to his mature and lusty Polish bride. They had ten children of whom

seven lived; six girls and one boy. However, after seventeen years of
Marie, Louis began to look around. One of his early favorites was
the Duchess of Châteauroux. The Duchess tried to shake her royal
lover out of his lethargy; unfortunately she died without succeeding
in doing so.

The King then fell in love with Jeanne Poisson, a beautiful commoner whom he ennobled by making her the Marquise de Pompadour.
The charming and intelligent Marquise moved into the palace at
Versailles; later on she had palaces of her own. From 1745 until her
death in 1764 Pompadour was the real power behind the throne. The
King appointed no prime minister; he imagined that he was prime
minister himself. Ministers and generals were appointed and removed at the whim of La Pompadour. The rudderless ship of state
drifted to disaster.

One good minister was Machault who replaced Orry as controller
of finance. After the War of the Austrian Succession it became imperative to levy a new tax. Machault proposed a five-per-cent tax on in-
comes from which no one was to be exempt. The privileged classes,
and especially the clergy, made frantic outcry. The King gave in and
allowed such exemptions that practically the entire burden of the new
tax fell upon the Third Estate, upon those who could least afford to
pay it. Then as now, the privileged groups were too shortsighted to
perceive that it was to their interest to support a just reform. Their
opposition to it hastened the day of their destruction.

The King, after Pompadour came into his life, became madly extravagant. The fêtes that he gave were even more expensive than those
of his glorious predecessor and the bills were paid without even a look
at them. The cost of "the little pleasures of the King" rose from half a
million *livres* each year to nearly three million. When any minister
suggested economy the King turned his back.

In 1750 the King had lost all the popularity that he had had a few
years before. Madame de Pompadour was hooted and jeered in the
streets of Paris and had to flee. There was talk of marching on Versailles and of burning the palace. A gentleman recorded in his journal
that the people hated the King with bitter hatred and talked of revolution in order to control him in the way that the king of England was
controlled.

The frivolity of the Court was reflected in the social life of the wealthy. The trickery in finance that Law had introduced, the system of farming out the taxes, and the general prosperity prior to 1750 produced many millionaires. Money was spent freely on art, on entertainment, and on libertinism. Upper-crust life in Paris became a spectacle that bewildered and delighted foreign visitors. There was an elegance, a carefreeness, and an immorality about it that could not fail to charm. In that atmosphere anxiety ceased to exist; to take anything seriously was not permissible. It was necessary to be gallant and urgent to be witty, but it was not important to be wise, charitable, or virtuous.

The artificiality of that society was as great as that of the Court of Louis XIV, but it was of a different sort. The difference was reflected in the popular art of the day. Solemnity, spaciousness, and majesty fell from favor. They were replaced by prettiness, intimacy, daintiness. There was more interest in boudoir decoration than in great halls hung with huge tapestries and heroic paintings. Slim-legged furniture came in and square solidity went out; everything had to be sinuous. Elegance replaced dignity. Watteau, whose paintings were sweet little poems, set a style under the regency. He had many imitators. Jupiter and Minerva disappeared in favor of Venus, nymphs, fat cupids, and pastoral scenes with shepherdesses. Architecture became rococo and interior decoration ran to pastel shades, mirrors in elaborate, curly frames, and painted woodwork ornamented with carved garlands, ribbon bows and furbelows. It was a triumph for the girlishness of both sexes.

There was another side to this picture. In the midst of elegance, insouciance, and unreality, serious thinking was done. The drift policy of Louis XV, through its very negligence, was favorable to the development of thought and expression about topics formerly taboo in polite society. There began to be much more talk about religion, about social justice, about the rights of man, about the achievement of opportunity for the fulfillment of human capacity. In this slack reign things were said, written, and printed that before were only whispered. Philosophers sat on slender chairs and discussed great subjects in frivolous environments. There was an emancipation of the mind.

The intellectual salons of Paris had ceased to exist when Louis XIV made everybody who was anybody come to Versailles. Under his successor they reappeared. One of the most famous was that of Madame de Lambert who said that "to philosophize is to shake the yoke of opinion and of authority." In her salon there was much shaking of that yoke.

There developed what was called "the philosophical movement," a tendency to make unprejudiced examination of the validity of all theories, beliefs and institutions. This movement was English as well as French. England, in two revolutions, had destroyed forever the absolutism of her kings. John Locke (1632-1704) had written of the rights of man, of the sovereignty of the people, and of religious tolerance. In the quarter-century of Franco-English friendship that followed the death of Louis XIV, the intellectuals of London and Paris frequently visited one another. Montesquieu and Voltaire passionately admired the tolerance and the liberty that they witnessed in England.

Montesquieu, once president of the *Parlement* of Bordeaux, published during the regency his *Lettres Persanes* (1721). La Fontaine had prudently camouflaged his criticisms in fables of animal life. Montesquieu, a little bolder, presented his in the form of a correspondence between Persians; that correspondence emphasized the stupidity of Church and governmental effort to impose a single form of religion. His great work, however, was his *L'Esprit des Lois* (1748), a critical examination of all forms of government. Montesquieu found the English system the best of those prevailing. He advocated separation of the legislative, executive, and judicial powers. His book had great influence. Forty years after its publication, principles that it recommended were followed in the making of the Constitution of the United States.

Voltaire, born in Paris in 1694, lived until 1778. He was the son of a lawyer named Arouet. When twenty-three he spent a year in the Bastille on the charge of having written a criticism of the Regent. When he was released he changed his name to Voltaire. Some years later he went to jail again for six months because he lodged complaint against a noble gentleman whose lackeys, by direction, had assaulted him. Once released, he left France in disgust and went to England. Returning after four years, he published his *Lettres Philosophiques*.

They presented the theories of Locke and Newton and they compared England and France much to the disadvantage of France. That book was burned by order and its author escaped a third term in the Bastille only by flight.

At thirty-five Voltaire decided to risk martyrdom no further. He had seen enough of prisons. From that time on he saw much of *salons* and of palaces. He became the great wit, satirist, and historian of his day. He had an enormous social success. He was a guest of Louis XV at Versailles and of Frederick the Great at Potsdam. In 1751 he published *Le Siècle de Louis XIV,* his most important historic work. However, it was as a pamphleteer that Voltaire was at his best. At sixty-four he retired to the château of Ferney that overlooks Lake Geneva, a château that his genius has made historic. In the twenty years that were left to him of life, the pen of Voltaire at Ferney was mightier than any sword in Europe. He was the Eighteenth Century's great champion of truth and justice.

Voltaire's philosophy and his superb criticisms of religious intolerance added to the flood of thought and feeling that swept on to the Revolution, but he was not a republican nor a believer in revolution. He was a believer in enlightened despotism. He was a humanist, but, for humanity's own sake, he had no confidence in popular government. By instinct he was an aristocrat, a lover of elegance who liked fine lace at his throat and frequented the seats of the mighty. But his brilliant and sensitive mind could never acquiesce in injustice. With "clarity and spiritual precision" he bared abuses to the bone and revealed the essential humanism of his philosophy.

It was fortunate for his fellow men that Voltaire's fondness for fashionable society kept him from spending his best years in jail. He had more influence in the *salons* than he could have had in the Bastille. Being what he was, he served humanity better by not sharing its suffering. He was its intellectual ambassador.

Before Voltaire's time there had been no open conflict between philosophy and the established order. Criticism had covered itself with literary camouflage, for the doors of the Bastille opened inward all too easily. After the publication of Voltaire's *Lettres,* the inevitable conflict moved into the open. The weakness of the government made the need for caution less. Montesquieu's great criticism was followed in 1750 by Jean-Jacques Rousseau's first *Discours*. In 1751 the first volume of Diderot's Encyclopedia appeared. Against absolutism and religious intolerance there arose an opponent that force could not defeat. The King and the Church could not imprison the new ideas that the philosophers no longer hesitated to advertise. *Parlement,* already in opposition to the old regime, found a new ally. The philosophers became an even more formidable opponent than the magistrates, for they shaped the vague and aimless discontent of the masses into definite desires. In the middle of the century, the people of France, submissive for centuries to the abuses of authority, found themselves on the threshold of a great discovery.

The new philosophical ideas owed much to the progress of science. The integrity of mathematical and empirical methods had been proved by Galileo in Italy, by Descartes in France, by Huygens in Holland, by Leibnitz in Germany, and by Newton in England. Respect for their work steadily increased. Science became fashionable. Private laboratories were as much in vogue as private art collections. The talk of the *salons* drifted from the drama of the stage to the drama of the universe.

Fontanelle, permanent secretary of the Academy of Science, was a pioneer in an art in which the French excel, the art of simplification. In his presentation of scientific theories, Fontanelle combined simplicity with an excellent literary style. He died in 1757, one hundred years old. His influence upon the French thought of his time was hardly less than that of Voltaire.

Herschel, 1738 to 1822, a German organist resident in England, made astronomical discoveries that gave rise to new conceptions of the universe. With the improvement of the telescope, thousands of stars were discovered that had been hitherto unseen. The suspicion grew that these stars might be other suns and that the universe is illimitable. Thought and imagination were given new dimensions. Bold minds became still more bold and kings seemed less important.

In the Eighteenth Century physics and chemistry were even more popular than astronomy. The thrill that comes in exploration of nature was described as "a forerunner of celestial bliss." Benjamin

Franklin's kite experiment was hailed with delight; it assured him a very favorable reception in France when he came as an ambassador. Thermometers appeared, Fahrenheit in England in 1724, Réaumur in France in 1730, and Celsius (centigrade) in Sweden in 1742. About 1775, the Scotsman James Watt invented the engine that was to give to England a century of unrivaled superiority in industry. In 1783 modern chemistry began with Lavoisier's synthesis of hydrogen and oxygen and his analysis of air. Another French chemist, Lebon, invented gas illumination. Buffon, 1707 to 1788, organizer of the *Jardin des Plantes* in Paris, was the great naturalist of that time. His *Histoire Naturelle* in twenty-nine volumes is a magnificent work. His *Epoques de la Nature* was philosophical as well as descriptive. It appeared just before the Revolution and had much influence upon popular thought.

Scientific and philosophical progress produced social and political effects. The ancient regime of Church and State rested upon religious assumptions that were held to be beyond dispute. There had been revolt on account of injustices and there had been war on account of religious differences, but there had never been any serious challenge of the fundamental basis of social organization. In the light of the new knowledge, however, the divine right of kings became no right at all and the supremacy of the Pope nothing more than an accepted technique. Hell began to lose its terrors. Science and philosophy had revealed a new foundation upon which a different political structure might be built. Attempts to build it were not to be long delayed. Unfortunately, the old structure had first to be destroyed, a destruction that could not be accomplished without tragedy.

Voltaire said that he believed in God, but no one was so successful as he in undermining belief in religious dogma or in shaking confidence in the virtue of the existing order. He was the great demolisher. Contemporary with him, and his rival in influence, there was another philosopher who was constructive rather than destructive. Jean-Jacques Rousseau, 1712 to 1778, passionate believer that virtue is inborn, had an enthusiasm for his beliefs that was contagious. Son of a poor clockmaker of Geneva, he was familiar with poverty. Unlike Voltaire, he wished to remain poor and "to share the miseries of the people"; at least he said he did. His *Contrat Social* appeared in 1762. Its fundamental thesis was human equality. For Rousseau, nature had no hand in the making of princes or of millionaires. Like John Locke, he maintained that all men are free and equal, that the first duty of the state is to safeguard the individual, but that the individual should submit to the will of the majority, which, alone, is sovereign.

Rousseau's *Contrat Social,* important when the Revolution came, produced little effect when it appeared, but his *Emile,* published in the same year, was very popular. It was a romantic book about how to bring up a boy. It was a pioneer in the return-to-nature movement. It extolled the beauties of motherhood and the joys of family life. It made the *salons* more interesting. Charming young mothers brought their babies along and proved that they did their own nursing. Rousseau's ideas about education still have effect; he was opposed to discipline; he found it impossible to believe that most children need it; he believed that nature should be trusted; some "progressive" schools still follow in his wake. About religion, Rousseau was sentimental; he was opposed to the atheism that gained ground at that time.

There was a group called the Encyclopedists. Denis Diderot, 1713 to 1784, the son of a knife-maker, was its leader. He was the most ardent, the boldest, and the most indefatigable of all the propagandists of the new philosophy. For openly declaring his atheism he was sent to prison; a century earlier he would have been sent to the stake. His fame rests especially upon the Encyclopedia of which he and the mathematician d'Alembert were the editors. Montesquieu, Voltaire, Rousseau, and Buffon contributed to it. It presented a general picture of the achievements of human intelligence. It was philosophical as well as practical. In 1752, after two volumes had appeared, it was suppressed as being subversive "of God and of Royal authority."

Diderot, fired with admirable enthusiasm, persuaded Madame de Pompadour to befriend his cause. Thanks to her influence, the Encyclopedia was completed in 1772 in thirty-four volumes. It was the most influential of all the presentations of the contemporary thought of the philosophers.

The philosophy of Rousseau had effect outside of France, especially in Germany. Goethe and Schiller were influenced by it.

A professor in the University of Glasgow, Adam Smith, published in 1765 his *Wealth of Nations*. That historic justification for a *laissez-faire* economy remained in good repute until recent years. The French economist Turgot sustained a similar thesis. The "hands-off-of-business" policy was better suited to those times than it is to ours. It led to increase of prosperity both in France and in England.

It would be too much to say that the philosophical movement was the direct cause of the Revolution, but it furnished to the Revolution its fundamental thesis and its interpretation of facts.

CHAPTER EIGHT

THE DECADENCE OF THE BOURBONS

THE DIPLOMATIC REVOLUTION AND THE DISASTROUS SEVEN YEARS' WAR.
PITT WON CANADA IN GERMANY AND FREDERICK THE GREAT MADE PRUSSIA
POWERFUL. FEEBLE LOUIS XVI AND FRIVOLOUS MARIE-ANTOINETTE. THE
REFORMS OF TURGOT AND NECKER WERE THWARTED AND
REVOLUTION BECAME INEVITABLE.

THE Peace of Aix-la-Chapelle of 1748 was an extremely precarious peace. For two major reasons it could not long continue. One reason was Maria-Theresa's determination to retake Silesia from Frederick the Great. The other was England's determination to prevail over France in India and America. France might have won the colonial war had she stood aloof from the struggle between Prussia and Austria, but there was no Richelieu or Mazarin to guide her destiny. When Maria-Theresa wished to have France at her side she addressed herself to Madame de Pompadour! A treaty that was made at Versailles in 1756 put an end to the old hostility between Austria and France and committed France to the fatal policy of fighting Austria's battles in Germany. England, seeing clearly where her interest lay, had become an ally of Frederick the Great. This was the Diplomatic Revolution. It cost France dear.

The Seven Years' War, 1756 to 1763, was as nearly a world war as could be managed in those days. France fought England in India, in America, on the sea, and in Germany. With Austria, Russia, and Saxony, she fought Frederick the Great. The winners were England and Frederick; the principal loser was France. The Seven Years' War revealed the weakness of her government and quickened the trend toward revolution.

After 1740 the colonial rivalry between France and England led to acts of war wherever their interests conflicted. From 1741 until 1760 they struggled for supremacy in India. There for years France held the upper hand thanks to the great energy and ability of Dupleix, governor of the French "establishments." Dupleix won the friendship and co-operation of many of the native princes in his effort to found a colonial empire. He was on the high road to success when he was checked by the enterprise and courage of a young English captain, Robert Clive. The French government did not support Dupleix. After he had expended his personal fortune in the interest of France, he went home and, unrewarded, died in poverty. Clive, following the policies that Dupleix had inaugurated, established the British power.

There was a similar rivalry in North America. There the French, holding Canada and New Orleans, claimed the whole Mississippi basin. The English opposed this claim. Their colonies controlled the coast from Georgia to Canada, but the French, by way of the Saint Lawrence and the Great Lakes, had easier access to the territory west of the Alleghenies. They constructed forts on tributaries of the Mississippi. They built Fort Duquesne on the headwaters of the Ohio. In 1754 the Governor of Virginia sent a militia officer named George Washington to attack Duquesne. He was repulsed. General Braddock, a veteran of European wars, was then sent at the head of trained troops. He too was defeated by the French and their Indian allies. England, without declaring war, attacked French shipping wherever it could be found and wrought great havoc. They blockaded French ports and attacked Cherbourg and Saint Malo.

England tried to make an alliance with Austria against France, but Maria-Theresa would have none of it. She never forgave England for having helped Frederick the Great to win Silesia. The new alignment developed. Maria won France to her support and the Seven Years' War began with France, Russia, and Saxony committed to co-operation with Austria against Frederick, and England ready to do all it could to injure France.

Definite hostilities began with capture by the French of English Minorca. An English fleet was defeated. This, coming after Braddock's defeat, caused a shake-up of the English cabinet. William Pitt, the elder, was given control of the war and soon proved himself the right man for that job.

At the end of 1756, Frederick the Great, knowing that delay would be fatal, invaded Saxony before his enemies were ready to fight.

England's Hanoverian king was still deeply interested in Hanover. His son, the Duke of Cumberland, was put in command of a Hanoverian army. Cumberland was compelled to surrender to French forces, but the French general made the mistake of allowing him to withdraw upon agreeing that his army would take no further part in the war. Pitt repudiated that agreement and the Hanoverian army returned to action. Frederick the Great never made a mistake like that; when he compelled the surrender of a Saxon army he made its soldiers fight for him.

In 1757 the combination of Pitt and Frederick proved its superiority over Maria-Theresa's more numerous coalition. England supplied funds for Frederick and supported the Hanoverian army. Pitt said, "I shall conquer America in Germany," and he made his word good.

Soubise, a favorite of Madame de Pompadour, was the French commander who opposed the Prussians. He had fifty thousand men. Frederick, with twenty thousand, defeated him in the Battle of Rossbach. George II sent Ferdinand of Brunswick to take command of the Hanoverian army; that army defeated another incapable French general in the Battle of Krefeld. Pompadour, all-powerful at Versailles, was responsible for disaster upon disaster. Napoleon said that "all the generals she selected were of the most perfect incapacity." Pitt's policy proved its virtue. France, compelled to fight in Germany, neglected her interests in India and America. Frederick the Great said, "England has at last produced a man."

In 1758 Montcalm was the French commander in Canada. Pitt sent thirty thousand men against him. Montcalm had hardly a third of that number. The French began to withdraw from their outposts. An English expedition found Fort Duquesne abandoned. They rechristened it Pittsburgh in honor of their great war minister. But the French defeated the English that year in an attack they made on Fort Ticonderoga on Lake Champlain.

In June of the following year a young British general named Wolfe reached the French stronghold of Quebec with nine thosand men, and camped below its cliffs. Montcalm's position was too strong for him to take by assault. Two attacks failed. The summer passed without success, and when September came the British admiral said he would have to withdraw the ships that were supporting Wolfe. Wolfe

decided to make a last desperate attempt. A weakly guarded path had
been found. It led up the cliff a mile and a half above Quebec. On a
dark night the guards of that path were surprised and overpowered.
When morning broke the whole English force had reached the Plains
of Abraham, a plateau above Quebec. Montcalm attacked at close
quarters. Wolfe and Montcalm were both mortally wounded, but
Quebec was won. In the following year Montreal surrendered and
Canada ceased to be a French possession. Heroic Montcalm, like
Dupleix in India, was the victim of a negligent government. Pompadour's personal allowance might have saved Canada for France.

The war was extremely unpopular in France. The alliance with
Austria had been disliked. After the defeats of Rossbach and Krefeld
the French generals were derided and Frederick the Great became a
popular hero in Paris. The Abbé de Bernis, who had perfected the
alliance with Austria, wrote, "In France there is no longer government, nor administration, nor army. Everything is in a state of de-
composition. We touch the final period of decadence. . . . The people
love the King of Prussia and detest the court of Vienna, regarding it a
bloodsucker at the throat of France."

Etienne Choiseul, an able man, became minister of foreign affairs
in 1758, but he could do little to check the tide of disaster that had set
in. Two fleets, as badly commanded as the army, were demolished by
the English. The prestige of the French land forces was lost. They
continued to fight in western Germany for possession of Hanover, but
achieved no success that was permanent.

Frederick the Great made desperate and heroic resistance to combined attacks by Russia and Austria. Attacked on two fronts by superior numbers, he was saved, as he himself wrote, "only by the mistakes of the enemy." In 1759 a Russian army came within three days'
march of Berlin and defeated Frederick in the Battle of Kunersdorf;
in that battle his army of forty-eight thousand was reduced to three
thousand and he lost all his artillery. He believed that his cause was
lost and asked for peace. What saved him was that the Austrian and
Russian forces did not unite. The Austrian army entered Saxony and
the Russians invaded Silesia. Frederick called that a miracle. He was
able to organize a new army, and, in the following year, he won two
important victories over the separated forces of the enemy.

Prussia, victorious, was exhausted. England, having attained her objectives in North America and in India, became less interested in the cause of Frederick. Her subsidies ceased. Austria and Russia continued their pressure, and again Frederick's defeat seemed certain. Again he was saved by a "miracle." In 1762 the Empress Elizabeth of Russia died and was succeeded by Peter III. Peter, a great admirer of Frederick, reversed Russia's position. Instead of an enemy of Prussia, she became her ally. That practically put an end to the war.

A treaty of peace was signed in 1763. Frederick kept Silesia. The coalition had failed in its purpose. Frederick emerged as the great man of Europe and Prussia as one of the great powers. France had lost her colonial empire and had left two hundred thousand dead in Germany. Never had a government shown greater inefficiency than the government of Louis XV.

France made a separate treaty with England. She surrendered all claim to Canada, to the valley of the Ohio, and to India except for five towns that she was allowed to keep for commercial purposes only. To Spain she ceded her claim to all between the Mississippi and the Rocky Mountains. Ten years earlier France had been in a position to become mistress of the world's greatest colonial empire, but when she signed the Treaty of Paris in 1763 the greatest colonial empire became England's. France did not realize what she had lost. Even Voltaire referred to Canada and the Ohio Valley as "some acres of ice, not worth fighting for." Montcalm, in desperate need, was sent three hundred and twenty-six men! Canada was lost while France was uselessly expending her blood and treasure on battlefields across the Rhine.

In this period of decadence Choiseul was the one man in the government who showed real ability. He was supported by Madame de Pompadour who seemed to acquire some wisdom as she grew older. He came to power too late to avert the disasters of the Seven Years' War, but, from 1758 to 1770, he gave to the government an intelligence that it had entirely lacked. In 1768 he negotiated the purchase of Corsica from Genoa. Two years prior to that, upon the death of King Stanislas, father-in-law of Louis XV, Lorraine reverted to France in accordance with the agreement made with Austria in 1738.

Choiseul reorganized the army and the navy with a view to a resumption of hostilities with England. Liberal in his internal administration, he made wise concessions to public opinion. He gave to *Parlement* more freedom of action. *Parlement* used this freedom to declare the order of the Jesuits illegal on the ground that it recognized no authority save that of the Pope. The King issued an edict that confirmed the decision of *Parlement* and suppressed Jesuitism in France.

There was much jealousy of Choiseul. Madame de Pompadour was no longer there to protect him; she died in 1764 and there was a new favorite, the Comtesse du Barry.

Du Barry was officially chosen to be the royal favorite in 1768, the year that Queen Marie Leczinska died. This beautiful young woman was the illegitimate daughter of a mother who had many lovers. When fifteen she left the convent in which her mother had installed her and became companion to an elderly lady of the nobility. The elderly lady dismissed her for misbehavior. She became a salesgirl in a dress shop and the mistress of Comte Jean du Barry. She married Comte Jean's brother and was presented at court. Louis XV, then fifty-eight, could not resist her blonde beauty and her lively wit. He installed her in a château at Louveciennes near Versailles. Du Barry became the rage in literary and artistic circles. Talleyrand wrote that this child of the street acquired an art of speech that was more pure and elegant than that of Madame de Pompadour. She was "gay, frivolous, and incapable of hate, but made to be a tool in the hands of a political party."

Choiseul's enemies secured Du Barry's co-operation; in 1770 she and they persuaded the King to dismiss him. He was replaced by the Chancellor Maupeou. Maupeou came into collision with the *Parlements*. He attempted to restrict their authority and to reorganize the judiciary. The magistrates responded by refusing to work; for that they were sent to the country. Although the reform that Maupeou proposed was a good reform, popular sympathy was with the magistrates. They had resisted royal authority. That alone was enough to recommend them to the people.

When Louis XV died, France was on the verge of revolution. His death retarded the revolution for fourteen years, but his reign had made it almost inevitable. Stricken with smallpox, the King died in

May, 1774. So strong was the feeling against him that they dared not pass through Paris when they conveyed his body to the royal crypt at Saint Denis. In the dead of night, without escort and without honor, the royal remains were hurried through the Bois de Boulogne. But, even at midnight, there were those who came to jeer the sorry cortege as it passed.

In the fifty-nine years of his reign Louis XV dissipated the glory and the power of France and made her people lose their ancient faith in royalty. Louis, once the "Well-loved," ended as Louis the despised.

Louis XV was succeeded by his grandson; his only son had died in 1765. Louis XVI, a fat and awkward young man with a robust appetite, was barely twenty when his grandfather died. His lively and lovely wife was nineteen. She was Marie-Antoinette, daughter of Maria-Theresa of Austria. They were together when the King's death was announced, and together they exclaimed, "May God protect us. We are too young to reign."

Nothing had been done to prepare Louis XVI for the responsibilities of kingship. He would have been glad to escape those responsibilities. His tastes ran in a different direction. He was happiest when tinkering with locks or old clocks. Simple and honest, he wished harm to no one, but his weakness brought harm to many. He was easily influenced by those less generous than he, and especially by Marie-Antoinette who never could see why concessions should be made. Innocent of the slightest comprehension of reality, she blithely led the Court toward its doom. She seemed to have inherited nothing of the mentality of the great stateswoman who was her mother.

Maurepas, then seventy-three, a former member of the cabinet with an uncertain record, was invited by Louis to be his chief adviser. He advised restoration of the *Parlements* and dismissal of the ministers of Louis XV. These measures met with popular approval. The new cabinet was very superior to its predecessor. It was intellectual rather than political. Certain members of it commanded the esteem of the philosophers and the public; it might nearly have been called a "brain-trust." Turgot, the famous economist, became Minister of Finance. Malesherbes, a distinguished magistrate and director of the royal library, became Secretary of State and the Comte de Saint Germain became Minister of War. Had these gentlemen been continued in office the Revolution might have been averted. Vergennes, a former ambassador, was made Minister of Foreign Affairs. He was the only one of the four who was able to continue in office long enough to produce important results.

The government was deeply in debt. Turgot was determined to balance the budget by economies, by equality in taxation, and by enlargement of production. His idea of equality in taxation insured his unpopularity with the privileged. He set an example by reducing his own salary by nearly one-half, and he suppressed a great number of well-paid positions that were unnecessary, but he could not prevail upon the King to reduce the extravagances of the Court; Marie-Antoinette was very much opposed to that.

The grain market was not a free market. It was controlled by regulations that enabled unscrupulous speculators to make large profits at the expense of the people. Turgot, believing in the freedom of trade, abolished these regulations. After a bad harvest the price of bread rose and Turgot was blamed. At the instigation of his enemies, bands of rebels sacked granaries, bakeries, and markets in Paris and in Versailles. They threatened to kill the King and all his ministers. It took twenty-five thousand soldiers to restore order. This "Flour War" occurred in May, 1775.

Turgot carried on. Early in 1776 he persuaded the King to issue an edict that abolished the guilds (corporations). They had existed since the Middle Ages. "In nearly all the towns of our kingdom," the edict declared, "the exercise of the arts and trades is under the control of a few master-workmen who prevent all other citizens from manufacturing or selling the articles on which they exercise a monopoly. . . . This system is contrary to the general interest and to natural rights. The right of a man to work in order to provide for his essential needs is a God-given right in which the state should sustain him."

Turgot already had all the privileged nobility and the ex-office-holders against him; this new measure assured for him the hostility of the privileged artisans. Against the opposition of organized labor, privileged capital, and Marie-Antoinette, Turgot's schemes for social justice had no chance at all. The choice lay between temporary sacrifice and the ruin of revolution. The privileged people did not hesitate. They chose the road that led to ruin.

Turgot planned other reasonable reforms, but he was given no opportunity to put them into effect. The theory of equal rights for all citizens was scorned by the ruling classes; it was held to be subversive. The hostility of the clergy to the theory of equality was no less than that of the nobility. *Parlement* became the mouthpiece of the privileged and joined with Marie-Antoinette in demanding Turgot's dismissal. In May, 1776, Turgot wrote to the King, "Do not forget, Sire, that it was feebleness that cost Charles I his head." A few days later the King proved his feebleness by abruptly dismissing his best minister.

Malesherbes, liberal and generous, sought to reform the brutal treatment of those charged with crime, and to increase religious tolerance. He tried to have civil rights restored to the Protestants. Realizing the futility of his efforts, he resigned on the same day that Turgot was dismissed.

The Comte de Saint Germain, an old soldier of strong and fearless character, reorganized the army in the manner of Louvois. He showed no favor to the nobles and restored the discipline that had been so disastrously lost in the days of Pompadour. Under him the French artillery became the best in Europe and her trained soldiery was doubled. Saint Germain's efficient methods were not pleasing to the courtiers who believed in favoritism; he soon had to yield his place to one who was more lenient.

Necker, a rich banker, Swiss by origin, was made "director general of finance"; he could not be named a minister because he was a Protestant. Necker did not agree with Turgot about the virtue of freedom of trade; he was an admirer of Colbert's system of controlled economy. He was honest, philanthropic, and highly esteemed as an expert in finance. He preferred to borrow money rather than to curtail expenses and to increase taxes. His excellent reputation in financial circles permitted him to float a huge government loan, much of which was used to help the American colonials in their war with England. He agreed with Turgot about the suppression of unnecessary offices and went him one better. He practically abolished the system of "farming" the taxes.

Necker's prestige was such that he was able to secure reforms that were outside of his department. He continued Malesherbes's work of prison and hospital reform. Until 1780 it was legal to put to torture anyone suspected of crime; admissions extorted by this method were used as evidence. Necker secured the abolition of this medieval procedure.

Turgot had a plan for provincial assemblies that would give the people some voice in the government. Necker, believing in this idea, secured its trial in Berry and in Guyenne. The assembly of Berry consisted of twelve representatives of the nobility, twelve of the clergy, and twenty-four of the Third Estate. They voted as individuals, but they were all royal appointees. This assembly requested that in the future its members should be elected by the people whom it represented. The trend toward belief in popular participation in government was unmistakable.

Necker, despite his great services to the state, was undermined. The clergy hated him because he was a Protestant, and old Maurepas, still the confidential adviser of the King, began to fear him as a rival. Necker published a report on the government budget for the year 1781. That was unprecedented in France, although an established custom in England. For the first time, the public saw put down in black and white the enormous sum of the pensions paid to the nobility, the "drones" of the kingdom. The nobility, aided by Maurepas, planned the downfall of the author of this indiscretion. Necker made the bold request that the provincial assemblies be extended throughout the kingdom. Maurepas told the King that any such move would be violently resisted by the *Parlements* and that most of the ministers would resign. The King denied Necker's request and Necker resigned. That was in May, 1781.

Necker's resignation was a fatal blow to the financial credit of the government. Government paper was offered on the Bourse without takers. The gentlemen who had made the heavy loan to the King's treasury felt that their money was lost. There was a general feeling that Necker's fall definitely marked the end of reform under the established regime and that no hope remained for social progress except through revolution.

Summary of Chapters One to Eight

The France of 1780 was very different from the France that emerged from the religious wars in 1610. Economic and political questions were to the fore. With the departure of the Huguenots and the growth of knowledge, religion had become a minor issue. The wealth and intelligence of the *bourgeoisie* had increased. Capability successfully to resist the royal government had developed. There were omens of a great change.

Richelieu and Mazarin, between 1624 and 1661, had made the power and prestige of the King greater than it had ever been before. Louis XIV continued their policy of subordination of the nobles, but he was less far-sighted than they in other matters. When he died in 1715, France's position was less strong than England's.

In the weak reign of Louis XV, great material losses were accompanied by notable intellectual progress. The condition of the lower classes remained deplorable, but many of the bourgeois became richer and better educated than the nobles. The philosophical movement developed. Those who followed it acquired more respect for the rights of man than for the divine right of the King. The prosperous *bourgeoisie* had no voice in an extravagant government that called upon them to pay its bills. Under Louis XV the nobility regained control of the army and of the government. Both were badly managed. Battles were lost through inefficiency and the financial situation went from bad to worse. When Louis XV died, France was on the verge of revolution, a revolution due to the new courage and philosophy of certain bourgeois leaders. The misery of the common people made them ready to support any movement which might change their situation.

Henri IV died in 1610. Louis XIII, his son, was then nine years old. Louis's mother, Marie de Medici, was regent from 1610 to 1617.

She paid dearly for the support of Condé and his friends, and was controlled by Concini and Leonora. When fifteen, King Louis married a Hapsburg princess, Anne of Austria. In 1617 he had Concini killed and banished his mother from the Court. Inefficient Luynes, the King's favorite, died in 1621. In 1624 Richelieu became prime minister.

The Huguenots were defeated at La Rochelle in 1628. Between that time and his death in 1642, the genius of Richelieu laid the foundation for the supremacy of France in Europe for one hundred and fifty years. In 1632 Lorraine was occupied. In 1635 France entered the Thirty Years' War. Protestant Gustavus Adolphus of Sweden became an ally of France; Richelieu did not let his religion interfere with his statecraft. In 1639 Richelieu gained control of Alsace for France. In 1642 he won Roussillon from Spain. France approached her natural frontiers.

Louis XIII died in 1642. Louis XIV was then five years old. Queen Anne became regent and Mazarin chief minister. In 1643 Condé brilliantly defeated the Spaniards at Rocroi, and, in the following year, with Turenne, won victories over the Bavarians. The Treaty of Westphalia, 1648, ended the Thirty Years' War. France's rights to Alsace and Lorraine were recognized. A civil war, the Fronde, ran from 1648 to 1653; after some reverses, Mazarin triumphed over those who opposed him, of whom Condé was the most important.

The royal family led a fugitive life during the Fronde. With English aid, the French, commanded by Turenne, defeated the Spaniards in the Battle of the Dunes, 1658; Condé, a traitor, fought with the Spaniards; Mazarin made an advantageous peace with Spain which involved King Louis's marriage with the Hapsburg Maria-Theresa. Mazarin died in 1661, and King Louis, then twenty-four, began his long and extremely personal reign. He weakened the nobility and strengthened the *bourgeoisie*. Colbert was his best minister. The Revocation of the Edict of Nantes occurred in 1685.

The Spanish succession involved France in unfortunate wars, especially with Holland. William of Orange, ruler of Holland, formed a coalition against France. In 1674 Germans who had invaded Alsace were driven out by Turenne. In 1678 Spain ceded Franche-Comté and part of Flanders to France. Louis XIV failed in his effort to restore James II to the throne of England; William and Mary began their reign there in 1688. In 1700 a grandson of Louis XIV became Philip V of Spain; a Bourbon had supplanted a Hapsburg. The War of the Spanish Succession followed. England, Holland, and Austria fought France; in 1704 a French army was defeated in Germany and the English took Gibraltar; as a result of this thirteen-year war, England gained ascendancy over France. Louis XIV died in 1715.

Louis XV was a great-grandson of Louis XIV. He was only five when his reign began. His uncle, the Duke of Orléans, acted as regent. An alliance was formed with England and Holland against Spain. From 1720 to 1740 there was an interlude of peace and prosperity. The regent died in 1723. In 1726 the King married Marie Leczinska, daughter of the dethroned King of Poland. From 1726 to 1743 the venerable Cardinal Fleury was prime minister.

In 1741 France became involved in the struggle between Maria-Theresa of Austria and Frederick the Great of Prussia; at Fontenoy in Belgium in 1745, the French, commanded by Maurice de Saxe, won a great victory over an English-Dutch army; a peace that gained nothing for France was made at Aix-la-Chapelle in 1748. The Seven Years' War was from 1756 to 1763; France, the principal loser, fought both England and Frederick the Great; in 1758 Wolfe captured Quebec and France thereby lost Canada. When Louis XV died in 1774, France was on the verge of revolution.

Louis XVI was a grandson of Louis XV. He was twenty when his grandfather died. He had married Marie-Antoinette of Austria, daughter of Queen Maria-Theresa. The early part of his reign was marked by reforms, but increase of financial embarrassment led to the summoning of the States-General, and that led, in turn, to the Revolution.

CHAPTER NINE

THE LAST YEARS OF THE OLD REGIME

VERGENNES MAINTAINED PEACE ON THE CONTINENT WHILE PREPARING
FOR WAR WITH ENGLAND. THE AMERICAN REVOLUTION AND THE TREATY
OF VERSAILLES OF 1783. THE VARIOUS CAUSES OF DISCONTENT. THE KING,
COMPELLED TO CAPITULATE, RECALLED NECKER AND
SUMMONED THE STATES-GENERAL.

SUCCESSFUL direction of the foreign policy of France called at this time (1774) for rare diplomatic ability. Vergennes had that ability. He realized that it was in France's interest that neither Austria nor Prussia should increase in strength at the expense of the other. He did all that was possible to keep peace between them, maintaining the neutrality of France despite her commitments to Austria.

Joseph II, son of Maria-Theresa, succeeded his father as emperor in 1765 and, upon the death of his mother in 1780, he became the ruler of Austria. Joseph was an extraordinary prince. Devoted to the philosophy of reason, he was one of the "enlightened despots" whose creed was "everything for the people, but nothing by the people." In that he was like Frederick the Great. Both were liberal about religion and admirable in their economic achievements, but Joseph had dangerous ambitions that would have caused renewal of a general war except that France strove steadily for Continental peace.

Vergennes often came into conflict with Marie-Antoinette because of his unwillingness to aid her brother in his efforts to enlarge Austria, but Vergennes, more diplomatic than Turgot, succeeded in keeping the King's favor. His main objective was to keep France out of any other war so that, when the time was ripe, she might have a better chance to win a war with England. He was unwilling to help Austria against Prussia, but he was willing to give discreet help to all who were hostile to the British. The American Revolution was a great help to the success of the Vergennes policy.

129

A grave threat of war came in 1777. The Elector of Bavaria died without leaving a direct heir. His nearest of kin was the Elector of the Palatinate. With him Joseph II made a bargain to divide Bavaria between them and Austrian troops occupied the territory that Joseph coveted. Frederick of Prussia opposed this aggrandizement of Austria. Hostilities began. France, then on the verge of renewing war with England, declined to support Austria. Vergennes, with the aid of Catherine of Russia, compelled Joseph to make peace with Frederick and to withdraw from all but a narrow strip of Bavarian territory.

In 1784 Joseph again attempted to acquire Bavaria. He offered to give his Flemish territory in exchange. He offered Namur and Luxembourg to France if she would approve this exchange. The offer was tempting, but again Vergennes opposed the fulfillment of Joseph's ambition. He realized that, for geographical reasons, Austrian possession of Flanders was more advantageous to France than Austrian possession of Bavaria. Joseph, thwarted in the west, turned eastward. He undertook to enlarge his territory at the expense of Turkey. Vergennes offered no objection to that. He believed that Joseph would have a great deal of trouble with the Turks.

The American Revolution was of intense interest to France. Her people passionately desired the success of the colonials. In fighting England they appeared to be defending principles that the philosophical movement had made dear to the hearts of Frenchmen. The Declaration of Independence was hailed with enthusiastic joy. Adequate reasons restrained the government from prompt recognition of American belligerency, but nothing restrained a number of young nobles from making a perilous journey and offering their services to Washington. The most notable of these volunteers was the young Marquis de La Fayette. He was barely twenty when, violating the formal order of the King, he went to America. He wrote to his wife, "The welfare of America and the welfare of humanity are one. America is destined to become the sure refuge of honesty, of tolerance, of equality, and of a tranquil liberty." La Fayette reflected the fervor of an optimism that became contagious. Widening breaches in the walls of the old despotic order made people believe that Utopia was attainable. The qualities of man that prevent that attainment were, for a time, obscured.

The government, though not ready to come into open conflict with England, was willing to permit unofficial help to America. The distinguished writer Beaumarchais organized a private business whose purpose was to provide the revolutionists with supplies. Through that channel the government sent money, artillery, and uniforms. Vergennes favored open co-operation, but Turgot was against it; he insisted that open warfare with England would bring financial ruin. However, after Turgot was dismissed and Franklin came to France, things took a different turn.

Franklin landed in Brittany in November, 1776. His reputation as scientist and philosopher had preceded him. He was seventy-five. He was strangely attired. His fur cap, his great spectacles, his long hair, his unusual shoes and his gallantry to the ladies added to his popularity. Shoes like his became the style. He remained in France until 1783, representing America both during the war and at the peace conference that followed.

In 1777 it looked as though the British would defeat the Americans. France still withheld official recognition of their cause. An American victory was needed. It came at the end of that year when Burgoyne surrendered at Saratoga. "Now our time has come," exclaimed Vergennes, "now or never!"

A few weeks later France signed a treaty of alliance with the new republic and entered into open warfare with England. Vergennes had left no stone unturned to strengthen France's position. He secured the alliance of Spain and he made the most of the feeling against England that had been aroused by her arrest and search of neutral vessels. The neutral powers agreed to resist England's "right of search." Holland broke with the British and entered into the coalition against them. For five years England was compelled to fight a maritime war with France, Holland, and Spain in addition to the land war in America. It was fortunate for the Americans that the British were thus prevented from concentrating on them.

The alliance with France was followed by a let-down of military effort by the Americans. The English again seemed near to victory.

However, in 1781, France sent Rochambeau with six thousand men and De Grasse with thirty-eight ships of war. These forces were placed under Washington's command. The surrender of Cornwallis at Yorktown followed. That victory achieved the independence of the United States.

In 1782 the English, having accumulated a staggering debt, suggested a peace conference. France, also short of money, welcomed the British overtures. The negotiations were difficult. The Americans had agreed not to make a separate peace, but, fearing "foreign entanglements," they signed a separate preliminary treaty with England. This violation of an agreement might have been disastrous except for Vergennes' admiration for Franklin. Nine months of discussion followed before the Treaty of Versailles of 1783 was perfected. England recognized the independence of the United States and its territorial rights as far west as the Mississippi. France and England, neither having gained important territorial advantages at the expense of the other, returned practically to the pre-war status. England kept Gibraltar, but ceded Minorca and Florida to Spain. Certain African territory was restored to France and her right to fortify Dunkirk was recognized.

The territorial gains of France were negligible compared with what she had lost in the Seven Years' War, but her moral victory was great. Her political and military prestige was re-established. England, having lost her most valuable colonies, regarded the future with grave anxiety. The younger Pitt, soon to prove himself a worthy successor of his father, said, "The glory of England has ended. She must now recognize the humiliating necessity of employing a language fitting to her new condition." Pitt was unduly pessimistic.

The success of the Americans had a profound effect upon France. Returning soldiers preached the gospel of liberty and equality. The Declaration of Independence was widely read. The Americans had expressed the philosophy of Rousseau, Voltaire, and Montesquieu in an eloquent summary that was like a call to arms. It made the new philosophy dynamic. There was a feeling that the Americans had won a victory for humanity as well as for themselves. The surrender of Cornwallis shortened the days of the King of France. Another thing that shortened them was the war debt that Turgot had sought to avoid. That debt necessitated the historic meeting of the States-General in which the Revolution began.

The Treaty of Versailles of 1783 improved the situation of France in her foreign relations, but it did not improve her internal situation. It secured peace abroad, but not at home. The threat of civil war remained.

France had long since lost the unity that Henri IV achieved and Richelieu perfected, and her people had begun to lose confidence in the virtue of royal government. They were ready to take desperate measures in an effort to improve their situation.

The system of *intendants* that Richelieu instituted contributed to disunion. The weak government of Louis XV permitted the *intendants* to increase their power until they were like little kings in the regions they controlled. These regions were called *généralités*. They did not follow the boundaries of the old provinces. There were thirty-four provinces and thirty-nine *généralités*. The provinces still possessed their noble governors but, since they had been deprived of civil powers and had become merely military directors, the noble governors were usually to be found in the crowd of preferment seekers at Versailles.

The burden of taxation was very unfairly distributed. The *intendants* did as they saw fit about that. Some of them were devoted to the general interest and did admirable administrative work. Turgot, as *intendant,* lifted the Limousin from poverty to prosperity and Saint-Sauveur transformed Roussillon. But in other regions, far more heavily taxed, the misery of the people increased.

Of the many kinds of taxes the *gabelle* was the most unpopular. It was the tax on salt. Its imposition was extremely irregular; in some regions it was twenty times as heavy as in others. This tax made the government hated by the peasants. Despite heavy penalties, they resisted it. Each year more than five hundred were sent to the galleys for evasion of the *gabelle* and for the smuggling of salt. The tax on wine was similarly detested. The wine of the south, in order to reach Paris, had to pay in taxes nearly as much as its original cost at retail sale. Taxation, in one form or another, reached a point that left to the peasant hardly one-fourth of the fruit of his labor.

The administration of justice was no less complicated and irregular than the administration of the finances. There were courts of the state, of the Church, of the lords, and of the municipalities whose competences were overlapping. A lawyer reported in 1763 that "it was sometimes necessary to plead for two or three years at great expense in order to discover before what judges one would finally have the misfortune to try the case." The government, having used the sale of judicial offices as a source of revenue, sold far more of them than were needed. A great number of hereditary legal posts were purely parasitic and the acceptance of bribes was an established custom to which no penalty was attached.

Punishment for crime remained medieval. Poachers risked being sent to the galleys for life. A servant was hanged for having stolen a sheet. Preliminary torture was abolished in 1780, but continued to be applied between the sentence and its execution. The public was encouraged to witness judicial tongue-piercings, the breaking of bodies on the wheel and their dismemberment by horses driven in different directions. Parisian mobs were taught to enjoy the sight of blood before they began to shed it.

The restoration of the nobility to their previous status was another cause of discontent. The days when Louis XIV gave preferment to the *bourgeoisie* were long since gone. For more than a century the nobility had steadily strengthened its grip on the important offices in army, Church, and government. Birth had come to count for more than merit. Even the magistrates of the *Parlements*, originally recruited from among the *bourgeoisie*, developed into a closed caste; they made it a rule to admit to sit with them only those who had at least four generations of noble rank behind them; the justices of the Supreme Courts, once the friends of the people and courageous advocates of social justice, became supporters of the ancient order and opponents of reform. They thought of many reasons why nothing should be changed and co-operated with the nobility in thwarting both Turgot and Necker in their efforts to save the state. In 1781 it was made a rule of the army that none except four-generation nobles could be appointed as officers without having worked up from the ranks; young men of the *bourgeoisie* were thus excluded from military careers.

The strangle hold that the nobility took upon the government was like the desperate clutch of a swimmer whose strength has been spent. The strength of the nobility in its own right had been spent; it could save itself only by seizure of rights and privileges for which it gave nothing in return. There had been a day when the commoners, believing themselves dependent upon the nobility for protection, had made little complaint about the special privileges of the lords, but, the less their justification became, the more tenaciously the lords clung to their ancient advantages. One reason for that was that forfeiture of their special privileges would have put most of the lords in the poorhouse.

The lavish expenditure of the Court at Versailles had made luxury a necessity for the nobility. They had to keep up with the parade or they were lost; if they were not seen at court they were forgotten, and to be properly seen at court cost a great deal of money. They either mortgaged their estates or sold them. The rules of their caste made it impossible for them to go into business, impossible for them to make their living by any productive work. Predestined to parasitism, the degeneracy of the nobles was inevitable. The pensions and perquisites they received from the government were usually spent before they were received. Since it was below the dignity of the nobility to haggle about costs, they were unmercifully fleeced on every purchase. Most of the money derived from the labor of the peasants passed into the hands of tradespeople. The *bourgeoisie* became more prosperous, but not more satisfied.

A bourgeois class that became richer and better educated than the nobility was barred from political and social recognition, but was called upon to support the government in which it had no voice. The extravagances of Versailles finally compelled the government to lay heavy hands upon the wealth of that class. The rich *bourgeoisie* loaned their money freely to Necker because they had confidence in Necker, but when he had gone confidence fled. The unenlightened workers and peasants, unable to do otherwise, might continue their endless struggle to exist upon the fourth or fifth of their earnings that was left to them, but no such resignation could be expected from the *bourgeoisie*. The lower classes rejoiced in the Revolution and made a regrettably bloody business of it, but the *bourgeoisie* started it.

Discontent was not confined to the *bourgeoisie* and to the down-trodden lower classes. It also abounded in the ranks of the nobility and the clergy. Many impoverished nobles had been unable to keep up with the parade and had secured no preferment. Counts of ancient lineage had been reduced nearly to beggary, and the miserable *curés* of the country looked with loathing upon the noble bishops who drew their purple robes close about them when rustic priests approached.

The contemptuous attitude of the nobility and the higher clergy had much to do with the breaking of the storm. The more parasitic the nobles became, the more intolerable became their attitude toward the commoners. They developed a fantastic exaggeration of polite-ness among themselves, but they treated the common people and the *bourgeoisie* like the dirt under their feet. In the days when the lords lived on their lands they had been able to keep in friendly touch with the people, but the court life of Versailles changed all that. In that fantastic center of unreality thousands of courtiers came to believe that they were as far removed from the common people as the heavens are above the earth. Confidence in their divine right extended from the King to all who came near him. "Whom the gods would destroy they first make mad."

From 1782 to 1787 the extravagance of Versailles knew no abate-ment. The defeat of England brought in its train a new feeling of con-fidence and a flush of national prosperity. The Atlantic ports were busy with a greater volume of overseas business than they had ever known before and the Continental trade increased. Regular passen-ger and freight service to America began in 1783. There was a feeling that a difficult corner had been successfully turned, and it might have been successfully turned had extravagance stopped and economy be-gun. The tremendous debt that had been incurred on account of co-operation with America was disregarded. On the part of the people there was great admiration for the new American republic, but there was little belief that a similar republic was suitable for France. The vast majority were still favorable to monarchy provided that mon-archy could be limited in its powers, as in England.

Versailles danced on. The feeble King went hunting, pottered about in his workshop, made childish entries in his diary, and, for all his good will, he had no understanding of the realities. And Marie-Antoinette! That lovely child of joy was even more remote from reality than her royal spouse. Madame de Pompadour had said, "After us the deluge," but Marie-Antoinette did not even believe in rain. Her lively goings-on estranged from her many who were influential at court. Rebellious against its etiquette, she ridiculed the King's aunts and preferred for playmates those whose reputation sullied her own. The King had been an inadequate husband. For years he had stuffed himself at dinner, bade Marie good night, and then snored alone while she stepped out. Malicious tongues made the most they could out of that.

The King presented Marie with the Petit-Trianon, a perfect palace in miniature that the great architect Gabriel had built for Louis XV. In it Louis XV had given notorious nudist parties at which only deaf and dumb servants were allowed to serve. Marie-Antoinette was never charged with having gone so far as that, but some of her parties went pretty far.

The Petit-Trianon is about a mile from the palace of Versailles. Marie embellished its park until it became the loveliest in the world. At one end of it she had a farmhouse built and a little mill. A lake was made between them. That group was called the *hameau;* reconstructed, the *hameau* is still there and is the most charming feature of Versailles; in its presence sympathy with the joyous queen who once played there is almost irresistible. On her miniature farm Marie-Antoinette and her maids of honor played at raking the hay and at milking the cows; the milk, caught in Sevres porcelain, stood in silver bowls on marble slabs. There was a temple of love on a little island. Marie lived at the Petit-Trianon, but Louis, less interested in love and gaiety, stayed stodgily at home where he could snore in peace.

In 1781 Necker retired and the venerable Maurepas died. Maurepas had been the most influential of the King's advisers. After he had gone, Marie-Antoinette had the most influence. Louis seemed incapable of making any important decision for himself.

Necker was succeeded by Fleury and Fleury by Ormesson. Neither of these gentlemen was able to relieve the government of its steadily increasing financial embarrassment. Suave and elegant Calonne, formerly an *intendant,* was put in charge in 1783. He did not believe in economy. He maintained that the first need was to restore confidence, and that the best way to do that was to act as though economy was unnecessary. For a short time this agreeable plan worked. Calonne was able to borrow enough to meet current expenses. The temporary prosperity of the nation permitted continuance of the spending policy for three years. Money flowed freely. Whatever debts the princes incurred, Calonne paid with a smile. Whatever Marie-Antoinette desired, he provided. He told her that, even though she asked for the impossible, he would make it possible. The new director of finances was very popular at court.

The day of reckoning came in August, 1786. Calonne had to tell the King that the credit of the government had failed; no more loans could be floated. Reversing his previous policy, he proposed financial reforms and tax-increases like those that Turgot and Necker had striven for. But it was too late to make such measures effective. *Parlement* would not admit their legality and the King was not strong enough to bend the magistrates to his will as Henri IV had done.

Calonne sought to have his proposals approved by an "Assembly of Notables" that convened at Versailles in February, 1787. Most of the members of this assembly were representatives of the privileged classes. Calonne asked for their endorsement of the abolition of some of their privileges. He might as well have asked for the moon. The Assembly was caricatured as a group of geese and turkeys asked in what sauce they would prefer to be cooked. They preferred not to be cooked at all. Marie-Antoinette supported the noble poultry in their objections. Calonne was dismissed. Demands for a meeting of the States-General began to be heard, demands that steadily became louder and more insistent.

Brienne, a distinguished archbishop, was appointed to succeed Calonne. The situation called for a genius and Brienne was not that. He had opposed Calonne in the Assembly, but, once in power, he found himself forced to become an advocate of the very measures he had helped to defeat. The Assembly continued to oppose these measures. In May the King thanked the "notables" and dismissed them. They had accomplished nothing.

The King realized at last that heroic measures were imperative. He tried to secure the endorsement by *Parlement* of certain edicts. *Parlement* took the position that only the States-General was competent to legalize the fiscal changes that were proposed. The obstructive magistrates were banished to Troyes where "they were received in triumph." The public failed to realize that the opposition of *Parlement* to the government had done more harm than good. The magistrates had suggested a meeting of the States-General and that was what the public wanted. Edicts would no longer suffice. The only choice left was between States-General and financial collapse. The Parisians began to make demonstrations against Marie-Antoinette. They called her "Madame Deficit" and "the Austrian," and dragged effigies of her friends in the gutters.

Brienne attempted an expedient of despair. He proposed a loan to the government under the stipulation that the States-General should be assembled at the end of five years. The King authorized this plan by edict. Objections that it was illegal he overruled, saying, "It is legal because I wish it." With all his feebleness of character, Louis XVI had not lost belief in divine right nor in absolutism. *Parlement* responded with a "declaration of the rights of the nation," and maintained the illegality of the royal edict. Brienne ordered the arrest of Epresmesnil and Montsabert, two of the leaders of this opposition. When an officer undertook to arrest them at the Palais de Justice, the members of the *Parlement* arose and cried out, "We are all Epresmesnil and Montsabert."

In July of 1788 it became clear that there would be a general refusal to pay taxes unless the States-General were convened. The King had to capitulate. A meeting of the States was called for May 1, 1789, but the call came too late to prevent insolvency. Government payment of its obligations ceased. The state was bankrupt.

Louis dismissed Brienne and reluctantly recalled Necker. Necker was able to secure a loan and government payments were resumed, but the country was less interested in that than in the meeting of the States-General. From that meeting a complete transformation of the system of government was expected to emerge.

CHAPTER TEN

THE NATIONAL ASSEMBLY AND THE KING'S FLIGHT

THE PEOPLE DEMANDED A CONSTITUTION. THE FALL OF THE BASTILLE
AND THE MARCH OF THE MARKET WOMEN TO VERSAILLES. THE ABOLITION
OF PRIVILEGES. THE BIRTH OF A NEW AND MORE ARDENT PATRIOTISM.
THE POLITICAL CLUBS. THE RETURN FROM VARENNES.

THERE had been no meeting of the States-General since 1614 when
Marie de Medici was regent. At that time the nobility, the clergy, and
the Third Estate had equal representation and these groups voted
separately; if the nobility and the clergy were in agreement, as they
usually were, the commoners had no chance. It was obvious that this
plan would not be acceptable to the commoners of 1789. They formed
ninety-six per cent of the population and they were far less submissive
than their predecessors had been. To the King's call for the assembling
of the States, *Parlement* added as a postscript "that it should follow the
form of 1614." This postscript ended the popularity of the magistrates;
it was seen that they shared the nobility's antipathy to any reform that
might curtail their privileges.

La Fayette, Condorcet, the Count Mirabeau, and the Abbé Sieyès
were leaders of the popular demand that the representatives of the
Third Estate should be equal in number to those of the clergy and
nobility combined, that the three groups should deliberate together,
and that voting should be individual. Upon Necker's advice, the King
conceded the first of these points; the others he left to be settled later.
Louis had made a just concession, but the nobility did not follow his
lead. The struggle became one between the commoners and the privileged classes with the government temporarily on the side lines. There
were disorders in several provinces that came near to developing into
civil war.

The situation was aggravated by unemployment and by a scarcity of
provisions. In 1786 a commercial treaty permitted free entry of

British manufactures. That had a bad effect upon French industry, especially the textile industry. In 1788 two hundred thousand workers had lost their jobs. There was a bad harvest that year. The poor were no longer able to buy bread. Marie-Antoinette is said to have suggested that they should eat cake! The winter that followed was of unusual severity. Hungry and cold, a fifth of the population of Paris was reduced to beggary. More than a hundred thousand desperate people were ready for any adventure. In the country, granaries and markets were pillaged. There was a riot in the Faubourg Saint Antoine that was suppressed only after many had been killed.

The election of deputies came in February, 1789. The disorder of the administration was shown by the list of election districts that it posted. These districts were based on the *bailliages* (bailiwicks); the official list included some that had ceased to exist and omitted others that had become important. The right to vote was extended to all men over twenty-five who were on the tax lists. The vote of a parish priest counted for as much as the vote of a bishop; that made it certain that most of the deputies of the clergy would be parish priests.

Eleven hundred and eighteen deputies were elected. The Abbé Sieyès and the Count Mirabeau, not acceptable to their own orders, were elected deputies of the Third Estate. The delegation of the nobles included a few liberals whose leaders were La Fayette and the Duke of Orléans, the King's cousin.

The nation, having been invited to express itself, did not hesitate to do so. Every district prepared a statement of its grievances. About minor matters there was much divergence of opinion, but there was practical unanimity about certain fundamentals. One of these was that royal authority should be controlled by a constitution. Many deputies had instructions to oppose all fiscal measures until after a constitution had been adopted. Equality of taxation was another fundamental about which there was agreement; the clergy and the nobles were willing to concede that point, but they were prepared to fight for all their other privileges.

The King was popular at this time. The people believed that he was ready to co-operate in making the needed reforms. It was officially announced that he favored equality in taxation, reorganization of the administration, and control of the budget by the States-General. The King's apparent support of these reforms led to the belief that they could be peacefully accomplished. The many *cahiers* (statements of grievances) contained no criticism of the King. Many of them praised him as the true friend of the people. Much additional misfortune was required before the nation abandoned its instinctive devotion to royalty.

All might have been well and bloodshed avoided had Louis XVI kept his promises. He wished to do well, but he was incapable of resisting influences that ran counter to the policies of Necker, influences that pushed him into such changes of attitude and action that no dependence could be placed upon him. It was the King's own fault that the people lost faith in him. Louis XVI was destroyed by a revolution that, except for his feebleness, he might have controlled.

The States-General assembled at Versailles May 5, 1789. The King desired that it should meet there so that he would not be inconvenienced about his hunting. The ceremonies of the opening session conformed to the old traditions and were humiliating to the deputies of the people. The King's speech was brief. He asked for financial aid, but he said nothing about a constitution. The liberals saw that any confidence in his support of their policies was misplaced. At heart the King was always a conservative.

The deputies of the Third Estate invited the clergy and the nobles to sit with them in a joint session. The nobles declined to do so, and the clergy, seeking a compromise, remained neutral. A month passed without agreement on this point; nothing had been accomplished. Then the Third Estate, strengthened by a fraction of the clergy, decided to go ahead on its own. Maintaining that it represented ninety-six per cent of the people, it called itself the National Assembly, and declared itself competent to legislate about taxation. On the nineteenth of June, the rest of the clergy abandoned the nobles and joined the commoners.

Badly advised, the King made no effort to secure a reconciliation of the three orders. He took a step that made the situation worse. When the deputies went to their place of meeting on the twentieth of June, they found the doors locked and guarded. They did not disperse.

They went in a body to an indoor tennis court near by. There they took the famous *Serment du Jeu de paume*. Standing, with arms up-stretched, they swore that "they would not disperse, and that they would continue to re-assemble wherever circumstances permitted until a constitution of the kingdom was firmly established."

A few days later the defiant deputies confronted their King in a *séance royale*. They heard him declare that their National Assembly was illegal and of no effect. He ordered them to adjourn forthwith and to resume on the following day the deliberations of the States-General, each order sitting separately.

The King left the hall, but the deputies of the Third Estate and some of the clergy did not leave. "You have heard the King's order," cried the noble master of ceremonies. "It seems to me that the National Assembly cannot receive orders," responded Bailly who was its president. "Only bayonets shall make us move," thundered Mirabeau.

Crowds in the streets were shouting, *"Vive le Tiers."* It was not certain that troops would obey an order to clear the hall. "Oh very well," said the King. "If they won't go, let them stay."

The Assembly had won the first victory of the Revolution. Abso-lutism ceased to exist when the King said "let them stay." On the twenty-seventh of June he directed that the clergy and the nobility should sit with the Assembly. Soon after that a committee to draft a constitution was appointed.

The King alone might have accepted the new situation and tried to make the best of it, but it was not so with those by whom he was surrounded. They planned a military suppression. A large force of hired foreign troops was concentrated near Versailles. The Assembly requested the King to withdraw these troops. He refused to do so. He dismissed Necker and formed a new cabinet of war dogs.

Necker's second dismissal caused a second panic. On the twelfth of July there were stirring scenes in Paris. In the gardens of the *Palais Royal* the young lawyer Camille Desmoulins, standing on a chair, made an impassioned speech. He cried out that a "Saint Bar-tholomew of the Patriots" was threatened. His hearers enthusias-tically pledged themselves to its prevention. For lack of any better symbol they fastened horse-chestnut leaves in their hats and rushed forth to find arms. Gun shops were raided and busts of Necker and of the Duke of Orléans were carried in triumph. In the Place Vendôme the excited crowd encountered a detachment of German cavalry and was driven back to the Tuileries gardens. Then French soldiers joined the retreating crowd and opened fire on the Germans. The hired defenders of the government fled, leaving a few dead behind them.

The next day the Parisian deputies to the States-General came to Paris and, at the *Hôtel de Ville,* organized a revolutionary municipal government. A bourgeois militia was authorized. In a few hours there were twelve thousand volunteers among whom there were many very respectable citizens. This little army represented the better element.

Then came the historic fourteenth of July. It began with pillage of the arsenal at the Invalides. Thousands of guns and some cannon were taken. Thus armed, a great crowd marched to the Bastille. Its surrender was demanded. While discussions were going on, someone fired on the crowd. Discussion ceased and the attack began. The attackers lost about two hundred, but they took the Bastille. The mob had tasted blood. De Launay, commander of the old prison, was murdered after he had surrendered. His head and some other heads, impaled on pikes, were paraded through the streets.

The Bastille was more than a prison. Built in 1375, that grim fortress had been for centuries the visible and convincing evidence of the royal power to punish. Its fall proved that royal power had been overthrown. The news, spreading like wildfire through the country, made the people realize, as they had not realized before, that the old order had passed. What would replace it?

Nervous nobles prepared to flee and the King capitulated. The deputies at the *Hôtel de Ville,* sleeping on benches or on the floor of the hall that they had not left since the thirteenth, were aroused on the fifteenth to be told that the King had ordered the withdrawal of his hired troops. On the sixteenth Necker was recalled. The deputies placed the volunteer militia under the command of La Fayette and gave it the name National Guard. On the seventeenth the flight of the nobles began and no one asked them to stay, but the King was invited to come to Paris in order to restore peace. Escorted by two hundred deputies, he was received with honor at the *Hôtel de Ville*. Bailly had been made the revolutionary mayor. He presented the keys of the city to the King, saying, "Sire, these are the keys that were given to Henri IV when he reconquered his people, but now the people have reconquered their king."

The King graciously accepted the keys. He also accepted and wore the tri-colored cockade that was the symbol of the new order. Blue and red were the colors of Paris; white, the color of the King, was placed between the blue and the red. Louis gave his approval to the formation of the National Guard and sanctioned the new municipal government. At that moment there seemed to be a chance that peace and order might be restored without further bloodshed.

Other cities followed the example of Paris in forming new local governments and in organizing militia that became part of the National Guard. The authority of the royal *intendants* was no longer recognized. The peasants, seeing their chance, rose against the nobles. Châteaux were pillaged and burned. It became clear that the restoration of peace and order would be a long and difficult business.

The Assembly, fully aware of its responsibility, did its utmost to quell the storm. Certain foresighted nobles were leaders in that effort. They proposed abolition of all the ancient rights and privileges of their own order. On the night of the fourth of August, 1789, the Assembly, with a great outburst of optimistic enthusiasm, legalized these proposals. In a single session of six hours a social revolution was accomplished. The principle of equality of rights was established. It was believed that this legislation would put a definite end to the Revolution.

Again the hope for peace was shattered. The King had been insincere. He and his friends were planning to regain control through force of arms. He did not sanction the Assembly's acts of August 4, and the garrison of Versailles was reinforced by a regiment from Flanders. The King appeared at a banquet given in honor of the officers of that regiment. Toasts were drunk to his health and to the confusion of all who resisted his authority. Exaggerated accounts of this banquet were published in Paris. It was reported that the tricolor had been trampled under foot.

Meanwhile the economic situation became worse. The flight of the nobles was a fatal blow to the luxury trades. Thousands of artisans and former servants swelled the ranks of the unemployed. There was still a shortage of food, and there was much division of opinion about what should be the next political step. There was a party that wished to replace Louis XVI by his liberal cousin, the Duke of Orléans. Other groups criticized the Assembly as too conservative and wished to move toward communism. The speeches of demagogues bewildered the people and their misery pushed them toward new acts of violence.

On the fifth of October the women of the markets organized a march on Versailles. They proposed to bring back to Paris "bread and the King." Thousands of men followed the thousands of women. This great armed mob massed itself about the palace. The King appeared. He promised to send wheat and to sanction the decrees of August 4. Then he prepared to follow his noble friends in flight, but Necker persuaded him to stay.

The distrustful mob remained at Versailles. On the following morning it forced its way into the palace, killed some of the guards, and reached the apartments of Marie-Antoinette. A massacre was prevented only by the arrival of La Fayette and his militia. The royal family, however, was forced to go to Paris, escorted by the mob as well as by the militia. The marching women cried that they were bringing back "the baker and the baker's little boy." That evening the King slept at the Tuileries. He had become a prisoner of the people.

A few days later the Assembly followed the King from Versailles to Paris and resumed its sessions in a hall near the Tuileries. This was a perilous thing to do. The rioters of Paris could not be expected to respect deputies who displeased them any more than they had respected the King. There was danger of intimidation.

The Assembly voted that the National Guard should use force if necessary in order to disperse all mobs that threatened violence. Only two voices were raised against this measure to control the mob. Those were the voices of Robespierre and of Marat.

The people of the provinces seemed to realize the peril of an ungoverned France. At Valence on the Rhône, at Pontivy in Brittany, and at Strasbourg on the Rhine great meetings were held. Declarations of loyalty to the Assembly were enthusiastically adopted. It seemed to be realized that a liberty so swiftly won would be lost again unless there was "fraternal co-operation." Without that, anarchy was inevitable. The established order that had been developed through centuries had been swept away as by a sudden storm, and nothing had been made ready to replace it. Almost overnight the people of France had the problem of governing themselves thrust upon them. There was evidence of a determination to be worthy of the great opportunity and to preserve the new-found liberty through fraternal effort. At a bridge-head on the Rhine the new flag of France was hoisted, and, under it, an inscription read, "Here the land of liberty begins."

The Assembly decided to strengthen the new fraternal feeling by a magnificent ceremony that was held in Paris on the first anniversary of the fall of the Bastille. Where the Eiffel Tower now stands an amphitheater was built with places for two hundred thousand spectators. Thousands of delegates came from all parts of France. An "altar of the Fatherland" was installed in the center of the scene. While the great crowd stood reverently in silence, Talleyrand, the bishop of Autun, celebrated a solemn mass. Then La Fayette, as commander of the National Guard of France, read the following oath: "I swear to be forever faithful to the Nation, to the Law, and to the King, and to support the Constitution decreed by the National Assembly . . . and to remain united with my fellow countrymen in indissoluble bonds of fraternity." The King, in his turn, swore to maintain the Constitution. A wave of wild enthusiasm swept through the crowd. The cries *"Vive l'Assemblée"* were almost drowned by cries *"Vive le roi."* It was very hard for the people to stop loving their King. It was still believed that loyalty to monarchy might not be inconsistent with loyalty to liberty. That point was cloudy, but another point was very clear. Whatever later form the government might take, king or no king, a new and a passionate patriotism had been born.

The newborn passion became contagious, but it did not facilitate co-operation nor strengthen fraternity. The removal of all restraints on thought and speech made the development of diversity of opinions inevitable. Political clubs became nurseries of passion as much as of patriotism. The solidarity of the liberals disappeared. Having attained their first great objective, their ranks broke into groups whose minds moved in different directions. There was no authority strong enough or respected enough to impose the harmony and co-operation that were sorely needed. The good temper and the reasonable idealism with which the Revolution began were lost in a new confusion.

A majority of the Assembly held for the original plan of limitation of royal authority, but there were dangerous minorities that favored more radical procedure. There was a group that wished for the abolition of monarchy. Another group, alarmed by the violence of the Revolution, wished for restoration of the old order.

There was a great deal of oratory and, in that, Mirabeau was easily the master. What a man! Forty years old when the Revolution began, he already enjoyed national reputation as an undesirable citizen. He came from a noble family of Provençe, but he had served several terms in jail and had even been condemned to death for seduction. Disowned by his family, he made his living by writing obscene literature. But he also wrote about history and politics. A series of brilliant speeches that he made in Provençe won him his seat in the Third Estate. His fellow nobles looked upon him with scorn, but he returned scorn for scorn. His swift and fearless eloquence gave him great influence, an influence that might have opened the door to the still larger place that he coveted, but Mirabeau died in 1791.

The most important of the political clubs was The Society of the Friends of the Constitution; its members were called *Jacobins* because they met in an old Jacobin convent; this club became the parent organization of hundreds of similar clubs in the provinces. The *Jacobins* perfected an organization that was, for a time, more powerful than the Assembly itself.

The Society of the Friends of the Citizen was called the *club des Cordeliers* because it met in a convent of that order. This club attracted those of the extreme left, those who wished to put an end to monarchy although not clear about what to do afterward. The main objective was to resist everything that seemed to encroach upon the "rights of man." Danton and Marat and Desmoulins were leaders of the *Cordeliers*. Other leaders were "men of the people" who could be counted on to lead thousands of fearless and fanatical followers in defense of whatever they thought to be their rights. The *Cordeliers* were a threat to the Assembly as well as to the King.

The religious question came to the fore and brought a crisis with it. In July of 1790 the Assembly legalized a "civil constitution of the clergy." That instrument did not touch upon Church beliefs, but it provided a new organization. Later, the Assembly decreed that all priests should take the civic oath provided in the national Constitution. The number of bishops was reduced from one hundred and thirty-four to eighty-three and the Pope was not even consulted. The King sanctioned this measure, believing that a compromise could be negotiated with the Vatican. The Pope, however, refused to compromise and most of the clergy would not take the civic oath. This premature requirement lost for the Assembly much support that it needed; the "refractory clergy" who would not take the oath became supporters of the "counter-revolution" movement.

Pious King Louis was much disturbed by the religious schism, and the people were much disturbed by the fact that only "refractory" priests were allowed to celebrate mass at the Tuileries. When Easter came in 1791 the King tried to go to the Church fêtes at Saint-Cloud, but a crowd stopped his carriage and would not let him go.

Louis decided that he had had enough of being the prisoner of such irreligious and disrespectful people. Flight was planned. Secret negotiations were under way with the Emperor Joseph II, Marie-Antoinette's brother. He had been asked to advance Austrian forces to the French frontier. There was a French army at Metz that was still loyal. It was decided to try to go to Metz.

On the night of the twentieth of June, the King, disguised as a lackey, fled with the Queen, his two children, and his sister Elizabeth. Troops had been posted to aid in the flight, but the bad roads caused delay. When the heavy royal carriage rolled into Varennes, the troops that should have been there to protect it, weary of waiting, had gone away. The postmaster at Sainte-Menehould had recognized the King when he passed. He was followed. At midnight his carriage was stopped on a little bridge at the entrance to Varennes. The royal family, despite the King's protests, was compelled to descend. They were conducted to a dingy loft over a grocery store. The grocer was the local representative of the *Commune.* Hastily he donned the insignia of his office. Then, in his torch-lit loft, surrounded by half-dressed and excited villagers, he compelled the King to admit his identity. In the name of the *Commune,* he placed him under arrest.

The carefully planned flight, so very near to success, failed when it had all but reached its goal. A village postmaster and a country grocer changed the fate of France and of her King.

Four days later, escorted by representatives of the Assembly, Louis re-entered Paris. A great crowd waited at the Tuileries to see him, but on that day no one shouted *Vive le roi!* As if on order, the people gazed at their King in stony and ominous silence. Their faith in him was dead.

CHAPTER ELEVEN

FIFTEEN FURIOUS MONTHS

THE CONSTITUTIONAL ASSEMBLY ENDED ITS HISTORIC LABORS. AUSTRIA AND PRUSSIA, URGED BY LOUIS, PLANNED TO INVADE FRANCE AND SUPPRESS THE REVOLUTION. THE BATTLE OF THE TUILERIES AND THE IMPRISONMENT OF THE ROYAL FAMILY. THE COMMUNE, STRONGER THAN THE NEW ASSEMBLY, PERMITTED A MASSACRE OF PRIESTS AND NOBLES. *"LA PATRIE EST EN DANGER."* THE MARSEILLAISE. VALMY WAS THE FRENCH BUNKER HILL.

WHEN Louis XVI was brought back from Varennes the silent crowd at the Tuileries saw more than a fat frightened man in a lumbering coach. In his dishonored return they saw the funeral of their long-cherished love of royalty, and they felt the fear that comes when there can no longer be retreat from perilous adventure. The people had new conceptions of "the rights of man," but they had hoped to enjoy those rights under the familiar rule of a king. They were skeptical about the abilities of their fellow men to govern with justice or efficiency. They had sought to preserve their King, but he himself had made his preservation impossible.

Prior to the flight there had been only a smoldering demand for a republic, but now that demand flared into the open and found new followers. It was argued that the flight of the King had created a *de facto* republic. In the streets there was heard for the first time the cry, "We need no king!" The *Cordeliers* petitioned the Assembly to establish republican government without further delay. Many demanded that the King should be brought to trial.

The Assembly was not stampeded. It made a final effort to preserve the form of monarchy, but that was not because of love for Louis. It was because of awareness that to declare France a republic and to depose the King would increase the probability of both foreign and civil war.

On the fifteenth of July, 1791, the Assembly voted down the proposal to bring the King to trial. That decision brought about a new

151

and a deep disharmony in the revolutionary party. Many of the *Jacobins* agreed with the *Cordeliers* in wishing for the abolition of monarchy. La Fayette and some others who held to the contrary resigned as *Jacobins* and formed another club. The flight to Varennes added enormously to the difficulty of the situation.

A petition was placed upon the Altar of the Fatherland at the *Champs de Mars*. It called for trial of the King and the establishment of a new executive power. This led to a riot upon the very spot where, a year before, the people of France had dedicated themselves to fraternal co-operation. La Fayette's National Guardsmen were compelled to fire upon the crowd to make it disperse. Some of the leaders of resistance to the Assembly were arrested. Danton and Marat went into hiding.

Order having been temporarily re-established, the Assembly decided to end its work. It had provided a constitution under which it was hoped that France might be governed with justice and order. On the fourteenth of September the King took oath before the Assembly "to employ all the power delegated to him in order to fulfill and to maintain the Constitution." There were manifestations that day in honor of the Assembly, of the King and of the Constitution, but there were more fervent manifestations in honor of two deputies who were known for their democratic opinions. Those two were Petion and Robespierre.

The *Assemblée Nationale* had changed its name to *Assemblée Constituante*. For two years it had labored to produce a constitution that remained in force for less than one. It is one of the ironies of history that the disinterested and patriotic work of the majority of the deputies had no chance to prove its merit. But the Constitution of 1791 was not a total loss. It put an end to absolutism and inaugurated a period that was rich in liberty. The Assembly established equality before the law and equality in taxation, and, by making ecclesiastical and royal property the property of the nation, it wiped out the deficit and stimulated private enterprise. It proved its disinterest by decreeing that none of its members should be eligible for the Legislative Assembly or for the King's cabinet that were provided for in the Constitution. That act alone entitles the Constitutional Assembly of France to high and exceptional honor in the history of legislative bodies.

The urgent necessity to pay debts compelled the Assembly to take extraordinary measures. When the bankruptcy of the government became imminent, Talleyrand and Mirabeau proposed that the property of the Church should be placed at the disposition of the nation. That seemed to be the only way out of the difficulty. It was argued that Church property had originally been deeded to the clergy in order that it might serve the general interest, and that the State was within its moral right if it used that property in order to avert catastrophe that threatened both Church and State. After long debate the proposed measure was carried. The blow to the clergy was softened by the provision that the State should assure a fair minimum income to the *curés*.

The value of the Church property that was taken over was in excess of the State debt, but its liquidation presented difficulties. Since there was immediate necessity for cash, the Assembly authorized the issuance in small denominations of four hundred millions in face value of five-per-cent bonds that were a lien on funds derived from sale of Church property. These small bonds were called *assignats*. They were not popular at first because it was realized that the liquidation of Church property would be a slow and difficult business; there was skepticism about the permanent validity of the titles. In order to make the *assignats* move, it was necessary to declare them legal currency. Their issuance later in much larger quantities constituted an inflation that brought disastrous results. The people who placed all their savings in *assignats* were ruined.

The flight of the nobles was another source of assistance to the state treasury. Their abandoned estates became government property that was much less difficult to liquidate than the property derived from the Church. Both bourgeois and peasants were delighted to acquire buildings and land that had once belonged to nobles who had despised them. Landed proprietorship became greatly extended. France began at that time to become a country of small farms. This had important social as well as economic effects.

The other European powers were uncertain about what effects the developments in France might have upon international relationships. Their first idea was that France would be so weakened that she might cease to be an important factor in European politics. There was little thought that the Revolution might become a threat to the peace and order of neighboring nations; the leaders of it were known to be pacifists. In 1790 the Assembly declared that "the French nation renounces the undertaking of any war of conquest and will never employ force against the liberty of any people." Not many years later Napoleon modified this policy.

Soon, however, it became clear that the French victory over absolutism gave encouragement to those who wished to resist it elsewhere. In 1789 there was a revolt of the Belgians against Joseph II and in 1790 the people of Avignon revolted against the Pope as their temporal ruler and demanded union with France.

Joseph II died in 1790 and was succeeded by his brother, Leopold II. To him Frederick William II of Prussia made the proposal that they should jointly undertake to put Louis XVI back into power with the understanding that France would have to pay the costs besides ceding to the saviors of her king Alsace and a large part of French Flanders. This plan was not fulfilled, but it led to an alliance between Austria and Prussia.

Certain German princes possessed fiefs in Alsace. When the Assembly abolished feudal rights, that abolition applied to these fiefs. The German princes protested that this constituted a violation of the Treaty of Westphalia. The Assembly, conciliatory in spirit, offered to pay indemnities. The Avignon question, however, was more difficult because it raised the point of annexation of new territory. In a plebiscite the people in the area concerned voted two to one in favor of annexation to France. The Assembly maintained that the result of this vote made annexation legal. It was obvious that the Assembly and the foreign rulers of the old order could not agree upon what constituted legality. The old order demanded respect for old treaties whereas the Assembly held that such treaties were invalid when the people concerned desired their abrogation. This divergence of opinion constituted an obstacle to mutual understanding that no diplomacy could surmount.

The most active if not the most influential agents in causing foreign intervention were the French nobles who had left France. The Comte d'Artois, who was the King's brother, and the Condé princes were

among the first to flee. Reinforced by many others, most of whom had
been officers, they organized a little army on the other side of the
Rhine and strove constantly to secure foreign support for suppression
of the Revolution. They deluded themselves into believing that the
new government had proved a failure and that most of the French
people would welcome their return. These fugitive nobles had less
effect upon foreign courts than the secret negotiations of Louis and
Marie-Antoinette. Intervention was imminent after the capture of
the King at Varennes, but it was postponed because of the Assembly's
wisdom in sustaining Louis as a constitutional monarch. It remained,
nonetheless, a constant threat that profoundly affected the procedures
of the new "Legislative Assembly."

Although the members of the Constitutional Assembly were not
eligible for membership in the new one, many of them continued to
have much political influence. Petion and Robespierre remained active in the club of the *Jacobins* whose formal meetings and discussions were like those of the Assembly. The club formed by those who
had resigned with La Fayette from the *Jacobins* was called the club of
the *Feuillants;* they were defenders of the Constitution and of the
King. In the new Assembly this moderate group outnumbered the
more radical *Jacobins* by two to one, but the *Jacobins* were more aggressive. The moderates sat on the right, the *Jacobins* on the left, and
in between sat those called *Indépendants.*

Those who sat on the left claimed that they wished to maintain the
Constitution, but they favored immediate deposition of the King
if he violated it. In this group the philosopher Condorcet and the
journalist Brissot were leaders. Three deputies from the Gironde were
able allies of Brissot; they and some others came to be called *Girondins.* The *Girondins* formed one faction among the *Jacobins;* Petion
and Robespierre were leaders of another.

The new Assembly began its sessions in October, 1791. It was confronted by the task of carrying on a form of government against which
many were in open rebellion. In the conservative west, in Brittany, in
Anjou, and in the Vendée, "refractory" priests encouraged the peasants to drive away all of the clergy who had taken the civic oath. In
many other places there was bloodshed and disorder. The pillage and

burning of châteaux had not ceased. It was obvious that, without loyal co-operation between the Assembly and the King, order could not be restored, and it was equally obvious that such co-operation was impossible.

The King did all that he could to hasten the failure of the system that he had sworn to support; he thought that the sooner it failed the sooner he might regain what he had lost. Instead of helping the moderates, who were his defenders, he helped the extremists. Royal influence made Petion mayor of Paris and Danton his chief assistant. Control of the city passed into the hands of believers in violence.

In December Louis wrote to one of his agents, "The absurd and detestable Constitution gives me less power than that of the king of Poland. . . . France is in such condition that it could not sustain even half a campaign, but I must seem to support it. My conduct must be such that in its misfortune the country shall see no other resource than to throw itself in my arms."

Louis, still pretending to be patriotic, sought to bring France into war so that he might profit by her defeat. The majority of the deputies also wished for war, but for different reasons. La Fayette and his friends believed that they would control the armies and could then suppress all trouble-makers. Many of their political opponents also favored war in the belief that war would sweep the King and his supporters out of the way and lead to the triumph of democracy. Only one of the influential leaders did his utmost in behalf of peace, but he was overruled by his fellow *Jacobins*. That leader was Robespierre.

The *Girondins,* on the floor of the Assembly, charged the King and the Queen with conspiracy and were loudly applauded. To save himself, Louis formed a new ministry composed of *Girondins*. Two of the new ministers were General Dumouriez and Jean-Marie Roland, an excellent administrator whose talented wife had much influence with the liberal members of the Assembly. Madame Roland's *salon* was a center of political discussion that was especially favored by the *Girondins*.

In March of 1792 the Emperor Leopold died. He had been successful in avoiding war with France, but his successor, Francis II, was not a pacifist. He demanded that the French government restore the rights of German princes with respect to their Alsatian fiefs, return Avignon to the Pope and repress republicanism. This large order the French government was not inclined to fulfill. It responded by declaring war, not against the Empire, but against the Emperor. The Assembly strove to make it clear that France did not wish to make war against any other nation, but only "in just defense against the aggression of a king."

The French army was in bad shape. It had become a political plaything. There was great lack of discipline. An attempted invasion of Belgium failed and a general was killed by his own soldiers. The Assembly decreed that a volunteer army of twenty thousand should be formed in Paris. The King, believing that help was near at hand, refused to sanction this decree, dismissed his *Girondin* ministry, and counted on the La Fayette group for support. This was another of Louis's blunders. The people of Paris arose again in defense of their liberty.

On the twentieth of June there was a great parade through the streets and the presentation to the Assembly of a "petition" that protested against the King's dismissal of the "patriot" ministers, and against his failure, through veto, to permit the will of the people to be fulfilled. The petition maintained that unless the King ceased to oppose the Assembly he should cease to be a king.

Having presented their petition, the people then proceeded to the Tuileries. The French guards at the gates made no effort to prevent their entrance. The King was cornered, but he showed courage. For nearly three hours he had to listen to such insults as he had never heard before. Standing at a window, he drank to the health of the nation and he put on the *bonnet rouge,* but he did not promise to cooperate with the Assembly. There was no violence that day, but there was no doubt about the threat of it.

Throughout France the manifestation of the Parisians was applauded. The enemy was approaching and the King was believed to be a traitor. Resolutions that called for the suspension of royal power were endorsed by many popular assemblies.

Early in July a force of Prussians and French fugitive royalists approached the Lorraine frontier. On the eleventh the Assembly enacted a decree entitled *"la Patrie en danger."* It was, in effect, an order of mobilization and it was addressed directly to the people. The King was ignored, and, for that, the decree had all the more effect. It was hailed with enthusiasm by an aroused nation.

Outside of the Assembly, *Jacobins* and *Cordeliers* co-operated in planning a *coup d'état* that would eliminate the King. They could count on the support of many provincial organizations. The fourteenth of July witnessed the arrival in Paris of many determined men who hoped to see more than a celebration. Five hundred patriots from Marseille came swinging through the streets and, as they marched, they sang a new song that Rouget de l'Isle had written. No song had ever stirred the French people as that one stirred them. It was the *Marseillaise*.

The Duke of Brunswick, who had been Frederick the Great's best general, was in command of the Prussian and Austrian forces that were to invade France. He issued at Coblentz a manifesto that threatened death to all the deputies and the total destruction of Paris if the premises of the Tuileries were again invaded or the King in any way molested. Nothing could have made another invasion of the Tuileries more certain. It was felt that Louis and Marie-Antoinette had had a good deal to do with the wording of that manifesto.

Control of Paris passed into the hands of what was called the *Commune insurrectional,* a body of citizens that made no secret of its intention to depose the King. On the tenth of August, 1792, the insurrectionists attacked the Tuileries. The royal family barely had time to flee through the gardens to the hall in which the Assembly was in session; they felt safer there. The Tuileries were defended by a force of four thousand, but only the nine hundred Swiss could be counted on to obey orders.

Led by the singing marchers from Marseille, the attacking forces reached the façade of the palace without opposition. It looked like a bloodless victory. But at last the Swiss, upon command of their officers, opened fire. The attackers withdrew in confusion, but reinforcements arrived and cannon were brought into action. After two hours of desperate resistance the Swiss received the King's order to cease firing, but that order came too late to save them. Six hundred of them were killed and the insurrectionists took possession of the palace. France on that day ceased to have a king.

There were three years and a month between the fall of the Bastille and the fall of the King. In those difficult years there had been disorders, but men of good will and moderation had been able to keep control and to avoid catastrophe. Now, however, catastrophe was at hand. The fall of the King involved the fall of the Assembly and of the Constitution. The *Commune insurrectional* was controlled by men who would not hesitate to use violence in order to attain their ends. They had the people behind them. The Assembly, confronted by a *fait accompli,* decreed the suspension of the King and the internment of the royal family in the Luxembourg palace. The *Commune,* disregarding this decree, imprisoned the King in the tower of the Temple and the Assembly could do nothing about it.

Realizing its impotence as well as its legal incompetence now that there was no king, the Assembly decreed that the French people should elect a *Convention* to determine what form the government should take; in the interim the affairs of the nation were to be directed by an executive council made up of Danton, leader of the *Commune,* and of the former *Girondin* ministers.

The Constitution of 1791 had restricted suffrage to citizens of property; it prudently provided for a limited electorate. But now the property qualification was removed. The right to vote was extended to all. The victory of the Tuileries made France a democracy without restraint. In defending their liberties the people had opened the door to chaos. Reason was replaced by passion. The *Commune* ordered the imprisonment of all who were believed to be its enemies.

Meanwhile the Prussians were approaching. At the end of August, 1792, they were at Verdun and the road to Paris was undefended. It was the *Commune* rather than the Assembly that met the crisis. In an impassioned appeal Danton cried, *"L'audace, encore de l'audace, toujours de l'audace, et la France est sauvée."* A new army was formed. Marat, Danton's colleague, suggested that, before marching against enemies without, the enemies within should be destroyed. The excited populace took him at his word. There was a massacre of more than a thousand prisoners, many of whom were priests. The Assembly was powerless to stop the slaughter. Danton intervened only when Marat and his murderous committee had issued orders for the arrest of the *Girondins.*

The fall of the King caused chaos in Paris, but it put order into the army. The people felt a new passion to defend a country that had become their own and not any king's. The generals Dumouriez and Kellermann were able to establish a discipline that had been lacking. The soldiers now knew where they were going and whom they were serving. There was new zeal and new confidence.

The invaders entered Champagne on the fourteenth of September, 1792. Dumouriez, outnumbered, did not retreat to cover Paris. He marched south and took a position on the flank of the enemy near Sainte-Menehould. Brunswick received orders to destroy the small army of Dumouriez before going on to Paris. That was what Dumouriez had hoped; he had saved Paris by deflecting the enemy and Kellermann had time to join him with reinforcements.

Valmy is a village a few miles west of Sainte-Menehould. Kellermann took position on a hill behind that village. The enemy bombarded the hill on the morning of the twentieth. There was heavy fog. When the fog lifted, the highly-trained Prussian infantry was seen advancing in perfect order against French recruits, most of whom had never seen a battle. Kellermann, rising in his stirrups and lifting high his hat on the point of his sword, cried *"Vive la Nation!"* The moment of uncertainty passed. All the French shouted, *"Vive la Nation"* and held their ground. They poured a murderous fire into the Prussian ranks. That was not what the Prussians had been led to expect. They had been told that the French army was little better than a rabble that would run as soon as it was attacked. The artillery duel continued, but the Prussian infantry did not advance again. Late in the afternoon a torrential rainstorm added to the disgust and discomfort of the invaders. Their heart was not in the business. They withdrew. Heavy rain continued for weeks and there was a contagion of dysentery. The Prussians, their ranks decimated by disease, trudged wearily homeward, a defeated army.

Valmy was a very small battle. Only a few hundred were killed.

But it was a victory that saved France. Its moral effect was tremendous. An untrained soldiery had repulsed an army that was thought to be invincible. Danton's slogan about audacity had been justified. After Valmy the French had a feeling that they could conquer the world.

The poet Goethe was with the Prussians. Asked what he thought of the battle, he said, "This day and this place mark a new epoch in the history of the world."

CHAPTER TWELVE

THE ROBESPIERRE PERIOD

THE CONVENTION. DEMOCRATIC RECKLESSNESS REPLACED BOURGEOIS PRU-
DENCE. *GIRONDINS* VS. *MONTAGNARDS*. ROBESPIERRE, MARAT, AND DAN-
TON. THE EXECUTION OF LOUIS XVI. CHARLOTTE CORDAY. THE TERROR.
LAZARE CARNOT, ARTISAN OF VICTORY. THE REVOLUTION WAS VICTORIOUS
IN BOTH CIVIL AND FOREIGN WAR. THE BETRAYAL AND DEATH OF A
BLOODSTAINED IDEALIST.

IN THAT fateful month of September, 1792, the month of the victory
of Valmy, France elected seven hundred and forty-nine deputies who
were to form her new governing body, the Convention. The right to
vote had been extended to all, but only a minority exercised that right.
The *Jacobins,* better organized than their opponents, became dominant
in the Convention. The conservative laws that the Assembly had enacted were soon supplanted by much more radical measures. Bourgeois
prudence was replaced by ultra-democratic recklessness.

The first meeting of the Convention was held on September 21,
the day after the Prussian retreat into the Argonne. At that first meeting the abolition of royalty was decreed. Paris was illuminated that
night and crowds marched through the streets crying, *"Vive la Re-
publique!"*

A new phase of human history had begun! The bad past should
be forgotten. A new calendar should mark the beginning of a new
world! The year I of man's liberation had come at last.

The new calendar was symbolic of the confidence, the optimism, the
new delight that possessed men's minds. The romance of human
brotherhood had become, for the moment, a reality. The new divisions
of the year should be expressive of man's equality and of his partnership with nature.

The republican calendar began with the autumnal equinox, which
conveniently occurred two days after the victory at Valmy. The year I
of the republican era began September 22, 1792. The year was di-

vided into twelve months of thirty days each; the five extra days were devoted to republican fêtes. The months were named:

Vendémiaire, September 22 to October 22, the month of the grape harvest, *vendange*.

Brumaire, October 22 to November 21, mist, *brume*.

Frimaire, November 21 to December 21, cold fog with frost, *frimas*.

Nivôse, December 21 to January 20, snow, *neige*.

Pluviose, January 20 to February 19, rain, *pluie*.

Ventôse, February 19 to March 21, wind, *vent*.

Germinal, March 21 to April 20, *germination*.

Floréal, April 20 to May 20, flowers, *fleurs*.

Prairial, May 20 to June 19, the month of haymaking in the *prairies*.

Messidor, June 19 to July 19, harvest, *moisson*.

Thermidor, July 19 to August 18, from a Greek word meaning heat.

Fructidor, August 18 to September 22, the month of fruits, *fruits*.

Weeks were suppressed. Each month was divided into three *decades*, the days being designated as *primidi, duodi, tridi*, etc., up to *decadi*. The author of the names of the new months was a poetic member of the *Convention* named Fabre d'Eglantine; *eglantine* means wild rose. The Gregorian calendar was not restored until January 1, 1806.

The brief and tragic history of the Convention falls into three periods. The first was the period of furious rivalry between the *Girondins* and the *Montagnards*. The *Girondins* resisted the rush toward pure democracy and opposed the execution of the King. The *Montagnards* (mountaineers), so called because they occupied the higher seats in the assembly hall, were led by Robespierre, Marat, and Danton. These "friends of the people" favored the destruction of everybody and everything that might hinder the fulfillment of their dream of pure democracy. Neither of these aggressive groups had a majority. There was a larger group of unorganized deputies called the *Plaine* or the *Marais* (swamp); the ascendancy that the *Montagnards* gained over the *Plaine* determined the outcome. The King was executed in January, 1793, and the *Girondins* followed him to the guillotine in the following October.

In the second period, the Terror, Robespierre was supreme. But he himself was executed in July, 1794. In the third period, pure democracy having been discredited, the country was plunged into a chaotic state from which only the genius of Napoleon Bonaparte was to rescue it.

In all three of these periods there was both foreign and civil war. Despite the sorry and uncertain state of their government, the French, fired by a new patriotism and drunk with freedom, performed prodigies of valor and won astounding victories.

Paris dominated France. Its *Commune,* controlled by the Robespierre group, was a menace to national legislation; it could override the Convention by force. The *Girondins* objected strenuously to that. They demanded a force strong enough to maintain peace and order in Paris; believers in legality, they hated violence. But the *Montagnards* maintained that the threat of violence was necessary for the success of true democracy. They feared return to bourgeois control.

The *Montagnards* accused the *Girondins* of wishing to make France a federated republic like the United States and to govern it in the interest of their own class. The *Girondins* responded by accusing Robespierre of wishing to reduce all citizens to the same economic level and to be their dictator.

Royalty having been abolished, the fate of the King remained to be settled. In November, 1792, documents were discovered that gave ample proof of the treason of Louis XVI. While professing fidelity to the new order, he had been plotting its overthrow. That sealed his fate. His trial by the Convention lasted more than a month. Louis, truly courageous in his last days, bore himself with admirable dignity. Much of the old respect for royalty was revived. Out of seven hundred and twenty-one votes, three hundred and thirty-four were cast against the death penalty. Condemned by this small majority, Louis was executed on Sunday, the twenty-first of January, 1793. He was thirty-nine years old.

The guillotine faced the Tuileries in the *Place de la Revolution,* now the *Place de la Concorde.* The King, unflinching, attempted to speak to the people who crowded close to the guards. A roll of the drums drowned his voice. The great knife fell. The established order of a thousand years fell with it. Respect for the "divine right" of royalty ceased on that day in France. The horrified monarchs of Europe, see-

The provinces of France which the Convention subdivided
into *départements*.

ing the handwriting on the wall, united to punish the people who had killed their King.

The execution of Louis XVI meant a death struggle between the Revolution and all its enemies. Austria, Prussia, England, Spain, Holland, and the states of the Empire and of Italy entered into a coalition against France. When the Convention decreed that an army of three hundred thousand should be raised, civil war broke out in Vendée. The General Dumouriez went over to the enemy. The situation seemed hopeless, but there was no thought of yielding. The desperate devotees of the Revolution prepared to fight to the last.

The division of France into provinces was too suggestive of the old order to please the Convention. They were abolished and, in their place, eighty-six *départements* were created. In nearly every case these new territorial divisions were named for rivers that traversed them or for mountains within their boundaries. Normandy, Brittany, Burgundy, and Provençe are familiar names still in common use, but they no longer have legal significance.

In the spring of 1793 the Convention sent into the *départements* agents *(Représentants en mission)* who were given full power to act against all who were suspected of hostility to the Revolution. A *Tribunal révolutionnaire* was set up and a *Comité de Salut public;* their purpose was to suppress all opposition. The *Girondins* opposed these measures, and succeeded in having the arrest of Marat authorized. But Marat was acquitted and returned to the Convention vowing death to the *Girondins.* He and his friends aroused the Parisians. On the second of June eighty thousand men surrounded the Tuileries where the Convention was in session and compelled the expulsion of the *Girondins.* Thenceforward the *Montagnards* were in control and enforced their policy of terror.

The great leaders of the *Montagnards* were Marat, Danton, and Robespierre. Marat, a journalist, a doctor, and a scholar, was the most extreme of the terrorists. He said every day in the Convention, "There are 270,000 nobles, priests, and their partisans who are a danger to the state. Therefore those 270,000 heads must fall." He, more than any of the others, urged the *sans-culottes* to violence. To prove his democracy, he wore wooden shoes and the red cap, insignia of liberty.

Danton, a lawyer, was called "the Mirabeau of the people." He resembled Mirabeau both in his massive ugliness and in his magnificent gift of oratory. Brutal and cynical in speech, in his actions he was more prudent and moderate than his colleagues.

After the execution of Danton, Maximilien de Robespierre was supreme. At thirty-five he was the most influential leader of the *Jacobins* and the most nearly perfect incarnation of their ideals. He was called "the incorruptible." He lived in the home of a carpenter and, though very meticulous in his dress, he carried his devotion to democratic ideals to the extreme. He believed that the cause of humanity and justice required the destruction of all who opposed democracy.

Within little more than a year, all three of these leaders were to meet violent deaths. On July 14, 1793, Charlotte Corday, an heroic young *Girondin* sympathizer, stabbed Marat to death in his bathtub. Danton became an opponent of Robespierre and was executed in April, 1794. Two months later, a conspiracy brought Robespierre to the guillotine. His death ended the period called the Terror.

In the summer of 1793 the Revolution came to the very brink of annihilation. Enemy armies entered France across all its frontiers. Civil war was added to foreign war. Bordeaux and Lyon, sympathetic with the *Girondins,* added their revolt to that of the Vendée. Normandy, the valley of the Rhône, and Provençe also rebelled. Marat was assassinated. Three-fourths of France was in arms against Paris. And yet, it was Paris and the revolutionary government that prevailed.

Under Robespierre's leadership the Convention became increasingly dictatorial, but the measures that it passed strengthened it with the masses. The *bourgeoisie* who had started the Revolution were now held to be its enemies. The people were led to believe that the middle classes were as hostile to true democracy as the nobility had been. Robespierre used the ignorance and the passion of the proletariat as instruments to serve his exalted and impractical ends.

After the suppression of the *Girondins,* the Convention tried to placate the provinces by its approval of a very liberal constitution that called for extreme decentralization. But the critical state of affairs did not permit this constitution to be put into operation. Even the provincial delegates agreed that it should not become effective until peace was restored. Meanwhile the "provisional revolutionary government" was to be continued. That meant extreme centralization and dictatorial powers. Robespierre declared that "the revolutionary government owes protection to all good citizens. To the enemies of the people it owes only death."

The Convention placed direction of the revolutionary government in the hands of the *Comité de Salut public*. Robespierre had supplanted Danton in control of that committee. A *Comité de Sûreté générale* was charged with the apprehension and arrest of all suspected of disloyalty, and the *Tribunal révolutionnaire* took care of trials and executions. These groups labored with an inspired and ferocious efficiency. They were aware of their peril. For them it was kill or be killed. The chief purpose of the Revolution was to destroy absolutism. It had destroyed one absolutism only to replace it by another that was even more tyrannical.

The accomplishments of the *Représentants en mission* were amazing. To them the Convention had delegated full powers. Some of them accompanied the armies and saw to the enforcement of rigid discipline. Officers who showed timidity or failed otherwise in their duty were promptly put to death. One of them was shot because he had left camp for a few hours without permission, and a private was executed because, contrary to orders, he had exchanged his bad hat for a better one. Such was the morale of the soldiers of the Revolution that discipline like this was applauded. Other *Représentants* were equally harsh in their suppression of civil revolts.

The situation that confronted the revolutionary government was desperate. Formidable foreign enemies had to be resisted, a civil war had to be won, and a famished nation had to be fed. Never have men undertaken a more titanic task, never has there been more prodigious accomplishment.

In August of 1793 the *levée en masse* was decreed. The entire population was conscripted for service with or for the armies. Any attempt to profiteer on necessities was made punishable by death. Prices were fixed. A forced loan of a billion francs was imposed. To break all

opposition, the Terror was established. In September all who were suspected of failure to perform their "civic duty" were made liable to
arrest and execution. The *Tribunal révolutionnaire* began sending
scores of innocent people to the guillotine every day.

One of the first victims of the Terror was Marie-Antoinette. Proud
and courageous to the last, she was executed on the sixteenth of October, 1793. After hers, the heads of the *Girondins* fell; they had been
kept under surveillance since their expulsion from the Convention in
June. Other famous victims were the Duke of Orléans, the cousin
of Louis XVI who had tried to save himself by changing his name to
Philippe Egalité; Bailly, the heroic mayor Paris; Lavoisier, the famous
chemist; and Madame Roland, "intrepid and smiling in the face of
death"; it was she whose last words were, "O liberty, what crimes are
committed in thy name!"

Between March of 1793 and July of 1794 nearly three thousand
people were executed in Paris and about fifteen thousand in the
provinces. At Nantes three or four thousand prisoners were thrust
into old boats that were sunk in the middle of the river; at Lyon they
were shot down in groups of as many as two hundred at a time.

While terror, fury, and bloodshed reigned in the heart of France, her
newly formed armies were developing in strength and experience that
was to enable them to change the map of Europe. After Valmy, in
the fall of 1792, the offensive had been taken. In the southeast,
French armies occupied Savoy and Nice; in the northeast they advanced to the Rhine. In Belgium the army of Dumouriez defeated
the Austrians in the battle of Jemmapes. In that fortunate autumn
the French had been received with joy by the people of the regions
they invaded; they were regarded as liberators. Goethe wrote in his
Hermann and Dorothea, "The French brought friendship. Gaily they
planted trees of liberty and promised justice to all. They opened our
eyes to new and brighter prospects." In November the Convention
declared in the name of the French people that "it would bring help
and fraternity to all who wished to gain their liberty."

This was too good to last. Financial needs and political traditions
soon dimmed the idealism that accompanied the first invasions. In
December the Convention decreed that in all occupied territory feudal

rights should be suppressed, existing officials replaced by "partisans of liberty," acceptance of *assignats* made compulsory, and all property of Church and nobles placed under the control of the French republic.

In Savoy an assembly of delegates voted in favor of annexation to France. France previously, in the case of Avignon, had recognized "the right of people to dispose of themselves." So Savoy was annexed. Early in 1793 the annexations of Nice, of Belgium, and of the left bank of the Rhine were decreed, but in these cases less attention was paid to the principle of self-determination. The harsh enforcement of the decrees of the previous December aroused bitter hostility in the Rhineland.

The successful campaigns of the fall of 1792 served to prepare for the far more difficult ones of 1793. The execution of Louis XVI in January multiplied the enemies of France. England took the lead in the new coalition. Pitt, the prime minister, had favored neutrality until the French occupied Belgium. Then England came in. Pitt declared that it would be a war of extermination. Hostilities between England and France did not cease from that time until 1815, except for the brief "peace of Amiens" of 1802.

In March, 1793, the army of Dumouriez was defeated at Neerwinden and the Austrians reoccupied Belgium. The Prussians recrossed the Rhine and blockaded French forces that were in Mainz. Early in April the defection of Dumouriez occurred; he went over to the enemy.

In July the French were compelled to surrender at Mainz and in August Toulon fell into the hands of the English. Spanish forces threatened both Perpignan and Bayonne, and the Austrians entered Alsace. In the north there was a combined attack by the English, the Dutch, and the Austrians; the century-old fortifications of Vauban resisted this attack, but the Austrians captured Valenciennes and laid siege to Maubeuge.

In this frightfully critical situation France was saved only by prodigies of energy. Lazare Carnot, a former captain of engineers, had become a member of the *Comité de Salut public*. As director of the national defense, he proved himself to be one of the great men of military history. By the end of 1793 he had a million men under arms and their organization perfected. Twenty thousand cannon were manu-

factured in a year and Paris alone produced a thousand muskets a day.
The whole nation either worked at the production of arms or carried
them. Despite Carnot's magnificent efforts the soldiers of the Republic
were very badly clothed. Most of them fought in rags, but that did not
diminish their ardor. The new liberty gave birth to new ambition, new
determination, and new recklessness. The old values and timidities
disappeared; the old restraints were gone. Life became a primitive
struggle in which home ties were forgotten and no quarter given.
The sheep became tigers. Defeats and endless hardships did not arrest
the magnificent contagion of their zeal.

Generals of the old army, if suspected of disloyalty or of too great
prudence, were either discharged or executed. They were replaced by
young officers who had risen from the ranks. The generals Jourdan,
Hoche, and Pichegru had been but corporals before the Revolution.
Hoche, a corporal in 1789, commanded an army in 1793; he was then
twenty-five. These young generals were untrained in military science,
but they were magnificent in leading reckless charges. The slogan,
l'audace, encore de l'audace, et toujours de l'audace, was theirs as well
as Danton's. Carnot instructed them to strike like lightning. They
joyfully fulfilled those instructions.

Fortunately there were no machine guns. When the soldiers of the
Republic made their reckless charges, singing and shouting the *Marseillaise,* they were opposed by slow infantry fire that could not stop
them. Nonetheless, their losses were enormous. Between 1792 and
1800, seven hundred thousand Frenchmen fell in battle.

Toward the end of 1793 the tide turned. Jourdan defeated the
Austrians in the battle of Wattagnies. Carnot was there and led an
infantry charge. This victory relieved besieged Maubeuge. Hoche, in
command of the army of the Moselle, attacked the Prussians twenty-
eight time in five weeks; he compelled their retreat.

In 1794 the strengthened armies invaded foreign territory. In June
Jourdan defeated the Austrians in the decisive battle of Fleurus in
Belgium. In October, having forced the enemy back of the Rhine,
French forces occupied Cologne and Coblentz. Pichegru drove the
English out of Flanders and occupied Antwerp in July. A few months
later Holland was invaded and the Dutch fleet, icebound in the Helder,
was captured by a few squadrons.

In 1795 Prussia, Spain, and Holland withdrew from the coalition and made peace with France. By the treaty of Bâle, Prussia recognized French occupation of her territories west of the Rhine. The Dutch ceded their part of Flanders and, having established a republic of their own, they became allies of France. Spain also made concessions. But the victory was not complete. England and Austria remained hostile.

The civil war of the Vendée began in 1793 and continued until 1796. Insurrection against the revolutionary government spread into Poitou, Anjou, and Brittany. A force of eighty thousand insurrectionists took the name "royal catholic army"; they desperately resisted all efforts to suppress them. While the regular forces were fighting foreign foes, the insurrectionists, popularly called *Chouans*, captured Saumur and threatened Nantes. The Convention sent fifteen thousand men against them commanded by Kléber and Marceau. The *Chouans* were disastrously defeated at Le Mans and at Savenay, but they were not pacified. Hoche, in 1796, in a just but merciful campaign, finally ended this civil war which had cost fifty thousand lives and made a desert out of a great extent of territory.

In Paris events had moved with great rapidity. By the end of 1793 Robespierre and his *Comité de Salut public* had been successful in suppressing the revolts in Lyon, Bordeaux, and Provençe. Most of the *Chouans* had been destroyed and the foreign invasions had been checked. But the economic policies of the government were less successful. Threat of famine compelled the rationing of food. There was much discontent on that account.

Another cause of discontent was the official contempt for Christianity. The new calendar ignored Sundays and obliterated the religious fêtes. Priests who still survived were compelled to renounce their sacred functions. In the cathedral of Notre Dame a *fête de la Liberté et de la Raison* was celebrated; a lightly clad ballet dancer personified liberty. After that the *Commune* ordered the closing of all the churches of Paris, but the Convention, realizing the danger of this measure, decreed that there should be no restraint of worship. A large proportion of the common people had not been won away from their devotion to the Church. The "dechristianization movement" weakened the hold that the *Montagnards* had on the populace.

Robespierre had secret enemies. Within his own political group there were some who were eager for an opportunity to bring about his downfall. Two factions in the Convention were loud in their criticisms of the *Comité de Salut public;* one demanded that the Terror should become still more terrible; the other faction, *les Indulgents,* favored clemency. The leader of the terrorists was the popular journalist, Hébert. Danton and Camille Desmoulins were leaders of the Indulgents. The struggles between these factions imperiled the administrative work of Robespierre's *Comité.* He decided that the leaders of both of them would have to be suppressed.

The Hébert group attempted to incite the famished people to an attack on the Convention. Robespierre acted swiftly. Hébert and his chief lieutenants went to the guillotine. That was in March, 1794.

The Indulgents were accused of defeatism, of cowardice, even of treason. It was believed that they wished for an immediate peace by which they themselves might profit. Less than a week after the execution of the *Hébertistes,* Danton, Desmoulins, and some of their friends were arrested on the charge of conspiracy against the republic. "Better a hundred times," cried Danton, "to be guillotined than to guillotine." The *Tribunal révolutionnaire,* fearful of the effects of Danton's fiery eloquence, obtained authority to prevent his attendance at his own trial. On the fifth of April he and his friends were put to death.

Robespierre, then thirty-five, became the uncontested master of the situation. From April to July, 1794, his authority was unchallenged. His most valuable ally was Saint-Just, a youth of twenty-seven whose feminine beauty was difficult to reconcile with his pitiless fulfillment of his principles. It was he who denounced Danton and the *Hébertistes;* he who as *représentant en mission* punished by death the slightest infraction of military discipline. His tireless work as a member of the *Comité de Salut public* was of the highest order, both for the sustenance and for the defense of his country.

After Danton's fall, Robespierre moved rapidly toward his goal of complete social equality. It was ordered that the confiscated properties of "enemies of the republic" should be given to "deserving patriots."

Saint-Just was charged with this distribution, and was authorized to revise the code of social institutions in the interest of pure democracy.

Equality attained, virtue was next to be extolled in Robespierre's ideal state. The Convention sought to popularize virtue through legislation. In May of 1794 the deputies unanimously approved a decree that set up a new form of worship. It ignored Christianity. The decree declared that, "the French people believe in a Supreme Being and in the immortality of the soul. . . . Worship of the Supreme Being is one of man's duties. . . . Fêtes shall be established to recall to man the divinity and dignity of his own being." There were to be fêtes to honor the Supreme Being and Nature, to honor Liberty, Equality, and Civic Virtue, to honor Love of Country, to honor Devotion to Parents, and to honor the whole Human Race.

The first of the new fêtes was held on the eighth of June. It was in honor of the Supreme Being. Robespierre played the principal role. Massed choirs sang a new hymn entitled *Père de l'Univers, suprême intelligence.* Robespierre lighted the fire that burned a statue representing atheism. Then, followed by all the members of the Convention and all carrying bouquets, he led a great parade from the Tuileries to the *Champs de Mars.* There a new tree of liberty had been set up, and there the fête reached its climax.

There had been another great ceremony in that same place in 1790. Then the people, amid similar scenes of enthusiasm, had pledged loyalty to a new constitution and to a new spirit of fraternity. But that constitution and that fraternity did not outlast the year. Robespierre and his new religion were doomed to fare no better.

Many believed that the fête of the Supreme Being would mark the end of the Terror, but that was not to be. Two days later the Convention passed a decree that enlarged the power of the *Tribunal révolutionnaire.* Trial by jury was denied to those suspected of "conspiracy," and the *Tribunal* was authorized to make condemnations without the hearing of witnesses. Heads began to fall faster than ever. It was the "Great Terror." In forty-five days there were 1285 executions.

The Great Terror was an expression of Robespierre's impatience to realize his ideal state. He wished to destroy all opposition to the establishment of social and economic equality. But he had overreached himself. The victory of Fleurus, in removing the threat of invasion, had allayed the fear that had formerly made the mob delight in the execution of all who were suspected of disloyalty. The "razor of the Republic" began to lose its popularity. The pitiless apostle of liberty, fraternity, and equality began to lose prestige. The word tyrant was murmured.

This new sentiment was quickly exploited by Robespierre's enemies. A dubious group of deputies planned to secure his condemnation by the Convention. That group was composed of former *Représentants en mission* whose hands were stained both with blood and with loot. Their record was known to Robespierre; they knew that he would bring them to the guillotine unless they brought him there first. These wolves sought to win the support of the *Plaine* by putting on sheep's clothing and advocating clemency. Fouché was the brains of the business.

Robespierre, aware of the plot, believed that he could still control a majority of the deputies. He might have done so, but on the twenty-sixth of July he made a fatal mistake. In an impassioned speech he told the Convention that many of its members were traitors. He named no names, but many feared that they were on his black list. He had multiplied his enemies.

That same night the plotters perfected their plot. They persuaded the presiding officer of the Convention not to allow Robespierre or his friends to have the floor. When, on the following day, Saint-Just rose to speak, Tallien cried out, "Let us unmask the traitors!" Billaud-Varennes, in the midst of frantic applause, denounced Robespierre as a tyrant and all the *Jacobins* as rebels. Tallien brandished a dagger. Robespierre tried to make himself heard, but his voice was drowned by the furious ringing of the president's bell. "President of assassins," he cried, "I demand to be heard." But he was not heard. Late in the afternoon his arrest was ordered. His brother demanded to share the same fate, and Saint-Just also shared it. "The Republic is lost," said Robespierre, "the brigands triumph."

When the order for the arrest became known, the *Commune* made an effort to prevent its execution. Robespierre and his friends had taken refuge in the *Hôtel de Ville*. Late in the evening many of the soldiers of the *Commune* assembled in front of that building, but they had no orders nor any effective leader. Toward midnight a storm broke. Drenched by torrents of rain and uncertain about their duty, the men of the *Commune* dispersed. At about two in the morning, soldiers of the Convention, having secured the password of the *Commune*, entered the building. They rushed into the hall where Robespierre was. A shot was fired that broke his jaw. Some said that he attempted suicide, but one of the soldiers claimed the honor of having fired that shot.

On the next day, July 28, 1794, Robespierre and his brother, Saint-Just, and nineteen others were executed. Eighty-three members of the *Commune* were executed in the two days that followed. That ended the Terror, and it all but ended the Republic. Democracy had followed autocracy to the guillotine. The Convention and the revolutionary government remained, but the death of Robespierre ended the dream of pure democracy and equality. No man dared to espouse the perilous cause that had brought death to its devotees. The time was ripe for a new leader who would point for a different goal. He was soon to appear.

CHAPTER THIRTEEN

THE REACTION FROM REVOLUTION

THE ROYALISTS BECAME AGGRESSIVE. THE WHITE TERROR. THE CONVEN-
TION, SAVED FROM THE MOB BY A CORSICAN ARTILLERY OFFICER, RETIRED
FROM OFFICE AND WAS SUCCEEDED BY THE *DIRECTOIRE*. THE REDISTRIBU-
TION OF LAND. NAPOLEON BONAPARTE'S CAMPAIGN IN ITALY. THE
TREATY OF CAMPO-FORMIO.

REACTION toward conservatism and greater clemency followed Robespierre's death, but there were strong radical forces still to be overcome. The government, in seeking to maintain itself, veered to the
right, then to the left, then back toward the right again. It used
the royalists to check the *Jacobins* and guns to check the royalists.

The administration was reorganized. Control by the *Comité de
Salut public* was limited to military and foreign affairs, and its membership was made subject to frequent change; strength and stability
were sacrificed in order that dictatorship might be avoided. The
Tribunal révolutionnaire and the *Commune* were shorn of their
extraordinary powers and the club of the *Jacobins* was closed. The
Robespierre legislation in the interest of equality was either suppressed
or ignored and, to the delight of the merchants, price-control was
abandoned. Some of the most ferocious of the terrorists were executed
and most of the imprisoned suspects were released. Those of the
Girondins who had survived were recalled to the Convention.

The reaction from antichristianism was even more rapid than the
reaction from political and economic radicalism. The majority of the
Convention were freethinkers, but they were compelled to make concessions to the increasing demand for re-establishment of the churches.
There was a resurrection of Catholicism. In May of 1795 the government restored to their rightful owners the churches it had seized.

Despite these conciliatory measures, the government was constantly
menaced by both royalists and *Jacobin* groups. It was the turn of the
royalists to become aggressive. Emerging from their hiding places, or

revealing themselves in their true colors, bands of young king-lovers began to persecute the radicals. There were demonstrations against democracy. No well-known *Jacobin* was safe in the streets. Violence reappeared, but it was a violence of the *jeunesse dorée* (gilded youth) rather than of the *sans-culottes*.

Pushed by the misery and hunger of a bitter winter, the people rose again. In April, 1795, a mob led by women invaded the hall of the Convention and intimidated the deputies. In May, the daily ration of bread having fallen to three ounces, the mob returned. A deputy was killed. His head, impaled on a pike, was brandished in the face of Boissy d'Anglas, the presiding officer. He calmly saluted it.

The Convention felt forced to act against this second insurrection. For the first time the army was called upon to restore order in Paris. Twenty thousand veterans came marching in. The people were compelled to surrender the arms that they had carried since 1789. The reaction toward conservatism was accelerated. All the surviving members of the Robespierre government were condemned with the exception of Carnot, the "artisan of victory." The *Tribunal révolutionnaire* was suppressed, and the liberal constitution of 1793 was abandoned even before it had been put into effect; it was replaced by a much less democratic one called the "Constitution of the Year III."

In the provinces a White Terror succeeded the Red Terror. Many *Jacobins* had their throats cut in Lyon, Aix, Tarascon, and Marseille. Royalism was revived. When it became known that the son of Louis XVI had died in prison, Louis's brother, the Count of Provence, took the title Louis XVIII. Vendée rebelled again and an English fleet brought to Brittany a large number of royalists who had taken refuge in England. They debarked at Quiberon. General Hoche compelled the surrender of this force and their *Chouan* allies. He took twelve thousand prisoners.

The Convention found itself frightfully embarrassed. The reaction toward conservatism had gone too fast and much too far. France had had its fill of *Jacobinism,* but it was far from ready for a restoration of royalty. Rigorous republicanism became again the order of the day. The old law against *emigrés* was applied to those who had returned too optimistically from England. More than seven hundred of them were shot.

A victory of the royalists was feared in the election that the new constitution called for. To prevent that result, it was decreed that two-thirds of the new legislative body should be composed of former members of the Convention. This two-thirds decree deprived the royalists of hope of advancing their cause by legal means. They determined to try force.

Twenty thousand men took arms against the Convention. There were only a few thousand to oppose them. Barras, in charge of the defense of the deputies, called to his aid a young artillery officer who had recently been promoted to the grade of general because his plan for gun emplacements had compelled an English fleet to abandon the harbor of Toulon. This officer placed forty guns at strategic points near the Tuileries. On the fifth of October, 1795, the royalists attacked. In their advance through narrow streets so many of them were shot down that the others retreated in disorder. Command of the army of the interior was conferred upon the officer who had saved the Convention. He made short work of breaking all resistance and restoring order. His name was Napoleon Bonaparte. Three weeks later the new constitution went into effect and the Convention adjourned.

In the three years of its dramatic existence, the work of the Convention had not been limited to military, political, and economic problems. In matters of internal organization its achievements were remarkable. Other committees worked no less laboriously than the *Comité de Salut public*. Among these were the committees on constitution, on finance, on legislation, and on public instruction. In the midst of tumult, peril, and uncertainty, legislation of the highest order was accomplished. Not France alone, but all civilization is indebted to the Convention for the precedents of social justice that it established.

The ultra-democratic constitution of 1793, which was to become effective when peace was restored, provided for the *referendum;* any legislation that was sufficiently opposed might be annulled by a vote of the people. The reaction from this extreme was reflected in the Constitution of the Year III. Its principal author was Daunou. Its preamble stressed the duties of citizenship as well as its rights. The earlier constitution had declared that, in case a government violated the rights of a people, insurrection was a "sacred duty"; the new one emphasized the obligation of citizens to respect law and order. Universal suffrage had been granted in 1793, but the new constitution restricted suffrage to taxpayers, and qualified even further the right to hold office; in many respects it was more conservative than the Constitution of the United States.

Legislative power was vested in seven hundred and fifty deputies who were to be divided into two Councils, the *Cinq-Cents* and the *Anciens*. The "Five Hundred," whose members had to be at least thirty years of age, were to prepare legislation which the "Elders," who had to be at least forty, were to adopt or reject. Each year there was to be a new election of one-third of all the deputies.

Executive power was entrusted to a *Directoire* of five members, and there was to be an election of one of these members each year. The members of the *Directoire* were to be selected by the *Anciens* from a list of ten prepared by the *Cinq-Cents*. There was, as in America, a strict application of Montesquieu's principle of the separation of powers; the *Directoire* was to have no control over legislation and the Councils were to have no control over the executive power save by the annual election of one member of the executive body. Dictatorship was made improbable, but the probability of conflict was increased. The success of this constitution was dependent upon a co-operation between the executive and legislative bodies that could hardly be expected.

Cambon of Montpellier was chairman of the committee on finance. That man's work was magnificent. He instituted, among many excellent measures, the *Grand Livre de la Dette publique*. In that great book those to whom the government owed money were given credit for the market value of their claims, and no more. Holders of bonds issued prior to the Revolution were placed on the same footing as those who loaned new money to the government. Complete repudiation was avoided and the public debt was unified. But Cambon could do nothing to prevent depreciation of the *assignats*. The Convention had forced their acceptance at par in 1793, but such inflation was necessitated in 1794 that nothing could then arrest their rapid fall. In July of 1795 they had fallen to three per cent of their face value.

When the Convention adjourned, the price of bread had risen to twenty francs a pound and a pair of shoes cost twelve hundred.

Although the Convention could not provide a stable currency, it did much in other ways to improve the status of the masses. It decreed the total abolition of feudal rights, caused all feudal titles to be burned, and established the peasants in ownership of their lands. Rural proprietorship became at that time, and has continued to be, more extensive in France than in any other country of Europe.

The sale of expropriated lands was not always conducted on a fair business basis. There was much profiteering. A story is recorded about a peasant who sold two pounds of butter in Amiens. On his way home he passed a building in which a public sale of land was proceeding. He stepped in and bought a small farm with the francs he had received for his two pounds of butter.

Lakanal, a former priest, was the leader in educational legislation. The *Jacobins* had subscribed to Danton's declaration: "After food, the first need of the people is for education. . . . The fatherland precedes the father in its claim on his child. . . . Parents must be compelled to bring their children to the public schools." A decree ordering the establishment of free schools was favored in Robespierre's time, but the reaction toward conservatism and the financial difficulties led to deletion of the word free; public primary schools were provided for, but only one-quarter of the pupils were to receive instruction without payment, and then only on account of the indigence of their parents.

Lakanal secured the foundation of secondary public schools (lycées), one for each department and five for Paris. Many special institutions were also established, notably the *Museum d'Histoire naturelle,* where Lamarck, Jussieu, and Saint-Hilaire did pioneer work in the study of organic evolution, the *Ecole Polytechnique,* the *Institut de France,* and the *Musée du Louvre.*

The Convention established a uniform system of weights and measures, the metric decimal system. The metre became the unit of linear measurement, the litre the unit of liquid measurement, and the gram the unit of weight,. The litre, a cubic decimetre, is a little less than a quart. The *livre* (pound) is five hundred grams, or 1.1 of the English pound. The gram is the weight of a cubic centimetre of water under standardized conditions of temperature and pressure. The metric system has great advantages over the antiquated units of weight and measure that are still used in England and the United States.

The Convention has an illustrious place in legislative history. Despite all the cruelties, intolerances, and absurdities that are a part of its record, no other body of lawmakers has ever worked more devotedly, more assiduously, or more disinterestedly for what it believed to be the general good.

The brief period in which the Constitution of the Year III was effective is known as the *Directoire*. It ran from October 27, 1795, until November 9, 1799. The first *Directeurs* were former members of the Convention. Carnot, the only survivor of a previous government, was the best of them. The change to a constitutional government did not change the problems that had to be faced. The legality of the government did little to lessen its difficulties.

England continued to aid the royalist movement and Austrian forces recrossed the Rhine. England had taken possession of Corsica. The government was without funds to finance new campaigns and the flotation of a new loan was impossible. After six years of war and revolution, the country was very weary; the reaction toward conservatism had brought in its train a deflation of spirit as well as of the currency.

This was the period of the *Incroyables* and the *Merveilleuses,* the incredibles and the marvelous; profiteers who advertised their incomprehension by eccentricity of dress and behavior. Women paraded the streets and the public gardens wearing fantastic hats, and long gowns that were made of the most transparent material obtainable. Men competed closely with the women in preposterous dress and behavior. Meanwhile the poor of Paris were starving. The nobles had blindly danced on at Versailles in the last days of the kingdom. Now commoners, similarly blind, behaved idiotically while their republic was tottering to its fall.

The *Directoire,* like the Convention, was compelled to incline, now to the right, now to the left. It used *Jacobins* against royalists, and royalists against the anarchistic tendencies of some of the *Jacobins.* There was a movement for communism. Its leader, Babeuf, declared that "the common good calls for common goods." He and his friends plotted the overthrow of the government. Arrested, Babeuf's trial lasted more than a year. He was executed in May, 1797. His was one of a number of similar plots.

The threats of anarchy and the government's weakness alarmed the property owners who, under the constitution, formed a majority of the electorate. Former republicans began to be sympathetic with the royalists. In the election of April, 1797, only thirteen deputies out of more than two hundred whose terms had expired were re-elected. For the vacant seat in the *Directoire*, Barthélemy was chosen; he favored a constitutional monarchy. Pichegru, who had become a partisan of Louis XVIII, was elected president of the *Cinq-Cents*.

It became clear that the *Directoire* could maintain itself only by illegal use of force. It could count on the army which was ardently republican, and upon its ablest generals, Hoche and Bonaparte. In violation of the Constitution, thirty thousand soldiers were used to intimidate the deputies. Barthélemy and Pichegru were arrested. A minority of the deputies declared the recent elections null and void. This was the *coup d'état* of September 4, 1797. It was highly irregular, but it gave the republicans back their majority.

The government was then compelled to turn left again. Its vanquished adversaries were not sent to the guillotine, but they were sent to Guiana which came to be called the "dry guillotine." Liberty of the press was suppressed for a year, and there was a return of "dechristianization"; all priests were required to swear to hatred of royalty and to fidelity to the Constitution. Republican forms of worship were re-established, but they were not popular. An agent of the *Directoire* reported that "all efforts to establish new religious habits appear to make the old ones dearer to the people."

Suppression of the royalists led to the election in 1798 of many *Jacobin* deputies. But *Jacobins* were no more popular with the *Directoire* than the royalists had been. Again the election was declared irregular. Governmental candidates were installed in spite of returns that indicated their defeat. Legality had ceased. The *Directoire* continued in power only because it had the support of the army. Economic conditions went from bad to worse, while a law of conscription brought two hundred thousand recruits each year into the army. It became evident that those who controlled the army would soon control the government. He who would soon control the army had already appeared.

Napoleon Bonaparte was born at Ajaccio in Corsica in 1769, only a year after Corsica had been purchased by France from Genoa in the latter part of the reign of Louis XV. His family was "of the little nobility and of modest fortune." He was accepted on a king's scholarship as a student in the *collège* at Brienne, and afterward in the military school in Paris. *"Bien noté"* as a student, he became at sixteen a sub-lieutenant of artillery.

As a boy Napoleon dreamed of the liberation of Corsica, but the Revolution dissipated that dream; it made a loyal Frenchman out of him, and a *Jacobin.* He became a captain in a regiment that was quartered in the *Midi,* the south of France. When in 1793 the French undertook to retake Toulon from the English, Captain Bonaparte was in charge of the artillery. The general in command directed him to make a breach in the city walls. Bonaparte insisted that it would be better to capture a fort that commanded the entrance of the harbor; possession of that fort would compel the withdrawal of the British fleet and the consequent surrender of Toulon. His plan was approved, the fort was captured, and the English abandoned both the harbor and the town. The Corsican captain, then twenty-four, was made a general and sent to command the artillery of the Army of Italy.

The fall of Robespierre in July, 1794 nearly put an end to Bonaparte's career. He was arrested on the charge of being a *Robespierriste,* but this charge was not sustained. In 1795 he was transferred to the "army of the West" as an infantry officer. But he did not care to be an infantry officer. Instead of reporting at the post to which he was assigned, he went to Paris in hope of securing appointment to service better suited to his training and his talents. He found work in the topographic office of the *Comité de Salut public,* but, stricken from the list and deprived of the pay of an active officer, he felt the pinch of poverty. Nonetheless, he frequented the *salons* of indulgent hostesses, attracted both by their sex-appeal and by their political influence.

A clever woman who made Napoleon's acquaintance is reported by Stendhal to have said, "He was the strangest and the thinnest young man I ever met. He wore his hair in 'dog-ears' that fell to his shoulders, and were not becoming to his strangely sombre expression. He looked like one you would not care to meet in a dark place. His coat was so threadbare that it was hard to believe he was a general. But, in spite of all that, he gave the impression of a rare intelligence. His way of looking at people suggested Rousseau. If he had not been thin to the point of illness, the fineness of his features would have been more apparent. At times he spoke with animation. He gave a most interesting account of the siege of Toulon, but there were days in which he was 'steeped in a sad silence.' He had nothing at all of the usual aggressive military manner."

Napoleon was at that time a youthful personification of angry and indomitable will. Sharp gestures marked his staccato speech. He had an imperious challenging manner to which his amazing eyes gave validity. They were eyes whose penetrating gaze made all evasion seem futile. They have often been described as *fulgurant* which means more than "shining"; it adds authority and force to gleam. He was a genius made to fit his time. The armies of France and their generals were in grave need of such authoritative leadership as Napoleon could provide.

Fed up with inactivity in Paris, Bonaparte asked to be sent to Turkey to reorganize the Sultan's artillery for use against Austria. Suddenly there came the royalist insurrection of October, 1795. He was summoned to aid in protection of the Convention. We have seen how successful he was in doing so. Five months later, in March of 1796, Carnot secured his appointment to command the Army of Italy.

The new commander was well aware of the difficulties that confronted him. He knew that some of the older generals, notably Augereau and Masséna, would not be happy about taking orders from a younger and less experienced man. The headquarters were at Nice. There the older generals received their new commander with frigid courtesy. Prepared for that, he made a short speech. He made it clear that he knew precisely what he intended to do and that opposition to his will would be useless. When the generals withdrew, Augereau, the least tractable of them all, said, "Gentlemen, that little bastard scared me. I cannot understand why his first look seemed to crush me and make him my master."

A ragged, underfed, and dispirited army had to be fired with a new zeal. Bonaparte began with personal investigations. He examined equipment and nourishment even to the minutest details, giving sharp and practical orders for whatever improvements were possible. That, better than words, won him the respect and admiration of the soldiers. When he spoke to them, they were ready to believe him.

"Soldiers," he said, "you have neither shoes, nor coats, nor shirts. You have hardly any bread. Our storehouses are empty, but those of the enemy are full. It is up to you to take them. You wish it. You can do it. Let's go!" (*Partons!* is the word he used, but shall we translate that "let us depart"?)

Austria and England were active enemies of France. Austria possessed Milan. Carnot's plan was for Bonaparte to capture Milan while the main French attack was going forward through Germany. The generals Jourdan and Moreau, taking different routes, were to converge on Vienna. The advance of their armies began in June, 1796. Moreau reached Munich and Jourdan reached the frontier of Bohemia. But the Austrians defeated Jourdan in the battle of Altenkirchen and compelled his retreat to the west of the Rhine. Moreau, isolated, withdrew into Alsace. A second invasion was begun in April, 1797, under the command of Hoche.

Meanwhile Bonaparte, whose campaign had been considered of secondary importance, was winning brilliant victories. Between the twelfth of April, 1796, and the eighteenth of April, 1797, he led his ragged army victoriously across Italy until he was within eighty miles of Vienna. In October, 1797, he compelled the Austrians at Campo-Formio to accept the terms that he imposed.

Napoleon had entered Italy with thirty-six thousand men. There were two enemy armies to be reckoned with, an Austrian army and an army of the King of Sardinia, seventy thousand men in all. The French marched in between these two armies. They attacked the Austrians first and compelled their retreat. Then the Sardinians were defeated. They asked for a truce and their King made peace with

Paris, recognizing French possession of Savoy and Nice which had been his.

Bonaparte was not yet satisfied. "Soldiers," he said, "in fifteen days you have won six victories, made fifteen thousand prisoners, and killed or wounded more than ten thousand. You have won battles without cannon, crossed rivers without a bridge, made forced marches without shoes, and bivouacked without brandy. But you have done nothing yet compared with what remains to be done. There are still battles to fight, cities to take, and rivers to cross. Is there any one of you whose courage falters? No. We all wish to achieve a glorious peace which will repay the fatherland for its immense sacrifices. We all wish, when we return to France, to be able to say with pride, 'I was with the victorious army of Italy.'"

Driving the Austrians ahead of him, Napoleon made a triumphal entry into Milan in May, 1796. There was a famous charge across a long bridge at Lodi which was defended by thirty Austrian cannon. Masséna led his men at full speed across the bridge, captured the cannon, and defeated an infantry force that outnumbered his men two to one.

As Gaston de Foix had done in the time of Louis XII, Napoleon swept through northern Italy like a tornado. In less than a month he conquered the country from the Alps to the Oglio. The Pope, the Dukes of Parma and Modena, and the King of Naples asked for peace. They secured it only upon payment of about fifty million francs. That afforded great relief to the financial stringency both of the army and of the *Directoire* in Paris. The *Directoire* could not have maintained itself except for the money that Napoleon sent. He also sent home many treasures of Italian art. Victory made the victors forgetful of the original idealism of the Republic.

To complete the success of the Italian campaign, Mantua had to be captured; its possession would give control of the two Alpine valleys by which Austrian armies entered Italy. Resistance by the enemy increased at that point. It took six months of hard fighting to win Mantua. In July, 1796, a tactical retreat was made. Wurmser, an Austrian general, had led seventy thousand men to the defense of the threatened city. The French waited until Wurmser had divided his army into two parts, and then defeated each part separately in the battles of Lonato and Castiglione. Wurmser withdrew his depleted forces into Mantua and the siege was resumed. That was in August.

After their defeat of the French in Germany, the Austrians increased their effort to defeat them in Italy. In November a fresh force of fifty thousand approached beleaguered Mantua; it was commanded by Alvinzi, a capable general. There was more difficulty with Alvinzi than there had been with Wurmser. There was another famous fight at a bridge; Napoleon led a charge across a fire-swept bridge at Arcola. The Austrians retreated, but Alvinzi came back again with seventy-five thousand and attempted to surround the French. On the fourteenth of January, 1797, the decisive battle of the campaign occurred, the battle of Rivoli. It was a crushing defeat for the Austrians. A fortnight later, Wurmser, starved out in Mantua, surrendered. That surrender completed the "pacification" of Italy.

The Pope, when the chances of defeating the French seemed good, had re-entered the struggle. Now he had to sue for peace again. He was compelled to recognize French possession of Avignon, and to cede Bologna, Ferrara, and the Romagna.

In March Napoleon advanced toward Vienna. Even with the advantage of position in high mountain passes, the Archduke Charles could not stop him. When the advance guard of the French had come within sixty miles of Vienna, the Austrians capitulated; an armistice was signed on the seventh of April. The peace negotiations which followed were conducted by Napoleon without waiting for instructions from Paris.

The campaign in Italy makes one of the great chapters in military history. Napoleon began it with a small army that was sunk in misery. He could count upon no assistance from his government. He had to create or to capture his supplies and his armament. Starting with thirty-six thousand men, he made one hundred thousand his prisoners and captured more than six hundred cannon. What he lacked in man power he overcame by speed and by tactical genius, and he was admirably seconded by the generals Augereau, Masséna, Joubert, and Berthier. Masséna's division in four days marched seventy miles and fought in three battles, one of them the great battle of Rivoli.

The genius of Napoleon's generalship was no greater than the audacity of his ambition. Accurately judging the state of his country, he believed, after Rivoli, that he might become her master, her savior, and even master of western Europe. He knew that his defeat of Austria would give him far greater prestige than that of any rival. He knew that he had nothing to fear from the *Directoire;* except for him that feeble group would have been long since swept out of office. He dictated terms to Austria as though he were himself the government of France.

Austria protracted the negotiations as long as possible, but at last, at Campo-Formio, a treaty was signed, October 17, 1797. Austrian Flanders and the Duchy of Milan became French possessions. In northern Italy the *République cisalpine* was to be organized as a dependency of France, and the Rhine frontier was to be extended northward. The treaty of Campo-Formio also involved an imperial division of Venetian territory between France and Austria; might made right; the humanitarian declarations of the Revolution were ignored. It was provided that there should be a congress at Rastadt to determine further details.

Campo-Formio marked a new orientation in the foreign policy of France and the beginning of a new epoch in the history of Europe. It completely ignored the right of peoples, and departed widely from the principle of equilibrium. It suited Napoleon's ambition that there should be instability in the new arrangements. His ambition had already run beyond the natural frontiers of France. Campo-Formio was a truce rather than a treaty.

CHAPTER FOURTEEN

THE MATERIAL FAILURE OF A SPIRITUAL VICTORY

FRANCE'S REVOLUTION SERVED HUMANITY AT FIRST BETTER THAN IT
SERVED FRANCE. THE COLLAPSE OF HER FIRST EXPERIMENT IN DEMOCRACY
LED INEVITABLY TO A DICTATORSHIP WHICH WAS ALSO DOOMED TO COL-
LAPSE. IT LEFT AS HERITAGE THE HANDICAP OF A GREAT ILLUSION.
NAPOLEON'S CAMPAIGN IN EGYPT. THE COUP D'ÉTAT AND THE ESTABLISH-
MENT OF THE CONSULATE.

AFTER Campo-Formio Napoleon might have gained control of the
government. He chose, however, to remain military rather than to
turn political. Austria subdued, England was the great obstacle to
fulfillment of his dreams. Impatient to override that obstacle, he believed that this could be done without waiting to strengthen France's
position on the Continent.

In 1797 England was still mistress of the seas, even though the
naval strength of Holland and Spain had been added to that of
France. The old project of a cross-Channel invasion was revived and
Napoleon was named general of "the Army of England." But the
English destruction of the Dutch fleet in the battle of Camperdown
compelled abandonment of that project. Talleyrand, returning to
prominence, had become minister of foreign affairs. He co-operated in
perfecting plans for an attack on Egypt which, if successful, would
enable France to cripple British commerce in the Mediterranean.
Napoleon said to his secretary in a burst of confidence, "Already my
glory fades. This little Europe does not suffice. I must go to the
Orient. All great glory comes from there." The occasional touch of
insanity that made his genius the more dynamic was already apparent.

The Egyptian campaign was even less sensible than the Crusades
had been. It was a colossal blunder. In depriving France of her
best general and her best soldiers it invited renewed attack by strong
and bitter enemies, and it added Russia and Turkey to the list of those

enemies. It came within a hair's breadth of causing complete disaster.

In May of 1798 Bonaparte sailed from Toulon. He took with him the generals Kléber and Desaix and a group of scholars, writers, and artists! Glory was provided for before a gun had been fired. There were three hundred and thirty-five ships, thirty-eight thousand soldiers, and sixteen thousand sailors. Nelson, in command of the British Mediterranean fleet, misjudging Napoleon's plan, was looking for him elsewhere. On the tenth of June Malta was captured and on the thirtieth, having landed without opposition, the French occupied Alexandria.

The hard-riding and hard-fighting Mamelukes were the masters of Egypt. After an exhausting march across the desert, the French defeated the Mamelukes in the battle of the Pyramids. On July 23 they occupied Cairo. A week later Nelson, having finally located the French fleet, destroyed it while it lay at anchor off Aboukir.

Napoleon refused to be dismayed. "Since our ships have been destroyed," he said, "we shall either die here or become heroes. We must do even greater things than we had thought to do. We may be destined to change the face of the Orient."

Turkey, at the instigation of England and Russia, declared war on France and undertook to attack the Egyptian expedition. Learning that a Turkish army was assembling in Syria, Napoleon went there. He defeated the Turks at Mont Thabor near Nazareth in April, 1799, but he failed in a siege of Saint-Jean d'Acre and had to return to Egypt. There was an epidemic of cholera. The return across the desert was marked by many deaths and by frightful suffering. In July an English fleet landed a second Turkish army in Egypt, an army that the French defeated before it had left the shore at Aboukir.

In the following month, learning that a new coalition of her enemies threatened France, Napoleon, without waiting for orders, sailed for home. Again he eluded Nelson. He had left Kléber in command in Egypt to save what could be saved of an expedition that had failed. He landed at Fréjus, October 9, 1799. It was none too soon. The Republic had great need of him.

Soon after Napoleon had landed in Egypt, England succeeded in securing the co-operation of Austria, Russia, Turkey, and Naples in her effort to defeat the French. These co-operators had become hostile to France on account of the Treaty of Campo-Formio, and as the result of aggressive acts that followed it. The *Directoire* had encouraged revolution in Switzerland, in the States of the Church, and in Naples.

The assassination of a French general officer was followed by French occupation of Rome. Pope Pius VI was exiled; he died in captivity in France. The States of the Church were declared to be the Roman republic. Switzerland was transformed into the Helvetian republic. These transformations were accompanied by heavy contributions to the needy treasury of France.

Paul I, the Czar of Russia, was extremely exasperated by the French aggressions. Eighty thousand Russians marched west, swelling the forces of the coalition to more than three hundred thousand. France had less than two-thirds that number to oppose them. In March of 1799 the Archduke Charles of Austria defeated Jourdan near the Rhine and prepared to invade Alsace. The Russian general, Souwaroff, a rude and very capable veteran of wars in Turkey and in Poland, drove the French out of Naples. After that he defeated them in a series of battles that compelled them to withdraw out of all of Italy except Genoa.

All that saved France was the lack of solidarity among her enemies and the alert generalship of Masséna. The Austrians, once Souwaroff had served their purpose, wished to get him out of Italy. They knew that his presence there would be an embarrassment to the success of their plan for repossession of the territories from which he had driven the French. They urged him to join a Russian corps that had reached Zürich in order that Austrian troops that were there might be moved forward to the Rhine; they pointed out that the climate of Switzerland would be better than that of Italy for Russian soldiers.

A French army commanded by Masséna was within striking distance of Zürich. When the Austrian troops moved out before Souwaroff's army had arrived, Masséna saw his chance. He swiftly attacked the Russian corps that had been left without support, crushed it in a two-day battle, and then turned to confront the Russians from Italy who were coming in by the Saint Gothard pass. They too were defeated. Souwaroff, having lost six thousand men and all his artillery, retreated into the mountains with his demoralized army. It was out of the campaign for good.

An Anglo-Russian force was defeated in Holland. The Czar, furious about defeats that were due to the tricky behavior of his allies, recalled his troops and withdrew from the coalition. When Bonaparte returned, France had escaped from foreign invasions as by a miracle, but she had lost nearly all that he had won for her in Italy, and, politically, she was in more perilous straits than ever. A grave internal situation had to be settled before further external action could be even considered.

The *Directoire* was discredited. The military reverses in Italy and Germany had increased its unpopularity. There was a strong group that favored revision of the Constitution; Sieyès, an able legist, was its leader. He prepared a plan that would strengthen the executive power. Elected a member of the *Directoire* in 1799, he induced the *Anciens* and the *Cinq-Cents* to compel the resignation of three of his colleagues. Then came the news of Bonaparte's unexpected return. His journey from Fréjus to Paris was an uninterrupted ovation; everywhere he was acclaimed by crowds so dense that his carriage could scarcely pass. Every town and every village was illuminated in his honor.

All the political groups solicited Bonaparte's support. Having studied the situation, he decided to give his support to Sieyès. Bonaparte's brother Lucien had been elected president of the *Cinq-Cents*. He, Roger Ducos who was one of the *Directoire,* Talleyrand, and Cambacérès, the minister of justice, were leaders of the Sieyès group. Their plan was for the *Directoire* to resign and for the *Anciens* and the *Cinq-Cents* then to name a committee to revise the Constitution. A majority of the *Anciens* could be counted on to support this plan, but opposition was to be expected from the *Cinq-Cents*.

For fear of popular resistance to any attempt to make the government less democratic, the *Anciens* voted that both Councils should meet at the château of Saint-Cloud, a few miles outside of Paris. They also voted that General Bonaparte should command the troops of the capital and prevent interference with legislative procedure. Bonaparte, on the ninth of November, came to the Tuileries at the head of an escort of resplendent generals. To the *Anciens* he declared, "We wish for a republic founded upon liberty, equality, and the sacred principles of national representation. That we shall have. I swear it."

There was a hitch in the plan when two members of the *Directoire* declined to resign. These two recalcitrants were detained under strong guard in the Luxembourg. France ceased to have any legalized executive authority.

On the following afternoon at two o'clock, November 10, 1799, the deputies assembled at Saint-Cloud. The opposition had had time to become organized. The *Cinq-Cents* and a minority of the *Anciens* declared their determination to uphold the Constitution of the Year III. Fruitless discussion followed. At four o'clock Napoleon appeared. He entered the hall where the *Cinq-Cents* were assembled. They were well aware of the role he had come to play. He was greeted with cries of, "Down with the dictator! Declare him outside the law!" Such a declaration was a death sentence. Some of the deputies tried to strike him. The guards had to come to his rescue. Frightfully humiliated, Napoleon was speechless. He could handle soldiers, but the politicians were too much for him. The *Cinq-Cents* were in favor of sentencing him to the guillotine.

It was brother Lucien who saved the situation. He was the presiding officer. When the deputies demanded the vote of *mise hors la loi,* the equivalent of a death sentence, he delayed the proceedings momentarily by removing his insignia of office which included a toga; no vote could have legal effect unless the presiding officer had on his toga. Lucien's presence of mind gave time for a squad of grenadiers to reach the hall.

Outside confusion reigned. A body of grenadiers was cheering Napoleon, but the *garde du Corps legislatif,* stationed in the court of the château, was not cheering; it was composed of veterans of the Revolution who were in a state of perplexity. Their duty was to protect the deputies from any outside interference. They could not easily become supporters of any movement to overthrow the republic for which they had fought for years, but the significance of the immediate situation was not clear to them. To this hesitant group Lucien made a timely speech.

"As president of the Council of the *Cinq-Cents* I declare to you," he said, "that the majority of that council is at this moment threatened

by the daggers of a minority. . . . I declare that these brigands, doubt-
less the paid agents of England, are in rebellion against the *Anciens*.
They are demanding the death penalty for the general charged with
executing a decree of the *Anciens*. It is they who deserve death because of their attack upon liberty. . . . These traitors are no longer
representatives of the people, but representatives of assassination."

This fiery and highly inaccurate speech increased the bewilderment
of the Legislative Guard. Then, with their drums beating the charge,
Napoleon's grenadiers led by General Murat rushed forward, drove
the *Cinq-Cents* out of their hall and dispersed them. The *coup d'état*
had been accomplished, but not in the manner planned. Napoleon,
hoping for general consent to his assumption of civil power, achieved
it only by trickery and the use of force.

On that same evening the *Anciens,* and some of the *Cinq-Cents*
who had quickly changed to the winning side, reconvened. They
decreed the suppression of the *Directoire* and its replacement by a
provisional *Consulat* composed of Sieyès, Roger Ducos, and Napoleon
Bonaparte. A commission was authorized which should modify the
Constitution under the direction of the consuls. As a matter of fact,
on that fateful tenth of November the Constitution had ceased to
exist. The Republic itself ceased to exist. A decade of revolution had
ended in the establishment of a dictatorship. The period of the Consulate was from November 10, 1799 to May 18, 1804.

The people of France did not at first realize the full significance of
the *coup d'état*. Like the staunch republicans of the Legislative Guard,
they were uncertain whether the Republic had been destroyed or not.
Even if it had been, they were not in a mood to fight for its preservation. Its inefficiency had been proved. The country was in the depths
of an economic depression. Brigandage flourished, and the *Chouans*
had risen again in the west. The wave of republican enthusiasm had
subsided. The people were ready to welcome any administration that
would restore order and improve business.

The leaders of the new adventure in government covered the shift
from democracy to autocracy with a camouflage that deceived no one
for long. In their own minds there was little doubt that the new government would be controlled by one man, and they knew who that

man would be, but they made no such avowal. They talked rather of a new constitution that would remedy the defects of the old one, and of provisional direction by a group of three of whom Napoleon was but one. Sieyès appeared to believe that one-man control could be avoided. He was soon undeceived.

Napoleon's thought was revealed in a conversation he had with a French diplomat while he was still in Italy. "Do you imagine," he said, "that it is for the glory of the *Directoire* that I am fighting? Or for the glory of a republic? What an idea! Republicanism is but a dream that will pass. The French love glory, but liberty would be their ruin. The soldiers of the Army of Italy have revealed the true French character. Because I have led them to victory, I am everything for them. The *Directoire* would not dare remove me from my command. . . . What the nation needs is not theories of government, fine phrases, and philosophical discourses that it does not understand. What it needs is a master. . . . I do not wish to return to France unless it be to play such a role there as I have played here. I can no longer take orders from others. I shall be the master, or I shall be nothing. But the moment has not yet come for that. The pear is not quite ripe."

The commission that was authorized to revise the Constitution under the direction of the *Consulat* waited for ten days before Sieyès submitted a tentative draft of his plan. Napoleon had become impatient. He summoned the commissioners and dictated to them a text in which Sieyès ideas were much modified by his own. The commission did not delay its approval of the Napoleonic text. The new Constitution of the Year VIII was put into effect December 15, 1799.

It was desirable to recognize the sovereignty of the people as a principle, however dead it was as a fact. So the people were permitted to approve the new constitution, but perfect precautions were taken against any chance of disapproval. The voting was done in public. It consisted merely of writing *oui* or *non* after the inscription of the voter's name. There were more than three million votes in favor of the constitution and less than two thousand against it. The *fait accompli* was ratified.

Bonaparte did not even await the people's ratification before putting his constitution into effect. In that ingenious document the fact of autocracy had been cleverly concealed behind a façade of democracy.

There was an enlargement of the electorate; every male citizen resident for one year in his community (*commune*) was given the right to vote. But he voted only to elect *notabilités communales.* The "notabilities" thus chosen met with those of other *communes* to designate one-tenth of their number as *notabilités departmentales,* and they, in similar manner, elected the *notabilités nationales.* From the "national notabilities" the government would select those who might serve as members of the National Assemblies, or otherwise serve the state.

Legislative power was entrusted to a *Tribunat* of one hundred members and a *Corps Législatif* numbering three hundred. One-fifth of the membership of these assemblies was renewable each year. They had no authority to initiate legislation; their authority was limited to ratification or non-ratification of legislation submitted by the *Consulat.* The *Tribunat* had the right to discuss such legislation but not to vote on it. The *Corps* had the right to vote on it, but not to discuss it. They were to be legislative bodies in name only.

A third assembly, called the *Senat conservateur,* was created. Its only legislative power was to confirm or annul acts declared unconstitutional by the *Tribunat.* Members of this assembly had to be at least forty years of age; they were to serve for life and to select their own successors.

Sieyès was responsible for the election and legislation features of the Constitution. Since they prevented any effective interference with the executive power, they were acceptable to Napoleon. But when it came to the *Consulat* he could not accept the Sieyès plan. That plan provided that one of the consuls should be charged with the administration of domestic affairs and another with foreign affairs. The third consul was to outrank these two, but he was to have no executive responsibility; appointed for life and paid a high salary, he was "to personify France" and to be called the *Grand Proclamateur Electeur.* Sieyès naïvely believed that the exalted but innocuous position of *Grand Electeur* might be acceptable to Napoleon. Napoleon declined it with scorn.

"Would you make of me," he exclaimed, "the fleshless shadow of a *roi fainéant?* Do you know any man vile enough to accept such a monkey job? Do you imagine that a man of talent would play the role of a pig even though fattened with millions? Do you wish that I who have made myself feared by all Europe should sit now with folded arms in the cushioned chair of a *Grand Electeur?* I shall do nothing so ridiculous. It is better to be nothing than to be ridiculous."

Bonaparte agreed for the sake of appearances that there should be three consuls, but he was to be the First Consul and the others would do his bidding. The promulgation of laws, as well as all executive authority, was to be entrusted to him, and he would appoint and dismiss all officers of the government as he saw fit. The other consuls might be consulted, and might express their opinions, but all final decisions were to be made by him. There was no one strong enough to oppose the dictatorship thus set up. Napoleon's dream was fulfilled. He had become the master of France. The other consuls, Cambacérès and Lebrun, could be counted on to serve that mastery rather than to challenge it.

Louis XIV had set the precedent of a definitely organized group of ministers called the *Conseil du Roi.* In similar manner Napoleon organized a *Conseil d'Etat* of thirty, and later forty-five, ministers and counselors; it was divided into the sections of legislation, finance, war, marine, and interior. Napoleon used this organization as his principal instrument for the fulfillment of his plans. It represented reality. The so-called legislative assemblies represented but the shadow of a republicanism that was fast fading out of the picture.

The First Consul gave preferential recognition to no party. "To govern through a party," he said, "is to end by making oneself dependent upon that party. I shall not do that. I am for the whole nation and love honest men whatever their color." In the interest of equilibrium and efficiency he selected his ministers from the most able men of different political groups. Fouché became his minister of police and Talleyrand his minister of foreign affairs; Napoleon did not trust either of these crafty gentlemen, but he knew how to make use of their great abilities.

In naming the prefects of the *départements* he chose without favor both former royalists and former republicans; even returned *emigrés* found places in the new administration. In the thousands of positions to be filled, men of all parties found place and payment. Thereby any organized opposition was forestalled. No group could maintain that it had been slighted.

A law passed in February, 1800, made the centralization of government greater than it had been before the Revolution. In the days of the monarchy, the *intendants* could be restrained by the *parlements* or by other provincial agencies. But the prefects appointed by Napoleon could be restrained only by Napoleon himself. *Parlements* had ceased to exist. In each *département* a prefect, in each *arrondissement* a sub-prefect, and in each *commune* a mayor *(maire)* were the direct representatives of the government. They depended directly upon the First Consul who appointed or replaced them at will, but while in office their authority was incontestible. Judges also were named by the First Consul. The power of the state was made greater and its organization more perfect than they had ever been before in the history of France.

Having established his authority and constructed his administrative machine, Napoleon at once put it to work in the interest of peace, order, and economic improvement. On the first day after the *coup d'état* he began his work of appeasement. On the thirteenth of November the banished royalists were pardoned, in December the imprisoned priests were released, and in March the proscription of *emigrés* was stopped. The movement for the restoration of the Bourbons became all but extinct. The nation accepted its First Consul as better than any king, and far better than the republic that he had helped to destroy.

Napoleon offered pardon and religious freedom to the *Chouans* provided they surrendered their arms within ten days. Most of them did so. Those who did not were suppressed, and peace was restored in that wide area of the west that they had terrorized for years.

The new order improved the financial situation. In less than a week after the crisis at Saint-Cloud, the low market value of government securities had nearly doubled. But that did not replenish the empty treasury. However, the suppression of forced loans and the appointment of an excellent minister of finance enabled the government to borrow enough from the bankers to meet immediate needs. Gaudin, the new minister, effected tax reforms that assured stability of government income. The assessment and collection of state taxes ceased

to be municipal functions; they were placed in the hands of a new organization called the *Direction des Contributions directes*. Within
a year a civil service of assessors and collectors was in operation. It
was entirely controlled from Paris. Leakage and evasion were stopped
and regularity of revenue was assured.

In order to diminish the national debt, a special service *(Caisse
d'Amortissement)* was set up for the purchase of outstanding governmental obligations. Skillful management of this service added much to
improvement of the situation. In February, 1800, the state-patronized
Banque de France was founded. Its success was so great that in
1803 it was granted a monopoly of the issuance of bank notes. Its
management was originally independent, but, after 1806, its three
directors were named by the government.

The new regime was hardly a half-year old when the payment of
government obligations in currency was resumed. When it was only
two years old the budget was balanced. The rapidity of this financial
recovery amazed the rest of Europe and made the people of France
more than content with their new master. They felt that their liberty
had been well lost.

CHAPTER FIFTEEN

THE CONSULATE

1800-1805

AUSTRIA DEFEATED AT MARENGO. THE TREATY OF LUNEVILLE. THE LIQUI-
DATION OF FAILURE IN EGYPT. THE *CONCORDAT*. THE *CODE CIVIL*. THE
EMASCULATION OF EDUCATION. THE ASSASSINATION OF THE DUKE OF
ENGHIEN. THE END OF THE CONSULATE AND THE ESTABLISHMENT OF
THE EMPIRE.

ON Christmas Day, 1799, Napoleon proposed peace to England and
to Austria. His proposal was declined and preparations were continued for a new campaign in the following spring.

Early in April, 1800, Masséna assembled in Genoa the French troops
that had remained in Italy. One Austrian army moved against him
while another one pursued Suchet into Provençe. Meanwhile the main
French offensive developed in the north. Moreau commanded an
army that crossed the Rhine, defeated Austrian forces in May, and
had them asking for a suspension of hostilities in July. But Masséna,
his supplies exhausted, was compelled to surrender at Genoa in June.

A reserve army of sixty thousand was secretly assembled southeast
of Dijon. In May Napoleon led that army into Switzerland and then,
from the eastern valley of the Rhône, up into the icy Alps. Through
deep snow the dismounted cannon were dragged on crude sledges
made from hollowed logs, twenty men to a sledge. Straining, slipping,
and struggling, the expedition made its way up and over the Saint-
Bernard pass following the perilous trail by which Hannibal had once
invaded Italy with elephants.

Napoleon recaptured Milan early in June without having to fight
for it. The Austrians were far away. The *République cisalpine* was
re-established. The army that passed over the Alps had taken the
Austrians by surprise. The valley of the Po was undefended. But
strong forces came up rapidly from the southwest, and, in their turn,

took Napoleon by surprise. On the fourteenth of June, on the plain of Marengo, he found himself confronted by fifty thousand. He had but twenty thousand. After six hours of battle the French lines were broken and defeat seemed certain. But, late in the afternoon, fresh troops arrived and a counterattack overcame the exhausted Austrians. An armistice followed the battle of Marengo.

Napoleon returned to Paris and peace negotiations were begun. They came to nothing and the war was resumed in November. Early in December, 1800, Moreau, having won a great victory at Hohenlinden, led his army down the Danube valley, and, with small losses, reached a point less than fifty miles from Vienna. The Austrians lost twelve thousand in killed and wounded and twenty-five thousand of them were taken prisoners. Meanwhile Brune had had similar success in repelling Austrians who had entered the valley of the Po. Again Vienna asked for an armistice.

The swift successes of Moreau and Brune were not pleasing to Napoleon. They came sooner than he had planned and deprived him of the glory of directing the final operations. The victorious generals discovered that their enterprise was not appreciated.

The first months of the new century were favorable for France. The Treaty of Lunéville was signed February 9, 1801. It renewed the concessions made by Austria at Campo-Formio in October, 1797, and recognized the establishment of French-controlled "republics" in Holland, Switzerland, and northern Italy. It left nothing to Austria in Italy except her control of Venice.

In the following month the King of Naples also sued for peace. He consented to French military occupation of three Neapolitan ports, and the closure of all of them to the English.

Paul I, Czar of Russia, still disgusted with his former allies, declared for neutrality, but went beyond neutrality in planning to cooperate in an attack upon British interests in India. This plan was frustrated by his assassination in March, 1801, but a definite peace pact was made between France and Russia some months later.

The end of the year found Napoleon in effective mastery of western Europe. With the exception of England and Turkey, his enemies had ceased to resist him. France had triumphed on the Continent, but

England had captured the French colonies, and some of those of Spain and Holland as well. British fleets commanded by Parker and Nelson had destroyed more than four hundred merchant ships of France and her allies.

Liquidation of the Egyptian expedition was humiliating and expensive. Kléber at Cairo was in command of twenty thousand imperiled and despondent soldiers. There was no more glory for them to win, no useful purpose for them to serve. They were sick for home. Early in 1800 Kléber made an evacuation agreement with the Turks, but the Turks could not persuade their English allies to ratify it. The French then attacked a Turkish army at Heliopolis and defeated it. All might have gone well after that if heroic Kléber had not been assassinated. His successor, Menou, lacked both courage and military ability. In the spring of 1801 the French were defeated by Anglo-Turkish forces; in August they agreed to lay down their arms if repatriated. The homesick remnant of a once proud army returned to France. The control of Egypt had been lost and England remained the mistress of the Mediterranean.

England, after the fall of the Pitt cabinet in March, 1801, had offered to stop the war and to recognize French control of Egypt if France would recognize British control of the colonies she had captured. Napoleon made the mistake of not accepting these terms, and then he lost Egypt.

In March of 1802 a brief peace was made on terms less favorable to France than those offered a year before. By the Treaty of Amiens, Turkish control of Egypt was recognized, France agreed to evacuate the Neapolitan ports she had occupied, and England relinquished most of the colonies she had captured, but she kept Ceylon. England also agreed to withdraw from Malta. This treaty did not touch upon the great Continental transformations that had occurred since 1793. Like the Treaty of Campo-Formio, it was but a truce.

Napoleon's ambition more than kept pace with his success. Having won peace by victory, he turned his attention to other difficult matters that had to be successfully settled in order to make his mastery of France secure. One of those matters was the religious question.

The great majority of the French had been republicans without giving up their Catholicism. But the Pope had been an implacable enemy of the Republic. It had massacred priests and confiscated Church property; the priests who had remained loyal to Rome had been active agents in arousing popular support for a restoration of the Bourbons. What would be the attitude of the Church toward the new regime, toward the dictatorship of the First Consul? If Napoleon could secure papal endorsement of his government, his position would be much strengthened thereby. If he could not secure it, there would be constant danger of Catholic-royalist plots to overthrow him.

The First Consul disavowed any personal feeling about religion. He was even more ready than Henry of Navarre to make whatever religious affiliation might seem to serve best the interests of the state. He is reported to have said "I shall be called a papist, but I am not. I was a Mohammedan in Egypt, and here, for the good of the people, I shall be a Catholic. I am not interested in religious differences." Napoleon believed, however, that religion was requisite in order to secure popular submission to law. "Society," he said, "cannot exist without economic inequality, and economic inequality cannot exist without religion. The only thing that can save the rich from destruction by the poor is an authority that can say to the poor 'God wills it so' and make them believe it, giving them the hope of bettering their condition in heaven."

For pacifying the underprivileged and making them submissive to law, Napoleon realized that the orthodox Catholic religion could serve him far better than any other; for centuries it had been in the business of preaching submission and had become expert at that. The naturalistic religion that the Revolution had attempted to establish invited to revolt rather than to submission to injustice or inequality.

The First Consul was disposed to seek reconciliation with Rome, but only under conditions that would be to his own advantage. A new Pope, Pius VII, had been elected in March, 1800. With him Napoleon began negotiations immediately after the victory of Marengo. There were many matters to be considered that were extremely difficult to adjust. The negotiations continued for more than a year. Finally the *Concordat* of August 15, 1801, was achieved. This elaborate document established the relationships between the Church and the new government of France. Mutual concessions had been made in which the Pope, in the light of subsequent developments, proved to have been a shrewd bargainer.

For more than a thousand years the Kings of France had accepted the Church of Rome as an authoritative element in their governments; Church and State were too closely allied to be separated. From Charlemagne in the Ninth Century to Louis XVI in the Eighteenth, they had all borne the title "Eldest Son of the Church." France had not been submissive to those sixteenth-century decrees of the Council of Trent which enlarged the Pope's authority; resistance of those decrees was the basis of what was known as *gallicanism*. Despite *gallicanism*, however, the Church had exerted for centuries a political influence in France to whose restoration Napoleon was firmly opposed. He would concede spiritual control; the Church in that capacity could aid him, but he wished to secure that aid without concessions that might open the door to the re-establishment of political influence.

In the preamble to the *Concordat* Napoleon recognized that "the Catholic religion is the religion of the great majority of the French people," and Pius VII stated that the Church expected "great good and glory to result from its re-establishment in France." Those were the best phrases they could find to cloak the wide divergence of their views.

It was agreed that all Catholic churches and chapels should be restored to ecclesiastical control and that public worship therein should be sanctioned and protected by the government. The First Consul was to select the new bishops, and the Pope to give to them canonical investiture. His right to remove them from office was recognized. The *curés* were to be named by the bishops from a list approved by the government. The sales that the Republic had made of Church property were declared irrevocable. The bishops and the *curés* were to take oath to support the existing government, and they were to be paid modest salaries by the State.

This new arrangement gained important advantages for the Church. It nearly put an end to the schism between "constitutional" and "refractory" priests that had developed with the Revolution, and recognition of the Pope's authority to remove bishops was a death-blow to *gallicanism*.

In exchange for the privileged position that the *Concordat* granted to it, the Church relinquished all claim upon its property that had been seized and sold. But that which interested Napoleon most was the hold that he secured upon the clergy. They were dependent upon him both for nomination and for compensation. In addition to that, all ecclesiastics were required to take the following oath:

"I swear to God and upon the Holy Evangels that I shall be obedient and faithful to the established government, and I promise to have nothing whatsoever to do with any anti-governmental effort made either within France or without, and to report to the government anything prejudicial to it of which I may become aware."

In his selection of the new bishops Napoleon was as impartial as he had been in the formation of his cabinet; twelve of those chosen had been of the "constitutional" clergy, and sixteen had been "refractory," but under the new regime they all became servants of the state. The clergy became, in effect, a part of that great force of functionaries that formed the structure of a more centralized government than France had ever known. About a third of the bishops of the old regime refused to submit to the conditions of the *Concordat,* and, for a time, formed what was called the *Petite Eglise.*

It was not to be expected that the *Concordat* would be acceptable to all. It was bitterly criticized by those whose ideas had flowered from the philosophical movement. The army did not like it; the soldiers of France had been separated from religious influence for years and they had fought the Pope as an enemy. Public sentiment had to be won; Chateaubriand's *Le Génie du Christianisme,* which appeared in 1802, did much to win it. The government sought to appease the opposition by legal recognition of the two Protestant sects. All religious organizations, Protestant as well as Catholic, were placed under state control and made, so far as possible, a dependent part of the civil structure.

The Revolution had gone too fast and too far in reckless efforts to fulfill its democratic ideal. In its haste to establish a reign of justice it committed monstrous injustices. The excellence of its ends were outweighed by the ruthlessness of its means. The Terror ended in the execution of the terrorists. There came the interlude of the *Directoire,* a halt in progress, a long pause in which bewildered France knew that its Republic had failed, but did not know what to put in its place, which way to go, or what political philosophy to believe. The one thing that seemed certain in that period of uncertainty was the imperative need for dynamic, unhesitating, and authoritative leadership. The people were weary of idealistic oratory that failed to fill their empty bellies; what they wanted was realistic leadership that would provide square meals. The political color of such leadership was of secondary importance. The first right of man was the right to eat. The time was ripe for "the man on horseback" who appeared.

One equally great in leadership might have fed the people without destroying the Republic. Napoleon saw fit to overthrow the Republic and to establish a dictatorship upon its ruins. But, though republicanism was ruined, the social gains of the Revolution were not all lost. The imperialism of the new regime could not do away with all the rights that had been so dearly won. The new autocracy was characterized by more of social justice than France had known in the reign of any of her kings. This synthesis of justice and tyranny was portrayed in the famous *Code civil*, which has come to be known as the Code Napoleon.

Napoleon assigned to three members of his cabinet the colossal task of codifying the civil laws. They took up this task where the Convention had left it in the time of the Terror. Cambacérès, one of the two secondary consuls, had been chairman of the Convention's committee on legislation. The excellent work of that committee was not lost; many of its proposals entered into the construction of the new code, but they rested upon different political premises. The new code was founded, not upon a theory of democracy that had failed, but upon a theory of beneficent despotism whose ultimate inefficiency was yet to be proved.

The Napoleonic code is one of the most definite and lucid of all historic legal documents. It reflects the amazing mental grasp and the constructive imagination of its final editor, Napoleon himself. It established the equality of all citizens before the law, their individual liberty, the abolition of feudal rights, and the equal division of inheritances; these provisions were souvenirs of the Revolution. The code also established the inviolability of private ownership, denied to workers the right to strike or to form unions, and gave to husbands despotic authority over wives and children; these items reflected the Napoleonic belief in the virtue of authority.

The educational system established by the Republic was too liberal to be acceptable to the new master of the country's destiny. The *Ecoles Centrales* established in all the *départements* had become very popular with both old and young. No restraints had been placed upon them. Since they had become centers of a free intellectual life, they might become centers of intellectual opposition to autocracy. In 1802 the *Ecoles Centrales* were replaced by *lycées* whose personnel was entirely under governmental control. The courses of study were rigidly standardized and military training and organization were made obligatory. The youth of France was to be severely trained to serve the fatherland through serving the power and glory of its master. The First Consul declared to the *Tribunat* that the new educational legislation was political as well as moral. "It is designed," he said, "to link fathers to the government through their sons, sons through their fathers, and thus to establish a paternity of the state."

In the same month that the educational system was reorganized, the Legion of Honor was created. It was to be composed of soldiers who had rendered distinguished service, and of citizens who had contributed importantly "to the establishment and the defense of the principles of the Republic." Despite this verbal tribute to the Republic, the Legion could not obscure its resemblance to the orders established by kings to protect and fortify their kingship. The project savored too strongly of monarchy to be popular. It barely missed disapproval by the assemblies and met with strong opposition in the cabinet. It was too soon for the legalization of a political aristocracy. Napoleon, realizing that the carrying out of this project would be premature, postponed its fulfillment.

The die-hard royalists had clung to a fond hope that Napoleon, like General Monk in England, would re-establish royal government, and be content to be the high-constable of the kingdom. When they discovered that his ambitions were far less modest than those of Monk, an attempt was made to win him by flattery. The Consulate was hardly three months old when, in February, 1800, the Count of Provençe, the future Louis XVIII, then resident in Russia, made a pathetic appeal. "You have acquired my high esteem," he wrote to Bonaparte. "If you doubt that I am capable of gratitude, name whatever places and rewards you would have for yourself and for your friends. . . . General, glory awaits you. I am impatient to restore peace to my people."

Napoleon believed that in his pursuit of glory he needed no help from a decadent Bourbon. He ignored both the first and a second royal appeal until after the victory of Marengo. Then he replied without regard for etiquette. "Sir," he wrote, "I have received your letter and thank you for it. You should not wish to return. You could return only by marching over one hundred thousand corpses. The peace and happiness of France require the relinquishment of your ambition, but I am not insensible to the misfortunes of your family and shall glady contribute to making its retirement comfortable." The Corsican commoner was willing to extend charity to the royal Bourbons, but the Czar saw fit to compel the pretender to leave Russia and to go to Warsaw, which was controlled at that time by Prussia.

Further to minimize the possibility of royalist trouble, the proscription of fifty-two thousand *émigrés* was annulled; that led to much loss of interest in the cause of the pretender. English subsidies had maintained a royalist army under the command of the Prince of Condé; in December, 1800, the subsidies having ceased, that army dispersed.

A group of desperate *émigrés* who were in England plotted the assassination of Napoleon. The Count of Artois, one of the numerous brothers of Louis XVI, was a leader in this plot; he was later to reign as Charles X. On Christmas Eve, 1800, the First Consul went to the opera. It was planned to blow up his carriage as it passed through the narrow *rue Saint-Nicaise*. A *machine infernale* was concealed on a cart, but Napoleon passed a few seconds before its explosion occurred. More than twenty were killed and more than fifty were wounded. This was believed to have been a plot of the *Jacobins*.

Fouché's investigation proved that it was not a *Jacobin* plot, but the opportunity to eliminate many undesirables was too good to be lost. Evidence was manufactured. One hundred were sent to tropical prisons where most of them died, nine were executed, and many others were arrested. The legal guarantees of personal liberty were disregarded; special tribunals from which there was no appeal passed more than seven hundred judgments. It was a momentary revival of the Terror.

Certain bold liberals in the assemblies opposed Napoleon's unrestrained use of authority, but this opposition was futile. Governmental control of the press prevented appeal to the people. Sixty out of seventy-three journals were suppressed. Bonaparte became increasingly impatient of all opposition, especially the opposition of the intellectuals. "There are twelve or fifteen metaphysicians in the assemblies," he said, "who are fit to be thrown into the river. They are vermin. But I know how to get rid of them. I am no Louis XVI. I am a soldier and a child of the Revolution. I came from the people and I shall not swallow insults as though I were a king."

When the time came for re-selection of one-fifth of the members of the assemblies as provided for in the constitution, Napoleon indicated to the Senate which fifth it should select for replacement. Thus, early in 1802, all the liberals were eliminated and their places taken by those about whose docility there was no doubt. The *Tribunat,* having taken its right of discussion too seriously, was effectively deprived of using that right to any advantage; it found itself divided into sections whose discussions were to be held in secret. Thus the "legislative power" became even more farcical than it had been before.

The peace that was made with England in March, 1802, by the Treaty of Amiens was followed by an amnesty extended to all *émigrés.* The government felt that former nobles, if pardoned and repatriated, would make less mischief than if kept in exile.

France had Napoleon's genius to thank for the restoration of peace and order. The Senate expressed the nation's desire as well as its gratitude when, May 8, 1802, it re-elected him to be First Consul for a period of ten years. But a period of ten years was not enough to satisfy Napoleon. He declared that he could accept extension of his tenure only "if he was commanded to do so by the expressed wish of the people." When the matter was placed before the people there had been a modification in the wording of the question. It was no longer a question of a ten-year extension; it was a question of naming Napoleon First Consul for life. More than three million voted in favor and only a few thousand against.

Having received this strong assurance of popular support, Napoleon enlarged his powers. A new constitution, promulgated by the Senate in August, 1802, gave him the right to name his successor, and also to name forty new members of the Senate. Control of new legislation was technically limited to this body, but control of the body itself was placed in the hands of the First Consul. The troublesome *Tribunat* was reduced from one hundred members to fifty. There had been much difficulty about fulfillment of the provision which called for the selection of a body of "notabilities" from whom officeholders might be chosen. The new plan called for "electoral colleges" in each *département* whose members were elected for life. These colleges would present two candidates for each governmental office to which it was entitled; the government would then choose between the two so named. This new plan made the camouflage of the dictatorship practically invisible. Monarchy was restored in all but name.

A final royalist-and-republican plot, financed by England, failed. Its active leader was Cadoudal, an heroic *Chouan*. The generals Pichegru and Moreau were involved. An effort was made to arouse the west of France and Cadoudal himself went to Paris to assassinate Napoleon. Fouché unmasked the plot, its leaders were arrested, and Cadoudal was executed. Pichegru committed suicide and Moreau, who was a republican and who had rendered great military services, was let off with a remitted two-year sentence and banishment from France. This happened in 1803.

A force of royalists was found to be hovering just beyond the Rhine, ready to enter France in case Cadoudal succeeded in killing Napoleon. With them was the young Duke of Enghien, grandson of the Prince of Condé. Upon an order from Paris, a squadron of dragoons crossed the frontier and made a night arrest of the Duke. He was taken to the château of Vincennes, subjected to a long interrogation, and then shot. Napoleon, by this murder, sought to terrify the royalists who had tried more than once to murder him. But in doing so he lost the friendship of Prussia, whose territory had been violated. That facilitated renewal of the coalition against France.

The feeling grew that the fatherland was again in danger and that conditions called for further proof of the nation's devotion to its leader. It was proposed in the Senate that Napoleon should be declared Emperor of France, and that that office and title should become hereditary in his family. Carnot's was the only vote cast against this proposal. On May 18, 1804, the Consulate ended and the Empire began.

CHAPTER SIXTEEN

THE FIRST YEARS OF THE EMPIRE

1805-1807

THE CORONATION. JOSEPHINE BEAUHARNAIS, EMPRESS. LIFE AT MALMAI-
SON. A MADE-TO-ORDER COURT. THE PERSECUTION OF MADAME DE STAËL
AND OF CHATEAUBRIAND. FURTHER RESTRICTIONS ON EDUCATION.
THOUGHT BECAME THAT WHICH NO ONE DARED TO EXPRESS. IMPRISON-
MENT OF THE POPE. ECONOMIC IMPROVEMENT. MILITARY ORGANIZATION.

THE First Empire began in 1804 and, except for the Hundred Days,
ended in 1814. The glory of that decade obscured the certainty of its
tragic end. Napoleon when First Consul served France far better than
when Emperor. His genius produced one of history's most dramatic
chapters, a chapter that opened with swift ascent through conquest to
glory, almost to world dominance, and ended in even swifter descent
through defeat to ultimate disaster.

Napoleon came to believe that he could surmount all obstacles. As
his power increased, his wisdom diminished. After he became Emperor he could brook no interference with the fulfillment of his will.
He disdained the lesser powers of other men, and believed that all
men could be controlled through self-interest. Prodigious in executive ability, he took into account all factors except that factor which
compels the ultimate downfall even of genius when it attempts to
throttle human freedom. All of Napoleon's astounding achievements
could not compensate for his misinterpretation of human nature. His
cynical philosophy was built upon a false assumption. Master of the
visible, he was overcome at last by that which, to him, was invisible.
He imposed order, but his order became intolerable to those who paid
for it with their freedom.

Napoleon was crowned December 2, 1804. The kings of France
had been crowned in the cathedral of Reims by the archbishop of

Reims. That did not suffice for the proud Corsican who believed himself to be greater than any king. For his coronation the Pope had to come from Rome and had to conduct the ceremony in Notre Dame in Paris. But even the Pope was not permitted to place the crown on Napoleon's head. He placed it there himself.

In 1795 an unkempt and undernourished young officer walked the streets of Paris in a threadbare coat and wondered whose hospitality might provide him with comfort. "He looked like one you would not care to meet in a dark place." People avoided him. To that lonely young officer with the burning eyes there came nine swift and eventful years. Then all the world turned its eyes toward Notre Dame where an emperor was being crowned. The gaunt young man in a thread-bare coat had become an emperor in a purple robe, and people feared him then in the daylight as well as in the dark.

Napoleon began his reign at thirty-five. The "dog-ears" that once concealed his own were gone. Gone too was the slenderness of his undernourished days. But the imperious flash of his eyes remained, and his consummate skill as an actor had increased with the years. In 1796, before he left for the campaign in Italy that made him master of France, he had married Josephine, a beautiful and languorous creole who was the widow of General Beauharnais. For her he had a mad infatuation. His letters to her rivaled for ardor those that Henry of Navarre wrote to the many ladies whom he loved. Napoleon and Josephine lived at the château of Malmaison which is about ten miles from Paris on the road to Saint-Germain. At Malmaison today there is a great collection of his personal belongings. You may see the desk at which he scribbled or dictated his swift orders, you may inspect the breeches and the tunic that he wore, and you may walk in the garden in which he made love and planned war.

Napoleon's violent temper became increasingly unrestrained. He would fly into a rage at remarks which displeased him. His chosen guests at Malmaison, the most distinguished men of the day, had to put a close guard on their tongues. Volney, an elderly senator and a celebrated author, made a remark that displeased his host. He was laid low by a hard kick in the abdomen. The Emperor's extreme nervousness made his handwriting an illegible scrawl. Into his official

correspondence he would introduce unprintable words which his secretaries modified as best they could. He often tore at his clothes, and
sometimes he had prolonged nervous fits. It is now believed that his
abnormalities, even his superhuman abilities, were associated with an
over-development of the pituitary body.

To Napoleon's nervous instability there was joined a prodigious
capacity for work and an infallible memory. He often worked eighteen
hours a day, begrudging the time necessary for sleep. He constantly
craved intense mental activity. It was natural for him to work; unnatural for him to be idle. But he prided himself upon the will power
which enabled him to fall to sleep quickly, in the saddle, or anywhere.

What a memory! In it, as in a well-ordered library, were kept
stored and up-to-date the infinite details of his government, both civil
and military. He seemed to visualize his armies, their equipment,
and their positions as clearly as though they were passing in review
before him. To this phenomenal memory there was linked a prodigious imagination.

Napoleon trusted no man. He believed neither in generosity nor in
disinterest, and could not understand either love of liberty or love of
God. Spirituality, virtue, all the higher qualities of the intellect, these
were for him but empty words. His once clear vision of reality became
distorted. As Emperor, he developed an egoism that surpassed even
that of Louis XIV. Scorn of his adversaries led him into fatal blunders. He would listen to no advice. "Carry out my orders to the
letter," he would command. "I alone know what should be done."
He used men as though they were mere machines, destroying the initiative of others until there was none left save his own.

There was no need for the Emperor to enlarge his powers after the
coronation. They could be no larger than they already were. He
allowed the fictional word *République* to remain on the coins, and the
republican calendar was not suppressed until 1806. He allowed a continuance of the assemblies in form if not in function. The docility of
their members was certain so long as they received their stipends. As
for the "constitution," he ignored it. New legislation took the form of
imperial decrees. His ministers and his counselors became mere
agents for the fufillment of his will.

Bonaparte, once a *Jacobin* and a passionate anti-royalist, sought to revive the pomp and panoply of royalty. While First Consul he had selected ladies-in-waiting for Josephine. When he became Emperor his brothers became princes. Monarchical offices and titles were created. Joseph Bonaparte became the *Grand Electeur,* Cambacérès the Arch-chancellor, Louis Bonaparte the Grand Constable, and Talleyrand the Great Chamberlain. To these and to other favorites land and money were given with lavish prodigality.

Elaborate fêtes were given at the Tuileries, at Saint-Cloud, and at Fontainebleau, but the easy grace and the aristocratic elegance of Versailles could not be recaught. There were magnificent uniforms and expensive gowns, but they only added to the stiffness and discomfort of those who wore them. No generations of aristocratic breeding lay behind the made-to-order ladies and gentlemen of the imperial court. Napoleon himself, very badly brought up, had deplorable manners. The solicited presence of some of the old nobility failed to produce the desired effect. They were all deathly afraid of offending their host. There was no spontaneity. They dared not relax. They were dreadfully bored.

But the Emperor had to have a court. To give it reality, he created a new nobility. Italy was his to parcel out as he might wish. He made his brother Joseph King of Naples, Cambacérès Duke of Parma, Talleyrand Prince of Benevento, and Fouché Duke of Otranto. More than twenty other Italian fiefs and titles were assigned to those whom he saw fit to honor. A decree of 1808 definitely established the Napoleonic nobility. A complete hierarchy of princes, dukes, counts, barons, and knights sprang into being. The first degree of the new nobility was the Legion of Honor, designed to be visible proof of partnership in the glory of France and of undying fidelity to her Emperor. In Paris and at Boulogne the first decorations of the legion were conferred with pomp and ceremony. The new legionnaires and all the assembled troops took oaths of devotion amid scenes of wild enthusiasm. Napoleon, on a similar occasion, wore a chaplet of laurel and the purple toga of a Roman emperor. He well knew how to arouse emotion that stifled reason. He transformed those who had once loved liberty into unwitting enemies of the very liberty they had loved. They became the devoted servants of an Emperor's despotic ambition. Never was the vain pursuit of glory begun with greater emotion or more delusive magnificence.

The Republic's guarantees of liberty ceased to exist. Napoleon's police arrested and imprisoned suspects with no authority except the imperial order. Judicial hearings were omitted. Distinguished citizens were exiled if they gave the least offense. An effort was made to imprison thought as well as thinkers. Books were suppressed as well as journals. The journals, reduced to nine under the Consulate, became but four under the Empire, and the government named the directors of the four that were permitted to continue. No comment on political matters could be printed. A journal that published a critical article by Chateaubriand was suppressed; Napoleon said he wished that its author might be "sabred on the steps of the Tuileries." The only papers permitted in the provinces were official sheets edited by the *Préfectures*. "The art of printing," said Napoleon, "is a dangerous weapon that I would have in the hands of none except those who have the confidence of the government." The printers of Paris were reduced to sixty.

The Emperor's bitter hostility to freedom of thought was exemplified by his treatment of Chateaubriand and of Madame de Staël. He objected both to the "Christianism" of the former and to the liberalism of the latter.

Chateaubriand, a melancholy genius, was a gentleman of Brittany who, under the Revolution, emigrated first to Germany and then to England. His most important works were contemporary with the Napoleonic ascendancy. His *Génie du Christianisme,* for its aid in overcoming opposition to the *Concordat,* won him favor that was quickly lost when he dared to protest about the murder of the Duke of Enghien. Chateaubriand was compelled to seclude himself in his rustic property in the Valley of the Wolves near Paris. This great writer looked upon the Christian religion as a fundamental source of artistic inspiration, but Napoleon came to regard the Christian party, which Chateaubriand represented, as hardly less dangerous than the philosophers and romanticists among whom none was more notable than Madame de Staël.

Madame de Staël was the daughter of Necker, the Protestant minister of finance under Louis XVI. She remained in Switzerland during the Terror. Later she traveled in Italy and Germany. In 1807 she revealed Europe to the French in her novel *Corinne*. In 1810 her *De l'Allemagne*, when in process of publication in Paris, was seized by the police. Both the proofs and the manuscript were destroyed. She had been too critical of Napoleon. Fortunately she had a copy of the manuscript and this book was published later in England where it had a great success. The lively wit, the keen intelligence, and the penetrating criticisms of Madame de Staël were intolerable to the Emperor who had a Roman contempt for women as thinkers. He forbade her to reside in Paris, and kept her under police observation when she went to live at Coppet in Switzerland. The only writers who found favor with Napoleon were those who extolled the virtue of submission to authority.

The beauty, charm, and wit of another woman made her influential in literary and political circles. Born in Lyon, Madame Jeanne Récamier married at fifteen a rich and indulgent banker who was old enough to be her father. From the early days of the Consulate until her death in 1849, her *salon* in Paris was a Mecca of fashion that was much frequented by distinguished literary and eminent political gentlemen.

Madame Récamier, like her friend Madame de Staël, fell into disfavor with Napoleon. Fearful of her influence, he ordered her to leave France. At Naples she persuaded Murat to oppose the Emperor after his return from Elba. After her own return to Paris in 1814, Chateaubriand became her closest friend. David's portrait of Récamier that hangs in the Louvre has contributed to her fame.

A decree of 1808 created the *Université imperiale*, and gave to it complete authority over both public and private education. The only instruction authorized above the primary level was instruction in the classic languages, in grammar and rhetoric, and in mathematics. All studies which might encourage a critical spirit were stricken out of the curriculum. The teaching of philosophy and history was forbidden. Higher instruction was all technical. Napoleon needed technicians, but he wanted no abstract thinkers. It appeared not to occur to him that the suppression of mental liberty leads to intellectual sterility. He said that the paucity of literary production was the fault of the Minister of the Interior. He might better have blamed his police. Constructive and imaginative thought had become that which no one dared to express.

Having re-established and subsidized the Church, Napoleon sought to make it serve his despotism. A revised catechism included in the list of Christian duties "love, respect, obedience, and fidelity to Napoleon I, our Emperor, and the cheerful rendering of military service, and of all else necessary for the preservation and defense of the Empire and the throne." Napoleon believed that he had bought the Church, but a conflict with the Pope became inevitable on account of certain territorial encroachments. The French possession of Naples was followed by gradual absorption of the States of the Church. Napoleon justified this procedure by alleging that Charlemagne, his "illustrious predecessor," had never yielded title to these States, and that even Rome itself was legally a fief of the Empire! The lapse of this claim for a thousand years meant nothing to him.

In 1809 Pius VII, in his extremity, ex-communicated the Emperor. Napoleon responded by declaring that thereby the Pope had ex-communicated himself. His soldiers were commanded to imprison the Head of the Church and to forward all the archives of the Vatican to Paris. Pius, confined at Savona near Genoa, was not allowed to communicate with the outside world. For some time prior to his imprisonment he had refused to give canonical investiture to new bishops in France. In 1811 there were twenty-seven French bishops who lacked papal authorization. Napoleon attempted to solve this difficulty by having a church council authorize the Archbishop of Paris to give the investiture. Bishops who declined to attend this council were imprisoned. The desired authority was extended to the Archbishop, but a delay of six months was imposed. It was expected that within that time the Pope would bend to the will of the Emperor. Since Pius showed no inclination to do so, Napoleon had him thrust into a locked carriage and brought from Italy to Fontainebleau. Isolated in that chilly castle, he had to await the Emperor's return from Russia.

Under duress the Pope signed, in January, 1813, a provisional draft of an agreement that Napoleon called the *Concordat de Fontainebleau.*

In that document endorsement was given to the decisions of the French church council, and the Pope agreed to reside at Avignon. Two months later he made a formal retraction of this document, but it was then too late. Napoleon had already forced its fulfillment. By that time, however, the Emperor's power was definitely waning. In 1814 he was forced to consent to the Pope's return to Rome where Pius was received in triumph by his faithful subjects. By his treatment of the Head of the Church, Napoleon turned all good Catholics against him and made them eager for a restoration of the Bourbons.

Under the Republic, ideas were abundant, but bread was scarce. The Empire, which reversed that situation, came to an even more disastrous end than the Republic. "Man does not live by bread alone." The suppression of ideas turned out to be as fatal as scarcity of food.

The Emperor's mechanistic conception of society was sustained by his genius for organization. He obtained results that appeared to justify his false social philosophy. Master technician that he was, the machine that he created might not have broken down had people been what he believed them to be. He did not fail because of his technique. He failed because his application of that technique rested upon a false assumption. The more he succeeded, the more inaccurate became his estimates of resistances to be overcome.

Napoleon sought to destroy the soul of France in order to save her body. His economic success obscured his less visible social failure. The return of prosperity made the people bless their tyrant for a time. Despite incessant warfare, and partly on account of it, he kept the wheels of industry turning and the people employed. There was an increase of population as well as of production. Growth of the nation from twenty-seven million to twenty-nine million occurred between 1802 and 1814. Paris grew from 548,000 to 650,000. Only the port cities shrank because they were deprived by the English of their overseas business.

The bulk of the population was rural. Rural conditions were vastly better than before the Revolution. Feudal oppression had given way to peasant proprietorship, and the taxes were far lighter than they had been in the days when the nobles were masters of the land. The cost of living was low. Good harvests favored the Empire from 1802 to 1810. There was more wine, more wheat, and more meat. There was important increase in the quantity of livestock and in the culture of potatoes.

France in this period enjoyed plenitude of all that she could herself produce, but England's command of the seas deprived her of tropical products. The use of chicory as a substitute for coffee was encouraged; even now through preference the French put chicory in their coffee, an objectionable habit for which Napoleon is responsible. Tobacco culture began in the *Midi*. But the greatest success was the derivation of sugar from beets instead of from sugar cane; this process, discovered in Germany, was a godsend to the French. The government paid liberal subsidies for the development of this and of other new industries.

There was great expansion of the European market. England blocked France from maritime trade, but France prevented British importation to the Continent. Napoleon saw to it that French goods followed in the wake of his victorious armies. He was an economic as well as political imperialist. The textile industries were especially benefited by greatly increased demands for their products. In 1812 the value of the industrial output of France attained for the first time an approximate equality with the value of all that her farms produced for sale.

The Emperor took especial pride and interest in useful physical improvements, new roads, new canals, the drainage of swamps and the building of dikes. Completion of the great dike at Cherbourg, begun under Louis XVI, transformed an open roadstead into an excellent harbor. The main roads were rebuilt and prolonged far beyond the old frontiers. Four military highways were built across the Alps: the *Simplon*, the *Mont Cenis*, the *Mont Genèvre*, and the *Grande Corniche*, familiar to tourists, which rises from Nice and, from a great height, overlooks the Mediterranean.

Paris, forecast to be the capital of Europe, was beautified in anticipation of her greater role. It was planned for kings to build palaces which they might occupy when they came to pay homage to their Emperor. The *Arc de Triomphe*, the Bourse, and the Madeleine were built, and a plan was made for wide avenues which were only partially completed. Of those which were completed, many radiate from the *Arc de Triomphe* and form the *Etoile* (star). The *rue de Rivoli,* the bridges of Austerlitz and Jena, the column on the *Place Vendôme,* and the arch of the *Carrousel* in the gardens of the Tuileries are other souvenirs of the Napoleonic glory.

The government concerned itself with the social and economic life of the nation more extensively than ever before. Public works, subsidies to industry, and war costs caused a constant deficit, but the currency was kept stable, and waste, leakage, and profiteering were largely eliminated. No monarch was more painstaking than Napoleon in seeing that full value was obtained for money expended. Government expenditure rose from seven hundred million in 1804 to twelve hundred and fifty million in 1813, army costs being more than one-half of that amount. Much of the income was derived from levies imposed upon conquered areas in Germany and Italy, but the failure of costly campaigns in Spain and Russia finally produced so huge a deficit that Napoleon left France in as desperate a financial situation as he had found her.

Minute attention to social, economic, and political matters appeared not to diminish Napoleon's devotion to his first love, the army. The Emperor was, first of all and last of all, a military genius. He made his *Grande Armée* a more perfect instrument of war than Europe had ever seen. There was compulsory recruitment in the form of an obligation for military service between the ages of twenty and twenty-five. However, not until 1813 were all young men made to fulfill this obligation. Prior to that, more than one-half of them were permitted to remain in civil life.

The *Grande Armée* was strengthened by foreign contingents. There were Swiss regiments, a Polish legion, and German and Italian troops. When the Russian campaign began, foreigners composed more than half of the effective strength.

The principal school for officers was at Saint-Cyr. Promotions were rapid. Napoleon preferred young leaders. The average age of his colonels and generals was only thirty-seven. His faith in artillery was such that he tripled what had previously been considered the normal ratio of cannon to men.

The *Garde impériale,* composed of the *élite de l'élite,* numbered ninety thousand. Napoleon boasted that with his *Garde* alone he could march victoriously across the whole of Europe. The guardsmen wore resplendent uniforms, but the infantry of the line was little better outfitted than the soldiers of the Republic had been.

The utter devotion of the army to the Emperor seemed hypnotic. His technique for making himself worshiped has never been surpassed. Once, at the distribution of eagle-crowned flags to new regiments, he asked the young soldiers to prefer death to the abandonment of their colors. "Never," said one of them afterward, "no never, shall I forget the thrill that came at the end of his speech, when, rising in his stirrups, he stretched out his arm toward us and shouted, *'Vous le jurez!'* It seemed to all of us then that he tore from the very depths of us as by force the cry, 'We swear it! *Vive l'Empereur!'* What power in that man! He brought tears to our eyes and put an invincible resolution into our hearts."

Napoleon permitted no general to sit in his presence, but he allowed the old soldiers of the *Garde* to treat him almost as though he were one of them. They called him "the little corporal" or "little baldy." When on campaign he would visit the campfires around which the soldiers huddled. He tasted their soup, called them by name, tweaked their ears, and sometimes explained to them the plan for a next day's battle. They adored him.

Discipline was not so severe as in the critical days of the Revolution when officers as well as soldiers were executed for minor offenses. There was much carousing in the imperial army, much absence without leave. Some of the most daring and able generals were guilty of drunken orgies and of pillage. Masséna and Murat, magnificent in battle, could never be expected to behave soberly after battles were won. But when it came to marching, or to fighting, or to enduring the utmost suffering and danger with stoical courage, Napoleon's veterans could not be surpassed.

Some historians have attempted to maintain that Napoleon was not the real aggressor in the wars of the Empire; that they were but a continuation of the defensive wars of the Republic, a resistance to the intention of other powers to force France back behind her natural frontiers and to restore the Bourbons. It is cited that England and Russia made a secret pact to that effect in 1805. However, this "pact" that was signed by Pitt and the Czar Alexander I was a statement of desires rather than an agreement to co-operate in their fulfillment. It was unknown to Napoleon, and it was not followed by military action. Numerous subsequent documents indicate a readiness of the other powers, even of England, to recognize the enlarged frontiers of France and to make peace with her emperor.

The wars of the Empire were due primarily to Napoleon's personal ambition. It was he who was the aggressor. "My power," he once said, "is due to my glory and my glory is due to my victories. My power will cease unless I continue to sustain it with the glory of new victories. Conquest has made me what I am, and conquest alone can maintain me. When a new-born government ceases to dazzle and to astonish, it falls."

Napoleon, after 1807, ceased to serve France. Having suppressed her soul in order to strengthen her body, he then sacrificed her body in service of his own ambition.

Chapter Seventeen

THE IMPERIAL PURSUIT OF GLORY

THE PREPARATIONS FOR AN INVASION OF ENGLAND. THE SWIFT TURN TO
THE EAST WHEN BAD NEWS CAME FROM THE SOUTH. THE BRILLIANT
VICTORIES OF ULM AND OF AUSTERLITZ. THE TREATY OF PRESSBURG.
TRAFALGAR. THE CONFEDERATION OF THE RHINE WHEREBY NAPOLEON
CONTRIBUTED TO THE DEVELOPMENT OF GERMAN SOLIDARITY. THE
DEFEAT OF PRUSSIA AT JENA AND AUERSTADT. THE FIRST CAMPAIGN IN
RUSSIA. THE TREATY OF TILSIT. THE CONTINENTAL BLOCKADE. UNFORTU-
NATE INTERVENTION IN SPAIN.

"Emperor of France! I am the Emperor of France! When I think
of what I was ten years ago! And Josephine! How wonderful, and
how delightful to possess is Josephine! But can she ever be an empress? Why did she weep when I put the crown on her head? She
will always be too soft, too sentimental. But there are many other
enjoyable women, and, after all, an emperor. . . . But I must not think
too much about women. I must concentrate on being Emperor. I must
be hard. I must stay hard to keep my generals submissive. They expect that. They would take any softness for weakness. And order;
there must be order, and softness leads to disorder. Order is the first
need of all Europe, and I am the only one who can create it. I have
proved that. I shall keep on proving it, and if the English interfere,
the worse for them. It may be difficult to cross the Channel, but even
that can be managed. People everywhere want what only I can give
them. Liberty! Democracy! Stuff and nonsense! My own people
have proved that. Five years ago they were still fighting for liberty
and democracy, but now they are all shouting, *Vive l'Empereur!* They
have made me an emperor, and I shall be one, court, conquests, glory
and all. They expect that. They shall have that. They shall be proud
to serve an emperor who brings them order and prosperity, and rides
all opposition down."

Napoleon's thought may have been like that. He had remade
France and held her in his grasp. All Europe was within his reach.

Ten years of triumph lay behind. Why not more triumphs? A few more might make him Emperor, not of France alone, but of all Europe. It was not difficult for him to believe that the whole world would be better off if he became its ruler. All those picturesque, medieval cities of middle Europe, the disordered glory of Italy, and the blue Mediterranean that lay beyond, the shining pathway to the Orient, all these should be his to rule and to put in order after his inevitable conquests. That was Napoleon's dream, a dream that might well have come true—except for England.

It was with England that the renewal of hostilities began. When peace was signed at Amiens in 1802, she had hoped for renewal of her trade with the Continent. But Napoleon would make no concessions about that; prohibitory tariffs kept British goods out of France, Spain, and Holland. British industry was threatened with ruin.

Napoleon foresaw that England would retaliate by fresh seizures of French colonies. He hastened to make a bargain sale to the United States of the Louisiana territory that had been ceded to France by Spain. In Santo Domingo, a French possession, there was a revolt under the leadership of a negro genius, Toussaint Louverture. Napoleon sent there an army commanded by one of his brothers-in-law. This expedition failed and France, in 1803, lost Santo Domingo.

The inevitable war began over the question of Malta. England had agreed to remove forces she had placed on that island, but did not do so, claiming that French encroachments in Holland, Switzerland, and Italy had changed the situation. Napoleon held that the Treaty of Amiens had nothing to do with changes on the Continent. England, however, was determined to keep Malta because of its importance for her control of the Mediterranean. In March, 1803, Napoleon told the English Ambassador that if the British stayed in Malta he would fight. England responded by the seizure of all French ships in British ports. Napoleon arrested all British residents in France. An eleven-year war began that ended only with the fall of the Empire.

Bonaparte's first move was to occupy Hanover, the King of England's personal domain. He began elaborate preparations for a cross-Channel invasion. One hundred and fifty thousand men were assembled at Boulogne. Twelve hundred boats were built. Five hundred cannon were mounted and forts were constructed even in the sea to make English interference impossible. From their camp the soldiers of the *Grande Armée* could see the patrolling ships of England, and, from the heights above, her shores were dimly visible. There was a vast enthusiasm. Poitiers, Crécy, and Agincourt were to be avenged. That was in the summer of 1805.

The main French fleet, commanded by Villeneuve, had been sent to the West Indies in order to draw Nelson away from Europe. The ruse succeeded. But the fleet, sailing back for Brest, was damaged in an engagement off the coast of Brittany. Villeneuve, overprudent, went to Cadiz for repairs. Nelson's fleet, returning from the Caribbean, blockaded him there. That ruined Napoleon's elaborate plan. He had counted upon the arrival of his fleet in August to protect the passage of his troops across the Channel. The invasion had to be abandoned.

Meanwhile Pitt had left no stone unturned in efforts to form a new coalition against France. In 1802 French troops had restored order in Switzerland where a civil war had broken out. The grateful Swiss accepted Napoleon's control of their country. In similar manner, Napoleonic order was established in Germany. Its three hundred and sixty governments were reduced to eighty-two; princes who paid liberally were rewarded with enlargements of their territories. Prussia gained a half-million new subjects and Austria lost most of her control of the German states; this was the death-knell of the Holy Roman Empire. In May of 1805 Napoleon was crowned King of Italy and Genoa was annexed. This rapid extension of French territory and influence facilitated Pitt's task because it greatly alarmed both Austria and Russia.

Alexander I, who had become Czar at twenty-three upon the assassination of his father, Paul I, was active in the new coalition. England agreed to furnish liberal subsidies, but no land forces. She had enough to do on the seas. In August of 1805, England, Russia, Austria, Sweden, and Bourbon-ruled Naples were all aligned against France and ready to march. An army of Swedes and Russians was to advance through Hanover, an Austro-Russian army was to move up the valley of the Danube, and two other armies were to attack France in Italy.

August brought to Napoleon at Boulogne news that might have stunned a lesser man. Hard upon the heels of the messenger who brought news of the blockade of the French fleet in Cadiz, there came another to announce that four enemy armies threatened France. Furious, but undaunted, still confident of his destiny, Napoleon turned eastward, swiftly to strike and brilliantly to win the greatest battles of his career. While still five hundred miles from the scene of action, he dictated the plan of his campaign in full detail. Never was his military genius more apparent. Ignoring the north and south armies of the coalition, he made his principal attack upon their center.

The headwaters of the Danube are in the Black Forest. There General Mack, commanding eighty thousand Austrians, expected to find the French. But Napoleon crossed the Rhine at Mainz, far to the north of the Black Forest, and by forced marches, entered the Danube valley eastward of the Austrians. Ney prevented their retreat to the north. At Ulm, on the twentieth of October, they were compelled to surrender. Eighteen generals and thirty-three thousand soldiers became prisoners. The captured army defiled before the Emperor, laying down arms as it passed. Thrilled with admiration for the brilliance of his generalship and the greatness of his victory, many of the prisoners cried, *"Vive l'Empereur!"* Even the enemy felt his hypnotic power.

A great Russian army was slowly moving toward France. Napoleon moved even more swiftly toward it, "to save them," he said, "half their journey." On the fifteenth of November he occupied Vienna after twenty-three days of uninterrupted marching. His soldiers had lived on the potatoes they found in the fields. The Emperor Francis II had not stayed to defend his capital; he had gone with his army to join the Russians led by the Czar.

Napoleon, moving north from Vienna, searched the Moravian countryside to find a battleground that suited him. Having found it, he proceeded by a series of masterly maneuvers to induce the enemy to fight him where he wished to fight. On the second of December, 1805, he fought and won what has been called the perfect battle, the battle of Austerlitz.

A high plateau that rose about three hundred feet above the valley of a marshy little stream was the key position of the battleground that

Napoleon selected. The town of Austerlitz lay a few miles east of that plateau, the stream lay west of it, and, still farther west, there ran from north to south the highroad to Vienna. To the north there were mountains.

On the twenty-ninth of November, Napoleon, feigning retreat, evacuated Austerlitz and moved westward across the plateau and across the marshy stream, the Goldbach. His forces took positions west of the Goldbach; that suggested intention to keep open a line of retreat along the Vienna road. On the thirtieth the enemy moved forward through Austerlitz and occupied the plateau that overlooked the Goldbach. They were ninety thousand to Napoleon's seventy-four thousand. Napoleon's idea was that the Russian general in command would send a large force to turn the French right flank and block its only practicable line of retreat.

The night of December 1 was clear and cold. Sound carried far. Napoleon waited under the stars and listened. At nightfall the enemy movement began. Hour after hour the sound of heavy caissons rolling along frost-bound roads came like sweet music to the Emperor's ears. The enemy was making the maneuver that he had hoped for; it was as though they were marching under his own orders. When, at three in the morning, he was sure that his forecast had been fulfilled, sure that the enemy's encircling movement had greatly reduced its force on the plateau of Pratzen, then he retired to his tent.

When dawn came the valley of the Goldbach was filled with mist that concealed French regiments advancing stealthily. They were halfway up the height before they were seen. Napoleon had launched his main attack directly at the enemy's weakened center, where the Czar and the Emperor of Austria were. By nine o'clock the French infantry had won the plateau, cutting through the enemy's center and dividing his forces into two parts that were without liason. Napoleon and the *Garde impériale* occupied the conquered ground. Realizing how greatly they had been deceived and imperiled, the enemy made desperate attempts to retake the heights, throwing in all the reserves. There was fierce fighting at close quarters. By one o'clock the enemy had been forced back into the ravines toward Austerlitz.

Meanwhile Davout, in command of the French right wing, had withstood with ten thousand men the attack of the thirty-five thousand who had been sent down from the plateau. Two villages, taken and retaken three times, were, at eleven o'clock, held by the Russians. But at two o'clock French troops, descending from the Pratzen by the same roads that the Russians had traversed the night before, attacked them from the rear. Fired upon from both sides, the Russians lost ten thousand men in less than an hour. To the north the sabers of Murat's four thousand cuirassiers cut down the Austrian cavalry, and Lannes continued pursuit of the infantry. When the sun set at four o'clock the battle was over. The enemy had lost thirty-five thousand to Napoleon's eight thousand. He had not used his reserves. With forty-five thousand he had defeated ninety thousand. Nearly all of the enemy's artillery was captured. The bronze of it was used to construct the great column on the Place Vendôme which is surmounted by a toga-clad figure of the Emperor.

Prussia had agreed to join the coalition, but after Austerlitz Frederick William III hastened to send his congratulations from Potsdam and to reaffirm his reluctant friendship for France. Napoleon was not deceived. He knew that if he had lost Frederick William would have joined joyfully in the march on Paris.

Defeated Austria signed the Treaty of Pressburg on December 26. She yielded to France all the territory in Germany and Italy that she had controlled. Austerlitz made Napoleon master of practically all Europe except Russia.

However, on October 20, the very day that an Austrian army surrendered to Napoleon at Ulm, Nelson crushingly defeated the French fleet in the battle of Trafalgar. Villeneuve had received at Cadiz the Emperor's order to proceed at all costs into the Mediterranean where his fleet could be used in an attack on Naples. That order led to disaster. Off Cape Trafalgar the English sank or captured more than half of Villeneuve's ships. Heroic Nelson lost his life, but he had won a victory at sea which counterbalanced Napoleon's victories on land. Trafalgar did more than save England; it gave to her that control of the seas which, in the end, enabled her and her allies to crush the Empire.

In the first half of 1806 Napoleon's mastery of western Europe was uncontested. Joseph, his oldest brother, became King of Naples;

the Bourbons who reigned there had fled to Sicily. Louis Bonaparte, who had married Josephine's daughter Hortense, became King of Holland. Only the Pope raised a protesting voice. We have seen what happened to him.

Germany was remade. The Holy Empire ceased to exist. The dukes of Bavaria and Wurtemberg had supported Napoleon; for that they became kings. Other friendly German princes became grand dukes. Hanover was given to that uncertain ally, Frederick William of Prussia. Murat, the brilliant cavalry commander, had married Napoleon's sister Caroline; for him the new grand duchy of Berg was created in the Rhineland. The Confederation of the Rhine was formed; it was composed of the new kingdoms and grand duchies that covered the south and west of Germany. Frankfort was its capital and Napoleon, called its Protector, was its master. His dream of mastery over the picturesque medieval cities of middle Europe had been fulfilled.

It looked as though all European resistance had been overcome. Pitt had died in January; it was said that the news of Austerlitz killed him. Fox, who succeeded him, opened peace negotiations with Talleyrand, Napoleon's foreign minister, and the Czar, for the same purpose, sent a representative to Paris. Napoleon could have had official recognition of his control of western Europe, but he wanted more than that. He wanted an open path to the Indies. His dream of oriental glory had not faded; he demanded the withdrawal of England and Russia from points that they held on the Mediterranean. But England would not withdraw, and Russia would not give up her Ionian isles. The negotiations came to nothing.

Frederick William of Prussia finally became a partner in a new coalition, the fourth that had been formed against Napoleon. Supported by Russia and England, and imagining himself a second Frederick the Great, he attempted to liberate Germany from French control. On October 7, 1806, he sent an ultimatum, demanding that all French troops be withdrawn to the west side of the Rhine. Napoleon, then in Germany, instantly took the offensive. Six days after receiving Frederick's ultimatum, he defeated part of the Prussian army at Jena, and, on the following day, Davout defeated the other part at Auerstadt. Prussia lost forty-five thousand men in these two battles. The venerable Duke of Brunswick, general-in-chief, was killed; it was he who had been repulsed at Valmy in 1792. Napoleon made a triumphal entry into Berlin on the twenty-seventh of October.

The once-formidable Prussians had been defeated in six days, but it took six months to defeat the Russians. Winter had come when the Emperor led his army into the great lonely plains of Poland. The few roads were very bad, food was very scarce, and the enemy extremely elusive. On February 8, 1807, the battle of Eylau was fought in a blinding snowstorm. It was indecisive. Hostilities were not resumed until winter was over. In June the Russians were defeated at Friedland and asked for an armistice.

The young Czar, like his father Paul before him, found England a very unsatisfactory ally. Her subsidies had ceased and she sent no men. Alexander decided to come to an understanding with Napoleon. He was a peace-lover. He had come to the conclusion that the peace of Europe could be best secured by co-operation with France, Napoleon to govern in the west and he in the east. He made a plan for the partition of the Continent into the Empires of the Orient and the Occident.

The two Emperors had their first interview on a raft in the middle of the river Niemen. Each wished to win the support of the other. Their discussions continued for several days and led to the Treaty of Tilsit, July 8, 1807, a treaty of peace and of alliance. Prussia lost Hanover, her part of Poland, and all that she possessed east of the Elbe; her population was reduced from ten million to five. It was only to please the Czar that Napoleon left anything of Prussia; Alexander interceded for Frederick with whom he had had a sentimental friendship. Napoleon agreed to aid Russia, if necessary, in expelling the Turks from Europe, and the Czar agreed to withdraw from the Ionian isles and to declare war on England.

Two new states were created out of the territory taken from Prussia; the kingdom of Westphalia with Jerome Napoleon for king, and the grand-duchy of Warsaw, to be ruled by the former elector, now king, of Saxony. These states entered into the Confederation of the Rhine. Napoleon's imperial control had reached to the Russian frontier.

Before the victories of Ulm and Austerlitz the new war had not been popular. Anxiety about its outcome led to a financial crisis. The interest rate rose to twenty-four per cent and the Bank of France came near to closing its doors. Napoleon's victories restored confidence, but he remained aware of the need to win victories of peace as well as of war, the need to finish his battles and turn his attention to business. After the victory of Austerlitz he proclaimed to his soldiers, "As soon as we have done what is necessary to assure the security *and prosperity* of the fatherland, we shall return to France. There you shall be the object of my most tender solicitude."

To the French people the Treaty of Tilsit was even more welcome than the victory of Austerlitz. It gave hope of peace to a war-weary nation. Only England remained to be conquered, and she was to be conquered through economic pressure rather than by force of arms. The idea of an invasion had been abandoned. Instead, there was to be a Continental blockade which might compel the obstinate British to sue for peace.

The British did not appear to be intimidated. They even invited an increase of European hostility by seizing French merchandise in transport on neutral ships. In May, 1806, England undertook to prevent all maritime commerce with France. In November Napoleon ordered cessation of all commerce with England; British merchandise was to be confiscated and British subjects made prisoners wherever found. There was to be no distinction between civilians and soldiers; all were in the war. What could not be accomplished with guns was to be accomplished by economic strangulation.

In September, 1807, the British attempted to commandeer the Danish fleet. When their demand was refused, they bombarded Copenhagen and seized the ships. In November England announced that she would undertake to seize all ships except those that paid duty and obtained clearance in a British port; Napoleon announced that he would seize all ships that did so. Neutrality became impossible.

The elimination of English competition in European trade would greatly benefit the industries of France. It was also evident that many thousand workers would become unemployed in England; she might have to accept Napoleon's terms in order to avoid a civil war. But the blockade also hurt France. The stoppage of both exports and im-

ports increased the cost of living. The port towns suffered greatly.
Marseille was ruined. The blockade was extremely distasteful to
other European states where industry was but slightly developed. It
could not be effectively enforced; there was much cargo-running.
Napoleon's brother Louis, King of Holland, refused to ruin his subjects by complete enforcement. So Holland was annexed to France,
and Bremen and Hamburg also. The little kingdom of Portugal
caused the most trouble. It was frankly pro-British. When its King
refused to close his ports, a French army occupied Lisbon. The King
fled to Brazil.

Intervention in Portugal facilitated intervention in Spain, and there
the decline of Napoleon's career began. A branch of the Bourbon
family had been reigning in Madrid since 1700 when the Duke of
Anjou, a grandson of Louis XIV, became Philip V of Spain. Throughout the Eighteenth Century, Spain had been a fairly consistent ally of
France, but the Spanish Bourbons degenerated. Charles IV, King in
1807, was an aged imbecile who was controlled by an unscrupulous
favorite named Godoï. Charles's son Ferdinand was popular with the
people, but the only sound basis for Ferdinand's popularity was his
opposition to Godoï. The Crown Prince had neither courage, virtue,
nor ability, but Godoï was universally detested. The political situation
was extremely tense.

Napoleon could be relied upon to take advantage of the instability
of the Spanish government. That pear was ripe for the plucking.
Under pretense of reinforcement for the French forces in Portugal,
Murat led a second army into the peninsula early in 1808. This army
did not go on to Portugal; it remained in Madrid. The enemies of
Godoï judged the moment opportune for a *coup d'état;* one of
Napoleon's secret agents was in touch with them. They compelled the
abdication of father Charles and declared son Ferdinand king. Both
father and son appealed to Murat for support. The situation was made
to order for intervention.

The Emperor went to Bayonne and summoned the royal family of
Spain to appear before him. They did so on the thirtieth of April.
Two days later there were disorders in Madrid in which French sol-
diers were killed. It became Napoleon's "duty" to restore order in

a country in which his soldiers had been assassinated. Cowardly
Ferdinand, terrified by the situation, surrendered his briefly-worn
crown. He was sent as a prisoner of state to Talleyrand's château at
Valençay. Old Charles abdicated again, this time in favor of "his
friend, the great Napoleon." The Emperor made his brother Joseph
King of Spain and sent Murat to succeed Joseph as King of Naples.

Napoleon's seizure of the throne of Spain contained no element of
glory. It was the act of a political bandit, a shameful business accomplished through trickery and accompanied by massacre. Murat, ful-
filling instructions, drowned the disorders in Madrid in "a bath of
blood." Monks and other blameless people were executed without
trial. Napoleon's conscience troubled him about that. In his memoirs
he expressed regret that the circumstances attending his overthrow of
the Spanish government had obscured his good intentions.

Spain was unlike middle Europe. The docility of the people of the
German states was lacking in the Spaniards. They were not intimidated by the Emperor's formidable military reputation. They bitterly
resented the trickery by which their rulers had been drawn into a trap
at Bayonne, and they were furious about Murat's massacre at Madrid.
Napoleon underestimated the resistance to the new regime. It required
a battle to open the Madrid road to Joseph when he went there to
reign. He wrote to his brother, "No one has told the truth to Your
Majesty. The truth is that I am supported by no more than a handful. . . . A brave and an irate nation is arrayed against me. . . . Sire,
you are in error. Your glory will be wrecked in Spain."

One hundred and fifty thousand Spaniards took up arms. In July,
1808, a French army, trapped in wild country and perishing from
hunger, thirst, and heat, was compelled to surrender. King Joseph
left for the frontier.

England saw her chance. She sent Wellington in command of
sixteen thousand to aid in driving the French out of Portugal. In
August, Junot, the French commander, surrendered at Cintra. The
whole peninsula was lost to France.

Meanwhile Napoleon, unable to believe the truth about Spain,
made grandiose plans for conquest of the Orient. Both he and the

Czar were impatient to profit by their new alliance. Napoleon urged Alexander to attack Sweden because Sweden had refused to co-operate in the Continental blockade; Alexander obliged by taking Finland away from the Swedes. But when he urged action about the partition of Turkey as agreed upon in the Treaty of Tilsit, Napoleon put him off with fine words; he wished for Alexander's aid, but he did not wish for any extension of Russian power that might interfere with the extension of his own. He proposed that the Tilsit project be enlarged; that, having driven the Turks out of Constantinople, Franco-Russian forces should enter Asia with India as their objective! Napoleon was unwilling to concede Constantinople to Russia; he wanted that important city for himself.

His dream of oriental conquest so dominated the Emperor's mind that, even while his armies were being defeated in Spain, he appeared to be thinking less of them than of victories in India. Troops and ships were assembled in Italy for the new expedition, and supplies were sent forward to Dalmatia. The advance was to begin in September. But, before September came, defeats in Spain that Napoleon believed could not happen did happen. The great project had to be postponed while the accident to a minor one was being repaired. Little did Napoleon realize in that fateful summer of 1808 that he had already surpassed the limit of his powers, that his plan for oriental conquest was forever dead, that he never would see Constantinople.

CHAPTER EIGHTEEN

THE EBB TIDE OF THE EMPIRE

ITS FRAGILITY BECAME VISIBLE. AUSTRIA AND RUSSIA CAME TO AN
UNDERSTANDING, BUT THE CORSICAN WON AGAIN AT MARENGO. HE
DIVORCED JOSEPHINE AND MARRIED AN AUSTRIAN PRINCESS. PROGRESS
IN PRUSSIA. THE FRANCO-RUSSIAN WAR. THE RETREAT FROM MOSCOW.

THE invincible armies of France had been defeated, defeated by the
untrained patriots of Spain and Portugal. That suggested Valmy.
There the invincible Prussians had been repulsed by a revolutionary
rabble. Now the roles were reversed. Out of that revolutionary
rabble there had evolved the most formidable military force of Europe.
And now it had met defeat at the hands of an enemy it had not taken
seriously. The news spread like wildfire. All the enemies of the
Emperor, all those whom he had conquered and who longed for revenge, lifted their heads again. Resignation was replaced by hope.

For the first time Napoleon felt compelled to make concessions.
He dared not go to Spain until he made sure that France would not
be attacked while he was gone. With Prussia he agreed to evacuate
her territory if she would pay a heavy indemnity and limit her army
to forty-two thousand. With the Czar he had an interview at Erfurt
that lasted more than a fortnight. He was worried about Austria. He
sought to obtain from Alexander a definite promise "to show his
teeth" and to keep Austria powerless, but Alexander made no such
promise; he agreed to co-operate against Austria only in case she declared war.

Talleyrand had a hand in determining Alexander's attitude at Erfurt. He believed that Napoleon had lost his grip on reality and would
bring disaster upon France. He believed that it was in France's interest
to keep Austria strong enough to hold Russia in check. In a secret
interview he urged the Czar "to save Europe" by not concurring in
Napoleon's plans. Talleyrand risked death as a traitor, but he suc-

ceeded in preventing Alexander from becoming a tool in Napoleon's hands.

The Emperor had to leave for Spain without assurance that Austria would not again rise against him in his absence. He had moved too rapidly in the development of his empire, seeking new enlargements before earlier gains had been made secure.

Minor victories opened the road to Madrid. There, in December, 1808, Napoleon undertook to win Spanish support for the new regime. He abolished the Inquisition, suppressed feudal rights, and required a solemn oath of fidelity. But his work of "pacification" was interrupted by bad news from Paris. Instant order was given for a quick departure. In bitter midwinter cold the imperial carriage rushed northward across the bleak Spanish highlands. Soult and Ney were left behind to finish the work of pacification.

The pacification of Spain was never accomplished. Her people would not accept Napoleonic control. Aided by the English, they kept up their resistance until the Empire crumbled. Between 1808 and 1813 more than three hundred thousand French soldiers were sent to Spain, but the Spaniards kept on fighting. The absence of these soldiers when they were needed in France was a primary cause of Napoleon's downfall.

The imprisonment of the Pope enabled the Spanish priests to preach a holy war against the French. The devout peasants were taught to believe that French soldiers were devils. In a Spanish catechism the question, "Is it a sin to kill a Frenchman?" was answered "No; to kill these dogs of heretics is to make sure of going to heaven." The peasants made sure of heaven whenever they had a chance, making doubly sure of it by adding torture to their assassinations. Atrocities led to reprisals. French soldiers put villages that resisted them to fire and sword, not sparing even the children.

Napoleon went from Madrid to Paris in six days. It had been reported that Austria was preparing an attack and that Talleyrand and Fouché were planning, in case anything happened to Napoleon, to make Murat his successor. The Emperor saw fit not to eliminate these able gentlemen of whose services he had need, but he told Talleyrand what he thought of him in no uncertain terms. That master diplomat bowed before the storm, merely saying when he emerged from it, "What a pity that so great a man has such bad manners."

There was need to enlarge the army, both for service in Spain and to meet the threat of an Austrian attack. But, due to the unpopularity of the Spanish war, enlargement was difficult to accomplish. In some *départements* more than one-half of those due for military service failed to respond to the summons. The army had to be reinforced with foreign contingents. Metternich, the Austrian Ambassador in Paris, reported to his government that the war in Spain had greatly reduced French military strength. Vienna believed that her chance had come to avenge Austerlitz.

For the first time Napoleon had a war forced upon him that was not to his liking. Austria had rebuilt her army. She had nearly a half-million men under arms. The Czar remained as neutral as possible. He warned Austria that, if she was the aggressor, the Treaty of Tilsit called upon him to co-operate with France, but to an Austrian general he expressed his sympathy. Vienna knew that there was nothing to fear from the Czar. It was understood that Austrian and Russian troops would manage to avoid each other.

Hostilities began with an invasion of Bavaria in April, 1809. The Austrians had hoped to surprise Napoleon, but his attack was swifter than their invasion. In five days he drove them out of Bavaria, and on the eleventh of May he again entered Vienna in triumph. A great army commanded by the Archduke Charles withdrew across the Danube, destroying the bridges behind it. Napoleon, having moved a few miles east of Vienna, attempted to cross by an improvised bridge of boats from the island of Lobau. A sudden rise of the river broke the bridge while the crossing was in progress. The situation was extremely critical, but the forces that had crossed resisted desperate Austrian attempts to overwhelm them and finally rejoined their comrades on the island. The losses were very heavy on both sides. General Lannes was mortally wounded.

Napoleon found himself compelled to remain in an entrenched position on the large island, and to await the arrival of the Army of Italy that he had summoned to his succor. More than a month passed before he was able again to take the offensive. Then, favored by a storm, he made a memorable night crossing of the Danube with one hundred and fifty thousand men.

On the fifth and sixth of July, 1809, the battle of Wagram was fought within sight of Vienna. As had been attempted at Austerlitz, the Archduke Charles tried to cut Napoleon's line of retreat. But Napoleon, instead of retreating, attacked the Austrian center. The fire of a hundred guns was followed by a massive infantry attack. The enemy lines were broken and more than thirty thousand of them were killed, wounded, or captured, but the victory was not so complete as at Austerlitz. Napoleon had to fight at Wagram with an army chiefly composed of green recruits and foreign contingents; half of his best soldiers were in Spain. He had to throw all of his reserves into action. The army was too exhausted to follow the retreating Austrians. The bulk of the Archduke's army withdrew in good order into Bohemia. Fortunately for Napoleon, his narrowly won victory was enough to terrify Vienna.

Austria again begged for peace. Harsh terms were imposed. By the Treaty of Vienna of October, 1809, Austria lost three and a half million inhabitants and nearly thirty thousand square miles of territory. Napoleon had reasserted his mastery of middle Europe, but the people there were no longer inclined to be docile under that mastery. They had heard of the French reverses in Spain and they knew that France had become less formidable. While Napoleon was fighting on the Danube, an English army landed in southern Holland and caused alarm in Paris; it was forced to withdraw on account of an epidemic. Insurrection broke out at various points in Germany and there was an attempt to assassinate the Emperor.

Despite his reverses in Spain, the narrow margin of his victory in Austria, and the growth of popular discontent throughout the territory of the Confederation of the Rhine, Napoleon, in the fall of 1809, believed himself to be stronger than ever. He believed that only one thing was lacking to insure the stability and power of the imperial dynasty he had founded. That Talleyrand and Fouché had dared to think of Murat as his successor enraged him, and yet he realized that there must be thought of the future, thought about what would hap-

A sketch to indicate the extent of Napoleon's empire in 1810.

pen if he should die. He knew that even while he lived his position was weakened because of uncertainty about his successor.

The Emperor must have a son. Since Josephine had been unable to give him one, another empress must be found, another of higher rank than Josephine Beauharnais had been, one in whom political advantage would be joined to maternal capacity.

Napoleon thought of marrying a sister of the Czar, but Alexander evaded the honor of this suggested alliance. If not Russia, then Austria. Austria was happy to oblige. The Emperor Francis had an eighteen-year-old daughter named Maria-Louisa. To her the great honor befell.

The divorce of Josephine was a simple matter. On the sixteenth of December, 1809, Napoleon's marriage to the beautiful creole was annulled. Josephine went into retirement at Malmaison, but Napoleon, the man, did not cease to love her. It was the Emperor who had divorced her.

In April, 1810, the Corsican of lowly birth who had become an emperor was allied by marriage to the Hapsburgs, the proudest and most illustrious of the European dynasties. In March, 1811, Maria-Louisa gave birth to a son, who, even in his cradle, bore the proud title, King of Rome. In him Austria was united with the new imperial dynasty of France. In him Napoleon saw assurance both of the stability of the Empire and of the peace of Europe.

After Wagram there came three comparatively peaceful years. Hostilities continued in Spain, and France won no glory there, but that was looked upon as a minor war and came to be accepted as a routine matter. In that period Napoleon's domination of western Europe attained its greatest extent; only Denmark and Sweden remained independent. France herself included one hundred and thirty *départements,* and beyond her new frontiers lay vassal states, and other states of which her Emperor was sovereign. Napoleon was master of nearly all of what had formerly been the Holy Roman Empire. He was the King of Italy; his step-son Eugène de Beauharnais ruled there as viceroy; divorce of Josephine had not ended Napoleon's attachment to her son. France alone formed no more than one-fourth of the area of Napoleon's domain.

The Emperor was too expert in administration to seek to impose everywhere an identical organization of government. He allowed local conditions to be determinative. Always generous to his family, he endowed his brothers and his sisters with kingdoms and with principalities, but they all took an oath of fidelity to him as their overlord. Certain states within the Napoleonic domain retained nominal autonomy, but they were obliged to pay tribute, to furnish soldiers, and to leave it to the Emperor to determine their foreign relations. Despite diversity in form, there was unity in the fundamental fact of Napoleon's direct control. Some material and political benefits resulted from this control.

Napoleon removed the burdens of the old feudal regime and introduced the efficient forms of administration which had been developed in France. His *Code civil* extended widely the principles of social equality, civil liberty, equality in inheritance, and trial by jury. The improvement of roads, canals, and harbors was undertaken throughout the *Grand Empire*. But there was another side to the picture. Military conscription and heavy taxes were imposed. The embargo on English goods was maintained, and England continued effectively to restrain all maritime commerce that might benefit France. The cost of living rose.

Some countries were less benefited than others. Holland was brought close to ruin by the Continental blockade and her federated republicanism was effaced; monarchy was continued there after Napoleon fell. In Spain the French were hated, but the insurrectional government adopted a constitution based on the one-time liberalism of France. In Italy Napoleon's control led to more of national feeling than there had been before; companionship in military service and identity of regime did much to diminish ancient rivalries that had made the Italian states non-co-operative. In Germany the effects were different on the different sides of the Rhine. The west side, annexed to France, was well administered and profited largely by the change, but east of the river there was much discontent. Dispossessed feudal lords kept this discontent alive. Forced conscription, abuses by the armies of occupation, and the economic effects of the blockade more than counterbalanced the benefits. As in Italy, the new regime facilitated the later emergence of a new German nationalism. Napoleon

gave to middle Europe the form that it had prior to 1919. Destroyer
of the ancient regime, wherever his power extended he made changes
which determined the nature of the new Europe that emerged from
the ruins of his empire.

Most significant of the reactions to French domination was that
which occurred in Prussia. Ever since the failure of the Duke of
Brunswick to win at Valmy, certain German thinkers had been trying
to explain that failure, and to account for the succession of French
victories that followed it. They believed that more than Napoleon
had to be accounted for. Before Napoleon there had been Jemmapes
and Fleurus as well as Valmy. For nearly twenty years the soldiers of
France had fought with a spirit, a dash, a transport of courage and
energy that their enemies lacked. They fought with a recklessness
that could not be denied, like men whose souls as well as their bodies
were pledged to victory or death.

Two ministers of Prussia, Stein and Hardenberg, and Scharnhorst,
a general officer, were students of this problem. They agreed upon
the necessity for firing the Prussian soldiers with a spirit to match
that of the French, but they disagreed about how to do it. The common people were apathetic in their attitude toward the state; a new
devotion to it had to be aroused. Hardenberg believed that this could
be done by acceptance of the principles of the French Revolution
without the Revolution; he held for democratic practice within the
frame of a monarchical government. Stein believed in administrative
reform, but he had a horror of democracy. He succeeded Hardenberg
as minister and continued the work of reform that his predecessor had
begun. By an edict of 1807, serfdom was abolished and the right to
own land was extended to others than the nobles. Later edicts established equality of taxation and freedom of industry. In 1811 and
1812 "assemblies of notables" were held in Berlin to consider governmental reform. It was French influence that led to this weakening
in Prussia of absolutism and feudalism.

Scharnhorst was convinced that French military superiority was
due to superior morale, and that, in turn, to "democratic nationalism."
He labored to introduce a similar spirit into the Prussian army.
Charged with its reorganization, he abolished the requirement that all

officers should be of noble rank and suppressed the brutalities of corporal punishment. Napoleon required that the Prussian army should not exceed forty-two thousand, but Scharnhorst provided military training for far more than that number without incorporating them in the army.

Due to the efforts of the Scientist Humboldt, the University of Berlin was founded in 1810. The philosopher Fichte was its first rector. His "Lectures to the German nation" did much to arouse the spirit of nationalism which was so essential to any hope of escape from French domination. Even in the days of Napoleon, Prussia was engaged in the inculcation of a philosophy which makes of the state a god that all good citizens must worship, a philosophy that denies the virtue of liberty and democracy, and extols the excellence of unquestioning obedience.

The Prussian leaders strove to secure a popular devotion to the state like that of the French, but without the freedom which was the basis of that devotion. Their success in doing so indicated that the Germans are more docile than the French.

The magnificence of the Empire could not conceal its fragility. As early as 1806 its collapse was predicted by thoughtful men. After Wagram, in 1809, when it reached its greatest extent, one of Napoleon's ministers is reported to have said, "The Emperor is crazy, completely crazy. He is heading straight for catastrophe and taking us all with him." Many shared that opinion.

Conscription, economic difficulties, police activities, and the imprisonment of the Pope undermined Napoleon's popularity even among his fellow countrymen. Thousands hid in the woods or in the mountains, or maimed themselves, in order to avoid military service. Peasants began to speak of "the ogre of Corsica." Outside of France, hatred of control by the Empire steadily increased. An army of three hundred thousand commanded by some of Napoleon's best generals was unable to overcome the resistance of the Spaniards, and of Wellington in Portugal. Prussia, Austria, and Russia were bound by treaties to be allies of France, but these treaties had been signed under the duress of military defeats; only fear of Napoleon's power made them effective. Sincere allegiance to him existed outside of France only in Poland, and there only because the Poles believed that he would restore their kingdom.

It was about Poland that Alexander and Napoleon came to definite disagreement. The Czar had waited five years for the help in the partition of Turkey that Napoleon had promised at Tilsit. He grew tired of waiting. Besides, he and his family had been overlooked when the invitations to Napoleon's wedding were sent out. Alexander began to believe that France was even less satisfactory as an ally than England had been. He was ready to tear up the Treaty of Tilsit as soon as he dared.

After his defeat of Prussia and Russia in 1807, Napoleon had created the Grand Duchy of Warsaw out of that part of the former kingdom of Poland that he took from Prussia. Recognition of this new duchy was one of the items in the treaty that the Czar had signed, but he did not like that item; he could not be happy about anything that suggested a resurrection of Russia's old enemy, Poland. His unhappiness was increased by the addition of western Galicia to the Grand Duchy of Warsaw after the defeat of Austria in 1809. One of his ministers told the French ambassador in Moscow that "Russia would fight to the last man to prevent re-establishment of the kingdom of Poland." In 1810 Alexander asked Napoleon to give a pledge not to restore Poland; Napoleon refused to do so. The Czar then mobilized troops on the Polish frontier, and so did the Emperor. In 1811 they both prepared to fight.

The Franco-Russian War began in June, 1812. Theoretically, Austria and Prussia were Napoleon's allies, but that was only because they were afraid not to be. They both kept in touch with the Czar and would have joined him in fighting the French had they dared. Metternich sent assurances to Alexander that the thirty thousand men Austria was required to provide would do as little harm as possible, and that Austria had the friendliest feelings for Russia. Sentimental Frederick William of Prussia wrote, "Good brother, friend, and ally of the heart and soul, we shall inflict no more damage than necessity compels. We always remember our former union and hope for its renewal."

For the Russian campaign Napoleon assembled the largest army he ever put into the field. It was composed of 200,000 French and 475,000 foreigners; the expeditionary force was to be composed of 400,000. There were German, Swiss, Italian, Dutch, Polish, and other contingents. It was called by its enemies "the army of twenty nations." The Russians, at the beginning of the campaign, were outnumbered nearly four to one.

The invasion of Russia began in early summer. Napoleon's first objective was Vilna. He knew that one Russian army was north of that point and another south of it; he planned to break their liason and defeat them one at a time. This plan failed. The Russian forces united and then retreated without offering battle. The imperial army advanced through country in which the villages had been burned and from which both people and provisions had been removed. They could not come to grips with the Russians, whose plan was to draw the invaders always farther on and to leave it to nature to defeat them. Cold and hunger were better protectors of Russia than all her armies.

After nearly two months of weary marching without a battle, the invaders came to Smolensk, a little more than halfway to Moscow. There was a battle there, but the Russians burned the town and escaped without serious loss. When Napoleon finally approached Moscow, he had lost more than a hundred and fifty thousand men by death or desertion; thousands of the foreign troops disappeared every day. The horses that drew the provision wagons had died; the soldiers had to find food as best they could.

Alexander decided to defend his capital. On the seventh of September, 1812, the battle of Borodino was fought. It was a frightfully bloody affair. The dead were piled up six or eight deep. The Russians finally retreated, but Napoleon's soldiers were too exhausted to pursue them. On the thirteenth the French marched into Moscow and found it deserted. Napoleon had believed that his occupation of "the holy city" would make the Czar sue for peace, but the Czar gave no indication of doing so. Emissaries sent by Napoleon were not even allowed to enter the Russian camp.

On the day after the occupation of Moscow a great fire destroyed most of the city. The French did not start that fire, but they were accused of it. Napoleon was called the new Attila. The Russian peasants, like those of Spain, were aroused to a fury of hatred for the invaders.

Napoleon originally planned to spend the winter in Moscow. In September he could not think of retreating. In October, however, he changed his mind. He decided that it would be better to march back. That was the most unfortunate decision the Emperor ever made. The retreat from Moscow is one of the great tragedies of history.

On the nineteenth of October the thousand-mile trek began. More than fifty days of bitter cold and cruel suffering lay ahead for those who survived, but hardly one in ten survived. When they left Moscow they had provisions for only fifteen days, and they were moving into country where provisions could not be found. Provision was certain only for the vast flocks of carrion crows that followed them. A bitter winter began before its time. The dreary landscape was lighted by a pale sun for only six hours each day. The nights were interminable and unendurable.

Nature was not the only enemy. Bands of Cossacks preyed upon the flanks of the retreating army, an army that soon became no more than a staggering mass of humanity dying of hunger and cold. The little meat they had became as hard as lumps of ice. They cut open dead horses with sabers and greedily ate the clotted blood. From dawn to dark they dragged their miserable bodies across snow and ice, and most of them were happier to lie down and die than to struggle on.

When November was nearly over they came to the Beresina, a wide river that they had expected to cross on the ice. To add to their misery there came a thaw that melted the ice, and there also came large forces of Russian cavalry that surrounded them. They could not fight. More than half of them had thrown away their guns.

In the crossing of the Beresina the great tragedy reached its peak. An heroic battalion of engineers sacrificed themselves to save their comrades. For a night and a day they worked in icy water to construct and to maintain two pontoon bridges, bridges that were swept by Russian fire, naked bridges from which thousands were pushed into the river by the rush of desperate men behind them, bridges that broke and had constantly to be repaired. The bridge-builders stayed at their posts until the end. Most of them died there, but they had saved the remnant of the army from annihilation.

The cold became more intense; thirty below zero. Nearly one-half of the pursuing Russians were frozen to death. On one of the last nights of the retreat, of a French division that numbered fifteen thousand at dusk only three thousand were alive at dawn.

On the sixteenth of December, 1812, the pathetic remnant of the invading army crossed the Niemen at Kovno. Three hundred and eighty thousand had gone from there; only eighteen thousand returned. Of the *Garde impériale,* once ninety thousand strong, only fifteen hundred remained alive. The glory of the Empire had been buried forever in the winter snow of invincible Russia.

CHAPTER NINETEEN

THE CAGING OF THE EAGLE

WITH RAW RECRUITS NAPOLEON DEFEATED PRUSSIAN AND RUSSIAN ARMIES,
BUT, WHEN AUSTRIA ALSO WENT AGAINST HIM, HE HAD TO RETREAT. HIS
DEFEAT AT LEIPZIG WAS FOLLOWED BY AN INVASION OF FRANCE. IN
MARCH, 1814, THE ALLIES ENTERED PARIS. LOUIS XVIII WAS DECLARED
KING. THE FRENCH PEOPLE HAD NOTHING TO SAY ABOUT THIS. NAPOLEON
ABDICATED AT FONTAINEBLEAU. THE ALLIES MADE THE MISTAKE OF
BELIEVING HIM. THE RETURN FROM ELBA.

FROM October 19 until December 5 Napoleon remained with the
wreck of his army. He marched with it. He was clad in heavy furs
and he had a horse, but to keep from freezing he had to walk more
often than he rode. For endless days and nights the ruin of his ambitions hemmed him in; for long weeks the miserable debris of the
Grande Armée surrounded him. Each day he saw the frozen bodies
of thousands whom he had led to inglorious death. He could not
escape this purgatory.

At Vilna on December 5 the Emperor received news that made him
leave the army and make full speed toward Paris. In October there
had been an intentional report of his death. A republican *coup d'état*
had been attempted. It had failed, but it had made clear that, if
Napoleon did die, his dynasty would die with him. No one had
thought of his infant son as his successor.

The Russian forces had suffered nearly as much as the French. It
became Prussia's turn to strike the next blow at the Empire. On the
last day of 1812 a Prussian army corps abandoned the French and
went over to the enemy. Stein, the Prussian minister, worked zeal-
ously to cement a new alliance with Russia. He assured the Czar that
Germany had become and would remain hostile to Napoleon. He declared that he would no longer seek to serve the special interests of
Prussia. "I have but one fatherland," he wrote. "A fatherland whose
name is Germany. Her various dynasties are meaningless to me save

as they may serve for the achievement of German unity. If that unity can be better achieved under Austrian rather than under Prussian government, so be it."

King Frederick William, hesitant and vacillating, found it difficult to approve the bold plans of Stein, Hardenberg, and Scharnhorst, hard to accept as a fact that his people could be aroused to overthrow Napoleon only by the concession of new rights. But each day brought increasing evidence that the new liberality of the government had aroused popular enthusiasm for nationality and for effort to throw off the Napoleonic yoke. Napoleon had brought the spirit of the Revolution into Germany. "Poets and philosophers made flaming appeals. . . . Fichte adjourned his university courses and gave rendezvous to his students upon the battlefield."

At the end of February, 1813, Frederick William made a treaty of alliance with the Czar and in March he declared war on France. Russian forces advanced into Germany to co-operate with the Prussians.

The greatly reduced French forces east of the Rhine assembled in Saxony, south of Berlin, under the command of Prince Eugène, Napoleon's stepson. Napoleon himself organized in France a new army of three hundred thousand young conscripts; later he had reason bitterly to regret that he did not recall the veterans who were in Spain. He needed the cavalry that was beyond the Pyrenees.

The fighting began in May, in Saxony. Prussian and Russian forces advanced westward across the Elbe. Napoleon defeated them at Lützen, and again at Bautzen, driving them back to the Oder, but his lack of cavalry permitted the enemy to retreat in good order.

The veteran Blucher commanded the Prussians. He had fought in the Seven Years' War; he was seventy-one, but he alone of the officers of the Allies had an ardor for combat like that of Napoleon's brilliant young generals. He alone refused to be discouraged after the defeat at Lützen. "So much blood shall not have been shed in vain," he cried. "I shall not retreat."

Austria remained aloof. She was in a position to determine the outcome; her aid might permit either side to win. Metternich, hesitant about commitment, proposed mediation. Napoleon's acceptance of this offer was a confession of weakness; he needed time in which to bring up his cavalry. An armistice was agreed upon. Hostilities were suspended from June 4 until August 10.

Historians have been unable to agree upon an interpretation of this armistice or of the subsequent negotiations. Some maintain that Austria proposed mediation merely to gain time for military preparation; that she had already decided to fight against France. Others maintain that Metternich was sincere; that he believed that alliance with Prussia and Russia might result in more harm to Austria than a continuation of the alliance with Napoleon. Austria feared Russian designs on Poland, and she feared even more the revolutionary tendencies which had developed in Prussia.

At Dresden on the twenty-sixth of June, 1813, Metternich had a memorable interview with Napoleon. He has left an account of it. Austria had proposed conditions of peace that were inacceptable to the Emperor.

"So you wish war," said Napoleon. "Very well, you shall have it. I defeated the Prussians at Lützen and the Russians at Bautzen. You shall have your turn. I give you rendezvous in Vienna."

Metternich replied, "The fate of Europe, its future as well as your own, depends upon Your Majesty. Between the aspirations of Europe and your desires there is an abyss. There is great need for peace. It can be had only by your withdrawal to the frontiers we have indicated. Today you can have peace; tomorrow it may be too late. The Emperor of Austria, my master, is guided only by his conscience; it is your turn, Sire, to consult your own."

Napoleon indicated that he was more interested in honor than in conscience. He said that he would dishonor himself if he yielded an inch of territory. "Evidently," Metternich responded, "Your Majesty and Europe cannot agree. You are lost, Sire. I felt that when I came. Now, upon leaving, I am sure of it."

On the next day Austria made a secret agreement with Prussia and Russia; she promised to fight with them against Napoleon unless he accepted by August 10 the terms of peace which had been proposed.

Napoleon remained obdurate. Despite the advice and desires of his weary and discouraged generals, despite the news that Wellington had entered Madrid, and despite the fact that the proposed terms left to France all her natural frontiers, he was determined to continue the war. He was confident that he could again defeat Prussia and Russia, and he believed that his father-in-law would not fight against him.

A "peace congress" was in session at Prague. France's representative, Caulaincourt, advised Napoleon to accept the terms proposed. But Napoleon would not agree to withdraw to the west of the Rhine and relinquish his control of Germany. On the day that the armistice was to end, the congress remained in session until midnight, hoping that a messenger might bring news at the last minute of Napoleon's acceptance of its terms; when midnight came and no message had arrived, it adjourned. Austria, through its secret agreement, became automatically at war with France. When the clocks of Prague struck twelve on the night of August 10, 1813, the *Grand Empire* ceased to exist.

Napoleon struck quickly, seeking to prevent concentration of the forces of his enemies. On the twenty-sixth of August he defeated an Austrian army at Dresden, but Blucher's Prussians defeated the French forces that were sent against them. Napoleon, greatly outnumbered, had to retreat westward from Dresden to Leipzig. There, in mid-October, the decisive battle was fought. For three days the Emperor with one hundred and fifty thousand men withstood the attack of twice that number. Shortage of munitions and the defection of German troops compelled a retreat across the Elster. A bridge was blown up before the crossing was completed. Twenty thousand French were captured.

Leipzig was the first great battle lost by Napoleon. There the Allies won all that the congress at Prague had asked for, and Napoleon lost more than a battle. He lost France. The defeat at Leipzig made an invasion of France certain, and almost certainly successful.

The end of October found Napoleon at Mainz on the Rhine. His army had been reduced to forty thousand. While the Allies were driving him out of Germany, Wellington drove the last of the French out of Spain. On the eighth of November English troops crossed the Bidassoa and advanced on Bayonne.

The Allies were hesitant about making a winter campaign in France.

Blucher and the Czar were for it, but Metternich advised delay. He wished for time in which to make the French people understand that invasion of their soil would be solely due to Napoleon's refusal to relinquish control of other people's soil. The news was spread that France might still have peace with preservation of her natural frontiers—the Rhine, the Alps, and the Pyrenees. Twenty thousand copies of a manifesto were circulated in France. "The allied powers," it stated, "do not make war against France, but only against that preponderance which, to the misfortune both of France and Europe, the Emperor Napoleon has for too long exercised beyond the limits of his own empire . . . The Allies confirm the extension of French territory beyond the limits that it ever had under its kings. . . ."

Metternich's plan was wise. The French people had little interest in fighting to preserve the *Grand Empire;* they preferred peace with the preservation of their natural frontiers. The legal representatives of the nation urged Napoleon to accept the terms the Allies offered. He refused to do so. When, subsequently, he felt compelled to do so, it was too late. The invasion had begun.

In the last week of 1813, three armies moved westward across the Rhine. By the first of February they had entered Champagne, three hundred thousand strong. They expected to reach Paris a week later. Napoleon, swift and unpredictable as he had been in his first Italian campaign, held them in check for two months.

Between the tenth and the thirteenth of February, 1814, Blucher's Prussians were beaten in four battles, one of them at Château-Thierry. An Austrian army commanded by Schwarzenberg approached Fontainebleau, but Napoleon compelled it to retreat to Troyes and then to Chaumont. The Emperor's genius never shone more brilliantly than in his defense of France. His failure to avert the invasion had been inexcusable, but when it came his resistance was magnificent. He very nearly compelled a complete retreat of the Allies; the Austrians and the Prussians were for giving up and going home; only the insistence of the Czar and the support of England induced them to continue hostilities.

Blucher advanced again and reached Meaux, less than thirty miles from Paris. When Napoleon approached, he retreated to the northeast and took up a position on the steep plateau of Laon. There he successfully resisted the French attacks. Compelled to leave the Prussians where they were, the Emperor hastened southward to stop a new advance by the Austrians. At Arcis-sur-Aube, on the twentieth of March, Schwarzenberg, outnumbering them four to one, compelled the French to retreat.

Napoleon, like Dumouriez in 1792, did not move west to defend Paris. He moved east, planning to cut the Allies' line of supplies and compel them to make an about-face. This bold plan came very close to success. The Allies united their forces at Chaumont and prepared to retreat. Then a letter to the Emperor was intercepted. It warned him that a strong royalist group was preparing to co-operate with the Allies if they were allowed to approach Paris. The intercepted letter made the Czar decide in favor of marching directly on the capital.

Unfortified Paris could not hope to make successful resistance. On the thirtieth of March its forty thousand miscellaneous defenders fought bravely, but on the thirty-first the Allies entered the city. Ten days earlier an Austrian army had occupied Lyon. Wellington was approaching Toulouse.

Talleyrand, disloyal to Napoleon but loyal to his conception of the best interests of France, gave his support to the movement for restoration of the Bourbons; since the son of Louis XVI was presumably dead, his brother, the Count of Provençe, was to become Louis XVIII. The Czar had many misgivings about that plan. He was unacquainted with the gentleman proposed for king, but he felt sure that any Bourbon would be unable to rule successfully over the new, the post-Revolution France. However, he had no alternative to propose. Talleyrand persuaded him that even a Louis XVIII would be preferable to a Napoleon II with Maria-Louisa as regent. As to Napoleon I, all were agreed that he should be compelled to abdicate. A proclamation declared that the Allies would no longer treat with Napoleon or any of his family. On the third of April the Senate decreed the dethronement of the Emperor.

Napoleon, rushing back from the east, had reached Fontainebleau with sixty thousand devoted followers. On the very day of his dethronement he made a brave speech to the veterans of the *Garde impériale*. He proposed to march on Paris, to drive out the Russians, and to crush the ungrateful royalists who had turned against him. *"Vive l'Empéreur,"* his faihful old soldiers cried. *"À Paris, à Paris!"* They would have gladly followed him anywhere, even to certain death.

The Emperor possessed the blind loyalty of his men, but the loyalty of his higher officers was less blind. Led by Ney, they bluntly told him that he would have to abdicate. On the fourth of April he did so in favor of his infant son, but that was not enough. On the sixth he was compelled to make a second abdication, relinquishing all claims to the throne by his family as well as himself. In his almost illegible handwriting he scrawled, "The allied powers having declared that the Emperor is the only obstacle to the re-establishment of the peace of Europe, the Emperor declares that he renounces for himself and for his heirs the thrones of France and of Italy, and that there is no sacrifice, even of life itself, that he is not prepared to make for France." On the same day, April 6, 1814, the Count of Provençe, a brother of Louis XVI, was declared by the Senate to be King of France as Louis XVIII; he had been baptized as Xavier-Stanislas. The exact fate of Louis XVII, the young son of Louis XVI, still remains somewhat a mystery.*

The Allies agreed that Napoleon should be allowed to keep the title of Emperor, and that he should have for his empire the tiny island of Elba which lies between Corsica and Italy. They also agreed that France should pay him a pension of two million francs a year.

On the twentieth of April, in the great court of the château, Napoleon said farewell to the heroic old soldiers of his *Garde*. Four hundred of them would not let him go without them; they insisted upon going with him to his island exile. There were no dry eyes at Fontainebleau that day.

---

* Louis-Charles de France, a handsome boy with beautiful, tragic eyes, was barely eight years old when, in August, 1792, he was imprisoned with his parents in the Temple. One week after his father's execution, on January 28, 1793, his uncle, the Count of Provençe, then in Belgium, issued a manifesto which declared little Louis-Charles to be king as Louis XVII; he was recognized as such by all who were loyal to the old order. The "official" record is that he died in the Temple in 1795, but many believed that another boy had been substituted for him, that he had been taken away, even that he had been taken to America. The claims of some of his alleged descendants were supported by influential men under the Second Empire, and as late as 1911.

The victorious Allies were no longer inclined to grant to France her natural frontiers. The Czar, master of the situation, remained in Paris throughout the spring months and determined the conditions of peace. France fared better than she might have fared had it not been spring, and had another than generous Alexander determined her fate. She had to surrender fifty-three fortified places in Germany, Italy, and Flanders that were still occupied by her troops, turn over thousands of cannon and fifty-three war vessels, and withdraw to her frontiers of 1792. By the Treaty of Paris of May 30, 1814, France lost not only all that Napoleon had gained; she lost almost all that the Revolution had gained.

Louis XVIII, a guest of England since 1807, could not come promptly to Paris. An attack of gout had him by the heels. April was nearly over when he landed at Calais. He was blissfully ignorant of the transformation his country had undergone in the twenty years of his absence. He believed in his God-given right to govern France, but in her effort to govern herself France had become a country to which he was a stranger. He expected to adjust her to his ideas rather than himself to hers. He scorned the red, white, and blue of the Revolution and restored the white banner of royalty. He would not accept the constitution that the Senate had prepared; if there had to be a constitution, he would make one himself.

The Czar, more skeptical than ever, stayed on in Paris to see that a constitution was actually produced. Early in June, an instrument called the *Charte constitutionelle* was promulgated. It provided for a government like that of England; there was to be a *Chambre des députés* and a *Chambre des Pairs* (peers). After that, the allied sovereigns and their armies left France. Everything considered, they had dealt with her gently.

The people were too weary of war to resist the restoration. There was apathetic acceptance of it. La Fayette, emerging from obscurity, made a ceremonial call and endorsed the new regime. Since he was as influential a spokesman for republican sentiment as was available, his approval helped. But the Czar had been right. It took the new King and his court only a few months to become obnoxious.

There was a flocking back to France by nobles who had been away for many years. They wore their old-fashioned clothes and put on their old-fashioned airs. These ghosts of Versailles lacked reality. At first they seemed to be more amusing than dangerous, but soon they showed their teeth.

The promises of liberal government made in the *Charte* were disregarded. The clergy held services of expiation for "the crimes of the Revolution." Censorship was imposed. For a time the University was closed. Experienced officers of the administration were replaced by inexperienced royalists. There was a breakdown of governmental efficiency. Talleyrand, the one minister who might have saved the situation, went to Vienna to represent France at the Congress which was to make the final liquidation of the *Grand Empire*.

Some of the nobles attempted to regain possession of the estates they had formerly owned. There were fights between the new proprietors and the old. In some localities the Church also sought repossession. The gravest threat to the new regime arose from its reorganization of the army. Thousands of officers with excellent records were discharged, and nobles were given high rank because of services in fighting *against* France. Carnot ridiculed the restoration in a publication of which more than a half-million copies were sold in a few weeks. Refusal to pay taxes became frequent.

It became evident that the new regime would be short-lived. It was hardly ten months old when two regiments revolted at Lille and Cambrai. They started to march on Paris. Suddenly there came news that stirred the nation as no other news could stir it. Napoleon had returned!

The island of Elba is five miles wide and less than fifteen miles long. To that tiny empire the dethroned Emperor seemed at first resigned. He interested himself in the setting out of mulberry trees and of grapevines. For months he seemed to have no other ambition than to live in peaceful retirement. But Louis XVIII was not wise enough to keep his predecessor content with that modest ambition. His family was not permitted to join him. The liberal pension that the Allies had prescribed was not paid. Napoleon lost interest in his mulberry trees.

Reports came to the island of the increasing unpopularity of the new

government, of the readiness of the army to revolt, and of the intention
of the Congress of Vienna to send Napoleon still farther away from
France. Abruptly the exiled Emperor decided to risk everything in a
desperate adventure.

On the first of March, 1815, Napoleon landed at *Golfe-Juan,* a tiny
fishing port behind the *Cap d'Antibes,* not far from Cannes. The
famous bathing beach of *Juan-les-Pins* lies just beyond it to the east.
There were but a few hundred men with him. All Europe was against
him, and yet all Europe trembled when it heard of the Corsican's
return. Such was the magic of the man that France gave her heart
again to him who had betrayed her. Months passed before the Allies,
concentrating all their forces and aided by good fortune, were able
again to defeat him. In the Hundred Days that lay between the land-
ing at *Golfe-Juan* and the battle of Waterloo, the fate of nations again
trembled in the balance.

Two proclamations had been sent from Elba into France. To the
people Napoleon said, "In my exile I have heard your lamentations.
You wish for restoration of the government of your choice. It alone
is legitimate. . . . I shall return to re-establish your rights and my
own." To the soldiers, "Tear down the flag which for twenty-five
years has been the flag of our enemies! Raise again the tricolor, the
flag of France and of victory! Our eagles shall carry it from belfry to
belfry, even to the towers of Notre Dame."

In his northward march Napoleon took the shortest way, avoiding
the valley of the Rhône where there were many royalists. He and his
few hundred men entered the Alps by way of Grasse, marching along
a military road that he had built. They call it now *la route Napoleon.*
Troops were sent south from Grenoble to arrest him. They had him at
their mercy. He advanced alone. When he had come where they could
hear him, he called out, "Soldiers, if there is one among you who
wishes to kill his Emperor, he may do so. Here I am." Then all of
them threw down their guns and rushed toward him, crying *"Vive
l'Empéreur!"*

The entry into Grenoble was triumphant. At Lyon Napoleon's
escort grew into an army. The people "acclaimed him madly." At
Auxerre, Ney, who had promised the King to deliver Napoleon in

irons, delivered himself up to Napoleon. On the nineteenth of March Louis XVIII fled to Flanders, and on the twentieth Napoleon entered the Tuileries.

The first political move of the restored Emperor recalled the days of the Revolution. He appealed to the passion of the mob. "The priests and the nobles," he declared, "have tried to restore the old feudal injustices. I shall restore justice. Those who would oppress you I shall hang from the lamp posts." He had discovered that the old hatred of priests and nobles was aflame again.

Napoleon made Carnot his chief minister, but he did not follow Carnot's advice. He tempered his initial liberalism, seeking to win bourgeois support. He said that he did not wish to become "king of a *Jacquerie.*" The new constitution that he published in April was no more liberal than the *Charte* of Louis XVIII. The first enthusiasm of the people waned. Old grievances were recalled. Reason began to encroach upon emotion. It became known that the Allies were planning a new offensive. Napoleon could count upon his old soldiers, but he could no longer count upon solid support by the people.

When the news of the return from Elba was brought to the Congress of Vienna, strong language was used by those who had argued against leaving Napoleon at liberty. Further study of maps and of frontier revisions was postponed. A new and ominous fact thrust the theorists into the background.

A fortnight after he had landed, the Allies declared that "Napoleon Bonaparte in violating his agreement has destroyed his only legal right to exist. By returning to France he has become an outlaw, a disturber of peace upon whom public vengeance is warranted."

Napoleon did his utmost to avoid war. He announced that he would accept all the conditions that the Allies had imposed upon France when they occupied Paris and that his only desire was to serve the cause of peace. He sent secret emissaries to the Czar and to his father-in-law, the Emperor of Austria. But his efforts were in vain. His former allies were convinced that he could not be trusted.

Less than a month after Napoleon had landed at *Golfe-Juan,* England, Austria, Prussia, and Russia again allied against him, pledging themselves to make no peace until he was once more in their power.

CHAPTER TWENTY

THE HUNDRED DAYS AND THE REIGN OF LOUIS XVIII

WHEN it became clear that war could not be avoided, Napoleon struck swiftly. He rallied the remnants of the *Grande Armée,* 124,000 in all, and marched north. Commanded by Wellington, an English army had landed at Antwerp, and a Prussian one, commanded by Blucher, was advancing from the Rhine to join the British in Flanders. Napoleon hoped to arrive in time to attack these two armies separately. United, they would outnumber him almost two to one.

On June 15, 1815, the French army entered Flanders. On the following day it fought the Prussians at Ligny and compelled their retreat. Napoleon sent General Grouchy with thirty thousand men to pursue them, and, at all costs, to prevent their juncture with the English. He himself marched toward Brussels where Wellington's officers were making merry, unwarned of his swift approach.

The village of Waterloo lies a few miles south of Brussels. Beyond it there rises a height of land called Mont-Saint-Jean. Wellington had previously decided to station his forces upon that height. When word came to Brussels that the French were approaching, the Iron Duke was in attendance at an officers' ball. Fortunately for him, his plans had been well made before. Despite alarm and confusion, he was able to establish his forces at the selected positions before the attack began. But it was not the advantage of position that saved him. What saved the English from defeat was the rain, the torrential rain that fell on the night of the seventeenth.

The French, marching through the night, reached the field of battle exhausted and drenched to the skin. The artillery was mired and the feet of the infantrymen were heavy with mud. The attack could not begin until the sun had begun to dry the ground. That delay enabled Prussian forces to arrive in time to save the day for the Allies. Having eluded Grouchy, they marched steadily toward Waterloo during the long morning wait that was fatal to the French.

Napoleon opened his attack a little before noon on Sunday, the eighteenth. For two hours Wellington's men withstood it. Then thirty thousand Prussians arrived and attacked the French right wing. It was necessary to use all the reserves to oppose the Prussians. That left only first-line troops with which to fight the English. They were not enough. Had Grouchy not gone astray the result would have been different.

All through the afternoon there was terrific fighting on the plateau Mont-Saint-Jean. Ten thousand cavalrymen followed Ney in a terrific uphill charge. They were thrown into disorder at the hollow way of Ohain, but Ney kept them moving forward. For hours they fought among the squares of British infantry without breaking them. Utterly exhausted, the survivors were compelled to withdraw.

Meanwhile the Prussians had been repulsed. The long summer day approached its end. At half-past seven, Napoleon, risking everything, played his last card. His *Garde impériale* charged again upon the English position. The deadly fire of the enemy repulsed them with great loss. Suddenly a second Prussian corps appeared and made a flank attack. That ended the battle. The exhausted French, under fire from two sides, retreated in disorder. They were pursued by Prussian cavalry all through the night.

But the survivors of the *Garde* would neither flee nor surrender. They formed themselves into squares. Hopelessly, desperately, they resisted both the Prussians and the English. Completely surrounded, they were called upon to surrender. Scornfully they refused. One of their officers retorted with a vulgarity that Victor Hugo has immortalized. They were true to their oath. "The *Garde* dies; it does not surrender."

It is said that Napoleon, when he saw that all was lost, drew his sword and attempted to rush into the thick of the fight, wishing to die with his *Garde*. Restrained by his generals, and saved from capture by the old soldiers who refused to surrender, he rode silently away. Not a shred of hope remained. The most amazing, the most fertile brain in the world could think of no new avenue of escape from complete defeat. At last he had been overcome by those forces which, disbelieving in them, he had left out of his reckoning. For years his magnificent abilities, and the technical perfections they created, prevailed over all resistance. But in the end it became evident that some men prefer freedom to order; that, even for security, they will not pay too dear a price.

The feeling of France for Napoleon was not like that of his old soldiers. There had been no national enthusiasm for his march into Flanders. Even had he won at Waterloo, he might not have maintained his mastery for long. Too many were against him. When he returned to Paris on the twenty-eighth of June, Fouché, master of intrigue, had already perfected plans for the second return of the Bourbons. The *Chambre des Représentants* demanded a new abdication of Napoleon and established a provisional government directed by Fouché. Finding that all had turned against him, Napoleon abdicated again in favor of the King of Rome, a pathetic favor to which no attention was paid. He made a little visit to Malmaison, guest there of Queen Hortense, his stepdaughter. Josephine was dead. He went from Malmaison to Rochefort.

It was decided to make no resistance to the second entry of the Allies into Paris. In the first days of July, 1815, what was left of the French military forces withdrew south of the Loire. An Anglo-Prussian army entered Paris, and Louis XVIII, eager to be back in the Tuileries, followed close upon its heels.

Fouché, who was as responsible as anyone for the execution of Louis XVI, became the right-hand man of the dead king's brother who succeeded to the throne. He and Talleyrand went to meet Louis XVIII at Saint Denis. Chateaubriand witnessed their arrival. Talleyrand entered, leaning on Fouché's arm; for Chateaubriand that was "vice" leaning on the arm of "crime"; he called it a *vision infernale*. Both had been leaders in the Revolution and ministers of the Empire; both knelt and swore fealty to the Bourbons whom they had helped dethrone.

Napoleon had hoped to sail from Rochefort for the United States. A blockading English squadron made that hope vain. Since even his own country had disowned him, it seemed best to throw himself upon the mercy of the English. He wrote to the Prince-Regent, "Your Royal Highness, attacked as I am by factions in my own country as well as by the Continental powers, my political career is ended . . . I place myself at the disposal of the British nation, asking its protection as the most powerful, the most constant, and the most generous of my enemies."

On the fifteenth of July the fallen Emperor was received on board the British ship *Bellerophon*. He was taken as a prisoner of war to the island of Saint-Helena, a thousand miles at sea off the coast of Africa. There he was allowed to live in a comfortable villa, but vigilant guard of him was never relaxed. There he died, May 5, 1821, at the age of fifty-two.

France would have been far better off had Napoleon remained among his mulberry trees on the island of Elba. The Hundred Days made the last act of the Emperor's career intensely dramatic. A "glorious" victory was all but won at the end of them, but when they were over their brief glory was quickly dissolved in new misery and misfortune.

After Waterloo, France was invaded by almost a million soldiers. There was no longer any inclination to treat the conquered country with respect or generosity. Whether truly at fault or not, France was to be punished for having permitted Napoleon to return to power. The Czar Alexander could no longer dictate moderation, even had he been so inclined. The Prussians favored systematic devastation. Blucher proposed to blow up the Vendôme column and the Jena bridge over the Seine. Only the strong opposition of Wellington and the Czar prevented the immediate annexation of Alsace and Lorraine by Prussia.

The Second Treaty of Paris was signed November 20, 1815. France lost Savoy. Her northeastern frontier was so modified that it became practically defenseless. She was required to pay an indemnity of seven hundred million francs, and for five years to maintain a foreign army of one hundred and fifty thousand within her frontiers. In 1815 France became smaller than she had been since the Revolution.

Napoleon caused a moral loss to France that far outweighed her material losses. His banishment to Saint-Helena could not repair that loss. The French people could not escape the stigma their Corsican Emperor had put upon them. When their republican idealism failed, when an economic and political breakdown threatened, in that moment of weakness they had chosen him for their leader. Hypnotized by his material successes, they appeared to accept his philosophy. Forgetting the humane ideals for which they had previously fought, his soldiers followed him with blind devotion upon a career of conquest and of plunder. It was not the true France that confided its destiny to Napoleon. It was a France that, discouraged by the failure of her humanitarian effort and seeing no other way, gave herself for a time into the keeping of the only one who seemed able to bring order out of chaos.

When France acclaimed Napoleon's achievements as First Consul, she had little thought of his subsequent career as Emperor. She did not see the danger. He never had his country's mandate for his conquests. His magnetism and his military genius so dazzled his soldiers that they ceased to reason. For them he could do no wrong. But there was another part of France that did not march with her armies, a part that Napoleon's police kept stifled and silent. The soul of France seemed to be dead; only her body marched, marched and ran joyously into battle, like trained dogs that run and bark for joy when their master sets them on the trail.

The people of Europe could not be aware of the stifled soul of France, but they were all too well aware of the brutal impact of her misguided body. They could not understand that the "Corsican ogre" was not a true Frenchman. They identified France with him, and no one could blame them for that. There are many who still confuse France with Napoleon. She still pays dearly for her seduction by a glory-seeking imperialist.

It was France that first in continental Europe broke the chains of absolutism and of tyranny, France that fought with heroic courage and enormous sacrifice to establish justice, liberty, and fraternity, France that was the pioneer in effort to improve the lot of the common man. It was of the French that Goethe wrote, "They brought friendship. They planted trees of liberty and promised justice to all. They opened our eyes to new and brighter prospects."

It was the France of 1792 about which Goethe wrote. The France of the Empire was not like that. The friend of humanity appeared to have become its enemy. The country that had fought first to make a better world could not be forgiven for her later sins, even when she was broken, prostrate, and at the mercy of her enemies. She paid very dearly for the evil turn that her great adventure took. Her trees of liberty bore seeds of hate. France had rendered immeasurable service to mankind, but a France beguiled by Napoleon reconstructed the inhuman system it had destroyed and imposed it upon others. In her years of "glory" she compelled a misunderstanding that still exists. It was not Europe that suffered most from Napoleon. It was France. Even today, because of him, the world finds it hard to believe that France is more interested in peace and justice than in glory.

The First Treaty of Paris, the one of May 30, 1814, provided for a Congress empowered to undo what Napoleon had done to the map of Europe. That Congress met in Vienna in November, 1814, and continued its deliberations until the following June. All the countries of Europe were represented. Austria spent more than forty million francs in lavish entertainment of the two hundred delegates. The principal figures were Metternich for Austria, Talleyrand for France, Wellington and Lord Castlereagh for England, Humboldt and Hardenberg for Prussia, and Nesselrode for Russia.

The four great powers had secretly agreed about some things before the Congress opened. They agreed that Belgium and Holland should be united into a single kingdom, the better to withstand France, and that northern Italy should be divided between Austria and Sardinia. But agreement stopped there and violent disagreement began, disagreement that almost led to war. Astute Talleyrand profited by this situation. Pretending to be neutral, he secretly encouraged each side against the other.

The Czar was keen to possess the Grand Duchy of Warsaw, formerly controlled by Prussia. He proposed that, in place of Warsaw, Saxony be given to Prussia and the King of Saxony deposed because he had been faithful to Napoleon. England was hostile to any such westward advance of the Russian frontier, and Austria did not care to have Prussia possess Saxony because that would enlarge her contact with Austrian Bohemia.

Talleyrand, for the sake of bargaining, asked for far more than he expected to get. He supported a principle of "legitimacy" that the Revolution had disavowed; "conquest does not confer sovereignty unless the legitimate sovereign cedes his rights to the conquered territory." It was in his interest to pose as a champion of monarchical rights; the allied sovereigns found it embarrassing to disregard a principle upon which their own sovereignty might rest.

Talleyrand asked, among other things, for the re-establishment of the Bourbons in Naples and for protection of the King of Saxony. By a secret treaty he made common cause with Austria and England to resist the Czar, thereby sabotaging the coalition of the Allies. The return of Napoleon complicated Talleyrand's task, but the Congress did not adjourn and the adroit minister of France went on plotting and planning all through the Hundred Days.

The Treaty of Vienna was signed on the ninth of June, 1815, nine days before the battle of Waterloo. Victory over Napoleon was assumed. Not since the Treaty of Westphalia in 1648 at the end of the Thirty Years' War had there been another treaty that so extensively modified the map of Europe. Russia gained the larger part of Poland, Prussia gained most of the left bank of the Rhine, and Austria was extended into Italy, including Lombardy and Venice in her domain. Spain and Portugal returned to their previous status. Switzerland was enlarged and her neutrality guaranteed. The kingdom of Sardinia was re-established; it included as outlying territory Nice, Piedmont, Genoa, and Savoy, touching Switzerland on the north and France on the west. Norway, formerly Danish, was given to Sweden; two German duchies were given to the King of Denmark as compensation for his loss of Norway. England kept all the colonies that she had won. She remained mistress of the seas and she succeeded in restoring that equilibrium on the Continent upon which her security and prosperity depended. It was England that profited most by the destruction of the Napoleonic empire.

The Congress of Vienna was guided by two principal considerations. First, to re-apportion the areas that Napoleon had conquered in such manner that an equality of national strength should be maintained among the major powers. Second, to strengthen the states that bordered France so that she should be effectually held in check. The rights of peoples to determine their own political status was given no consideration. It was a definite return to the *ancien régime*.

The German patriots were especially disillusioned. They had been aroused to fight in 1813 by hope of a free and united Germany. Austria, Russia, and England prevented German union, and the Congress was unanimously opposed to any enlargement of political freedom. Metternich suggested that enlargement of interest in art and music would tend to keep people's minds off of politics. The reaction to a harsh absolutism was inevitable. The sovereigns whom the Revolution and Napoleon had terrified planned henceforward to keep the people in more rigid subjection than ever.

Murat, who ruled as King of Naples, tried to come to terms with the Allies in 1813. He had no scruples about deserting the cause of his brother-in-law who had made him a king, when he thought that cause was lost. During the Hundred Days, he attempted to enlarge his kingdom by an invasion of the States of the Church; he had a dream of conquering all Italy. The Austrians defeated him. He fled from Naples, disguised as a sailor. Later, attempting to imitate Napoleon, he returned. On October 13, 1815, he was captured and shot. The Bourbons were restored to the throne which the adventurous cavalryman had occupied in the great days of the Empire.

Louis XVIII was a heavy gentleman so greatly afflicted with gout that he could hardly walk without assistance. He was chiefly interested in etiquette and genealogy. Affairs of state he left to his ministers. One of them said, "To make a report to the King is of no more advantage than to make it to the figure of a saint in its niche. I merely present papers for his signature. He signs them all without question. The only annoyance is that he takes so long to write his name."

To his ineptitude for government the King added a belief in absolutism and divine right that his fellow countrymen had long since outgrown. France would not have been submissive to his rule if she had not been compelled to be. The army of occupation was there to sustain the figurehead whom the Allies had placed on the throne.

Louis XVIII was sixty years old when, on the eighth of July, 1815, he entered the Tuileries for the second time as king; Versailles with its painful memories had been abandoned as a royal residence. He was to reign until his death on the sixth of September, 1824.

The legal basis of the new government was the *Charte constitutionelle* of 1814; it was called a charter rather than a constitution in order to suggest that it was granted by the King, and not wrested from him. Louis XVIII stuck to the medieval theory of monarchy which France had long since discarded. In the preamble to the *Charte,* he declared that, "All authority resides in the person of the King. Our first duty to our people is, in their own interest, to defend the rights and prerogatives of the crown. . . . It is in free exercise of our royal authority that we have granted the *Charte."* The King stated that his awareness of human progress and "illumination" justified the granting of the *Charte,* but he did not believe that the people were sufficiently illuminated to direct their own destiny. There was no concession to the principle of the sovereignty of the people, no suggestion that the right of a king to govern derived from the consent of those governed; for Louis XVIII that was still a God-given right. His royal power remained absolute except for concessions specifically granted.

The equality of all before the law was recognized. There were no restrictions in eligibility to civil and military positions. Individual liberty was guaranteed. The Napoleonic civil code was preserved and representatives of the nation were to be allowed to "collaborate" in the making of new laws. That much remained of what the Revolution had gained. But there were reactionary restrictions about religion and about freedom of expression. Catholicism was made the religion of the state, and publications were to be rigidly controlled. The centralization of authority that the Consulate had developed was preserved.

Suffrage was limited to those over thirty who paid at least three hundred francs in taxes and membership in the elective *Chambre des députés* was limited to those over forty who paid at least a thousand francs. The *Pairs de France,* corresponding to the English House of Lords, was a nonelective and hereditary body to which the King made appointments without restriction as to number. Participation in the making of new laws was thus limited to those who were either rich or noble, and even they did not have the right to propose legislation; they could merely discuss measures proposed by the King; no amendment could be made without his consent.

Louis XVIII, despite his many shortcomings, was far more liberal and moderate than his brother Charles, the Count of Artois, who was to succeed him. He planned to be patient with his misguided people who had gone astray. "It is necessary," he said, "to nationalize the royalty and to 'royalize' the nation." He had a naïve belief that people might return to their ancient love for their king, that they might believe again that monarchy was ordained of God. Surely they had had bitter experience with the evils of democracy!

France had to find herself again. Under Napoleon she had lost her normal consciousness. She slowly awakened from the anesthesia of the Empire and found herself under the rule of a government about whose establishment she had had nothing to say. The Allies had imposed that government. The Revolution had made ruthless destruction of royalty and nobility; France had thought never to see their like again. But the First Republic, the fruit of the Revolution, had collapsed in the debris of its dreams. The Empire, built on the ruins of the republican experiment, had achieved an amazing success that numbed the people by its brilliance. But it too failed, and its failure left France weaker than she had been for centuries. Now, unasked and undesired, the Bourbons were back and the nobles with them! What could France do? In what could she believe? There were those who believed that everything had been tried and that nothing had succeeded. There was great apathy.

Napoleon had destroyed the political parties. There were many intriguers, but no parties. These had to form themselves again. But a party cannot be formed without a program, a program that can command a following. In 1815 there was no program except that of the uninvited government.

The political theorists had been silenced by Napoleon until they had lost their tongues. The republicans had not even rebuked La Fayette for his formal acquiescence in the restoration. Acquiescence was the order of the day. The spirit of republicanism, if not dead, was dormant.

The country had never been completely won either by the Republic or the Empire. Old soldiers glorified the Empire and created a legend about Napoleon wherever they went; that led to the Napoleonic restoration in 1851. Others talked of the Utopia that the Revolution had nearly won and turned thought toward a new trial of republicanism. France might turn either to the right or to the left, but only new events or new injustices would determine the direction of that turning. There was moral inertia. The workers were oppressed. They were not allowed to organize, they were required to work more than twelve hours a day, and they were miserably paid. The Continental blockade had ceased, but the industries were protected by high tariffs. The economic life of the nation was largely controlled by a small group of bourgeois industrialists. The cost of living rose. The peasants, more prosperous, but as ignorant as ever, remained docile. They were largely controlled by the *curés,* and, to the *curés,* Louis XVIII was a great relief after Napoleon.

News traveled slowly, and ideas, in this period, hardly traveled at all. The post-coaches made less than five miles an hour, and they were the fastest; they could carry but four passengers. Only one *commune* out of twenty boasted a post office. It took five days to go from Bordeaux to Paris. Newspapers were few, small, and very dear; advertising in them was unknown; they were not allowed to discuss politics or in any way to criticize the government. Usually several people combined to subscribe to a paper that one read aloud to the others; the reading of it was a social occasion; its moral precepts and its literary comments were well calculated to induce mental stupor; provincial ladies wearing the new leg-of-mutton sleeves were frightfully bored at the reading parties. Opportunity for political education existed only for the rich. The intellectual life had become mediocre.

Talleyrand and Fouché, expert schemers, proved to be poor executives. The King kept them in his cabinet for less than three months.

In September, 1815, the Duke of Richelieu, an honest man, became prime minister, but the real leader of the government from 1816 to 1820 was the young and handsome Count Decazes for whom the King had a great affection.

Immediately after Waterloo, royalists in certain parts of the country took bloody vengeance upon "Bonapartists." Two hundred were massacred in Marseille and even more at Avignon. Old religious feuds were revived. This was called the White Terror. It had an influence upon the election that was held in August. The *Chambre des députés* that was elected was "more royalist than the King."

Chateaubriand was one of the leaders in the demand for punishment of those who had supported Napoleon in the Hundred Days. The *députés* echoed that demand and the government was not strong enough to resist it. Sixteen generals were condemned to death. The most illustrious of them was Ney. His statue at the *Carrefour de l'Observatoire* in Paris marks the spot where this greatest of the Emperor's lieutenants was shot. Carnot and the famous painter David were exiled for life.

The leaders of the vengeance movement formed the first of the new parties, the Ultraroyalists. The Count of Artois, the King's brother, was its leader. The clergy were gradually induced to support this party. Its ambition was to destroy the *Charte* and to return to the days of unrestrained absolutism. It controlled the *Chambre des députés* and violently opposed the liberal policies of the government. The ministry realized the danger. Advised to do so by the Czar, Louis XVIII dissolved the *Chambre* whose too great zeal for reaction threatened to bring on disaster.

The Constitutional party became a rival of the Ultraroyalists. Richelieu, Decazes, and the historian Guizot were leaders of it. Their program was simple: opposition to modification of the *Charte* and honest enforcement of it. The Constitutionalists obtained a majority in the *Chambre* that was elected in October, 1816. This victory of the moderates enabled Decazes and his colleagues to correct many abuses. There was notable success in meeting the financial difficulties.

In 1818 a third party began its growth, a liberal party called the

Independents. The White Terror, the execution of the generals, and other abuses reacted against the Ultraroyalists and made this third party possible. La Fayette was identified with it. It was frankly hostile to the Bourbons and to the royalist clergy, among whom the returned Jesuits had become influential. In 1818 the Independents elected twenty-five *députés;* in 1819, forty-five. It gave promise of becoming an opposition party strong enough usefully to serve the interests of the country.

A law of 1819 lightened the restraints on the press. New and more liberal papers appeared. The country was moving in the direction of greater freedom and more justice when suddenly a political assassination caused a violent reaction.

The Duke of Berry was a nephew of the King. Only his father, the Count of Artois, and a childless older brother stood between him and succession to the throne. There was reason to believe that the Bourbon dynasty would become extinct if the young Duke died before he had a son. That is what the workman Louvel thought. On the thirteenth of February, 1820, while the Duke was escorting his wife from the door of the Opera to her carriage, he was fatally stabbed by Louvel. The assassination failed of its purpose because the Duchess of Berry soon gave birth to a son who became the Duke of Bordeaux.

The Ultraroyalists held Decazes responsible for the death of the Duke. It was claimed, even by Chateaubriand, that the liberal policies of the government had armed the assassin! Such pressure was brought to bear upon Louis XVIII that he reluctantly dismissed his best minister.

The fall of Decazes ended the liberal period of the Bourbon restoration. From 1820 until his death in 1824, the King did not attempt to oppose his Ultraroyalist brother. The Independents were compelled to bow to the storm. The reaction was strengthened by the discovery of military plots to overthrow the government. Liberty of the press and of the individual was suspended. Villèle, an able financier, became prime minister. He yielded to the control of the reactionaries.

When Louis XVIII died, September 6, 1824, France was in a state of repression, injustice, and hardship that could not long endure.

Summary of Chapters Nine to Twenty

The course of history is erratic. The evolution of human society may make little advance for centuries, and then suddenly move by leaps and bounds. There come times when fundamental changes are crowded into a single generation. In the twenty-six years between 1789 and 1815 France knew such a period. It was not France alone that knew it. She was but the center of the stage on which, in those eventful years, there was played a drama that profoundly affected civilized society throughout the western world.

The Revolution caused the breakdown of an order that had existed for a thousand years. Men became transformed. It was as though they had found a new world. When the forces of oppression were overthrown, the ashes of sullen submission were replaced by the fire of a passionate hope. The new freedom, more intoxicating than wine, led foolish men to frenzy, a frenzy that drove them to blind destruction, destruction of all that represented the old oppressive order or held a threat of its re-establishment. The prudent men responsible for the procedures that led to the Revolution lost control. The Terror came, and, after it, came chaos.

France proved the ardor of her new spirit in defeating the armies sent against her, she proved the sincerity for a time of her idealism and the greatness of her courage, but she also proved that she was not yet able to make a success of democratic government.

A dictator arose. France welcomed him because he defeated her enemies and brought order out of confusion. The people did not see in him at first the tyrant. They believed that the Corsican was one of themselves, the needed leader who would create an order in which the rights for which they had fought would not be lost. But Napoleon did not believe in preservation of those rights. For him the order that he established was but a framework for the power and glory that he coveted. For a time his genius made Frenchmen believe that they too cared more for power and glory than for freedom. But men could not be for long content with the order that a tyrant imposed. Gradually it was discovered that glory was a poor substitute for freedom, and that an emperor could be as ruthless as a king in the suppression of human rights. The downfall of Napoleon was as welcome to many of the French as it was to the Allies.

The American Revolution helped France to win in her struggle with England, and France helped the Americans. The United States failed to keep its promise not to make a separate peace; that led to complications. The Treaty of Versailles of 1783. France regained lost prestige as a world power, but her internal situation did not improve.

Bankruptcy compelled the King to call a meeting of the States-General in 1789. It met at Versailles, May 5. The Oath of the Tennis Court was taken, June 20. The Bastille fell, July 14. The flight of the nobles began. The King went to Paris and approved the new order, July 17. A mob invaded Versailles and brought the royal family to Paris, October 6.

The flight that ended at Varennes, June 20, 1791. On September 14 the King swore to maintain the Constitution, but he did not keep his word; he sought to bring France into war so that he might regain his lost power.

On August 10, 1792, the palace of the Tuileries was attacked, six hundred of the Swiss guard were killed, and the royal family became prisoners. An invading Prussian army was defeated at Valmy, September 20. In that same month France elected the *Convention* which was to be her provisional governing body. The extremists *(Montagnards)*, led by Robespierre, Marat, and Danton, gained control of the *Convention*.

Proof of the treason of Louis XVI was discovered; he was executed, January 21, 1793. The Terror began. On July 14 Marat was stabbed by Charlotte Corday. Danton was executed, April 5, 1794. Then Robespierre became supreme. Between March, 1793, and July, 1794, about three thousand were executed in Paris and fifteen thousand in the provinces. July 28, 1794, Robespierre was executed; then the Terror ended.

Victories by the Revolutionary armies led to the temporary annexation of Nice, Savoy, Belgium, and the left bank of the Rhine. England, under Pitt, took the lead in the coalition that almost continuously opposed France until the final defeat of Napoleon in 1815. In July,

1793, the English captured Toulon. Spanish and Austrian forces entered France. Lazare Carnot organized armies that young generals led to victories. In 1794 the Austrians were defeated in the battle of Fleurus. In 1795 Prussia, Spain, and Holland made peace with France.

The *Convention,* attacked on October 8, 1795, was saved by the ability of a young officer named Napoleon Bonaparte. In that same month the *Convention,* having established a new form of government, was replaced by the *Directoire.*

Napoleon was sent to conduct a campaign in Italy against the Austrians. After brilliant victories, he compelled Austria to make the Treaty of Campo-Formio, October 17, 1797; Belgium and Milan became French possessions and part of northern Italy a French dependency.

In May, 1798, Napoleon led an expedition to Egypt which failed. He returned to France, October 9, 1799. On November 10 occurred the *coup d'état* which made him First Consul; with that his dictatorship began.

On June 14, 1800, Napoleon defeated the Austrians at Marengo in Italy. Late in that year, French forces approached Vienna. On February 9, 1801, the Treaty of Lunéville was signed; it recognized French control of Holland, Switzerland, and northern Italy.

In March, 1802, peace was made with England by the Treaty of Amiens, but it endured for only a year. Napoleon prepared to invade England, but, in August, 1805, he was compelled to turn eastward and to fight Austria and Russia. He won a series of brilliant victories, the most notable one being that of Austerlitz, December 2. On October 20, Nelson had crushingly defeated the French fleet in the battle of Trafalgar. England's support induced Prussia and Russia to renew hostilities against Napoleon. In 1806 he defeated Prussia in a quick campaign, but it took six months to subdue the Russians.

In July, 1807, Napoleon made a treaty of alliance with Czar Alexander, the Treaty of Tilsit. At that time his control of western Europe extended to the Russian frontier. He inaugurated the Continental Blockade against England. In 1808 he made his brother Joseph King of Spain; his intervention there marked the beginning of his downfall.

In 1809 Austria renewed the struggle. Early in July Napoleon won the battle of Wagram, near Vienna. In the fall of that year he appeared to be more powerful than ever, but discontent with his rule was steadily increasing. In December he divorced Josephine. In April, 1810, he married Maria-Louisa, a Hapsburg princess from Vienna. Except for Spain, there was peace until 1812.

In June, 1812, Napoleon and Czar Alexander went to war on account of disagreement about Poland. Austria and Prussia, conquered by Napoleon, secretly sympathized with Russia. The French invasion of Russia ended in the tragic retreat from Moscow. Prussia struck at Napoleon's weakened forces. When he would not agree to withdraw to France's natural frontiers, Austria and Russia joined Prussia in a campaign against him.

In the last week of 1813 France was invaded. Napoleon made a brilliant defense, but in March, 1814, the Allies entered Paris. In April Napoleon was compelled to abdicate and to retire to the island of Elba. The eldest brother of Louis XVI was declared king as Louis XVIII. A congress in which all the Powers of Europe were represented was in session in Vienna from November, 1814, to June, 1815; the Treaty of Vienna remade the map of Europe.

Napoleon, violating his agreement, returned to France, March 1, 1815. The Hundred Days followed. Defeated at Waterloo, June 18, he returned to Paris; he surrendered to the British at Rochefort on July 3. He died on Saint-Helena, May 5, 1821, at the age of fifty-two.

The forces of the Allies entered Paris; Louis XVIII was re-established on the throne and a treaty was made whereby France became smaller than she had been even before the Revolution; she lost all that Napoleon had gained and more besides.

The Holy Alliance, conceived by Czar Alexander, came into existence in 1815; its purpose was to maintain the conditions of the Treaty of Vienna and to assure peace in Europe. However, the nations that entered into the Alliance could not agree about matters that involved intervention; the Alliance was short-lived.

Louis XVIII reigned from 1815 to 1824 over a broken and apathetic nation whose king had been imposed upon it.

CHAPTER TWENTY-ONE

CHARLES X AND LOUIS-PHILIPPE

THE HOLY ALLIANCE. ANOTHER UNJUSTIFIABLE FRENCH INTERVENTION IN
SPAIN. THE JULY REVOLUTION. THE REPUBLICANS WERE TRICKED OUT OF
THE FRUITS OF THEIR VICTORY AND A NEW KING WAS IMPOSED UPON THE
PEOPLE. INSTALLATION OF LOUIS-PHILIPPE. LIBERAL MODIFICATION OF THE
CHARTE. THE BOURGEOIS KING WAS A PACIFIST WHO CARRIED AN UM-
BRELLA. THE BEGINNING OF THE *ENTENTE CORDIALE* WITH ENGLAND.
BELGIUM WON HER INDEPENDENCE.

NAPOLEON's effect upon Europe did not end with Waterloo. He
became a prisoner upon a lonely island, a thousand miles at sea, but
the ideas he had set in motion could not be imprisoned. They
marched on.

Europe had seen the defeat of her most formidable troops by the
untrained soldiers of the French Revolution. She had seen an obscure
Corsican lead a ragged army to victory over proud Austria. She had
seen that same Corsican humiliate all her monarchs and become, for
a time, their master. Imperial though he came to be, he had risen
from the people and represented their revolt and triumph. His victorious armies carried revolutionary ideas in their wake. Throughout
western Europe a spirit of revolt against absolutism had been aroused.
The monarchs whom Napoleon had humiliated found it difficult to
regain their composure.

An immediate aftermath of Waterloo was an effort rigidly to suppress all that recalled the dominance of the Empire. Royal authority
became more severe than ever; censorship was rigidly enforced and the
state prisons became crowded with new prisoners. In Rome vaccina-
tion was forbidden and the street lamps were destroyed because the
French had introduced them! In Spain, Ferdinand VII, whom Napoleon had confined at Valençay in France, celebrated his restoration
by re-establishment of the Inquisition. The reactionary policy of the
monarchs served but to strengthen liberal aspirations. The demands
for constitutional restraints of royal authority increased. There was

an outbreak of conspiracies to overthrow oppressive governments.

The monarchs and their ministers made common cause against the tendency to rebellion. Czar Alexander was the leader in the formation of what was called the Holy Alliance. Mystical and increasingly unstable, Alexander dreamed of using religion as a means for securing peace, and as a justification for absolutism. He prepared an elaborate document to which he, the King of Prussia, and the Emperor of Austria affixed their signatures. It stated: "In conformity with the Holy Scriptures, which direct all men to act as brothers, the three monarchs declare themselves united in an indissoluble fraternity, and pledge themselves to mutual aid. Regarding themselves as the fathers of their subjects, they will act toward them in the spirit of family and fraternity. United in Christianity, the three monarchs regard themselves delegated by God to govern three branches of the same family."

The other powers endorsed this fantastic document, but did not take it seriously. Castlereagh called it sublime stupidity, and Metternich said it was meaningless and sonorous.

The Holy Alliance, as conceived by Alexander, came into existence September 26, 1815. The original document upon which it was founded may have been almost meaningless, but it transferred its name to a pact signed by the Allies two months later that was full of meaning. That pact was a definite commitment to co-operate in maintenance of the map of Europe as it had been drawn at Vienna, and to hold conferences from time to time "to examine measures judged salutary for the continuance of peace and prosperity." Castlereagh was the author of this pact. His object was to prevent developments in Europe which would be unfavorable to England. The pact was used later as justification for intervention to suppress liberal movements wherever they developed, but Castlereagh himself was opposed to intervention.

From 1815 to 1830 Metternich was the most influential statesman in Europe. Devoted to absolutism, he considered the religious and fraternal pretentions of the Czar ridiculous nonsense. Democratic tendencies were abhorrent to him. He favored intervention to suppress them—whenever such intervention did not conflict with the interests of Austria.

The first Congress of the Allies called for by their new pact was held at Aix-la-Chapelle in 1818. The Czar urged that the Holy Alliance co-operate with the King of Spain in suppressing the revolt of the Spanish colonies in South America. Castlereagh and Metternich, as practical men, successfully opposed this project.

France having paid the indemnity imposed by the Allies, the Congress agreed that the army of occupation should be withdrawn from French territory. France was even invited to become a member of the Congress, but there was a secret agreement to intervene in case of developments in France that might seem to threaten the peace and security of her neighbors.

There was much discontent in Germany. Disillusioned Germans found themselves without any more political liberty than they had had under the Holy Roman Empire. Metternich co-operated with the King of Prussia in suppressing German liberal tendencies. The movement for national unity was effectively held in check, but constitutions were granted by the princes of Saxony, Bavaria, Baden, and Wurtemburg.

In Spain there was a military revolt. Ferdinand VII was compelled in 1820 to re-establish and to swear allegiance to the constitution of 1812 that he had suppressed. In Italy another revolt was led by the *Carbonari,* a society so-called because its first secret meetings were held in the woods in the huts of charcoal burners. Ferdinand of Naples was compelled to grant a constitution like that of Spain; he swore to support it and publicly prayed that "God should strike his head with the lightning of His vengeance if he ever violated his oath." Both the Ferdinands were liars. The Spanish one appealed to the Czar to intervene; the other one appealed to Metternich.

An Austrian army defeated the liberal forces of Naples, and, a little later, suppressed a similar revolt in Piedmont. In both cases the leaders of the liberal movement were either executed or thrust into dungeons.

In 1822 the Congress of the Holy Alliance met at Verona. The Spanish situation had become acute. The Czar was all for intervention, but Canning, who had become prime minister of England after Castlereagh's death, was opposed to intervention anywhere. Chateaubriand was one of the representatives of France. Believing that the prestige of France and of the Bourbons would be enhanced thereby, he sided with the Czar against England. Intervention was decided upon, and France was to be the intervener.

There was violent opposition in Paris to the project of intervention. In the *Chambre des députés* it was recalled that foreign intervention had led to the execution of Louis XVI and the Terror. The Ultra-royalists argued that it was the duty of France to keep the descendants of Henri IV upon the throne of Spain and thus "to preserve this fair kingdom from ruin." The Ultraroyalists had their way. In April of 1823 a French army of one hundred thousand invaded Spain and defeated the forces of the liberals. Ferdinand promised to grant amnesty to those who had fought for constitutional government, but he did not do so. After the French had left, there was a massacre of those who had opposed him.

The intervention in Spain led to disruption of the Holy Alliance. England would have no more to do with it. Canning had no sympathy with the idea of policing Europe, and the Czar and Metternich soon came into disagreement over a war that developed between Greece and Turkey.

Charles X, more than any of the other Bourbons, had "learned nothing and forgotten nothing." It was his boast that he had not changed. The fall of the Bastille, the Revolution, the Empire—all that meant nothing to him. When he became king at sixty-eight in 1824 he was no less blind to reality than he had been at thirty-three in 1789. He was more affable than Louis XVIII, but less intelligent. Entirely immune to new ideas, he re-established so far as he could the *ancien régime* to the last detail of etiquette, ceremony, frivolity, and seduction. His coronation at Reims was a revival of ancient flubdub-bery that the nation had all but forgotten.

Even before the death of his brother, Charles and his party succeeded in reactionary modification of the election law. In each *département* the top fourth of the *électeurs* were to form a *collège;* these *collèges* were to elect 172 of the 430 *députés;* members of them could also vote for the other 258. This gave a double vote to the rich, and increased the majority of the royalists in the *Chambre;* under the new law only eighty liberal *députés* were elected. New restraints were placed upon the freedom of the press and censorship was re-established.

Deprived of all legal means of correcting abuses, young liberals plotted to overthrow the reactionary dynasty that had been imposed by the Allies. In imitation of the *Carbonari* of Italy, and even taking its name, a vast secret society, the *Charbonnerie,* rapidly developed. Its avowed aims were to give to the nation an opportunity to choose its own form of government, and to prevent that government from depriving the people of power to change it. There was to be no repetition of the nation's experience with Napoleon.

The *Charbonnerie* gained ground among the young intellectuals and in the army. It attained a membership of forty thousand. Its secrecy was a source of weakness as well as of strength. The majority of the people would have been actively sympathetic with it had its true aims been known. As it was, the secret police were able to thwart its insurrectional movements before they gained headway. Military revolts failed at Belfort, Toulon, Saumur, and Colmar. The *Quatre sergents de La Rochelle* have become legendary. They were four heroic young men who suffered death rather than reveal the names of those who stood high in the *Charbonnerie.* One of those names was La Fayette. The old Marquis might have saved the sergeants and even made a success of the movement had he dared come into the open.

The destruction of the *Charbonnerie* was followed by new repressive measures. When the new reign began the Ultraroyalists controlled all but fifteen of the *députés.* Their tenure had been extended to seven years. The University was placed under the control of the Church, the courses given by Guizot and other liberal professors were suspended, and the *Ecole Normale* was closed. A law of sacrilege was passed. The Church became a partner in the return to repression.

In 1825 the *Chambre* voted that 650,000,000 francs should be raised by the government and paid to the *émigrés* as indemnification for their properties that had been seized and sold. That caused depreciation of the *rentes* (government bonds). The *députés* also voted in favor of changing the law of equality of inheritance, and of suppressing political newspapers. The *Chambre des Pairs,* realizing the danger of these measures, prevented their enactment. Public opinion had become definitely hostile to the government. At a military review in 1827 the *Garde nationale* jeered the ministers, but the King still failed to realize the thinness of the ice on which he was skating.

The liberals had gained a valuable ally in 1824; Chateaubriand, dismissed as foreign minister, became one of them. He made a bitter literary campaign against Villèle whom the King had retained in office. An important group of *députés* and peers followed Chateaubriand's lead. There also developed a split in the Church party on account of the increased influence of the unpopular Jesuits. In August of 1827, Guizot led in the formation of a society for liberal propaganda which had a great success. Villèle thought to strengthen the perilous position of his government by dissolving the *Chambre* and calling for a new election, but such was the activity of Guizot's society that the government lost the election; the charge of "jesuitism" helped to defeat it. The liberals controlled the new *Chambre*. Villèle resigned.

The King replaced Villèle by Martignac. This new minister excluded the Jesuits from the schools, but that measure of appeasement did not suffice; he was defeated on other measures and the King dismissed him. Charles X then threw away his last chance to survive by appointing as Martignac's successor one of the most *ultra* of the Ultra-royalists.

The Prince of Polignac, son of Marie Antoinette's closest friend, had spent his youth as an *émigré* and had fought against France. He rivaled the King in inability to understand the new spirit of his country. Medieval in religion as well as in politics, he believed that he was guided by the Holy Virgin.

The *députés* reassembled in March, 1830. The King declared to them: "If obstacles are placed in the way of my government I shall know how to surmount them. I shall maintain peace, confident of the love that the French people have always had for their king." In a prepared statement, a majority of the *Chambre* responded, "The *Charte* makes our intervention a sacred right. . . . It makes agreement between your government and a majority of the representatives of the people indispensable. . . . Sire, our loyalty and our devotion compel us to state that such agreement does not exist." Thereupon the King dismissed the *députés*.

Polignac hoped to win popularity for his government by a firm foreign policy. Discord having developed among the Allies, he planned to abrogate the Treaty of Paris of 1815 and to regain the frontier of the Rhine. He failed in that but, by an expedition in the summer of 1830, he succeeded in winning Algiers. But Algiers did not win him more votes. A new election increased the majority of the liberals. Many were returned to the *Chambre* with a mandate to make an end of the Bourbons.

Even conservative old Talleyrand believed that only a change of dynasty could prevent another revolution and a return to republicanism. To him and to some other influential gentlemen it seemed desirable to try to place on the throne the fifty-seven-year-old Duke of Orléans whose loyalty to the Revolution would assure him of a certain popularity. Thiers, a young writer whose *History of the Revolution* had had a great success, directed propaganda that was favorable to the Duke.

The King would make no concessions. "Concessions," he said, "cost Louis XVI his head. I had rather ride on a horse into battle than in a cart to the guillotine." The *Charte* gave to the crown the right to make "decrees necessary for the execution of laws, and for the safety of the state." On the twenty-sixth of July, 1830, the King, abusing that right, issued four decrees, two of which were flagrant violations of the *Charte*. One of them ordered suppression of the liberal papers. That was enough to start the fighting.

On the morning of the twenty-seventh, the liberal papers appeared in defiance of the decree against them. The narrow streets were barricaded. The people of Paris rose again to fight for their rights. The King was hunting at Saint-Cloud. He had said that "one military helmet on a tower of Notre Dame" would be enough to keep order. Neither he nor Polignac had realized the necessity for organizing resistance to a popular uprising.

There were but a few thousand royal troops in Paris. They were commanded by Marmont, who had been a traitor in 1814. On the morning of the twenty-eighth the people, aided by the *Garde nationale,* took possession of the Arsenal, the Hôtel de Ville, and Notre Dame. They carried the tricolor. Marmont made vain efforts to clear the streets. There were bloody fights at many barricades. From the roofs and upper stories of the high houses, tiles, furniture, pots, kettles and other domestic vessels rained down upon the heads of the unhappy royal cavalrymen. They could preserve neither their equilibrium nor their dignity. The barricades were rebuilt as fast as they were destroyed. The Parisians, despite their casualties, made a very merry day of it. At nightfall Marmont had to withdraw to the Louvre and the Place Vendôme.

On the morning of the twenty-ninth the troops stationed on the Place Vendôme went over to the insurgents. By noon the Palais-Bourbon and the Louvre were taken. Marmont was compelled to retreat to Saint-Cloud and report to the King that his capital was in the hands of the insurgents. There is a street in Paris named *rue 29 Juillet* in honor of that day of 1830 when, behind crude barricades, the people defeated the troopers of the King.

One of King Charles's four objectionable decrees had ordered the dissolution of the *Chambre*. The enforcement of those decrees having been successfully resisted, Paris was without legal authority; only the moral authority of the *députés* remained. They issued a manifesto in which they declared that they considered themselves legally in authority despite the decree of dissolution. Prompt action was necessary if anarchy was to be avoided. At Guizot's suggestion, La Fayette was appointed to command the *Garde nationale* and five liberal *députés* were named municipal commissioners.

Knowledge of the seriousness of the situation finally penetrated the King's thick skull. A messenger was sent to the Hôtel de Ville to announce withdrawal of the four decrees. "It is too late," Paris responded. "The King has fallen in the blood that had been shed. Let him lie there."

The *députés* were confronted by a delicate and critical situation. Differ though they might in politics, they were all lovers of order. There was grave threat of disorder. The popular demand for a republic was rapidly gaining ground. Cooler heads realized that the King had been dethroned at the risk of foreign intervention and that the establishment of a republic would make intervention certain. There was immediate need for the establishment of a government which might be acceptable both to the European powers and to the aroused republicanism of France.

The group that believed that the Duke of Orléans might provide a solution of the dilemma acted quickly. Thiers drafted a manifesto; the morning of the thirtieth found the walls of Paris placarded with it. It read, "Charles X shall not return. He has shed the blood of his people. But a republic would find us disastrously divided among ourselves and would embroil us with Europe. . . . The Duke of Orléans was devoted to the cause of the Revolution, he has never fought against France, he fought for her at Valmy and at Jemmapes, he is a citizen-king, he has carried the tricolor under fire and he alone can carry it victoriously again. He has made no demand. He awaits the expression of our wish. He would accept the *Charte* as we have understood it and wished it. It would be from the French people that he would receive the crown."

A majority of the *députés,* though not enthusiastic about the Duke, were willing to accept him rather than republican disorder. In the afternoon of the thirtieth, the lieutenant-generalship of the kingdom was offered to Orléans. He accepted.

The people of the "quarters" were less amenable than the *députés.* They had done the fighting and they wanted no king. They were massed at the Hôtel de Ville and were making preparations to declare a republic. The issue trembled in the balance. At the right dramatic moment, Orléans appeared on the balcony with La Fayette. "Here," the old Marquis cried, "is your best republic!" The Duke kissed the Marquis. That settled it. The crowd cheered and the die-hard republicans went home disgusted.

When the bad news reached Saint-Cloud, Charles X decided that he had better go farther away from Paris. He went to Rambouillet. There he abdicated in favor of the Duke of Bordeaux, the nine-year-old posthumous son of the Duke of Berry. No more attention was paid to this than had been paid to Napoleon's abdication in favor of the King of Rome.

On the third of August a column of the *Garde nationale,* accompanied by a crowd of men and women who had fought at the barricades, marched toward Rambouillet. They wanted Charles X still farther away from Paris. He obliged by leaving at once for Cherbourg and sailing from there to England.

The Duke of Orléans was not definitely called to the throne until August 7, and then only after certain modifications had been made in the *Charte* by way of appeasement of the republicans. The declaration made by the *Chambre* stipulated, "Upon condition of his acceptance of the revised *Charte*, the *Chambre* declares that it is the urgent need of the French people to call to the throne Louis-Philippe of Orléans. He will be invited to appear before the *Chambre* and to make solemn oath to sustain the *Charte;* having made this oath, he will take the title, King of the French people."

On the ninth of August, Louis-Philippe took the required oath and received the insignia of royalty from the hands of four marshals of France.

Louis-Philippe was a son of that Duke of Orléans, a cousin of Louis XVI, who, at the time of the Revolution, changed his name to Philippe Egalité; he hoped thereby to save his head, but he lost it nonetheless. Louis-Philippe's governess was a disciple of Rousseau. He was educated as a peace-lover and a friend of the people. He was so much their friend that, when there was a demonstration against him in 1848, he abdicated without argument or resistance. His reign was followed by the short-lived Second Republic of 1848-1852. Then came the Second Empire.

"The King reigns, but does not govern." That was one of the slogans invented by those who sought, in July, 1830, to arrest the blind rush toward republicanism. Louis XVIII had graciously "granted" the *Charte* to the people on whom his rule had been imposed, but the people imposed the *Charte* on Louis-Philippe when they elected him to reign rather than to rule. They thought of him as president rather than king of a France that was to be republican in all but name. They did not call the new government a royal government; they called it "the government of July."

The July modifications of the *Charte* abolished heredity in the peerage and gave liberty back to the press. The tax-qualification for suffrage was lowered to two hundred francs and the eligibility-to-office qualification to five hundred. The age limit of *députés* was lowered from forty to thirty, and the *Chambre* gained the right to initiate legislation. The article that recognized Catholicism as the religion of the state was annulled.

News of the success of the revolt in Paris aroused all Europe. It stimulated to new and bolder efforts all those who wished similarly to overthrow or to liberalize their governments. There were widespread repercussions. Even in 1830 the political developments in one country had prompt effects upon the political situation in other countries. A German author wrote, "On the seventh of September I saw at Kehl a peasant who had come from Strasbourg. He wore on his hat a rosette of red, white and blue. . . . It was like a first glimpse of a rainbow after a storm. . . . And when I saw the tricolor of France wave again, I wept for joy." The example of France redoubled liberal efforts in all the countries of western Europe.

Belgium revolted against her enforced union with Holland and succeeded in breaking it. Poland revolted against Russian domination and had a temporary success. Switzerland revolted against control by her aristocrats and won a more liberal constitution. The alarmed princes of some of the German states found it prudent to grant constitutions before they were forced to do so. There were revolts in unhappy Italy, but there the iron hand of Austria continued to crush those who revolted. Spain and Portugal became constitutional monarchies.

England, less inclined than ever to aid her former allies in repression of liberalism, showed sympathy with the new government of France. England had become more liberalized herself through increase of Whig resistance to the Tories. Austria, Prussia, and Russia were the only strongholds of absolutism that remained. Alexander had been succeeded by Nicholas; the new Czar surpassed even Metternich in his hatred of liberal tendencies.

It remained to be seen whether the new King of France had the power or the will to curb his people in their suddenly aroused ambition to crusade for republicanism. There was strong popular demand for advance to the natural frontiers and for participation in other people's struggles for liberty. The spirit of 1792 was abroad. There was especial sympathy with Poland's heroic effort to regain her independence.

Fortunately for the peace of Europe, "the King of the barricades" was temperamentally opposed to the use of force. The other powers soon discovered that if they would recognize the legality of his government, they could count on Louis-Philippe heartily to co-operate in maintenance of the existing order. Czar Nicholas favored intervention in France and restoration of the Bourbons, but he found no support for this idea. The other powers followed the lead of England in recognizing Louis-Philippe as King of France.

Talleyrand was appointed ambassador at the Court of Saint James. The King had spent much time in England and ardently desired friendship with that country. Talleyrand succeeded in establishing an unwritten understanding that came to be called the *entente cordiale*. The revolution in Belgium put this *entente* to a severe test.

Always on the alert about the edge of Europe that comes closest to her shores, England was sure to oppose French domination of Belgium. Belgium, having won her independence from Holland, invited the Duke of Nemours, a son of Louis-Philippe, to become her king. Louis-Philippe, in order to cause no offense to England, did not permit his son to accept this flattering invitation. Belgium then invited Leopold of Saxe-Cobourg to her throne. This German prince was acceptable to England. He was the widower of an English princess. This occurred in 1831.

Leopold I was no sooner seated on his new throne than a Dutch army marched into Belgium and threatened Brussels. France sent forces that compelled the Dutch to retreat. Then the French withdrew, leaving the fate of Belgium to be settled by a conference of the powers held in London. There the independence and neutrality of Leopold's kingdom was guaranteed by the five great powers—England, France, Austria, Russia, and Prussia. This was a diplomatic triumph for England. France had gained the friendship of Belgium, but England prevented that friendship from flowering into a political alliance.

Chapter Twenty-two

THE "GOVERNMENT OF JULY"

CASIMIR PERIER, THIERS, AND GUIZOT. THE *GARDE NATIONALE*. REVOLT
AT LYON. GODEFROY CAVAIGNAC SUCCESSFULLY DEFIED THE GOVERN-
MENT. THE AMAZING MÉHÉMET-ALI. THE CRISIS OF 1840 ON ACCOUNT OF
EGYPT. THE *LE LOI GUIZOT*. GOLDEN YEARS FOR THE BOURGEOISIE. THE
CONQUEST OF ALGIERS. AN ACCIDENTAL REVOLUTION.

REVOLUTION made Louis-Philippe King of France, but he was no
friend of revolution. He was bound by law to respect the *Charte,* but
he was bound by temperament and self-interest to oppose any further
enlargement of popular rights. His regime was sure to become unpopular with ardent liberals. Its personnel became increasingly monarchical. Louis-Philippe was not such a throwback as Charles X, but
his political philosophy was not reflective of the spirit of the majority
of his people. His desire for improvement of the lot of the common
man was much weaker than his desire for peace and personal power.

The King was very prudent. His experience as an *émigré* made
him prudent about money as well as about political policies. Before
the Restoration he earned his living as a teacher of mathematics in
Switzerland, in England, and in the United States. Like most of the
émigrés, he also gave lessons in music and dancing.

After the Restoration, Louis-Philippe lived like a bourgeois in an
apartment in the *Palais-Royal;* he took pains not to be identified with
his reactionary cousins at the Tuileries; even when he replaced them
there he kept up his bourgeois habits. Dressed like any well-to-do
citizen, his umbrella under his arm, he used to walk unescorted in
the streets, stopping occasionally to talk with workmen. He put an
end to excess in royal ceremony; Queen Marie-Amélie sat in an easy
chair and crocheted, surrounded by a respectful but informal group.
But, under his simplicity and gentle, bourgeois manners, the "citizen-
King" concealed strong ambition for personal power.

The new reign began with an economic depression. Parades of workers gave almost daily evidence of the social unrest. The Prince of Polignac and three of his colleagues in the hated ministry of Charles X were sentenced to prison. Their trial was accompanied by violent manifestations. There was a popular demand for their execution that nearly led to insurrection.

Charles X had abdicated in favor of his grandson, the nine-year-old Duke of Bordeaux; the "legitimists" claimed that the kingship of France legally belonged to this direct heir of the deposed king. The priests added to their unpopularity by supporting this claim; to avoid assault they were compelled to dress as ordinary citizens. A memorial service in honor of the Duke of Berry was held in the church of Saint-Germain l'Auxerrois. A crowd showed its displeasure by sacking the church. There were similar outbreaks in several provincial cities.

The first ministers of Louis-Philippe were leaders of the movement that had made him king. Three of them, Guizot, the Duke of Broglie, and Casimir-Perier, favored restraint of the popular movement for greater liberty. Their colleagues favored giving full sway to that movement. The Guizot group, finding that they could not have their way, resigned. In November, 1830, Laffitte, popular in spite of being a banker, became prime minister. He had the support of La Fayette, who remained in command of the *Garde nationale*.

The Laffitte ministry proposed "to develop the consequences of July" by encouraging revolutionary movements outside of France. There was talk of a *"Sacred Alliance of the people of Europe"!* But the economic crisis soon dispelled this dream. The *rentes* fell to half their face value. The *députés* opposed the impracticable plans of the ministry. In March, 1831, the King replaced Laffitte by another banker, the energetic, strong-willed and practical Casimir-Perier.

The new minister, though he had favored the dethronement of Charles X, shared the King's prejudice against any further leftward movement. He believed that, unless respect for the authority of the new government was enforced, a new Terror might develop. The lure of a regenerated and democratized Europe did not appeal to him. He devoted all his energies to putting the brakes on a movement that he had helped to start. He declared that the government "would not recognize the right of popular uprisings to compel either war or political innovations." His colleagues, and even the King himself, bent to Casimir-Perier's inflexible will. He caused a dissolution of the *Chambre*. The new one, elected in July, 1831, gave him "a compact and faithful majority."

The government could not have maintained order except for the dependability and efficiency of the reorganized *Garde nationale*. A law of March, 1831, stated that the duty of the *Garde* was "to defend the constitutional monarchy and the rights conferred by the *Charte*, to maintain order and obedience to the laws, and, if necessary, to second the regular army in defense of the frontiers." This governmental police force was recruited from those whose prosperity made it in their interest to oppose any insurrectional movement. Those who joined it had to buy their own uniforms and arms; that provision excluded from it most of the young apostles of republicanism.

In November of 1831 the miserably paid silk workers of Lyon revolted. A minimum wage-scale had been agreed upon by a joint-commission of employers and employees, but some of the employers refused to abide by it. For two days the revolted workers were in control of the city. The government had to send in twenty thousand troops. The workers were disarmed and compelled to accept again whatever their employers chose to pay.

The adventurous Duchess of Berry believed that "legitimate" sentiment was strong enough to justify an attempt to win the crown for her small son. In April, 1832, she returned to France in disguise. In royalist and religious Vendée a few groups rallied to her support. They were easily dispersed and the Duchess was imprisoned in the fortress of Blaye. There she gave birth to a child of doubtful paternity. That inconvenient birth ended the political career of the Duchess, but it also opened for her the doors of her prison. In becoming a mother she had ceased to be a menace.

The greatest threat to the government lay in the strength and persistence of republican sentiment. The republicans had borne the brunt of the July revolution, and they had been defrauded, they felt, of the fruits of their victory. Though victorious, they had not won what they had fought for. Sons of fathers who had fought in the Revolution, still fired by their fathers' zeal, would not give up their republicanism. They formed clubs and they published papers that the government sought to suppress by bringing them into court on charges of sedition.

At the trial of a group of fifteen, one of them, Godefroy Cavaignac, declared, "My father sat in the Convention that proclaimed the Republic. He fought in its armies to defend it against all Europe. For doing that he died in a foreign land after twelve years of exile. Others, who betrayed the cause of the Republic, were honored by the restored Bourbons. . . . France has enjoyed the fruits of the Revolution. The only ones who have suffered are those who fought to win them, and who, like my father, would not betray the Republic. Today I declare what many others would, but dare not. I am a republican." He was acquitted.

It took all the persistence of Casimir-Perier, backed up by the constant vigilance of the *Garde,* to keep in subjection the sentiment that Cavaignac represented. On the fifth of June, 1832, barricades again appeared in the streets. It took two days for the *Garde,* reinforced by troops of the line, to restore order.

There was much sympathy in France for the Poles in their struggle for independence. That also caused trouble for the government. There was a popular demand that military aid should be extended to the people who for twenty years had been Napoleon's most loyal allies. Casimir-Perier remained unmoved by this sentimental appeal. He did not confuse Napoleon with France. He declared that "the blood of the French belongs only to France." When the news reached Paris that the Russians had entered Warsaw, September, 1831, there was a demonstration against the government that the *Garde* suppressed with difficulty.

The most serious foreign problem with which Casimir-Perier and his successors had to deal arose in connection with Egypt. Méhémet-Ali, an uneducated illiterate of amazing ability, became pasha of Egypt in 1805. He was an Albanian who had been a tobacco merchant before he became an officer in the Turkish army. It was his ambition to make Egypt independent of Turkey and to found there a ruling dynasty. He disposed of the feudal Mamelukes by having them all massacred in Cairo in 1811. Enriched by the development of great cotton plantations, he engaged French officers to train his army. This army proved its worth in aiding Turkey against Greece. In compensation for that aid, Méhémet-Ali demanded that his authority in Egypt should be made hereditary and that Syria should also come under his control. The Sultan's refusal of these demands led to war.

Mahmoud II, the Sultan, was no less ambitious than Méhémet-Ali. He had strengthened his position by a massacre of the Janissaries, and he too had engaged European officers. One of them was Von Moltke, later to become the great Prussian general. Mahmoud wished to Europeanize his Mohammedan subjects. He shocked them by drinking wine and dressing like an unbeliever.

The first Turco-Egyptian war began in 1831. It ended disastrously for the Turks. The Russians had defeated them with difficulty, but Méhémet's army defeated them with ease; it was commanded by his very capable son Ibrahim. In 1832 Ibrahim threatened Constantinople. Mahmoud appealed for help to his old enemy the Czar, saying, "A drowning man will clutch even a serpent." Nicholas sent fifteen thousand men to the Straits of the Bosphorus. That alarmed both France and England. It would not do for Russia to control the Straits and thereby have easy access to the Mediterranean.

A conflict of interests developed in the Levant which put a heavy strain on Anglo-French friendship. The *entente cordiale* became, for a time, a fiction. Lord Palmerston, the foreign minister of England, supported Mahmoud, but France supported Méhémet-Ali; they were in accord about resistance to the Russian advance, but they took opposite sides in the Turco-Egyptian conflict. Palmerston was determined to prevent increase of French influence in Egypt.

A treaty of 1833 conceded control of Syria to Méhémet and another conceded control of the Straits to the Czar. Neither of these treaties pleased Palmerston. Determined to let neither Russia nor France threaten England's interests in the Orient, he made a commercial treaty with Mahmoud and encouraged him to reopen hostilities with Méhémet. Mahmoud did so in 1839 and was again disastrously defeated. He died that year and was succeeded by a sixteen-year-old son.

The Turkish fleet sailed to Alexandria and placed itself at the service of Méhémet. At that time the Albanian adventurer seemed almost certain to become master of the Turkish Empire.

Palmerston, playing his double game against Russia and France, succeeded in having the failing cause of the Sultan placed under the control of the five great powers; in doing so he had the able assistance of Metternich. This arrangement pleased France so far as restraint of Russia was concerned; its effect upon the fortunes of her friend Méhémet was not clearly foreseen.

Thiers, prime minister of France in 1840, attempted to put through a treaty between Turkey and Egypt which would be favorable both to Méhémet and to France. He was outmaneuvered by Palmerston. The English minister secured the adherence of Russia, Austria, and Prussia to an agreement to sustain the cause of the young Sultan. That agreement constituted a four-power opposition to the French policy in Egypt.

France felt that she had been double-crossed. She had not even been consulted about the four-power pact. What Palmerston ironically called "a useful lesson to France" the French called "an intolerable humiliation." This situation played into the hands of republican sentiment. Those whose interests the French government had greatly served by its anti-revolutionary policy had repaid that service with a blow below the belt. It was argued that France should repay that treacherous blow by encouragement of insurrection against the governments that had delivered it. There was popular demand for a military advance whose first objective would be the Rhine.

Even peace-loving and prudent Louis-Philippe lost his temper. He felt that the other powers had shown base ingratitude. "For ten years," he said, "I have incurred great risks, even the risk of my life, in preventing French support of revolutionary movements, and this is the way they repay me!" His son, the Duke of Orléans, declared, "I had rather die on the Rhine than in a gutter of the *rue Saint-Denis*." The King was sorely tempted to take the side of the republican revolutionaries. Preparations for war were begun.

Thiers was for war, but Louis-Philippe, upon sober second thought, decided for peace. Thiers resigned and was replaced by Guizot. An Austro-English fleet operated against Méhémet-Ali and compelled him to accept conditions imposed by the four powers. That put an end to the dominance of French influence in Egypt. In 1841 France joined the other powers in requiring Turkey to block the Straits of the Bosphorus to all war vessels; Russia was thus deprived of the advantage she had sought to gain; she could no longer be a threat in the Mediterranean; her warships could not sail out from the Black Sea.

The outcome of the "oriental crisis" was a triumph for Palmerston's diplomacy. France suffered from loss of her advantage in Egypt, but even more, in later years, from the reaction against her in Germany that was aroused by her threat of war to win back the Rhine frontier. Germany was far less interested in republicanism than she was in becoming a strong and united nation.

Casimir-Perier was prime minister when the east-Mediterranean difficulties first developed, but he died long before they came to an end. Never robust, he undermined his health by overwork. A visit to a cholera hospital brought to an end his notable services to the state. He had succeeded in thwarting the efforts both of republicans and of "legitimists" to overthrow the government; he had given definite direction to its policy; he had organized the conservative party that controlled the *Chambre des députés.* His brief and efficient ministry had been the salvation of the "monarchy of July." He died in 1832 at the age of fifty-five. The death of Napoleon's son in that same year strengthened the position of Louis-Philippe; the infant "King of Rome" had become, as the Duke of Reichstadt, a graceful and tragic young man whose movements were controlled by the court of Austria.

Casimir-Perier held republicanism in check, but it was impossible to suppress it. For sixteen years after his death the conservative party he had organized was able to maintain a majority in the *Chambre,* but it was always doubtful whether it had a majority in the country. By persistent propaganda the liberal opposition kept alive a popular demand for more democracy than the government of Louis-Philippe would grant. Finally the opposition became strong enough to prevail. The revolution of 1848 proved the vigor and the continuity of the republican spirit. It strengthened the evidence that, after the fall of the Bastille, only force and economic pressures prevented France from expressing in the form of her government her faith in the ideals of democracy.

In 1832 Casimir-Perier caused the dissolution of the *Societé des Amis du Peuple,* but that did not prevent dissemination of this strong organization's program. Some of the items in it were universal suffrage, decentralization of the administration, free schools, freedom to form organizations, and a sliding scale of taxation.

There was a group of young idealists of the educated bourgeois who spent much of their time in jail on account of their republican speeches and writings. Among these were Raspail, Louis Blanc, Ledru-Rollin, Arago, Barbès, and Blanqui. Not one of these fails to have an important avenue of modern Paris named in his honor. Barbès and Blanqui, leaders of a secret society that attempted an insurrection in 1839, were imprisoned at Mont-Saint-Michel.

In the period between 1832 and 1848 the ministry changed frequently, but, whether its chief was Thiers, Guizot, Molé, or the Duke of Broglie, the vigor of its effort to suppress republicanism never ceased. However, the *Charte* did not permit it, nor did it dare, to use the methods of Napoleon or of the Bourbons. Imprisonment could be made only after fair trial by jury. The attitude of the public may be judged by the fact that hardly more than a third of the government's charges were sustained.

The *Societé des Droits de l'Homme* was organized in 1833. It was a league in defense of civil liberties. It raised money for the defense of political prisoners and to protect the freedom of the press. Thousands of young republicans throughout the nation became members of this society. It supported the silk workers of Lyon when they revolted again in 1834. It tried to extend that revolt to other cities in which workers were unfairly exploited. Barricades appeared again in the streets of Paris. But the government was always on the alert. The revolts were ruthlessly crushed. Propaganda continued, but insurrectional efforts ceased after 1839. There came a period of calm in which the republicans felt compelled to bide their time.

The Duke of Broglie succeeded Casimir-Perier as *Président du Conseil.* Thiers was minister of the interior and Guizot minister of education. The most notable achievement of this ministry was the *loi Guizot* of 1833 which compelled the establishment of elementary schools in all *communes;* there had been twenty-five thousand *communes* without them.

Eminent historian as well as politician, Guizot, an advanced liberal under the Restoration, had been converted to conservatism by the events of 1830. Primarily a lover of order, he was unwilling to accept disorder as the price of social progress. He believed that revolutionary tendencies were the offspring of ignorance and of moral laxity. His plan for the schools called for much emphasis upon character formation. The *loi Guizot* formed the legal basis of public elementary instruction until the formation of the Third Republic in 1871.

So long as Guizot, Thiers, and the Duke of Broglie were in accord, they determined the policies of the government. Only when they disagreed did Louis-Philippe become the determining factor. They disagreed in 1836. Thiers favored the English system; he invented the phrase, "The king should reign, but not govern." Guizot was opposed to such restriction of royal authority. This divergence of views between the leaders of the conservative party enabled the King to appoint as chief minister the Count Molé, his close personal friend. From 1836 to 1839 Louis-Philippe governed as well as reigned.

The passing of the years dimmed the faults of Napoleon and magnified his virtues. His old soldiers told spellbound audiences of the glories of the Empire and made Frenchmen believe again in the genius of Bonaparte. Louis-Philippe seemed pitiful in comparison. The "Bonapartists" grew in number. Louis Napoleon, a nephew of the Emperor, made an attempt to emulate his uncle. In October, 1836, he attempted a *coup d'état* that collapsed before it was fairly started. He was arrested. To escape the embarrassment of putting a Bonaparte on trial, the government sent Louis to America.

Guizot and Thiers, having composed their differences, formed a coalition whose objective was to put an end to the "personal government" of Louis-Philippe. Their campaign for restoration of parliamentary control was successful. The coalition won the election of 1839. Molé was compelled to resign. In the months of uncertainty that followed, Barbès and Blanqui made their unsuccessful revolutionary effort.

In 1840 Thiers became chief minister for the second time and Guizot went to London as ambassador. That was the year in which the Egyptian difficulty brought France to the brink of war. Thiers resigned and Guizot returned from London.

In the new ministry, Guizot was not the *Président,* but his was the dominating influence. Soult was the *Président,* but the government was really directed by Louis-Philippe and Guizot. The King gradually came to have great confidence in the frosty and precise professor-statesman. In diligence, intelligence, and eloquence Guizot surpassed his colleagues. He and Louis-Philippe, despite their differences of temperament, were alike in belief in the fundamental importance of order and authority.

Guizot's foreign policy was based on revival and strengthening of the *entente cordiale* with England. His domestic policy was based on opposition to all innovations. He strove for "the moral and material amelioration of France," but sought to attain that objective by use of a technique whose rigidity and disregard of justice led to his downfall. Inflexible in his opposition to political reform, his constant effort was to strengthen the existing framework of the state. He was the complete conservative. Lamartine, the poet-politician, compared Guizot's immobile statesmanship to the stones which definitely demark the limits of a surveyed field.

The years of the Guizot ministry were golden years for the *bourgeoisie.* They had a monopoly of culture, of political influence, and of wealth. They profiteered on this monopoly, showing slight regard for the welfare of the workers. The Industrial Revolution gave opportunity for the development of large fortunes. The property qualification made the electorate almost wholly bourgeois. The labor of twenty-eight million enriched the two million who controlled them. The foundations of an economic feudalism were laid.

In application of the new inventions England and Germany made even more rapid progress than France. The French merchant marine lost more than half of its carrying trade to foreign steamships. The industrial steam power developed in England was six times that of

France. Stephenson constructed his first locomotive in 1814; twenty-four years later the *Chambre des députés* rejected a proposal for railroad-building. Thiers declared that he did not believe in the future of the railroad. Arago argued that to transport soldiers by rail would make them effeminate. In 1848 France had less than 1,200 miles of railroad while England had 3,800 and Prussia 2,200.

The industrialists were able to maintain a high tariff against English products. The *maîtres de forges* (iron-masters) of Lorraine and of the north had great political influence. Iron and steel cost nearly three times as much in France as in England. The political situation favored the success of new companies that were formed to exploit the new inventions. In 1830 the trading on the Bourse was limited to forty-four stocks; in 1847 there were nearly two hundred. The five-per-cent *rentes* rose from 52 in 1831 to 125 in 1845. The cost of living did not decrease. Underpaid labor bore the burden. The workers, as in England, were not permitted to organize. The average wage was about sixty cents for a twelve-hour day; women and children were employed for less. A merciful law of 1842 forbade the employment in factories of children under eight, and those under twelve could not be compelled to work at night! Labor conditions were equally bad in England.

Polignac's expedition had conquered Algiers in 1830. The excuse for this conquest was that the Turkish Dey who ruled there had insulted the French Consul; he had struck him with a fly swatter. The Dey was annoyed because he had not been paid for wheat furnished to France many years before.

Under Louis-Philippe the French extended the area of their control in Algeria. Bugeaud, an able general, made a successful campaign in 1844 against Abd-el-Kader, an equally able chief of the Arabs. Comfortably imprisoned for years in the château of Amboise, Abd-el-Kader later became a loyal ally of France. Stripped of her American and Asiatic colonies by England, France, under Louis-Philippe, acquired a new empire in Africa.

In 1847 an enlargement of the electorate was proposed. Guizot remained inflexible in his opposition. "Universal suffrage is absurd," he said. "The question does not deserve that I give it my attention." The vote of the *députés* was 154 for the proposed reform and 252 against it.

The defeated reformers took the question to the country. Bad harvests and floods in 1846 had caused hunger and unemployment. The prosperity which had sustained the government disappeared. The lesser *bourgeoisie* began to favor the reform movement. The minister of public works was convicted of having sold mineral concessions. Support of the government diminished more rapidly than Guizot or Louis-Philippe realized.

In May of 1847 the republicans, supported by the "left center" (liberal conservatives), opened a campaign in favor of electoral reform. A series of political banquets was held in many cities. The toast to the King was omitted. The right of labor to organize and the enlargement of the electorate were the principal themes.

A grand final banquet was planned to be held in Paris late in February, 1848. The public was invited to show its approval by assembling on the *Place de la Concorde*. The government forbade this assembly. It occurred nonetheless. The bourgeois *Garde nationale* was called out. But the *Garde* itself had become imbued with the ideas of reform. It joined in the cries of *"Vive la Reforme!"* and *"A bas Guizot!"* When Louis-Philippe realized that the *Garde* had turned against him, he abruptly dismissed Guizot and called on Molé to form a new cabinet. The people in the streets received this news with enthusiasm. They were satisfied. Order might have been restored except for an unfortunate and unplanned incident.

In the celebration that followed the victory of the reformers, a clash occurred between the crowd and the soldiers on duty at the Ministry of Foreign Affairs which was in the *Boulevard des Capucines*. The soldiers fired and sixteen of the people were killed. Instantly the celebration became a revolution. The shooting occurred at half-past nine on the evening of February 23. The corpses were laid on a huge uncovered wagon where all might see them. Lighted by torches, they were paraded through the streets until two in the morning, accompanied by a furious crowd crying, *"Vengeance! Aux armes! Aux barricades!"* Dawn saw the barricades arise again.

The government had soldiers available under Bugeaud's command who could have suppressed this insurrection. But Louis-Philippe would not give the command. The defection of the *Garde nationale* had taken the heart out of him. At mid-day on the twenty-fourth he abdicated in favor of his grandson, the Count of Paris; his son, the Duke of Orléans, had died. On the same afternoon he and Marie-Amélie drove up the Champs-Elysées and on out of Paris. At four o'clock the revolution was over. On the second of March Louis-Philippe sailed from Trouville for England where he died in 1850.

Slight attention was paid to the Duchess of Orléans and her young son in whose favor the King had abdicated. A Republic was proclaimed and a provisional government was set up. It had been proved once more that the defense of order and of property ultimately fails when social justice is disregarded.

Chapter Twenty-three

THE SECOND RENAISSANCE

THE INEVITABLE ALLIANCE OF THE DEMOCRACIES. PROGRESS IN ENGLAND.
ROMANTICISM IN LITERATURE, ART, MUSIC, AND RELIGION. LAMENNAIS
PROPOSED AN ALLIANCE BETWEEN CATHOLICISM AND DEMOCRACY. ROBERT
OWEN AND THE COUNT SAINT-SIMON. THE BEGINNINGS OF SOCIALISM.

INEVITABLE antagonists through centuries, France and England were destined to become inevitable allies. Their antagonism in the Feudal Ages was an affair of the lords and kings. In the economic conflicts and the colonial wars that followed, the people had a larger interest. When the Napoleonic blockade deprived England of her best markets, the whole economic life of England was affected. But, once England had helped France to rid herself of Napoleon, their similarity of interest in political reform gradually became evident. The strength of their people's devotion to liberalism outlined itself against the somber background of Central Europe's tyranny.

Napoleon instinctively threw himself upon the mercy of his "most loyal and most generous enemy." He appealed "to the justice of English law"; there was no such justice elsewhere. After Waterloo the French were compelled to submit to a restoration of the Bourbons, but they soon put an end to that restoration. Louis-Philippe did not seek first an alliance with the repressive powers. He sought first an alliance with England. He sent Talleyrand to London in search of an *entente cordiale* with that nation whose political ideals most closely resembled those of France.

The inevitable alliance between France and England is based on common concepts of social justice. It is based on thought rather than on things. It is a mental alliance that intense economic rivalry has been unable to prevent. The people of France and of England, more than the people of any other great power in Europe, have been resistant to tyranny. They have compelled autocracy to yield to democratic progress. In other countries people have been more submissive to autocracy. They have preferred to submit rather than to struggle. Such economic benefits and such order as autocracy has provided, they have preferred to the uncertainties and disorder of an enfranchisement about whose benefits they have had no clear vision.

In Central Europe there has developed through more than a century a political philosophy that is definitely opposed to the democratic concepts of France and England. To that ideological conflict there has been added the stress of economic inequality. These fundamental differences of ideas and of status constitute the major obstacle to human peace and progress. The divergence of their ideas and of their economic interests is such that the great powers have the same difficulty that the French Revolution had with the rest of Europe; they have ceased to speak the same language; their conceptions of justice are not the same.

The contemporary situation is rooted in the past with which we are dealing; a brief comment on that situation may be permissible. The growth in strength of the autocracies has hastened the inevitable *rapprochement* of the democracies. A definite alliance of the democratic powers to defend their common idealism, coupled with a co-operative effort to alleviate the economic needs of the submissive peoples—that may yet provide a peaceful solution of the great difficulty. But nothing short of that will provide it.

The democracies will either stand together or they will fall, and the longer they defer their alliance, the more they risk certainty of their fall. Co-operation is commanded. It alone can prevent war, a war which, won or lost, would be catastrophic. A democracy that remains neutral and aloof facilitates thereby the triumph of force over reason. Isolation plays into the hands of the dictators. Their best allies are those who advocate isolation, or sabotage the mutual confidence that is essential to co-operation. Freedom can be saved and war avoided only by the co-operation of all who believe in freedom and in peace. Minor differences must be forgotten. Such is the greatness of the issue that mutual confidence can beget its own justification.

The evolution of political sympathy between France and England points to the conclusion that the people of these two countries have

excelled in courage, in initiative, and in readiness to resist social injustice. Their political philosophy was more advanced than that of
most of their eastern neighbors—advanced, that is, in the direction of
belief in the virtue of individualism. Their devotion to democratic
ideals was based on confidence in the potentialities of the common
man, tempered by reservations about his present capacity as a political
animal. These reservations are indicated by the slowness of enlargement of the electorate. A long series of political reforms preceded any
popular demand for universal suffrage.

Since political reform was accomplished in England with less of
revolution and of bloodshed than in France, it is reasonable to believe
that the English were more devoted to orderly procedure than the
French, or that the rulers of Britain were more sagacious than those of
France in timing their concessions to popular demands. England
benefited, however, both from her geographic position and from the
object lesson of her neighbor across the Channel. After the revolutions
of 1830 and 1848 the rulers of England made concessions that might
not have been made save that they wished to avoid the sort of thing
that had happened in France. Also, Charles X and Louis-Philippe
were sustained in the error of their ways by autocratic European courts
whose influence upon England's domestic policies was negligible.

England's record in political evolution is more orderly than France's,
but France helped to make it so. Her people, for a century and a half,
have done more fighting than any other people for liberty and for
justice. They had to do it, and they did it. The other democracies may
not appreciate how much they have benefited from the fact that the
French have not been a submissive people. They will appreciate that
benefit, however, if through blindness to their own interests they
permit France's resistance to autocracy to be overcome.

For England the first half of the Nineteenth Century was a period of
political progress and of great commercial expansion. A quarter-
century of war had arrested her development and absorbed her energy.
She emerged from her long struggle with Napoleon exhausted, but in
a more favorable position for economic development than she had
ever been in before. After 1815 the new inventions, coupled with
her coal and iron supply, permitted rapid increase of an industrial

output for which her colonies provided profitable markets. England became transformed from an agricultural to a manufacturing country. Increase of the wealth and influence of the industrial and commercial groups had important political effects.

The population increased from ten million in 1800 to fourteen million in 1820. London, with a million inhabitants in 1811, was by far the largest city of Europe. Manchester, Liverpool, and Birmingham grew by leaps and bounds.

Protestant England was ruled by an aristocracy whose right to rule was endorsed by the clergy. Protestantism took the side of peace and order rather than the side of reform and social progress. The two political parties were the Whigs and the Tories. The Whigs favored removal of the disenfranchisement of the Catholics, but apart from that the differences between the parties were more personal than political. Wellington, the national hero, was a Tory. His party was almost continuously in power from 1783 to 1831.

George, the profligate and heartless son of dull and respectable George III, was Prince Regent from 1810 to 1820 on account of the insanity of his father. Despised, and so far as possible disregarded, he reigned as George IV from 1820 to 1830. His brother, the "bluff and honest" sailor king, was William IV from 1830 to 1837. William was succeeded by his niece Victoria.

Parliamentary authority had developed in England to such extent that her monarchs had less control over government than the monarchs in any other country of Europe. In France Charles X and his Polignac ministry had overridden the representatives of the people and had violated the Charter; George IV could have done no such thing in England. But the people of England, no less than those of France, were insistent about electoral reform. New conditions called for a new deal.

The landed aristocracy dominated Parliament at the expense of the enlarged and enriched commercial and industrial groups; business had outstripped agriculture in economic importance, but, under an outworn system of representation, those interested in agriculture held a majority of the seats in the House of Commons. The House of Lords was almost exclusively made up of owners of large estates who stub-

bornly opposed reform. A reform bill passed the Commons by a majority of one. Its rejection by the Lords led to riots. That was in 1831.
Many buildings were burned. Bristol was for days in the hands of a
mob. The people showed their teeth. It became clear that choice had
to be made between reform or insurrection. The French had overthrown their government the year before. That example was contagious.

The Whigs were in power. They compelled the King to agree to
create enough new peers to assure passage of the Reform Bill through
the House of Lords. The Lords capitulated before the new peers were
appointed. The bill was passed in 1832. Thus England accomplished
a political revolution, avoiding violence in the nick of time. It might
not have been avoided except for the blood that was shed in the streets
of Paris in July, 1830.

The Reform Bill abolished 143 of the old seats in the House of
Commons, gave proper representation to the great industrial centers,
and enlarged the electorate. The property qualification for the right
to vote was so reduced that political power was extended to thousands
of workers and small tradesmen; subsequent amendments enlarged
the electorate even further.

The threat of revolt in Ireland had already led in 1829 to restoration of civil rights to the Catholics. In 1833 slavery was abolished in
all British dominions. In that same year the Factory Bill was passed;
it forbade employment in industry of children under nine, and limited
the working day of those between thirteen and eighteen to twelve
hours a day! The shift in political power from the large landowners to
the industrialists was accompanied by no increase of solicitude for the
workers.

Victoria was eighteen when she became Queen. Her youth and
her sex facilitated parliamentary progress in further restriction of
royal authority. The German Prince Albert whom she married in
1840 became her most influential adviser, but he never advised her to
oppose Parliament. He was a wise and tactful gentleman whom the
British aristocracy never liked until after he was dead. For forty years
after his death in 1861, Victoria became a model widow as well as
Queen of the British Empire. Her long and gentle reign gave more of

blessing than of restraint to the social evolution of her people. For over a century the English monarchy has not opposed the progress of its people toward democracy. The British respect and affection for the royal family is justified by experience. There is an understandable belief that the crown in its century-old tradition unifies and stabilizes the nation, exercising a conservative influence that is desirable.

The ministry of Sir Robert Peel from 1841 to 1846 was notable. Gladstone called Peel the greatest man he ever knew. He was a Tory who cared more for social justice than he did for party regularity. Canning, also a Tory, had broken with his party in 1827 because it opposed the restoration of civil liberty to the Catholics; it was with Whig support that the Catholic Relief Bill was passed. Similarly, Peel broke with his party on the question of the Corn Laws. The landed aristocracy bitterly opposed repeal of the act of 1815 that excluded foreign wheat. But enforcement of that act worked great hardship upon workers in industry; in the cities bread was twice as dear as in France. Richard Cobden and John Bright were leaders in an Anti-Corn-Law league that was formed in 1838; Cobden's forceful writings and Bright's great eloquence won much support for the movement in favor of cheaper bread, but it took eight years to wear down the combined Whig and Tory opposition to a measure that would put an end to the profiteering of the landowners.

Again the danger line of popular insurrection was approached. Finally, in 1846, Peel, supported by Whigs and cursed by his former Tory colleagues, was able to secure passage of the bill which led to the free entry of wheat. This led in turn to gradual abolition of all tariffs. England made the discovery that free trade was for her a better economic policy than a protective tariff which favored certain groups at the expense of the nation as a whole. For many years she had nothing to fear from competition by the industrial products of other countries.

The effect upon England of the French revolution of 1848 was less than the effect of the one of 1830, but it was unmistakable. The Whigs had split into the Liberals and the Radicals, and the Tories had split into the "Peelites" and those who preferred to be called Conservatives.

The Radicals demanded a "People's Charter" which would confer manhood suffrage, abolish property qualification for membership in the House of Commons, and provide payment of its members so that poor men could belong to it. These demands were direct echoes of those that the people of France were making.

The "Chartists" in 1848 planned a great demonstration with presentation to Parliament of a petition that had more than a million signatures. The government was so alarmed about this that it placed the Duke of Wellington in charge of the defense of London and authorized the swearing-in of nearly two hundred thousand special constables, one of whom was Louis-Napoleon Bonaparte. That was a force that the Radicals could not expect to overcome.

Wisely advised, the new party decided to work for votes rather than to resort to violence. Its leaders had encountered difficulty in uniting the ranks of the workers. One of them reported, "Our movement is unanimously supported only by the worst paid of the workers. Those who earn thirty shillings a week have little sympathy for those who earn only fifteen, and those who earn fifteen are not interested in the hardships of those who earn only five or six. There is an aristocracy of the workers as well as of the *bourgeoisie.*"

The first half of the Nineteenth Century was marked by intellectual as well as by material and political progress. In literature and art the classic traditions were broken by the new "romanticism." In science, the use of more exact and more empirical methods led to discoveries which raised many new social and political problems; progress in material co-operation with nature far outstripped progress in human co-operation, even as it does today. In religion, Protestantism did not lessen its rigidities, but Catholicism became more liberal. In human relations, thought began to run beyond democracy to consideration of socialistic doctrines and programs. On all the fronts of progress there was new activity. There was a great tumbling down of outworn traditions and discredited beliefs. It was a second Renaissance.

Until nearly the end of the Eighteenth Century Versailles had set the fashion for European culture. Intellectual progress was an affair of the polite world in which French influence was dominant. The Revolution put a stop to that; to republican France the polite world became *anti* rather than *pro*. After that, for fifteen years Napoleon clamped down the iron lid of his imperialism upon all "subversive" thought. The Bourbon governments did what they could to keep that lid in place, but ideas spread under it and increased their pressure. When the lid was finally blown off, the Bourbons were blown away with it. Abstract thought had ceased to be an affair of the polite world alone. The lid of repression could not easily be replaced again in France.

Culture, escaping the domination of French influence, became nationalized. Independent schools of thought and of expression developed in England and in Germany. The volume of printing increased. France became familiar with the works of Dante, Milton, and Shakespeare.

Rousseau and Diderot laid the intellectual foundation for revolt against the classical traditions that hindered freedom of expression. They made it popular to believe that nature rather than authority should be the decisive factor in determining behavior; they expressed more respect for the human urge than for the human heritage; they argued that self-fulfillment is more virtuous than self-repression. The Rousseau-Diderot influence had great effects in the realm of politics and morals, but in the field of art its immediate effect was negligible; in that field the classic standards continued to be respected in France with an almost superstitious veneration.

Early in the new century, however, the current of the times began to run heavily against authority in art as well as in politics. Those who had bathed in the blood of the Revolution and shared in the great adventure of the Empire could not be content with the pallid stuff of the classicists. They wanted life, life and action. *Au diable avec la formule classique!* After the wars there was discontent with peace. Readjustment was difficult. Men were bored, irritable, and inclined to the melancholia of which Chateaubriand was the arch-priest. It was hard to return from a battlefield to a garden. There had to be a new adventuring; if not of the body, then of the mind.

The break with the classical traditions in literature occurred in

Germany and in England before it occurred in France. Lessing began it in the middle of the Eighteenth Century, and Goethe and Schiller came soon after Lessing. Goethe's *Werther* of 1774, beloved of youth, and his *Faust* of 1798 gave strong impetus to romanticism. Schiller, ignoring the classic models altogether, wrote lyric poetry that went straight to the heart.

England contributed more than its fair share to the literary emancipation of feeling. The poetry of Wordsworth and Coleridge appeared at the end of the old century and Sir Walter Scott's historical novels ushered in the new one. But the most perfect expression of English romanticism was given by Byron and Shelley and Keats, all three of whom, "as though spent with passion," died tragically while both they and the century were young.

Chateaubriand was a pioneer of literary freedom in France, and Madame de Staël, "passionate, persecuted, and in revolt against all restraint," typified romanticism in her life as well as in her writings. There is a brief account of both of them in Chapter Sixteen.

In 1823 Stendhal, whose real name was Henri Beyle, published in Paris a small work entitled *Racine et Shakespeare.* In it he wrote, "Romanticism is the art of producing literature which is of interest to people now living. Classicism is the art of producing literature which might have been of interest to our great-grandparents."

A literary feud developed between the classicists and romanticists. The public's passionate partisanship helped make this feud historic.

The newspapers began to publish stories written by the romanticists, stories that broke the classic rules by presenting emotional portrayals of contemporary life. The classicists sought in vain to arrest the increasing popularity of this sort of writing. The best-sellers were romance and romanticized history.

The *Méditations poétiques* of Lamartine, then an unknown young writer, appeared in 1820. They were followed by the *Odes* of Victor Hugo and the *Poèmes* of Alfred de Vigny. All three of these romantic productions delighted the public. But the Academy disapproved of them; the Forty Immortals formed the chief citadel of literary conservatism. The rebel romanticists called the Academicians old wigs. The conservatives countered by calling romanticism "a disease like epilepsy which should be a fit subject for a medical thesis."

The struggle reached its crisis at the first presentation of Hugo's *Hernani*. That was in February, 1830. The crowded theater became a bedlam. The loud *bravos* of Hugo's admirers were not loud enough to drown out the derisive shrieks of his enemies. Young intellectuals hurled insults at one another with the bitter hatred of sworn enemies. They seemed to feel that civilization itself was at stake.

The first performance of *Hernani* all but ended in a battle royal, but its popular success could not be denied. Victor Hugo, then but thirty, became a sort of god for the romanticists. Eleven years later, in 1841, his election to the Academy definitely marked the defeat of the classicists.

Other romantic writers of this fecund period were Alfred de Musset, Balzac, and George Sand. England had Carlyle, Macaulay, Thackeray, and Dickens. The poet Heinrich Heine was the one contemporary German who enjoyed a European reputation. There was also a Dane, Hans Christian Andersen.

The painters no less than the writers disagreed about what constituted art. David, 1748 to 1825, was the official artist of the Revolution and of Napoleon. For him, and for the architects of his time, classic models were the foundation of art. They went in for the heroic and the sublime, scorning the prettiness of their predecessors. In Paris the Madeleine and the Bourse show what their idea of art was. No one dared dispute David's prestige so long as Napoleon was his patron, but the excellent artist Prudhon in his portrait of the Empress Josephine showed fidelity to the charm of the Eighteenth Century.

In England there were the great landscape artists Turner and Constable. French painters went to London to admire their work. They influenced Delacroix who, when David was an old man, was able to make color as much respected as design. But Delacroix found a rival in Ingres, whose years of work in Italy had made him a thorough classicist. For years the struggle continued between these two leaders of rival schools. Mid-century brought the early work of the famous French painters of landscapes of whom Corot and Theodore Rousseau are the best known.

Growth-pains were also suffered in sculpture. When it came to making a statue of Napoleon, the classicists decreed that his boots and breeches were impossible. So Canova presented him nude with a toga thrown over his left arm. But the sculptors could not for long resist the movement toward more of life and action. Rude's magnificent *Départ des Volontaires* is the one live part of the *Arc de Triomphe;* its figures are classically clad, but to them there has been given an *élan prodigieux.*

In music the conflicting tendencies of the period were shown, but the great new compositions were in the forms of the sonata and the symphony which the Eighteenth Century had produced. In this field German supremacy was incontestable. Beethoven was born at Bonn in 1770. Deafness, solitude, and poverty could not stifle the magnificent expression of his genius. In his immortal symphonies he put romantic inspiration into forms whose clarity was classic. Weber, Schubert, and Schumann who followed him in Vienna were romanticists in the strength of their feeling and in their interpretation of nature.

The operas of the Italian Rossini and of the German Meyerbeer had great successes in Paris. Chopin, a Polish refugee befriended in France by George Sand, and Berlioz, who composed *The Damnation of Faust,* definitely belong to the romantic school—all inspiration.

In religion these was also a movement toward a new orientation. Neo-Catholicism was akin to the romantic movement; it too demanded closer alignment with the realities of life.

Lamennais, born at Saint-Malo, became a priest in 1816. He was one of many young Catholics who realized that the unpopularity of the clergy was due to the Church's support of reactionary political parties.

In co-operation with the Abbé Lacordaire and the Count Montalembert, he founded a liberal Catholic newspaper called *l'Avenir.* Its motto was, "God and liberty." It appeared in 1830 when the Church had espoused the cause of the Ultraroyalists and the priests were being driven to cover.

"Catholics!" Lamennais wrote, "we must save our faith, and there is but one way to save it,—the way of liberty. . . . Henceforth the only way of life is liberty. . . . Liberty does not kill God." *L'Avenir* demanded cessation of the government's subsidy of the clergy established by Napoleon's *Concordat.* "Whoever is paid is dependent upon the source of his pay," Lamennais claimed. "The morsel of bread that the government tosses to a priest deprives him of his liberty." The ardent and enlightened reformer proposed nothing less than an alliance between Catholicism and democracy. He foresaw that only by such an alliance could both democracy and Christianity, in the long run, be saved. It has taken the Church, Protestant as well as Catholic, more than a century to discover how right Lamennais was. The cause of Christ and the cause of human freedom are inseparable.

The Church was not ready to approve of liberty. Bishops forbade the priests to read *l'Avenir.* It had to suspend publication. Lamennais and his colleagues went to Rome and tried to persuade the Pope that their ideas were right. They had better not have tried. A result of their efforts was that Gregory XVI issued a formal denunciation of "liberal catholicism"; he described liberty of conscience as madness and liberty of the press as "the worst of all things, which can never be sufficiently abhorred and cursed."

Lamennais resigned from the Church. In 1848 he became a republican *député.* Neo-Catholicism could not resist its definite condemnation by the Pope, but the movement that Lamennais had started did not die. Many of the clergy who shared his ideas, though outwardly submissive to the Pope, were nonetheless able to convince the people of their sympathy. Societies were formed whose charitable work brought the priests and the people into closer understanding. There was a renewal of confidence in the Church. In the revolution of 1848 the people and the clergy made common cause against injustice.

The development of factories using the new machinery did not alleviate the misery of the working classes. The pre-Revolutionary guilds had protected the economic status of craftsmen who were fortunate enough to belong to them, but when they disappeared nothing replaced them. Their abolition gave freedom of employment but, since organization and strikes were forbidden, the situation of the workers was not improved. Employees were at the mercy of employers and little mercy was shown. Wages were very close to the starvation level.

Obvious injustices led certain theorists to propose the reorganization of society on a more rational basis. Those who favored such reorganization were called Socialists. Rousseau, Robespierre, and Saint-Just had all been advocates of the principles which the Socialists espoused.

Robert Owen, who left home at the age of ten with a few shillings in his pocket, became the manager of a cotton mill before he was twenty. He became one of the most successful manufacturers in the textile industry of England. He was unique in his concern for the welfare of his employees. Finding that there was no hope for securing legislation which would improve the status of the workers, he devoted his fortune to a communistic experiment which was made at New Harmony in Indiana, 1825 to 1829. It was his ambition to develop an economically self-sufficient community of two or three thousand persons in which the community itself, "as the mother of all," should justly apportion both work and profit. The Owen experiment in Indiana failed, but its example led to successful co-operative undertakings by workers in England.

In France the best-known Socialist was the Count Saint-Simon, 1760-1825. This aristocrat came to the conclusion that society was almost precisely upside-down. He believed that those who did most of the work were deprived of their just rewards by those who did the least. He held that the wealth of the world belongs primarily to those who do productive or otherwise useful work, and that all who profiteer upon the labor of others, or upon their incapacity to co-operate, are parasites; that included the politicians, the lawyers, and the bankers; advertising agencies, insurance experts, investment brokers, and the host of high-pressure salesmen had not yet appeared.

"Work," Saint-Simon wrote, "is the source of all virtue. That work which is most necessary should be the most esteemed. It is those who do the most necessary work who should play the first role in society. . . . Religion should direct society primarily to the amelioration of the status of its poorest classes." Some enthusiastic disciples of Saint-Simon formed a party and published a paper which kept his ideas alive long after his death. They were for the most part young engineers who had come under his influence while they were students. One of them was Ferdinand de Lesseps, the builder of the Suez canal.

The Utopian dreams of the early Socialists were too detached from the reality of human nature to have practical results. But from them there were distilled ideas which workers and philanthropists used later to advantage. Successors of Owen and Saint-Simon descended from the clouds of idealism and made the world conscious of the justice of their claims. Their devotion and disinterest was often in striking contrast with the selfishness of the privileged classes. When the middle of the century was reached, the forces of resistance to social injustice were stronger than they had ever been before.

Early in the Nineteenth Century some men became aware of the fact that nature has made the permanence of civilization dependent upon the evolution of competition into co-operation. This command of nature was heard, but the technique as well as the will to obey it were lacking. They still lack, but the choice between co-operation or destruction has become a more imperative choice than ever.

CHAPTER TWENTY-FOUR

THE SECOND REPUBLIC

DISREGARD OF THE DUCHESS WHOSE SON HAD INHERITED THE THRONE, IF THERE WAS TO BE A THRONE. THE PROVISIONAL GOVERNMENT. DECLARATION OF THE SECOND REPUBLIC. THE ABOLITION OF AN EMPLOY-MENT EXPERIMENT LED TO FOUR DAYS OF BLOODY STREET-FIGHTING. THE ELECTION OF A PRESIDENT WHO HAD NOTHING BUT HIS NAME TO RECOMMEND HIM. THE NEW *MONTAGNARDS* BECAME A MENACE. THE COUP D'ÉTAT OF THE LESSER NAPOLEON, DECEMBER 2, 1851.

THE SECOND REPUBLIC was a tragic demonstration of befuddled humanity's major weakness—its inability to co-operate in general improvement. Those who had the will to co-operate were deficient in technique and those who possessed the necessary technique lacked the will. The result was the loss of a dearly won opportunity. A bad framework had been broken, but it proved impossible to construct a better one. High hope was succeeded by disillusion and apathy. To social progress the old brakes of reaction were firmly reapplied. Even in name, the Second Republic endured but for three years, 1848 to 1851. It was succeeded by the Second Empire.

The carriage of Louis-Philippe and Marie-Amélie had no sooner left the Tuileries and headed up the Champs-Elysées than his daughter-in-law, the widowed Duchess of Orléans, crossed the Seine to the Palais Bourbon. There the *députés* were in session. That was on the twenty-fourth of February, 1848. The King had abdicated in favor of the Duchess' young son. His mother took him along with her to present him to the *Chambre*.

A majority of the *députés* were inclined to accept the regency of the Duchess; that was the slight recognition that she received. Suddenly the hall was invaded by a clamorous crowd of the insurgents. Bedlam broke loose. No further attention was paid to the Duchess. Her boy who had come to claim a crown got lost in the crowd. It became obvious that a regency would not do.

317

Many of the *députés* were in sympathy with the demands of the insurgents. In the midst of tumult and disorder it was decided that seven of them should constitute a provisional government with headquarters at the Hôtel de Ville. These seven had no more than begun their first meeting when a rival group walked in. It too had been authorized to constitute a provisional government, authorized by the socialistic left-wing republicans and some of their ardent followers among the workers. In an effort to make everybody happy, the provisional government was enlarged to include the unofficially appointed newcomers. The poet Lamartine, the scholar Arago, and the orator Ledru-Rollin were the best known of those who had been appointed at the Palais Bourbon. Louis Blanc was the leader of the other group. None of them had had practical experience with the difficulties of administration.

A manifesto announced, "The provisional government favors a republic if ratified by the people." That was not enough to satisfy the insurgents. They did not care to wait for an uncertain ratification; they demanded that a republic be proclaimed without further delay. It was deemed prudent to accede to this demand. *"République française"* and *"Liberté, égalité, fraternité"* were printed at the head of the placards which announced that France would forthwith undertake its second experiment in democracy.

The Terror of 1793 had not been forgotten by the republicans of 1848. They had great desire to avoid violence and to be definitely humanitarian. There was no longer the opposition of a powerful nobility to be overcome, but its role had been taken by privileged bourgeois whose opposition to free democracy might be no less; they could be counted upon openly to oppose or secretly to sabotage any measures which threatened to take toll of their privileges or their wealth. The threat to peace lay more on the side of reaction than on the side of republicanism.

The provisional government suppressed the death penalty for political offenses, abolished slavery in the colonies, set free those imprisoned for debt, restored liberty of the press, and established universal suffrage. It decreed that a Constitutional Assembly of nine hundred members should be elected and that all citizens over twenty-

one should have the right to vote. Removal of the property qualification increased the electorate from two hundred thousand to over
nine million. Unfortunately the vast majority of the new electorate
had no political education.

At first all went well. The bourgeois fear of anarchy was allayed.
The Orléans family made no effort for restoration and there was no
threat of foreign intervention. The clergy made public pledges of
loyalty to the new regime and blessed the trees of liberty that were
planted with joyful ceremony in towns and villages throughout the
country. Lamennais was delighted. In his paper he urged the workers
to bear with fortitude the inevitable delays in the improvement of
their lot. "They have," he wrote, "three months more of misery to
endure in the service of the Republic."

A Catholic journal stated, "France believed that it was monarchical
when it was already republican. . . . If the Republic will give to the
Church the freedom which autocratic powers do not give, there will
be no better nor more sincere republicans than the Catholics of
France."

It was the economic situation, of course, which brought disaster.
The inexperienced provisional government was unable to relieve the
depression. The revolution, largely a result of the depression, had
made economic conditions worse. Unemployment increased. Those
who had money hoarded it, thereby proving their incapacity to co-
operate. Fearful of insecurity, they made security less certain. People
tried to save their skins instead of trying to save that upon which the
safety of their skins depended. The brave dream of fraternal co-
operation turned gradually into a nightmare of unintelligent selfishness.

On the second day of its existence the provisional government
rashly promised to find employment for all. In order to do so, it decreed the establishment of national work-projects. It appointed
Louis Blanc, the workingman's friend, head of a commission authorized to deal with labor problems. Blanc's commission established a
ten-hour work day for Paris; eleven hours for the provinces. The right
of labor to organize was recognized.

The impression gained ground that Louis Blanc was a dangerous man. Bourgeois employers and shareholders did all they could to strengthen and enlarge that impression. With the workers of Paris behind him, Blanc had dominated and intimidated the provisional government. It began to be believed that his socialism, if unrestrained, might lead to a division of property. That settled the case of socialism with the farmers. They instantly became allies of the *bourgeoisie*.

In the April election of the Constitutional Assembly, the socialists were crushingly defeated. The moderate republicans gained an overwhelming majority. The provisional government resigned and was replaced by an executive committee of five, not one of whom was a socialist. Lamartine, Arago, and Ledru-Rollin were members of that committee.

The bourgeois *Garde nationale* had been unable to prevent frequent manifestations by the workers of Paris. It was supplemented by a new force of volunteers called the *Garde mobile*. Both of these forces had to be called out on the fifteenth of May, 1848, to suppress an armed mob that invaded the hall in which the Constitutional Assembly was in session, and tried to set up a rival government at the Hôtel de Ville.

The new executive committee suppressed Louis Blanc's labor commission, but it was more difficult to put an end to the national work-projects. Direction of that work had been entrusted to an efficient double-crosser whose secret purpose was to make this scheme fail. Blanc's plan was to provide work for each man according to his trade. What actually happened was that they were all put to work shoveling dirt, dirt that there was no sense in shoveling. They were paid two francs a day for tearing up streets and then smoothing them down again. They piled up paving stones and then put them back where they had been before. Their numbers increased until this project cost the government 150,000 francs a day.

On the twenty-first of June the executive committee ordered that all of the two-franc a day men who were between seventeen and twenty-five should join the army, and that the others should be sent to shovel dirt in the provinces. Up went the barricades, more than four hundred of them. But the government had expected that. It had brought into Paris thirty thousand troops to reinforce the *Garde nationale* and the *Garde mobile*. Command of this force was given to General Cavaignac, a brother of that Godefroy Cavaignac who had successfully defied the government of Louis-Philippe to punish him for his republicanism.

"Work, bread, or lead!" the workers cried. Arago attempted to reason with them. "Why do you resist the law?" he asked. "Because the lawmakers have not kept their promises," they replied. "One cannot argue with men who are on the barricades," said Arago. "But, Monsieur Arago," someone answered, "do you not remember that you were with us on the barricades of 1832?" "Ah! Monsieur Arago," a woman cried, "you have never known what it is to have no bread!"

There followed the most terrible street-fighting Paris has ever seen. It took the troops four days to crush the resistance of the desperate and famished workers. Thousands were killed, among whom there were six generals. The Archbishop of Paris was mortally wounded when he made a brave attempt to stop the slaughter. Finally driven back to the *Place de la Bastille* and the *Faubourg Saint-Antoine,* the workers were compelled to surrender. Many of the eleven thousand prisoners were shot without trial. They were all treated as criminals. Four thousand of them were shipped in one lot to Algeria. That was what it cost to abandon the policy of feeding the hungry. When those who "have" evade their responsibility for those who "have not," some blood is fairly sure to be shed. And history suggests that, in the long run, the only way definitely to avoid violence and destruction by the "have nots" is to transform them into "haves."

The *bourgeoisie* were responsible for the slaughter of the workers. The Republic, established in February, found itself controlled in June by those who had not favored its establishment. Its body was to survive for three more years, but the soul of it died on the barricades. *Liberté, égalité, fraternité* became a fiction on the day that the Republic gave to the famished workers bullets instead of bread.

Louis Blanc had no part in the insurrection, but he escaped trial and probable execution only by flight to England; today a wide avenue in Paris bears his name.

The government gave to General Cavaignac complete executive authority. Cavaignac was a republican, but he was more interested in order than he was in justice. Certain political clubs appeared to reverse that interest. He suppressed them. A deposit of twenty-one

thousand francs was required from publishers of journals. That caused
the suspension of those with leftist tendencies. Lamennais, in the last
issue of his paper, wrote, "One must pay dearly now for the right to
speak. We are not rich enough. Silence to the poor!"

The workers, defeated and disillusioned, became indifferent to the
fate of the republic that they had fostered. The child whose birth
had delighted them was now in the hands of their enemies. Those
who had captured the infant Republic were sure to strangle it before
it gained strength. Their hoarded government bonds had lost more
than half their value! A republic might be very well in theory, but, for
them, it must be a republic immune from any folly about social justice,
a republic whose first obligation would be to maintain that particular
variety of order which would insure continuation of their profits, a
republic, in short, which they themselves could control. If they could
not have that sort of republic, then back to monarchy!

The landowning peasants were also skeptical about the virtues of
republicanism. What they wanted was a government which would
protect their proprietorship and reduce their taxes. The rumor that
Louis Blanc believed in reapportionment of the land had given them
a frightful scare. Far better a king than a socialist! They also noticed
with strong disfavor that the new government had increased their
taxes.

The new constitution was promulgated in November, 1848. The
rights and duties of citizenship were set forth in its preamble in the
form that had become traditional, but specific commitments of the
government were carefully avoided. The Republic should "fraternally
assist" needy citizens to find work, but only "insofar as its resources
permitted."

There was to be but one legislative body. It was to be composed
of 750 members elected for three-year terms. Its dissolution could
be ordered only by itself. The executive power was vested in a president elected for four years and ineligible to succeed himself. He
would appoint his ministers, and he was authorized to "dispose" of
the army, but could never himself command it.

The election occurred in December. There were five candidates
for the presidency. The moderate republicans favored General Cavaig-

nac. A million and a half votes were cast for the General, but he was defeated by one who had nothing to recommend him but his name. That name was Bonaparte. Old soldiers had created a Napoleonic legend; the order, the prosperity, and the glory that the Little Corporal once brought to France were recalled; the evils that came in their train were forgotten. Seven million votes were cast. Three-fourths of them were for Louis-Napoleon Bonaparte. The enlargement of the electorate had brought no improvement.

When Waterloo was fought Louis-Napoleon was seven years old. His father was Louis Bonaparte, one-time King of Holland. When the Empire collapsed, his mother, Queen Hortense, daughter of the Empress Josephine, took him to Switzerland. There he had a military education. In his early twenties he went to Italy, where he became affiliated with the *carbonari;* he had a part in their insurrection of 1831. The death of the Duke of Reichstadt in 1832 made him the titular head of the Bonaparte family.

There was nothing about Napoleon's nephew to suggest the genius of his uncle except the name. He spoke but little, and what he did say was disappointing to thoughtful minds. He appeared to be in a perpetual doze, having the air of a dreamer reluctant to abandon his dreams. He may have dreamed of glory. Once he wrote to a girl friend, "Certain men are born to serve the progress of the human race . . . I feel myself to be one of them . . . I await my destiny with courage and resignation."

This dopey, glassy-eyed Bonaparte did not wait with resignation for the French people to ask him "to serve their progress." In 1836 he attempted a *coup d'état* at Strasbourg; as noted in Chapter Twenty-two, that *coup* was suppressed before it was fairly started, and the government, to save trouble, sent Louis to America. Four years later he was back again and started a rebellion at Boulogne. It also collapsed before it had accomplished anything. After that second attempt, the Peers of France condemned troublesome Louis to life imprisonment. In 1846, disguised as a workman, he escaped from the fortress at Ham and fled to England. There, two years later, he might have welcomed Louis-Philippe, but he did not. He did, however, provide a house in Berkeley Street for a blonde Miss Howard, and, as one of an army of special constables, he stood resolutely with the Tories in preventing an open demonstration in favor of an enlargement of the electorate.

There was no Bonapartist party in France at the time of Louis-Philippe's abdication, but, when the difficulties of the Second Republic began, there were many who saw that it might profit them to drum up interest in a candidate who had a great name behind him. It was not difficult to persuade even some of the workers that Bonaparte was the man for them. Certainly they would not vote for General Cavaignac who had murdered many of their relatives and sent others into exile.

The ex-rebel candidate was not unwelcome to the bourgeois lovers of order. Virtuous Cavaignac refused to strengthen his own candidacy by making any pre-election promises, but Louis-Napoleon helped destiny by promising all that anybody asked. He gained support from the clergy by promising to remove all restraints on Church schools. The wealthy voted for him because of confidence that he spoke their language, and all who wished for the re-establishment of royalty voted for him because they knew that he shared that wish.

The rich and the royalists had combined to form a party whose anti-republican objectives were camouflaged under the name "the party of order." President Bonaparte chose his ministers from that party. The republicans, excluded from all executive power, could hope to keep the Republic alive only through control of legislation. But in the election of 1849 even that control escaped them. The majority of those elected to the new Assembly were of "the party of order." The Republic was in the hands of its enemies.

Ledru-Rollin, after the slaughter of the workers in June, 1848, had gone over to their side, abandoning the moderates. He received more than three hundred thousand votes for president and became the recognized leader of the socialist workers. From their prototypes of 1793 his party inherited the name *Montagnards*. Their conservative opponents considered the *Montagnards* no better than brigands. The fact that these brigands elected one hundred and eighty members of the Legislative Assembly put fear into the hearts of the lovers of order and comfort.

In April, 1849, four months after his election, President Bonaparte authorized a military expedition to Italy. Its purpose was to prevent Austria from extending her control southward so that it would include the States of the Church. A revolt against the temporal power of the Pope was led by that amazing soldier of liberty, Giuseppe Garibaldi. Pius IX invited Austria to intervene. But France intervened first. Her stated intention was to re-establish the Pope's authority with such reforms of administration as might satisfy his rebellious subjects. What actually happened was that the French expedition besieged a Rome defended by Garibaldi. An army of the Second Republic had intervened against republicanism. That gave the *Montagnards* plenty to talk about on the floor of the Legislative Assembly.

The Constitution expressly forbade intervention against the liberty of any people. Ledru-Rollin charged the government with violation of that provision. The government ignored his charge. His party responded on the thirteenth of June, 1849, by insurrection. Some barricades were built. But the government was on the alert. The insurrection was quickly suppressed and Ledru-Rollin fled to England. The French expedition entered Rome and restored the Pope to power.

The legislation enacted in 1850 was definitely anti-republican. One of the fundamental tenets of the republicans had been that the State rather than the Church should control the schools. Neo-Catholic sympathy with republicanism was outweighed by the Church's long record of reaction. Socialist-republicans believed that Catholic schools would teach youth to favor the maintenance of privilege and order, and to leave the achievement of social justice to God. The Church could not be expected to favor social or economic changes that might put its own privileges in jeopardy.

Falloux was a Catholic *député* who had great influence. In March, 1850, the *loi Falloux* was enacted. It gave to all who possessed prescribed academic qualifications the right to establish both primary and secondary schools, it placed all primary schools under the surveillance of the clergy, and it gave to the Church membership in the Superior Council of Public Instruction.

Thiers, formerly hostile to Catholic schools, supported the *loi Falloux*. He explained his inconsistency as follows, "I have changed my attitude, not because of a change of conviction, but because of a change of conditions. . . . The public school teachers have become anti-social. Thirty-seven thousand of them are socialists or communists. . . . It will be better to put all primary instruction in the hands of the clergy. They will propagate the good philosophy, which is that man's lot here below is to suffer. . . . Education is not a good thing for all. It makes for covetousness of a standard of living which cannot be attained by all. I am opposed to building a fire under an empty pot."

The *loi Falloux* did not have all the effect that was anticipated. The University was able to maintain its independence, and socialist teachers continued to teach. But the new law did have the effect of establishing two rival systems of instruction whose rivalry continues to this day. Public opinion of the respective merits of these two systems remains divided.

The "party of order" twisted and turned in search for a way to reduce the strength of the *Montagnards*. So long as there was universal suffrage they remained a horrid threat to the kind of order that was so dear to the hearts of the *bourgeoisie;* in 1848 there was but a handful of socialist *députés;* in 1849 there were a hundred and eighty.

A lawyer found a solution. The Constitution guaranteed universal suffrage without restriction about property, but it was within the technical if not the moral right of the Assembly to modify the restriction about residence. A law enacted in May, 1850, restricted suffrage to those who had resided in the same *commune* for three years.

This measure diminished the electorate by more than one third. Of the three million who were disenfranchised the great majority were workers, because, in search for employment, they often had to move from one *commune* to another.

Thiers felt called upon also to explain his support of suffrage restriction. "Those whom we are depriving of the vote," he said, "are not the poor. They are the vagabonds. They are a part of that vile multitude which has destroyed all republics. Friends of true liberty and true republicanism must always dread the multitude."

The trickily disenfranchised multitude that Thiers dreaded, and all their friends, "conceived a lively animosity" for him and for the Assembly. That animosity was not lessened when further restrictions on the press compelled many liberal republican and socialist journals to suspend publication. The Assembly seemed not to realize that its restrictive measures hastened the approach of a new and more objectionable autocracy.

The majority of the *députés* were united in their hatred of the *Montagnards* and in their desire to put an end to the Republic, but they had different ideas about what monarchy to put in its place. Napoleon, Charles X, and Louis-Philippe had all abdicated in favor of their heirs. Which heir should be chosen? One who had no doubt about which one should be chosen was the Napoleonic heir who was already president of the fast-sinking Republic. He was determined to remain in power.

The President did all he could to assist destiny in his metamorphosis into an emperor. That change could not be accomplished if the army opposed it. The President made ardent love to the army, and the army found a thrill in the old cry, *"Vive Napoleon! Vive l'Empereur!"*

Bonaparte won the army with the magic of his name, but not the Assembly. The *députés* knew him too well to wish to increase his power. They would have preferred either the young grandson of Louis-Philippe, or the Count of Chambord, grandson of Charles X. Louis-Napoleon had to act quickly because his term would expire in 1852; a vote on a constitutional amendment which would have made him eligible for re-election failed to secure the necessary three-fourths majority. That was in July, 1851.

When the President found that the Assembly would not support him, he decided on a *coup d'état*. In order to win popular support, he proposed abolition of the residential requirement for suffrage. When this proposal was rejected by the Assembly, he felt that he might count on the sympathy of the proletariat as well as the support of the army. As for the Assembly, he planned to suppress it.

The day chosen for the *coup d'état* was the forty-sixth anniversary of Austerlitz, December 2, 1851. All who might effectively oppose it were placed under arrest the night before. Thiers and Cavaignac were among these. Troops occupied the hall of the Legislative Assembly. Two decrees which were entirely illegal were posted up on the walls of the city. One of them announced that the Assembly was dissolved and that universal suffrage was restored. The other one ordered that on the fourteenth of December the people of France should vote yes or no upon the question of giving full power to Louis-Napoleon Bonaparte for a period of ten years. The President called upon the people "to be the judge between him and the Assembly." Arch-demagogue, he declared that "the only sovereignty he would recognize was the sovereignty of the people."

Strict military control prevented successful resistance by the *députés*. Three hundred of them, assembled in one of the town halls, declared Bonaparte to be a traitor to the Republic whose perjury had automatically deprived him of office; all of this courageous group were promptly arrested and imprisoned. Victor Hugo was one of the *députés* of the *Montagne;* he helped in an attempt to organize armed resistance, but the people of Paris did not care again to risk a slaughter like that of June, 1848. Besides, the workers had been seduced by the promise of universal suffrage.

The country was less content with the *coup d'état* than Bonaparte had hoped. In many *départements* the republicans armed themselves and prepared to fight. The repression of such efforts was merciless. Military law was established in thirty-two *départements*. More than thirty thousand were imprisoned. About ten thousand were transported to Algeria. Sixty-six *députés* were exiled; Victor Hugo was one of them. Thus was autocracy again imposed upon France.

The yes-or-no plebiscite occurred under conditions which have been revived in modern times. Over seven million voted in favor of giving full power for ten years to the new president-dictator; not one out of ten had the courage to vote no.

On the twenty-first of December, 1851, Louis-Napoleon Bonaparte, elected theoretically as president, became Emperor of France in all but name.

CHAPTER TWENTY-FIVE

THE MID-CENTURY CONTAGION OF INSURGENCE

IN ITALY, MAZZINI, PIUS IX, CHARLES-ALBERT, CAVOUR, VICTOR-
EMMANUEL II, AND GARIBALDI. IN AUSTRIA, KOSSUTH, THE EMPEROR
FERDINAND, METTERNICH, AND SCHWARZENBERG. IN GERMANY, FREDERICK
WILLIAM IV, AND THE PARLIAMENT AT FRANKFORT. FRENCH INFLUENCE
AND EXAMPLE HAD MUCH TO DO WITH THE INSURGENCE AGAINST
TYRANNY IN ALL THESE COUNTRIES, BUT IN GERMANY, THE MOVEMENT
WAS MORE NATIONALISTIC THAN DEMOCRATIC.

PHENOMENA in the evolution of European society in the first half
of the Nineteenth Century suggest analogous phenomena of the
Sixteenth. New discoveries in the field of applied science contributed
to intellectual as well as to material progress. The discovery of America by Columbus and of Italy by the French were similarly contributory
to the enlargement of the scope of the Renaissance. The Renaissance
was followed by the Reformation which had its political as well as its
religious aspects. Similarly the enlarged intellectual activity of the
early part of the Nineteenth Century was followed by widespread
efforts for political reform. There occurred in many different areas the
insurgence of men so convinced of the validity of new ideals that
they were willing to fight and to die for them.

To diminish autocracy was a common aim of this contagious insurgence, but, beyond that, its objectives varied. In Germany and in
Italy the reformers fought for nationalization; in Austria they fought
to escape from it. One was a struggle for natural unification, the other
was a fight to end a unification that was unnatural. Both were heroic
efforts to make political organization conform to people's desire rather
than to enforced dictation.

The evolution of society is marked by changes which are dominantly
either spiritual, organic, and natural or material, inorganic, and, in that
sense, artificial. The general European insurgence of 1848 was of the
former rather than the latter type. Essentially it was a revolt of the
human spirit against asphyxiation. It was an admirable revolt, but

like most revolts that have a spiritual rather than a material impulse, it was weak on the side of organization and material equipment. Its final gains, though real, were at the time almost imperceptible. Reaction put tyrannical autocracy again in the saddle, but the horse under that saddle had acquired a new restiveness.

The stage of constitutional monarchy had been attained in England, France, Belgium, Spain, Portugal, and the states of southern Germany, but in Prussia, Russia, Austria, and the Italian states the Metternich type of absolutism was supreme. Everywhere, however, there were varying degrees of discontent. England was the most liberal of the constitutional monarchies, and, as we have noted, she suffered less than the others from the mid-century wave of insurgence.

In January, 1848, there were revolts at Palermo and Naples against the Bourbon Ferdinand II, King of the Two-Sicilies. In February the French compelled Louis-Philippe's abdication. As quickly as the success of the Parisians became known, it was imitated. In March there were revolutions in Vienna, in Berlin, in Milan, and in Venice. In April a semi-united Italy fought Austria, and in May the movement for German unity terminated in a "national parliament" at Frankfort which failed of its purpose.

The Treaty of Vienna of 1815 had divided Italy into seven states. The kingdom of Sardinia, with Corsica lying between its widely divided northern and southern parts, belonged to the House of Savoy, Bourbons had the Two-Sicilies, the Pope had the States of the Church, and Austria had the kingdom of Lombardy-Venice. There were also the three duchies of Parma, Modena, and Tuscany; Florence was the capital of Tuscany.

Metternich made it his especial business to see that Italy remained submissive both to absolutism and to the arbitrary partition of her territory. But even the most rigorous repressive measures did not intimidate a group of patriots whose triple objective was to destroy absolutism, to unify Italy, and to drive out the Austrians.

Mazzini of Genoa organized the society "Young Italy." That society did much to propagate the new ideas, but all its physical efforts were thwarted. The patriots then undertook to form an Italian confeder-

The political divisions of Italy in 1848.

ation of liberalized monarchies. Books and pamphlets devoted to this thesis were widely read. Ambition for national unity and for liberal reforms became more general than it had ever been before. This movement was called the *Risorgimento*.

A new pope, Pius IX, gained wide popularity in 1846 by liberal decrees which were a great shock to Metternich. The Austrian arch-priest of absolutism said "I believed that I had foreseen everything that could happen in Europe, and that I was prepared for everything, but the possibility of a liberal pope had never occurred to me."

The Pope's example and the *agitation populaire* induced the Duke of Tuscany and King Charles-Albert of Sardinia to make some concessions, but Bourbon Ferdinand conceded nothing; he even decreed that in the Two-Sicilies a cheer for the Pope should be considered an act of sedition. His obstinacy led to the successful revolts in Naples and Palermo in January, 1848. Ferdinand was compelled to grant a constitution. Charles-Albert, the Duke of Tuscany, and Pius IX followed suit.

In March a sudden insurrection occurred in Vienna. When Venice and Milan heard of that, they too revolted and drove out the Austrians. There were five days of bloody fighting in Milan. The Austrian Dukes of Parma and Modena did not wait to be driven out. They hastily sought refuge elsewhere.

The patriot Cavour wrote in his journal, *Risorgimento,* "Events in Lombardy and Vienna put an end to hesitation. We must fight. Prudence at this moment calls for audacity."

Charles-Albert of the House of Savoy became the military leader of the patriots. They spurned an offer of French help made by Lamartine. They believed they could defeat the Austrians without foreign aid, aid that might end in demands for territorial concessions.

Unfortunately, Charles-Albert's military ability was inferior to his good intentions. After some minor victories, the forces of the patriots were defeated at Custozza. Austria regained control of northern Italy, and Ferdinand, who had only pretended interest in the cause of the patriots, renewed his grip on the south.

Italy, after the defeat at Custozza, abandoned the idea of unification under the leadership of her monarchs. They had failed her. A pure republic became the new objective of the patriots. Rome and Florence were the centers of the new movement. The popularity of Pius IX had ceased because he had refused to declare war against Austria. In November, 1848, Rossi, the principal political adviser of the Vatican, was assassinated. He had formerly been an ambassador of France. The republicans demanded a constitution and a declaration by the Pope of war against Austria. They besieged the papal palace and shot one of the prelates.

These events changed Pius's sympathy for liberalism into hatred of it. He could not accept progress at the price of disorder and bloodshed. He took refuge in the Two-Sicilies. In February, 1849, the Roman republic was declared both at Rome and at Florence, the Duke of Tuscany having followed his fellow dukes in flight. Mazzini was elected chief of a directing triumvirate.

The patriots of the north were encouraged to renew the struggle with Austria. Radetsky, the Austrian general, crushed their army at Novara, March 23, 1849. Charles-Albert, who had been pushed into this renewal of hostilities, abdicated in favor of his son, Victor-Emmanuel II, and left for Portugal; he died there a few months later. Austria enlarged her grip on northern Italy by military occupation of a large part of Piedmont.

At this point President Louis-Napoleon intervened in favor of the Pope. An army of the French republic fought against the forces of the Roman republic led by Garibaldi. This anomalous intervention was described in the preceding chapter.

France was not favorable to Austria, but Napoleon was favorable to reaction. His intervention ruined the cause of the patriots. Authoritarian control was re-established throughout Italy and her prisons became gorged with political prisoners. Pope Pius would not even listen to suggestions of prudent reforms which were made to him by the French. King Ferdinand at Naples treated his political opponents as though they were murderers. Twenty thousand of them were packed into horrible prisons among condemned criminals. Gladstone of England, visiting Naples, was a witness of Ferdinand's brutal procedures; in letters that were published he bitterly denounced King Ferdinand.

The one bright and shining exception in the renewal of tyranny was young Victor-Emmanuel. Austria put great pressure upon him to make him abrogate the constitution which his father had granted. He was offered the duchy of Parma as a bribe, but he preferred to remain faithful "to the memory of his father, to the honor of the House of Savoy, and to the sanctity of promises made to his people." Italy was not to be forgetful of Victor-Emmanuel.

Piedmont, the northwest corner of Italy where the House of Savoy reigned, became the refuge of the patriots. Cavour declared, "So long as liberty exists even in a single corner of the peninsula, there is hope for the future. So long as Piedmont escapes despotism the cause of the regeneration of all Italy has not been lost."

For centuries Austria had been the most artificial of all the European states. Only her uncompromising absolutism enabled her to control her heterogeneous population. Her empire was a mosaic of mutually antagonistic peoples whose intense racial prejudices have been but slightly modified in the march of time. In 1848 her control extended far beyond this mosaic, into Italy on the south and into Germany on the north.

Four principal languages were spoken in Austria. Her revolution of 1848 followed as many lines as there were languages. Each language was spoken by a racial group that sought political independence of the other groups. There were Slavs, Latins, Germans, and Magyars; all of them wished for states of their own. Separatism was the keynote.

The Slavs were the most numerous, but they were also the most divided, both geographically and sub-racially. They included Poles, Croats, Serbs, the Czechs of Bohemia, the Slovacs of the Carpathian hills, and the Ruthenians of Galicia. They occupied frontier areas of Austria on all sides except the west.

The Latin group included the Roumanians in Transylvania and the Italians of the Tyrol who were at the other extremity of the Empire.

The Magyars lived in Hungary. They and the Germans occupied the center, the Danube valley. The Germans were in Vienna and upstream from it; the Magyars were below it, spreading out over the great Hungarian plains on both sides of Buda and Pest.

All of these peoples had once been loosely organized in states of their own, vestiges of whose rights and institutions Austrian conquest

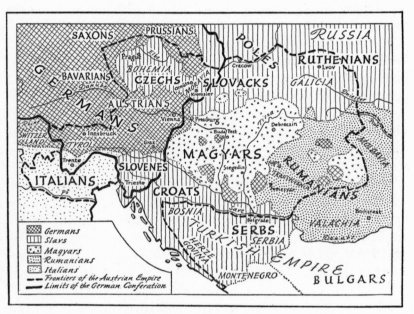

The racial mosaic of the Austrian Empire in 1848.

had been unable completely to eradicate. They had lost their independence, but none of them had lost the ambition to regain it.

The government at Vienna was Germanic. German was the official language. Among the conquered peoples certain assemblies of the nobles continued to be held from time to time; they preserved their form, but they had lost their power. Hungary was the only exception to that; the Magyar nobility maintained a semi-independence in the empire of which their country was a part.

The Austrian government was never guilty of any concession to freedom, but the laxity of its administration made a weak spot in the iron ring of its tyranny. Negligence permitted in Vienna, Prague, and Pest a spread of liberal ideas that should have been prevented. In 1848 there came a lively revival of separatist aspirations. There were writers who sought to fan nationalist embers into flames. One of them, Louis Gaj, a Croat, wrote, "A people without nationality is like a body without bones."

There was a tendency for the Magyars and Czechs to make common cause against the Germans, and for the Serbs and Croats to unite against the Magyars. The only thing which these mutually hostile people held in common was a keen desire for independence. The inextricable tangle of their separate revolts facilitated Austria's recovery of the control of all of them.

When the news of Louis-Philippe's abdication reached Pest, Lajos Kossuth, leader of the Hungarian patriots, made a demand in the Diet (the assembly of nobles) for national independence, a demand that was enthusiastically supported by his colleagues. That was on the third day of March, 1848. On the eleventh Czech patriots demanded at Prague the re-establishment of an independent government of Bohemia with equal representation of Czechs and Germans. On the thirteenth the contagion reached Vienna. A crowd burned Metternich's villa. The proud and inflexible minister saved his skin only by taking flight in a laundry cart, hidden under the washing.

The Emperor Ferdinand, deprived of the services of his chief minister, made concessions which produced a temporary calm, but a new storm that broke in May so alarmed him and his court that they fled to the Tyrol.

The cause of reform, and of a variety of political independences, might have been won at this time except for that mechanized, non-reflective force which established authority can usually count upon for support—the army. While one imperial army was crushing rebellion in Italy, another one crushed it in Austria. The Croats were encouraged also to fight against their traditional enemies, the Magyars, with whom they had better reason to make common cause. The only reward the Croats received later for important services rendered was the detachment of their territory from Hungary and its division into separate provinces. The benefit they derived from fighting on the side of the Empire was less than nothing at all.

In June of 1848 the Czechs were defeated at Prague, and Bohemia was placed under military dictatorship. Vienna presented greater difficulties. There the insurgent elements remained in control but not in accord all through the summer. Late in October, after a five-day bombardment, an imperial army entered the city.

Prince Felix Schwarzenberg became the man of the hour. His prompt decisions and his audacity saved the day for the old order. Prince Felix would have gone much farther than he did except that he died suddenly in 1852; to him belongs the credit of having restrained Prussia as well as crushing the revolution. Appointed prime minister in November, Schwarzenberg persuaded Ferdinand to abdicate in favor of his eighteen-year-old nephew, Francis-Joseph. At the same time, as a further measure of appeasement, he promulgated a constitution, but did not specify at what date it would go into effect. It never did go into effect.

The case of Hungary remained to be settled. The imperial government's difficulties in Bohemia, Vienna, and Italy had prevented interference with Hungary's organization of an independent democratic state. Its chief was Kossuth. But the Serbian, Croatian, and Roumanian minorities of Hungary could not accept absorption into a state controlled by the Magyars. The call for an assembly of Slavs at Zagreb was declared by the assembly at Pest to be an act of sedition. The Serbs and the Croats then allied themselves to fight the Magyars.

That alliance of the southern Slavs facilitated the task of the Austrian army. The Kossuth government, driven out of Pest, was compelled to take refuge in the midst of the great swamps of the Tisza. But in the spring of 1849 Kossuth emerged from the swamps and defeated the Austrians. The independence of Hungary was again declared.

Austria was compelled to seek the aid of Russia. Czar Nicholas I, an autocrat of the Metternich school, was delighted to help in crushing the Hungarian democracy, the poison of whose liberal ideas might infect the Russian part of Poland. Co-operating Austrian and Russian forces soon choked the life out of the new state. Kossuth escaped to Turkey, but all the other revolutionists who were captured were either hanged, shot, or imprisoned. Hungary lost all of its previous privileges and was placed under martial law until 1854; it was divided into provinces that were governed by Germans who did not even speak the Magyar language.

The two years of struggle in central Europe for freedom and autonomy were succeeded by a decade of reaction and tyrannical absolutism. But the flames which had been kindled were not extinguished. A Czech publicist wrote, "In two or three years one may not expect to repair evils that have endured for centuries. No matter! Austria shall become what we wish her to be, or *she shall cease to exist. . . .* The bayonets of our oppressors are carried by our own people; today they do not understand, but they shall come to understand." Events have proved that, as seen from a democratic standpoint, the second part of this prediction was less accurate than the first part.

Germany, like Italy, was the scene of a mid-century struggle for national unity, but the German struggle was different in that two major powers, Prussia and Austria, had to be reckoned with as German states.

The German Confederation of 1815 was a sketch of the dream of the nationalists. It was a confederation in name more than in reality, but it forecast the shape of a great nation that was yet to find itself.

The Confederation was composed of thirty-nine member states whose inequality in importance was almost as great as inequality could be. They ranged from the great powers, Austria and Prussia, down to tiny principalities of less than twenty thousand inhabitants. Intermediate in importance were the kingdoms of Bavaria, Wurtemberg, Hanover, and Saxony, and the free cities of Hamburg and Frankfort.

The president of the Confederation was the Emperor of Austria. Its Diet, which met at Frankfort, was authorized to propose measures relating to the common peace and security of the member states, but any such proposals had to be approved by all the states before they became effective. In 1815 the Diet proposed the construction of a line of fortresses along the western frontier; ten years later no agreement had been reached even about the location of these projected fortresses. This was typical of the inefficiency of the Confederation. Its Diet was little more than a social foregathering of major and minor diplomats who enjoyed the excellent beer of Frankfort.

Germany was even more fragmented than Italy, but some of her states were in advance of Italy in political organization. Absolutism prevailed in Austria, and in the states of the north including Prussia, but the states of the south had constitutions. Everywhere, however, men who were outspoken in the cause of liberalism risked persecution. Democracy had no better social standing in the monarchies than communism has today in the democracies.

The states of southern Germany were the most exposed to French influence. That influence, despite Napoleon, was a democratic influence throughout the Nineteenth Century. Baden, Wurtemberg, and Bavaria shared the pre-Napoleon aspirations of the French. But in the north, no less than in Austria, the seeds of democracy found few crevices in which to sprout. Where age-old feudalism held sway, sustained by the absolutism of Berlin and Vienna, democracy seemed but a futile fairy tale.

Another cause was more dear to German hearts than the cause of liberalism. That was the cause of German unity. Democracy they might dismiss with a shrug, but, at the suggestion of a union of all Germans to form the world's mightiest nation, their eyes took fire. They were more interested in becoming strong than in becoming free.

Napoleon contributed importantly to the birth of the German passion for unity. It had its birth in 1813 with the realization that only by united effort and common inspiration could the yoke of the Corsican be lifted. From its establishment in 1810, with Fichte as its first rector, the influence of the University of Berlin constantly contributed to the growth of national feeling. Other universities and many ardent writers stimulated the German pride of race and passion for power. If France had fulfilled her threat of war in 1840, German unity would probably have been achieved at that time.

The objective of the nationalists was to transform the shadowy Confederation into a substantial union of its member states. The leadership of Prussia seemed essential to the attainment of this end. Prussia was pure German; Austria was not. Indolent and romantic Vienna looked to the past; vigorous and realistic Berlin, looking to the future, worked tirelessly in service of her materialistic ambition. In 1831 Edgar Quinet wrote, "Prussia, more than any other German state, satisfies the German thirst for power and for material achievement. . . . She needs but a ruler who can see clearly the star of her destiny. She does not dream of the past as they do on the banks of the Danube. She dreams of the triumphant future of a united Germany."

Austrian influence in the German states was political. Prussia built hers upon a more solid foundation. She created an economic confederation called the *Zollverein* to which most of the German states belonged, but not Austria. The suppression of duties led to a great increase of trade between members of the *Zollverein,* an increase which benefited the others as well as Prussia.

In 1840 Frederick William IV succeeded his father. Mature when he began his reign, Frederick had a gift of eloquence and a reputation for scholarship, generosity, and patriotism. The nationalists, with whose views he had expressed entire sympathy, had great hopes of him. But Frederick's fortitude proved to be inferior to his eloquence. His impressive façade rested upon an inadequate foundation. When it came to a pinch, he was hesitant and timid. The cold audacity of Austria's Schwarzenberg took all the starch out of Prussia's Frederick. Frederick coveted the leadership of a united Germany, but he wished to receive that high office from the hands of the princes rather than from the representatives of the people; at least that was the excuse he offered for not taking it when Austria opposed the popular movement.

Frederick, like all weak monarchs, craved popularity. He wished to make himself beloved by conferring new privileges, but, like Louis

XVIII, he wished to confer privileges without diminution of his power. For seven years he sought for a way to eat his cake and still to have it. At last, in 1847, he created the *Landtag,* an assembly whose power was limited to voting new taxes and to expressing opinions about other matters only when called upon to do so. Frederick explained his position to the *Landtag* as follows:

"I shall never accept that between God in heaven and our country there shall be inserted any written document, or that paragraphs shall ever become a substitute for our ancient fidelity. . . . Your mission, gentlemen, is not to give effect to academic opinions. That would be definitely not German. It would lead to insoluble difficulties with the crown, which, in accordance with the laws of God, should rule of its own free will and never be submissive to the will of majorities."

The *Landtag* was not content with the limitations of its assignment. Some of its members expressed their "academic opinions" and their disagreement with Frederick's association of himself with God rather than with the majority of his subjects. Five months after he had created it, God's partner dissolved the *Landtag* and thereby increased the general discontent.

The news that came from Paris late in February, 1848, stirred the German discontent into action. Early in March a group of liberal patriots met at Heidelberg in Baden. They called for the assembly at Frankfort of an all-German "preliminary parliament" whose purpose should be to establish a permanent parliament of federated states. Public opinion about unity had become so aroused that the monarchs did not dare at first to interfere with the assembly at Frankfort.

There, early in April, representatives of the people met and called for a Constitutional Parliament to be elected by universal suffrage. Riotous crowds in the capitals showed readiness to fight in support of the patriots at Frankfort. The revolution in Vienna of March 15 was followed three days later by revolution in Berlin. Behind barricades the people fought the royal troops in the Parisian manner. But Frederick, like Louis-Philippe, had no stomach for fighting. He called off his troops. The people then invaded the court of the palace and compelled the King to salute the corpses of those whom his troopers had slain.

Frederick, greatly alarmed, ceased temporarily to be a deputy of God and came over to the side of the people. Hardly one year after he had told the *Landtag* that he should never submit to the will of majorities, he rode through the streets wearing the red, black, and gold colors of the democratic united-Germany movement, and he promised a constitution that would grant equality of rights.

In May the all-Germany parliament at Frankfort created a provisional federal government and placed at its head an archduke who was an uncle of the young Emperor of Austria. This duke was popular because he had married a postmaster's daughter.

In Germany as in Austria, the revolution was short-lived because of the canine fidelity of the soldiers to the hands that fed them. Frederick, taking courage from Schwarzenberg's bloody success in Vienna, turned his troopers loose again upon the people whose cause he had momentarily espoused. With the free use of bayonets he re-established his divine right to rule. But he deemed it prudent to grant a constitution; he swore to observe it, but he added, "It is necessary that the king govern. I do not govern because that is my pleasure, but because that is God's order. . . . There must be a free people[!] governed by a free king." The Prussian constitution of 1850 remained in effect until 1918; its ingenious electoral provisions restricted to the propertied classes the limited political power which it conferred.

The restoration of royal power in Vienna and Berlin was a forecast of death to the Parliament at Frankfort. The restored monarchs could not be expected to support a movement which was essentially democratic. Austria might be the only member of the Confederation to oppose the principle of German unity, but all the monarchs would oppose a unity based on democratic ideals.

In March, 1849, the Parliament invited Frederick William to become the emperor of a federation of the German states exclusive of Austria. Austria at once ordered her deputies to leave Frankfort, and Schwarzenberg warned Frederick that his acceptance of the Parliament's invitation would mean war.

Frightened Frederick cloaked his fear in pompous and preposterous phrases. He wrote, "I do not wish to accept, like Louis-Philippe, a crown soiled by the mud and slime of the streets. . . . The crown that is offered to me bears neither the Holy Cross nor the mark of God's grace. The descendant of more than eighty monarchs may not accept a crown from the hands of rebel serfs. . . . The only right of the Frankfort assembly is to submit to the princes a proposal for a constitution. Its failure to do that is a monstrous sin."

Frederick's refusal of leadership killed all hope for a unified and democratized Germany. Desperately the patriots attempted to arouse the people. There was no response that was effective. Saxony and Baden compelled the flight of their princes, but Prussian soldiers quickly suppressed this insurrection. The Parliament, reduced to a hundred deputies, moved from Frankfort to Stuttgart. There some of them were arrested and the others were dispersed. Many liberals, realizing that the vast majority of their fellow-countrymen were more interested in force than in freedom, left at this time for foreign shores. America was particularly enriched by this migration.

The crown which Frederick William had declined to accept from the people he made a futile attempt to secure from the princes. But Austria, completely restored after her victory over Hungary, had no difficulty in thwarting Frederick's ambition. In the summer of 1850 Schwarzenberg sent an ultimatum to Berlin. Frederick caved in. He renounced all claim to govern more than Prussia alone. The old weak Confederation was re-established and the Emperor of Austria was re-elected as its president.

CHAPTER TWENTY-SIX

AN EMPEROR BY ASSASSINATION

THE BONAPARTISM DELUSION MISLED THE PEOPLE. A RETURN TO AUTOC-
RACY. FRANCE PAID DEARLY FOR THE REDEEMER COMPLEX OF HER EMPEROR.
THE CRIMEAN WAR. INTERVENTION IN ITALY. CAVOUR AND BISMARCK
BEGAN TO SHAPE HISTORY.

IN NOVEMBER, 1848, Louis-Napoleon, candidate for the presidency
of the Republic of France, issued a manifesto in which he stated, "I
promise, if elected, to be always faithful to the duties which the Legislative Assembly may impose upon me . . . I pledge my honor to leave
to my successor 'liberty intact.'." In the following month, having been
elected, he took oath that, "Before God and the French people, I
swear to remain faithful to the democratic Republic and to fulfill all
the duties imposed upon me by its Constitution. I shall regard as
enemies all who attempt by illegal means to change that which all
France has established." In November, 1850, while plotting to destroy the Republic, he declared to the Assembly, "I charge with great
guilt all who seek through personal ambition to compromise the stability which the Constitution affords. The invariable rule of my
political life is, under all circumstances, to do my duty, nothing less
than my duty. Today it is permitted to all, except to me, to desire a
revision of our laws. I, bound by my oath, am held within the strict
limits of the existing statutes. Loyally I have opened to you my heart.
You will respond by giving me your confidence, and God will do the
rest."

One year later, President Louis-Napoleon, having gained control of
the army, placed the Assembly under arrest and illegally proclaimed
to the people that they might have the privilege of extending full
powers to him for a period of ten years. Thus the little Napoleon
proved his resemblance to the great one in more than name alone. He
proved that he shared his illustrious uncle's contempt for such nonsense as truth and honor. In the practice of perfidy he even surpassed
the greater Napoleon's notable record.

The nation's tolerance of the little, perfidious Bonaparte requires explanation. This tolerance, inconsistent with the essential character of the French people, was compounded of various elements. First and most important, there was the great illusion called Bonapartism. Artists, writers, politicians, and the instinctive love of romance contributed to the strength of this illusion. The *Mémoires* of Napoleon, written for as well as by him at Saint-Helena, presented the Corsican despoiler as, at heart, a true friend of the people and a believer in democracy. Only foreign interference had prevented his fashioning for the people of France a form of government that would have fulfilled their heart's desire! Destiny had preserved a nephew who would fulfill the dream that Waterloo had so rudely shattered!

Even Victor Hugo's ardent republicanism could not resist the lure of the Napoleonic legend. In 1828 he wrote:

> *"Toujours lui! Lui partout!*
> *Tu domines notre âge; ange ou démon, qu'importe!*
> *Ton aigle dans son vol haletant nous emporte.*
> *L'oeil même qui te fuit te retrouve partout.*
> *Toujours dans nos tableaux tu jettes ta grande ombre.*
> *Toujours Napoleon, éblouissant et sombre,*
> *Sur le seuil du siècle est debout!"*

The colorless and comparatively joyless period that succeeded the Empire also facilitated the enlargement of Bonapartism. The elderly and drably garbed statesmen of Louis-Philippe made sad contrast with the swift and brilliantly attired young men who once frequented Paris, bringing with them the fragrance of new glories won on far frontiers. Ah! Those were the days!

"The appearance in public life of large numbers of elderly gentlemen, speaking with the accent of the last century and gloomily disapproving of the generation with which they found themselves surrounded, was inadequate compensation for the loss of those bronzed and booted men of the Empire who had ridden triumphantly into every capital of Europe. . . . The reign of Louis-Philippe was a dismal triumph of middle age, an age of reason as depressing as the administration of Walpole in

England; old men might stir their memories and young men
their imaginations with the picture of a more vivid period when
the Grenadiers of the Guard went swinging through the Carrousel and France was unacquainted with the less heroic figures
of M. Thiers and M. Guizot."—*Guedalla's Second Empire.*

Emergence from the folklore of hero-worship was still far distant.
Artists portrayed the victories of the Empire, sculptors made sympathetic figures of the Little Corporal, and *chansonniers* made Napoleonic glory the theme of songs that the people sang. Hardly a home
was without some stirring picture that made even battle seem preferable to the drab routine of peace. The people dreamed of more thrill-
ing days, days filled with color, movement, the spice of danger and
the roll of drums. They dreamed of freedom wedded happily to imperial glory and adventure. One name alone could find a place in this
fantastic dream. Again the magic of that name became an opiate to
reason and made impossibility seem possible. That name was Bonaparte.

In those mid-century days romanticism was more popular than
realism. Seventy more years of painful experience were to pass before
France removed from the foundation of her political philosophy all
but the hard stones of fact. She gave up her long-cherished illusions
only after they had led her into disaster after disaster. Her modern
realism is a fruit of adversity, and, because of adversity, that fruit has
a tough skin. It is difficult now for the common mind of France to re-
adjust itself to an economically unbalanced world in which some of its
assumptions may be no longer valid. A realism that is too rigid risks
inconsistency with reality.

The workers of France, in the thirty-three years after Waterloo, had
no more to eat and vastly less to thrill them than they had had under
the Empire. That period was golden for the *bourgeoisie;* they kept
the gold and to those whose work produced their wealth they gave
but dross. So, when France went to the polls in November, 1848, the
romance of the workers won an easy victory over the realism of the
bourgeoisie. Three-fourths of all who voted voted for an iridescent
dream, a dream that was to end in nightmare. He whom they elected

was a dreamer but half-awake whose grasp of reality was no more firm than that of his partisans.

Romance made Louis-Napoleon a president in 1848, but a more solid force was necessary in 1851 to overcome the realism of the Assembly. He found that force in a well-organized body, a body that begins to think only when it ceases to be fed. He kept it well fed and he sharpened its bayonets. When the day came for the *coup d'état* he could rely upon the army to suppress the realists and upon the romanticism of the proletariat to facilitate confirmation of his dictatorship.

The plebiscite of December 20, 1851, gave to Louis-Napoleon a mandate to make a constitution as he saw fit. He made one very quickly. It was published on January 14, 1852. It confirmed the full powers of the Prince-President and bore a striking resemblance to the one his uncle had issued in the Year VIII, December 15, 1799. Louis-Napoleon's constitution, like the First Consul's, established a monarchy without admitting it. It was little more than a secondhand democratic disguise to cover the nakedness of a dictator while his imperial robes were in the making.

In the spring and summer of 1852 the Prince-President traveled about. In the principal cities he dispensed the same sort of sonorous nonsense that had ended by boring the realists of the Assembly. But that honeyed palaver appealed to the crowd. It was easy for a well-trained *claque* to make the yokels join in shouting, *"Vive l'Empereur!"*

In a plebiscite held in November an overwhelming vote was cast in favor of "re-establishment of the imperial dignity in the person of Louis-Napoleon." Upon December 2, 1852, the first anniversary of the *coup d'état,* and the forty-seventh of Austerlitz, Napoleon III was declared to be the hereditary Emperor of the French People.

France's second emperor was in his forty-fifth year when he began his reign, a reign that was marked by two distinct periods. From 1852 to 1860 it was as much like the First Empire as a less gifted Napoleon could make it. After that, and until its disastrous end in 1870, it relapsed into a liberalism for which the philanthropy of the Emperor may be given slight credit.

Louis-Napoleon's obsession about destiny amounted to fatalism. His nature made co-operation with others extremely difficult. He had a mystic, Sphinxlike air that contradicted his assertions of sincerity. The Austrian Ambassador, who did not like the Emperor's fishy eye, said, "He does not wish to discuss; he does not know how to discuss." He seemed to wish to create the impression that he always had a trump card up his sleeve. There were symptoms of an inferiority complex that clashed with his conviction of magnificent destiny. His six years of prison life may have had to do with that. Men found it impossible to give him their confidence.

This enigmatic Bonaparte has been defended by some as a benevolent and generous idealist. Others have called him immoral, pitiless, unscrupulous, and ungrateful. Thiers maintained that the Emperor's incapacity was greatly underestimated! His youth and young manhood had been devoted to conspiracy. Having acquired the habit, he carried the air of a conspirator to the end. His technique was a technique of secrecy, surprise, and *coup d'états*.

Napoleon brought the blonde Miss Howard to France and took her with him on his travels. Some provincial republicans were slightly scandalized. There was an embarrassment at Saumur when a prominent but puritanical citizen declined the honor of having the Emperor and his blonde lady as house guests at the same time.

Since none of the reigning dynasties appeared to be interested in offering a princess as legal replacement for Miss Howard, the Emperor was spared the discomforts of a political marriage. He took to his bosom a bride of his own choosing. Eugénie de Montijo was a Spanish lady of great beauty whose father had served as an officer under Napoleon I. In January, 1853, she was wed to Napoleon III.

The Emperor was compelled to form a cabinet of mediocrities who were little known. "He lacked the esteem of honest men. . . . All who were eminent remained either hostile or aloof." Persigny, prominent from the beginning in all the Prince's conspiracies, Morny, a clever speculator, and Rouher, a lawyer "able in the defense of any cause,"—these men were the Emperor's first lieutenants.

There was immediate restoration of press censorship and of governmental control of education and of elections. The form of a legislative body had to be kept alive, if not its function. The usual precautions were taken to prevent the election of any except wholly sympathetic *députés*. The ballot boxes were guarded by officials named by the government and the prefects were instructed to see to it, "by use of whatsoever means they saw fit," that the returns would be favorable to the "friends" rather than the "enemies" of the government. An official list of approved candidates was published. In 1852, out of 261 *députés* elected, only five were not on the approved list. Political life suffered for a time a complete paralysis.

Popular interest shifted from politics to speculation. The brokers were kept busy at the Bourse. To profiteer on the perspiration of others became the fashion. Unearned money, unsocially acquired, was freely spent. Paris became again a capital of frivolity whose *insouciance* was echoed in the *éclat* of the imperial *fêtes*. The intellectuals either became melancholy or ceased to be intellectual. Taine, a young professor of philosophy, resigned rather than submit to the restrictions imposed by his superiors. Reuss, an Alsatian historian, wrote of the "intellectual atrophy" which seemed inescapable, and Victor Hugo, exiled in Jersey, exhausted his magnificent vocabulary in the verbal shafts that, between chapters of *Les Miserables,* he found time to launch at the head of the "criminal" who had "assassinated" the republican government of France.

Between his promises to the Legislative Assembly and his promises to the people, Louis-Napoleon made no distinction. He was false to all of them. One of his campaign slogans had been, *"On a dit que l'Empire, c'est la guerre. Moi je dis, l'Empire, c'est la paix."* The empire that was to be synonymous with peace was almost continuously at war. Its final act was to plunge blindly into a fatal struggle with Prussia, a struggle in which the physically wrecked and mentally vacillating Emperor was no match for the keen and cold-blooded intelligence of Bismarck.

Napoleon III, like Napoleon I, could not keep his mind off the rest of Europe. He had a similar thirst for glory, a cruel thirst that sent young Frenchmen to their death in all quarters of the globe. Europe alone was too small a graveyard for Napoleon. The bayonets that had made him Emperor were rewarded by more distant and more perilous tasks, and the bodies of those who bore them were buried in lands remote from France. Their graves are in Africa, in the Orient, and even in Mexico.

The first military adventure into which Napoleon pushed his people was the intervention of 1849 in Italy whereby the Republic of France choked the life out of an infant Republic of Rome. In 1854 France entered the Crimean War against Russia, in 1857 to 1860 she made campaigns in Africa and Asia, in 1859 she fought Austria in Italy, in 1861 she intervened to place a candidate whom Napoleon had chosen upon the throne of Mexico, and in 1870 her deteriorated military power was crushed by Prussia. Nonetheless, Napoleon always maintained that he was a pacifist. He had no stomach for war. The sight of a wound made him ill. He was not a warrior, but he was even more dangerous as an intriguer whose lack of understanding led to slaughter that he could not bear to witness. He was unable to foresee the inevitable results of his secretive and ill-judged schemes. His incapacity, as Thiers suggested, was underestimated.

The Emperor's great ambition was to correct the errors of the Congress of Vienna. He wished to destroy the treaties of 1815 and to be the guiding spirit in the making of new frontiers and new states which would be more consistent with geography and with racial affinity. Such consistency would justify extension eastward again of the frontier of France to the Alps and the Rhine. The Italians of Lombardy-Venice were to be freed of Austrian control and the kingdom of unhappy Poland was to be restored. Napoleon even favored the union of the German as well as the Italian states. He helped to increase the strength of the very power which was to crush him.

Eugénie, who had a mind of her own, told her husband that he would be an idiot to attempt to do all this. *"Le métier de rédempteur,"* she said, *"est un métier de sot."* French diplomats who were far more familiar than Napoleon with the European situation agreed with Eugénie. The Emperor, who could not be talked out of his conviction that destiny had called him to be Europe's redeemer, entered into secret negotiations. Secrecy was always congenial to him. The official diplomats of France were not consulted. Napoleon said to a representative of Prussia, "What my ministers may say is of no weight. I alone know what the foreign policy of France shall be." He made a treaty with Cavour of which his own foreign minister was ignorant. When that minister opposed Cavour, the Italian patriot produced a letter from the Emperor which caused great embarrassment.

The European monarchies had mixed feelings about the Second Empire. They were glad about the extinction of republicanism, but they were anxious about a Bonaparte upon a throne. That name stood for conquest. Having known the uncle, they placed little confidence in the peaceful protestations of the nephew. The nephew, however, was extremely anxious to secure co-operation in his self-appointed task of redemption. He could not expect to make progress on that until he was certain that Czar Alexander's Holy Alliance would not be revived to resist him. Czar Nicholas, who had succeeded his brother Alexander in 1828, had been the least cordial of all the monarchs in recognition of the new Emperor. Napoleon began to look for an adequate basis for a Franco-British alliance against Russia, an alliance strong enough to prevent new co-operation by the one-time allies who had united to destroy his uncle.

England's opposition to increase of Russian influence in Turkey was sure to be seconded by France. France was already involved in the trouble that was brewing in the Levant. Priests of the Greek Church, supported by the Czar, had replaced Roman Catholics in guardianship of the Holy Cities of Palestine. This violated an agreement to which Turkey had subscribed in 1740. France brought pressure upon the Sultan and succeeded in having their former rights restored to the Roman clergy.

The Sultan's displacement of the Greek priests gave to the Czar an opportunity he had long desired. The dismemberment of Turkey was one of his pet projects. He attempted to secure the consent of England for a proposed operation on "the sick man of Europe." Failing in that, he moved troops toward Constantinople. But the Sultan was not to be intimidated. French and British ships of war having arrived to support him if necessary, he declared war against Russia. That was in November, 1853.

In January, 1854, the French and British ships entered the Black Sea. The Russians had destroyed a Turkish fleet. In March, England and France as allies of the Sultan declared war against Russia. They made a joint agreement to guarantee the independence of the Turkish Empire without territorial diminution, and the Sultan agreed to put an end to all persecution of Christians, a promise which he was entirely unable to fulfill.

The Crimea is a peninsula whose shape suggests a heavy pendant with a slender stem, a huge pendant that is suspended from the north shore of the Black Sea. Sebastopol was a fortified harbor near the peninsula's southern extremity. There the Russians established a navy yard and arsenal. This military headquarters became the key position of the Czar's campaign against Turkey. Since the Franco-British forces did most of their fighting in the Crimea in an effort to capture Sebastopol, their war with Russia was called the Crimean War.

Strong forts and a cordon of sunken ships at the harbor entrance made Sebastopol secure from attack by sea. French and British forces were compelled to disembark some distance north of it and attack by land. The lack of unified command, a shortage of supplies, the marshy nature of the country, and epidemics of fatal diseases all contributed to make this campaign a slow and extremely difficult business. The Russians had ample time in which to organize their defense. They constructed earthworks which were repaired as fast as they were demolished. Assault after assault was repulsed. The misery and tedium of trench warfare was protracted for nearly a year. The siege of Sebastopol lasted from October in 1854 until September in 1855. The French lost ninety-five thousand men; the English twenty thousand. More than three-fourths of this loss was due to disease. Malakoff, the principal fortress of the defense, was finally captured by a French division commanded by General MacMahon. That compelled the Russians to retreat.

Czar Nicholas died while the siege of Sebastopol was in progress. Alexander II, his successor, was disinclined to continue the struggle. He agreed to terms that were developed in detail at a conference in which Austria and Prussia participated as well as the powers which had been at war. The result of that conference was the Treaty of Paris of March, 1856. The major features were the de-militarization of the Black Sea and recognition of the independence and territorial integrity of the Turkish Empire.

The French took the major loss in the Crimean War, and the English took the major gain. Russia's defeat kept her out of the Mediterranean, but that, in the end, was more to England's advantage than to France's. Napoleon, however, was delighted. His prestige had been increased. He had sent nearly a hundred thousand Frenchmen to suffer and to die in the cold and clammy muck of the Crimean marshes, but what of that? He had been true, he believed, to the role of redeemer to which destiny had so obviously called him. When, in response to his invitation, the powers met in Paris in 1856, the assassin of the republic felt himself to be upon the threshold of immortal glory.

The people of France showed less interest in glory and in the redemption of Europe than they did in the redemption of their own freedom. In 1855 the Emperor's minister of justice reported that "the democratic party is suppressed, but not corrected." Hugo's passionately anti-Bonaparte *Châtiments* and other forbidden literature continued to circulate and kept the flame of democracy alive. Arrests and imprisonments failed of their purpose. In 1857, despite the impossibility of campaigning, five out of ten *députés* elected by the Parisians were republicans.

Orsini was an Italian patriot who hated Napoleon because of his interference with the cause of Italian independence. In front of the Opera, on a January evening of 1858, Orsini threw three bombs at the Emperor's carriage. He missed the Emperor, but the flying fragments wounded more than a hundred people. That gave the government excuse for still greater severity. Some hundreds who had nothing to do with Orsini's plot were either exiled or deported. Thenceforward, all candidates for office were required to swear to a written statement that they would loyally support the government that had illegally destroyed the Republic.

Orsini, having failed to kill the Emperor, tried to persuade him. He urged him to help Italy. From his prison cell he wrote, "May Your Majesty not spurn the supreme entreaty of a patriot who is about to die. Liberate my fatherland and receive the blessings of its twenty-five million citizens and of their posterity forever."

Orsini's letter so impressed the Emperor that he had it published in the *Moniteur,* the official journal. A copy of it was sent to Cavour. Its publication in Italy caused a great stir. It began to be understood that Napoleon favored Italian independence even though his expedition to Rome in 1849 had seemed to be hostile to it. The intention behind that expedition had been to restrain Austria rather than to restrain the *Risorgimento.* Napoleon, when a very young man, had been associated with the *Carbonari;* as Emperor he found that the objectives to which Cavour's genius was devoted harmonized with his own dream of European redemption. Some gentlemen of his cabinet, more gifted as thinkers than as dreamers, were unable to see that co-operation with Cavour would be beneficial to France. Such co-operation would extend to thousands of young Frenchmen the privilege of dying in Italy rather than in the Crimea for a cause equally not their own, and it might hasten the day, already faintly discernible to the farsighted, when the armies of a united Germany might march victoriously into France. The Emperor seemed to see nothing of all that. But he did see that he could avoid argument with his ministers by dealing directly and secretly with Cavour.

The Count of Cavour, more than any other man, was the maker of Italy. In 1847 he founded a journal which took the name of the Italian movement for unity and for reform, *Risorgimento.* When Austria, in 1849, put a stop to that movement except in Piedmont, Cavour, undismayed, carried on. For years his perseverant genius was devoted to achieving the union of Italy under the leadership of his own liberal sovereign, Victor-Emmanuel II, King of Sardinia and head of the House of Savoy.

Victor-Emmanuel, much shorter than Henry of Navarre and much more be-whiskered, was akin to Henry in personality. He had a similar simplicity, brusqueness of decision, easy comradeship, courage in battle, and excellence of judgment. Cavour, almost equal to Henry's Sully in diligence, was vastly his superior in diplomacy.

Turin was the capital of a small but far-extended kingdom. There, for seven years, 1852 to 1859, Cavour served as the chief minister of the kingdom as well as artisan of the future of all Italy. His policy was based on maintenance of order and authority through steadily progressive reform by a monarchical government. He had the solidarity of Sardinia to perfect before he could proceed with his greater plans. And he knew that France must be secured as an actively co-operating ally before there could be any hope of eliminating Austria from Italy. He courted France's favor by sending Sardinian troops to fight with the French in the Crimea. That gained him a place in the conference of the powers at Paris in 1856. There he suggested that the reduction of Austrian influence in Italy would be contributory to the peace of Europe. Austria vigorously opposed this suggestion and nothing was done about it, but Napoleon indicated to Cavour that he was inclined to sympathize with that statesman's point of view.

Plombières is a delightfully situated health resort in the Vosges. Napoleon went there in the summer of 1858, hoping to find relief from his gall and bladder pains. His pains, unfortunately, were not great enough to keep his mind off of other matters. He invited Cavour to slip up from Turin to Plombières as secretly as possible. They took a long ride in the woods together. That evening, by dim light on the corner of a table in a little inn, Cavour drafted an agreement that was, in effect, a new map for Italy. He went back to Turin with the French army in his pocket.

Napoleon, recalling for a moment that he was a Frenchman as well as the redeemer of Europe, held out for Savoy and Nice as compensation for all the French lives that were to be lost for Italy. Cavour did not like that. He knew what Garibaldi would think about the cession of his beloved birthplace, but, even with the loss of Nice, Cavour had the best of the bargain. The Emperor of France had agreed to come to the aid of Sardinia as soon as Austria committed an aggressive act. All that remained for Cavour to do was to irritate Austria.

Shrewd Bismarck was delighted with the way in which the situation was developing, but England and Russia were not. They feared the outbreak of a general war. As the tension increased between Austria and Sardinia, they did what they could to prevent hostilities. And hostilities might have been prevented except that Austria finally fell into Cavour's trap. Sardinia had armed. Emperor Francis-Joseph, believing that his troops could crush the Sardinians before French help arrived, sent an ultimatum from Vienna to Turin demanding disarmament within three days. The ultimatum was rejected and war began.

The French were no more ready to move than Francis-Joseph had believed, but they moved. On April 29, 1859, Austrian forces invaded Piedmont. On the same day part of the French army started over the mountains for Turin and the rest of it disembarked at Genoa. Fighting began on the tenth of May and continued until the eighth of July. There were two principal battles. MacMahon, by a timely arrival, won the battle of Magenta for the French on the fourth of June, and on the twenty-fourth, near beautiful *Lago di Garda,* the slaughter of Solferino occurred. There the Austrians lost twenty-two thousand and the allies seventeen thousand. The only virtue of Solferino was that its horrors, added to those of the Crimea, led to the formation of the Red Cross.

Napoleon had had enough of it. He had agreed at Plombières to go on to Venice, but he did not. Having seen the shambles of Solferino, he wanted to go home. An added reason for going was his tardy discovery that by fighting Austria he had been playing into the hands of Prussia. Bismarck was not idle in that summer of 1859. Napoleon's furtherance of national unity in Italy also furthered unity in Germany, a unity that could not fail to increase the power of Prussia. Bismarck had proposed to the Diet at Frankfort that Prussia take charge of the Rhine frontier.

Napoleon offered peace to Francis-Joseph. On July 11, 1859, they met at Villafranca and agreed to an armistice whereby Sardinia gained Lombardy, but Austria remained mistress of Venice. Cavour, in utter disgust, resigned. Napoleon, having failed to fulfill his contract, relinquished his claim on Nice and Savoy, thereby losing all material as well as all moral benefits of his costly intervention.

An Italian statesman wrote, "Napoleon went to Italy with an army of two hundred thousand, expended half a billion francs, won several battles, lost thousands of men, restored Lombardy to the Italians, took nothing in return, and then departed amid the curses of those whom he had aided." The way of a redeemer is hard.

CHAPTER TWENTY-SEVEN

FOREIGN DEVELOPMENTS THAT AFFECTED FRANCE

ITALY BECAME ITALIAN AND NICE BECAME FRENCH. CAPABLE CAVOUR AND GLAMOROUS GARIBALDI. POPE PIUS IX PERCEIVED THE DANGERS OF DEMOCRACY. THE SITUATION IN GERMANY. NAPOLEON III CONTINUED TO BLUNDER. BISMARCK, THE DANISH DUCHIES, AND THE TREATY OF GASTEIN.

THE Franco-Austrian readjustment of Italy was, of course, not acceptable to the Italians. The repair work of Napoleon and Francis-Joseph was an emergency job which could not stand the first strains that were put upon it. At Zurich, in November, 1859, the armistice terms were incorporated into a treaty whose humor must have been apparent even to those who signed it. The Dukes of Tuscany, Parma, and Modena had been swept out of their duchies by the first breath of the revolutionary storm. The Treaty of Zurich stipulated that these dukes should be restored "without recourse to force"! The only item of this farcical treaty that was respected was its cession of Lombardy to Sardinia.

The Emperors of France and Austria appeared to believe that the determination of Italy's destiny was one of the duties which God had laid upon them, but they were soon to be relieved of that duty by two Italian patriots who claimed no celestial mandate. For Cavour and Garibaldi the mandate of their fellow countrymen was enough. Cavour's discouragement did not last for long. Having resigned in disgust in July, he returned to office with renewed zeal the following January.

The patriots who were in control in Tuscany, Modena, Parma, and Romagna found cause for laughter in Franco-Austrian dictation that was not backed up by bayonets. Instead of inviting their former dukes to return, they invited annexation by Sardinia. Victor-Emmanuel wisely responded that this annexation would be imprudent at that time unless it was approved by the Powers; Europe was already nervous about what was going on in Italy. Modena, Parma, and Romagna then united and chose a cousin of Victor-Emmanuel to be their regent. Cavour, though out of office, directed this movement.

Again Napoleon came into the picture. Victor-Emmanuel decided that he would risk enlargement of his kingdom if he could secure France's approval. Napoleon was hesitant. Pius IX was violently opposed to any further advance toward Rome of the liberalism which Victor-Emmanuel represented, an advance which would be a threat to his authority as a temporal ruler. If Bonaparte renewed his support of Sardinia, he would lose Catholic support in France which he had assiduously cultivated. Finally, however, the Emperor agreed to approve the proposed annexations if they were supported by plebiscites, and, more importantly, if plebiscites were held at the same time in Savoy and in Nice on the question of annexation to France. He had not forgotten the concession he had wrung from Cavour in the woods of Plombières.

Both Cavour and the Emperor had a good deal of explaining to do at home. Savoy and Nice are on the French side of the Alps. Napoleon maintained that France's support of the development of Sardinia into a powerful state made it his duty to secure for France the crest of the Alps as the Franco-Sardinian frontier. It would not do to leave easy access to the Rhône valley in the possession of a strengthened neighbor who might, in the future, become unfriendly. Napoleon's foresight was better when he looked across the Rhône than when he looked across the Rhine. Despite his plausible arguments his deal with Sardinia hurt him with the Catholics.

Cavour's task was more difficult than the Emperor's. Garibaldi bitterly opposed the cession of Nice whatever the will of its people. Cavour's argument was that Garibaldi should not insist upon the right of people in one place to determine their nationality and deny it to people in another place; since he supported self-determination for Florence, he should not oppose it for Nice.

The treaty with France which involved the proposed annexations was ratified by the Sardinian parliament by a vote of 223 to 36. Plebiscites were held at the same time on both sides of the Alps. By overwhelming majorities the people of Nice and of Savoy voted in favor of annexation to France and the people of Tuscany, Modena, Parma, and Romagna voted to become subjects of Victor-Emmanuel. That was in March, 1860.

Irrepressible Giuseppe Garibaldi was the most amazing adventurer of the Nineteenth Century. Having lost his beloved Nice, he found solace in a bold attempt to free the south.

When a young man, Garibaldi had been compelled to flee to Tunis on account of complicity in one of the plots of Mazzini's Young Italy society. Then he became a cattle-rancher in Uruguay. There he led a free-lance company that fought on the liberal side in various South American revolutions. He and his followers became famous for their daring and for their red shirts; the only cloth available when the shirts were needed happened to be red. In 1849 Garibaldi was back in Italy, fighting against the French for the republicans of Rome. He was then forty-two. Miraculously escaping capture by the Austrians, he next reappeared in New York as a candle manufacturer. Then Peru. Then China. In 1859, Italy again. In 1860, with Cavour's support, he organized at Genoa a new and greater company of Red-Shirts. He led this company of one thousand to fight for the liberation of his countrymen from the tyranny of the Bourbon King of the Two-Sicilies. "So long as there are chains in Italy to be broken," he said, "I shall fight on there, or there I shall leave my bones."

In the spring of 1860 there was an insurrection in Sicily against King Francis II, who was extremely obstinate about concessions. The Red-Shirts landed there in May. Within a few weeks Garibaldi was master of all Sicily and proclaimed himself its dictator in the name of Victor-Emmanuel. In August he crossed to the mainland and in September he made a triumphal entry into Naples, obstinate King Francis having departed.

Garibaldi and his devoted Red-Shirts began to think less about Victor-Emmanuel and more about Mazzini. Perhaps the republicanism that the Genoese patriot preached would be the better thing for Italy after all! Disregarding Turin, Garibaldi planned to lead his company from Naples to the conquest of Rome. Then Venice, and finally the recovery of his beloved Nice. Over all these cities there should fly the flag of liberated, united, and perhaps republican Italy.

Cavour saw that Garibaldi was capable of spoiling everything. Ever since Napoleon's intervention of 1849, a French force had remained on duty at Rome to protect the Pope and to assure Napoleon of Catholic support in France. Venice was still held by Austria. Unless Garibaldi was restrained, Austria and France might intervene again and undo all that had been accomplished.

In this critical moment Cavour was admirable. Audacity, intelligence and swift action were required. Cavour supplied them all. He asked Napoleon's approval for sending Sardinian forces to the south. Taking silence for consent, he sent an army into the States of the Church. That army dispersed a papal force that was commanded by a French general! The situation was extremely delicate.

The Sardinian army, led by Victor-Emmanuel, pushed on to Naples. There Garibaldi loyally agreed to take orders from his sovereign. The dual danger of foreign intervention and of republican revolution was averted. Cavour's intelligent audacity had won. The people of the Two-Sicilies and of the States of the Church voted almost unanimously in favor of annexation to the kingdom of Sardinia.

Thus Sardinia, a nation of five million in July, 1859, became, eighteen months later, a nation of twenty-two million that included nearly all of Italy. This was not what Napoleon had planned or desired. It was what Cavour and Garibaldi did.

On the fourteenth of March, 1861, a representative parliament met in Turin and declared Victor-Emmanuel "King of Italy, by the grace of God and the will of the nation." Italian unity was established on the basis of a liberal sovereignty to which the people gave their free consent.

Three months later Cavour died. Great patriot and great statesman, he had achieved the unification of his country except for Venice and Rome. The people loved him and called him "Papa Camillo." He was one who understood his fellow men and found happiness in devotion of his life to enlargement of their opportunity.

Rome and Venice! Italy could not be Italy without them. So long as Austria held the beautiful Queen of the Adriatic in her grasp, so long as the Pope ruled in Imperial Rome, the dream of the patriots would be but half fulfilled. Venice was attainable; there the obstacles to be surmounted were tangible; purely practical considerations would determine Austria's holding on or letting go. But Rome presented a far more difficult and more complicated problem. There the resistance to be overcome was not a purely practical resistance. It was stronger than that. It was a spiritual resistance that was supported by all good Catholics.

The pontificate of Pius IX was the longest in the history of the Church, and one of the most notable. It began in 1846 and ended in 1878. In this period the papacy was deprived of the temporal powers that it had possessed for eleven centuries, but such was the strength of the Pope's leadership that the Church's spiritual gains more than offset her material losses.

Upon his accession, Pope Pius, as monarch of the States of the Church, granted amnesty to all political prisoners and exiles. At the same time he promised to establish a Council of State. That led to belief that he was in sympathy with the *Risorgimento*. A few years later, however, he witnessed the disorder and bloodshed that accompanied republican insurgence in Rome. He felt compelled to flee from the Vatican to Gaëta. From that day until his death, he was the sworn enemy of liberalism. Even to discuss man's right to freedom was, he maintained, a violation of the will of God.

In 1864 Pope Pius published an encyclical which clarified the irreconcilability, from his point of view, of Catholic and democratic ideals. He asserted that society had fallen into "monstrous error." "There are those," he proclaimed, "who dare to teach that social progress requires disregard of religion, that liberty of conscience and belief is a natural right, and that all should enjoy freedom of speech without restraint by Church or State." He contended that, under such conditions, materialism would strengthen its domination of men's minds, that the influence of religion would diminish, and that, with free play for individualism, man's inhumanity to man would increase. Evidence that supports the Pope's contention is not difficult to discern.

In his judgment of human nature Pope Pius was far more realistic than Rousseau. The argument for democracy may have been based less upon the contemporary status of human nature than upon its theoretical capacity for improvement. However, in the three-quarters of a century that have passed since Pope Pius's encyclical was issued, that improvement has been slight. The perfectability of human nature remains the basic argument for democracy, but the intellectual and spiritual progress of those who have had the benefit of it has not been great enough to prove that Pius IX was wrong. Little in the modern world might tempt him to change his views. "My children," he might sadly say, "I warned you."

"Certain people," the encyclical continued, "dare to assert that the will of the people constitutes the supreme law. Thereby the victory of material force over right and justice is facilitated. *Faits accomplis* are acknowledged to be superior to divine and human rights. . . . Those who have undertaken to destroy social and religious order seek also to prevent the Church from fulfillment of its duty to educate. They would eliminate religion from the schools and replace it by perversion and misguidance. They would thereby deprive youth of the understanding of God which is their rightful heritage, and substitute for it a confusion of ideas which obscures the divine plan. . . . They have the impudence to assert that certain laws of the Church are invalid unless they are endorsed by the State. This pretention disregards the God-given authority of the Pope. . . . We hereby order all the children of the Church to regard the evil opinions and doctrines which we have specified as reproved, proscribed, and condemned." (This translation of excerpts from the encyclical departs from the letter of the text, but not, it is believed, from its sense.)

It became clear that the Pope would yield none of his territorial rights and that he could rely upon solidarity of Catholic opinion to support him. Good Catholics maintained that the Pope could not give up his temporal authority without sacrifice of his spiritual influence. Pius, untroubled by doubt, believed that his right to rule the States of the Church was no less God-given than his right to rule the Church itself.

The Pope's obstinacy was extremely embarrassing to Napoleon. There was a French military force at Rome whose duty it was to support the Pope. So long as that force remained there, it would aggravate Italy's irritation with France; gratitude for Napoleon's indispensable aid in the development of her unity was soon obliterated by resentment of his interference with completion of that unity.

The Emperor wished to withdraw his troops from Rome, but he

could not do so without increasing the hostility of the Catholics in France who already bitterly criticized his noninterference with Sardinia's acquisition of the major portion of Vatican-ruled territory. For nine years this situation caused difficulties within France and Italy, as well as troubling their relations with each other.

Garibaldi could not be restrained. Sicily responded to his cry of "Rome or death!" Again he led his Red-Shirts to the attack. Napoleon, insistent upon avoiding another clash between his troops and a force led by Garibaldi, put all the pressure he could upon Victor-Emmanuel to have him stop the march of the great adventurer. Sardinian soldiers had to wound him in order to stop him. That was in 1862.

Pope Pius showed no gratitude to Napoleon for having kept Garibaldi away from Rome. On the contrary, he accused the Emperor of treason because of his official recognition of the kingdom of Italy. Napoleon, bitterly criticized by both sides, tried to extricate himself from the difficulty by promising to take his troops out of Rome in 1866 if the Italian government would agree to make no further encroachment upon papal territory. An agreement to this effect was reached in September, 1864. As evidence of the sincerity of its renunciation of designs on Rome, the Italian parliament declared that Florence should be the capital of the nation. The people of Turin registered their disapproval of this step by staging a riot.

Napoleon, having bound Italy by treaty to keep her hands off Rome, attempted to regain something of his lost popularity by helping her to secure Venice. In the spring of 1866 Prussia and Austria were on the brink of war over the question of control of a united Germany. Napoleon encouraged Italy to make an alliance with Prussia against Austria. Emperor Francis-Joseph countered by offering Venice to France if Napoleon would guarantee both French and Italian neutrality in Austria's struggle with Prussia; it was understood that France would generously cede Venice to Italy. Napoleon took full advantage of the greatness of Francis-Joseph's need. All that he promised was French neutrality, and that only upon Austria's agreement both to cede Venice and to make no new encroachment upon Italy. Thus, thanks to Napoleon, Italy remained free to fight Austria without risk of territorial loss.

Italy won no glory in the three-cornered war of 1866; she merely made it easier for Prussia to defeat Austria; Napoleon had again played into the hands of Bismarck. Prussia defeated Austria at Sadowa, but Austria defeated Italy at Custozza. The Italians were also defeated in an attempt to win Venice by arms, but, through the mediation of Napoleon and after a plebiscite, Venice became a part of united Italy in October, 1866.

In that same year, in accordance with the agreement of 1864, the French garrison was withdrawn from Rome. That was the signal for irrepressible Garibaldi to break loose again. The government's promise that the Pope should not be molested meant nothing to him. He and his red-shirted volunteers proposed to make Rome the capital of Italy or die in the attempt. French forces, returning at top speed, arrived just in time to prevent this, and thereby to make France more unpopular in Italy than ever.

It was Prussia's invasion of France in 1870 that finally opened the gates of Rome to Italy. The fall of Napoleon freed Victor-Emmanuel from his promise to leave the Pope in peace. He tried to persuade Pius IX to make voluntary renunciation of his temporal powers. Failing in that, he sent an army which occupied Rome on the twentieth of September, 1870. Annexation of the ancient capital was "consecrated" by a plebiscite of its inhabitants who gave abundant proof that annexation was what they wanted.

Victor-Emmanuel did all that he could to allay Catholic fear of interference with the Pope's administration of the Church. He pledged himself "to protect the liberty of the Church and the independence of its Sovereign Pontiff." Parliament enacted a law which declared the Pope to be "holy and inviolable" and entitled to all the prerogatives of a sovereign. That law also directed that three million lire should be paid annually to the Vatican from the Italian treasury, and that the Pope should have full authority over the Italian clergy.

All these efforts for appeasement did not modify the attitude of Pius IX. He would not recognize a government which had deprived him of his rights by force. He would not leave the Vatican, maintaining that he had been "morally imprisoned" there. For nearly seventy years this situation remained unchanged. It was only in 1929 that Pius XI came to an understanding with the State which ended the long "imprisonment" of the Pope.

The achievement of unity in Italy gave a new impulse to efforts to achieve unity in Germany. There Prussia played the role of Sardinia and Bismarck the role of Cavour. But Bismarck's technique was in striking contrast to that of Cavour. They were alike only in intelligence and perseverance. The Italian statesman was a gentle and prudent diplomat whose eyes twinkled above his smile. Bismarck's eyes were steely and he was not inclined to smile. His technique was a technique of force, audacity, and brutality. His sole objective was enlargement of the power of Prussia. For him, all means that might serve that end were justified. He was not a believer in plebiscites.

Bismarck's task was less complicated than Cavour's. Prussia was far more powerful than Sardinia, and not so much hampered as Sardinia by republican tendencies. Her monarchy, traditionally militaristic, had made but negligible concessions to liberalism. It made none in its conquest of Germany. Prussia unified Germany by the force of arms.

William I, whose magnificent side-whiskers contributed to his fame, began his reign in 1861. He was then sixty-four, but still full of vigor. He lived to be ninety-one. Industrious, economical, authoritative, and of limited intelligence, he was a typical Hohenzollern. The army was his especial interest and pride. He built it up to an effective strength of nearly half a million. He lacked Bismarck's courage and audacity, but he was even more avaricious than Bismarck after victories were won.

The Baron Otto von Bismarck, an expert beet-grower in Brandenburg, entered politics as a member of the *Landtag* at the age of thirty-two. In 1862, when forty-seven, he became King William's chief minister. An avowed enemy of liberalism, Bismarck prevailed upon the King to dissolve the *Landtag* every time it refused to vote the credits necessary for the fulfillment of his military plans. The credits that the *Landtag* refused to authorize were established by royal decree. From 1862 to 1866, dictatorship was re-established. Bismarck was hated by all German liberals, but he did not mind that. He got the army that he wanted. That army enabled him to become the real master of Europe for nearly a quarter of a century.

For seven years Bismarck had served as Prussia's representative in the Diet at Frankfort. There he came to see that, if German unity was accomplished, Germany would be dominated either by Prussia or by Austria. Determined that it should not be Austria, he sabotaged all plans for union that Austria espoused.

"The Hapsburg monarchy," he said, "is a worm-eaten three-master to which it would be madness to attach the fine Prussian corvette." At another time he said, "In foreign policy one should be without either sympathy or aversion for any country. . . . If I believed it to be in the interest of Prussia, I would feel the same satisfaction in having our troops fire on Russians, English, Austrians, or French. The interest of Prussia is the sole determinant of my policy."

Napoleon had ample opportunity to prevent the fulfillment of Bismarck's plans. Instead of doing so, he continued to play into the hands of his shrewd opponent, piling blunder upon blunder.

When Bismarck became the Prussian pilot, the European governments were in a state of mutual distrust that was greater than usual. That favored the success of his policy. He was more expert than any of his contemporaries at fishing in troubled waters. The Italian revolution had troubled the water. For one thing, it had increased the demand for German unity. In 1863 Francis-Joseph brought the princes together at Frankfort to discuss federal reform. Nothing was accomplished because Bismarck refused to co-operate.

The breakdown of international co-operation appeared to be contagious. The prestige which France gained in the Crimea and in Italy gave her an opportunity to determine the direction of political development in Europe. Even a second-rate statesman might have taken advantage of that opportunity and dispelled the threat of storm that was brewing. But Napoleon, obsessed by unreality, speeded the coming of the storm.

In 1861 the Emperor plunged into a mad and disastrous adventure in Mexico. In 1863, by espousing the cause of Poland against Russia, he gained nothing for Poland, but much for Prussia. The Czar's natural position in a Franco-Prussian struggle would have been on the side of France, but Napoleon enabled Bismarck to win the Czar to his side. Prussia aided Russia in crushing Polish insurgence. Gain of the friendship of Russia was the diplomatic victory which enabled Bismarck thenceforward to assume a major rather than a minor role on the stage of Europe.

Napoleon, vaguely alarmed by developments that suggested disregard of his redeemership, proposed a Congress of the Powers whose objective would be "the pacification of Europe without shock." England, despite France's co-operation with her in the Crimea, declined Napoleon's invitation. She would have nothing to do with such a Congress. It did not convene.

Schleswig and Holstein were two duchies that occupied the stem of the fragmented peninsula which is Denmark. They were not a part of Denmark, but the King of Denmark was their duke. Holstein, at the base of the stem, was populated by Germans; it was a member of the German Confederation. Schleswig, north of it, had a mixed population of Germans and Danes; the Germans wanted attachment to the Confederation, and the Danes wanted annexation by Denmark. Denmark undertook to make the Danish constitution effective also in Schleswig.

Childless Frederick VII, Denmark's king, designated the Duke of Glücksburg as his heir. But the Germans of the two duchies maintained that another duke was the rightful heir. A Congress of the Powers that was held in London in 1852 recognized the Duke of Glücksburg as the rightful heir, but the Diet of the German Federation did not.

In 1863 Frederick VII died. Forces of the Federation entered Holstein with view to establishing the authority of its candidate to the succession, the Duke of Augustenburg.

Bismarck did not overlook the economic and military importance of the stem of the Danish peninsula. Its position between the Baltic and the North Seas gave it great value for maritime commerce; Kiel was its principal harbor. However, to establish Prussian control of the duchies was a delicate business which could not be hurried. Both Austria and Prussia had signed the London agreement of 1852. They could not, therefore, concur in the Diet's denial of the legitimacy of King Frederick's successor. But Bismarck craftily allied Austria with him in a demand for Schleswig's independence of Denmark.

Danish resistance of this demand led to a brief war in which Austro-Prussian forces defeated the Danes. The Duke of Glücksburg, having become King of Denmark as Christian IX, was compelled by the

Treaty of Gastein to cede control of Schleswig and Kiel to Prussia and of Holstein to Austria. No plebiscites were held. The Treaty of Gastein of 1865 marked the beginning of Bismarck's policy of remaking frontiers by force of arms.

Napoleon, bewildered, and more out of patience with England, Russia, and Austria than he was with Prussia, indicated sympathy with Bismarck's ambition to enlarge his state to the detriment of Austria. He stated that, "if the populations of the duchies consented, he had no objection to their becoming a part of Prussia." Napoleon's approval was helpful to Bismarck, even though the Iron Chancellor had no thought of giving "populations" a chance to say anything about who should rule them.

The Treaty of Gastein was satisfactory to Bismarck because of its fragility. It left much that was uncertain about Austro-Prussian relations in the Danish duchies. It provided a situation in which Prussia might easily find a *casus belli* whenever her armies were ready to march.

CHAPTER TWENTY-EIGHT

BISMARCK AND BONAPARTE

THE IRON CHANCELLOR MADE A CALL AT BIARRITZ. PRUSSIA'S QUICK DEFEAT
OF AUSTRIA WAS A SHOCK TO NAPOLEON. THE CONFEDERATION OF NORTH-
ERN GERMANY. POWER MADE PLEBISCITES SUPERFLUOUS. THE MEXICAN
BLUNDER. COLONIAL EXPANSION. LIBERALISM BECAME EXPEDIENT. THE
VERGE OF REVOLUTION. MATERIAL IMPROVEMENTS. THE REASONABLENESS
OF CERTAIN EARLY LABOR LEADERS.

HAVING arranged affairs in the Danish duchies in a manner that served his purpose, and having made certain of the neutrality of Russia, Bismarck was almost ready for his long-planned attack upon Austria. It remained only to secure the neutrality of France, and, if possible, the co-operation of Italy.

Napoleon had become fond of Biarritz, a picturesque spot on the Biscayan coast. He was there, at the imperial Villa Eugénie, when, on an autumn day of 1865, bald and solemn Bismarck came lumbering in to make a polite call. Politeness was, for the steely Prussian, the most difficult feature of his complicated task. He perspired freely at it. "Blood and iron," to use his own words, were more in his line.

Before going to Biarritz, Bismarck suggested to Napoleon's representative at Berlin the desirability of a friendly understanding between France and Prussia. He said that Prussia was disposed to recognize the right of France eventually to control all territory in which the French language was spoken; obviously it would be in France's interest to protect Prussia from whatever dangers might threaten her.

Despite the Emperor's characteristic vagueness and his glassy stare, Bismarck left Biarritz feeling that his call had not been in vain. No paper had been signed and no definite promise had been given, but Napoleon had made no objection to Bismack's anti-Austria plans. The Emperor appeared to be more interested in securing Venice for Italy than in any question about Germany. The idea that the growth of Prussia might endanger France seemed not to occur to him.

Bismarck found that Napoleon was favorable to an Italo-Prussian alliance because that would help Italy toward winning Venice from Austria. Victor-Emmanuel, reluctant to make this dangerous alliance, probably would not have made it except that Napoleon urged him to do so. A treaty of temporary military co-operation between Prussia and Italy was made in April, 1866.

The final step into war was easily taken. Austria indicated that she would ask the Diet to settle the fate of the Danish duchies. Bismarck, maintaining that this was a violation of the Treaty of Gastein, ordered the advance of Prussian troops into the duchy that had been assigned to Austria. Two days later he proposed a reorganization of the Confederation with the exclusion of Austria. Austria then called upon the Diet to order mobilization against Prussia. That amounted to a declaration of war.

A majority of the German states preferred Austria to Prussia. Saxony, Hanover, Bavaria, and Wurtemburg were among those for whom the political climate of Vienna was more agreeable than that of Berlin. They reluctantly prepared to fight on the side of their choice. Prussia was outnumbered, but she was ready to strike. The others were not.

Von Moltke, the Prussian commander-in-chief, struck swiftly. A Hanoverian army was compelled to surrender in June, 1866, and a Bavarian army was scattered early in July. But most of the action in this brief war occurred in Bohemia. There, on July 3, the main forces of Prussia and Austria fought at Sadowa. A half-million men were engaged. Austria, defeated, lost more than forty thousand. Her victories in Italy availed her nothing. On July 22, when Prussian forces were less than forty miles from Vienna, an armistice was signed. Prussia held Austria and all Germany in her power.

Only then did Napoleon begin to realize that, in aiding Prussia, he had strengthened a young giant whose iron jaws might close next on France. He had tragically underestimated that young giant's strength. He had believed that Prussia would be weakened in her struggle with Austria, but she emerged from it stronger than before.

Early in July Napoleon had missed his last opportunity to prevent Prussian victory. After the battle of Sadowa, Austria asked for his

mediation. Some of his ministers favored intervention by arms to
arrest the Prussian advance on Vienna. Napoleon played with that
idea for a time, but, sick and vacillating, he lacked the courage to
carry it out. Years later Bismarck admitted in the Reichstag that if a
French force had advanced to the Rhine and rallied to it the dispersed troops of southern Germany, the Prussian army would have
been compelled to abandon its advance on Vienna in order to protect
Berlin.

After Austria had capitulated, it became Napoleon's turn to be
polite. Without consulting his ministers, he dealt directly with the
Prussian Ambassador. He gave his approval to annexation by Prussia
of several German states and to her control of a new federation of
northern Germany. All he asked was that the southern states should
be allowed to form a federation of their own, and he asked nothing
for France.

The conditions imposed upon Austria were more lenient than
either Von Moltke or King William desired. Bismarck, more far-
sighted than they, opposed any greater enlargement of Prussian control than Prussia was prepared successfully to administer. Austria
relinquished her claim to any authority in the Danish duchies, consented to dissolution of the old Confederation, and recognized
Prussia's right to organize and control Germany north of the river
Main.

Austria's territorial loss was negligible, but that had not been
Bismarck's objective. His main objective had been to put an end to
Austrian influence in Germany. In that, his success was complete.
Once Austria ceased to be an obstacle to Prussia's domination of the
German states, Bismarck's policy called for renewal of friendship with
her.

Thiers saw clearly what Prussia's defeat of Austria meant to
France; he predicted that it would lead to greater misfortune than the
Hundred Years' War. Edgar Quinet, the historian, wrote in 1866,
"Now that Germany is unchained she will not stop. I know her too
well. She will grow, she will feel her strength, and she will make
France feel it. She will seek to replace us, to discredit us, to efface us."

Too late, Napoleon tried to secure some compensation, some *"pour-*

boire," for the service he had rendered Prussia. He asked for that part of Bavaria which lay west of the Rhine. The only result of this unfortunate request was to end the friendship of the southern states for France and to hasten their acceptance of Prussian control. The Emperor then suggested that Luxembourg and Belgium should be annexed by France; France's guarantee of Belgian independence appeared to mean nothing to him. Bismarck placed this suggestion on file and made no response to it; he foresaw that disclosure of it might be helpful at a later date.

Prussia proceeded to annex German states without regard to the will of their people. There were no plebiscites. Schleswig, Hanover, and Frankfort were incorporated in Prussia against the will of most of their inhabitants. When the King announced these annexations to the *Landtag* he spoke of "the judgment of God and the interest of Prussia." Bismarck said, "Our right is the right of the German nation to establish the basis necessary for its existence." The principle of annexations was endorsed by a vote of 273 to 14. In the face of a brutal success, liberal opposition subsided to a whisper. After the defeat of Austria there was no more difficulty with the *Landtag.*

Bismarck was the author of the constitution of the Confederation of Northern Germany. It became effective in April, 1867. It created a *Bundesrath* and a *Reichstag,* but executive power was vested in the King of Prussia as hereditary president and in a federal chancellor whose name was Otto von Bismarck. The states of the south were not included in the new Confederation, but they were bound to it by treaties which, in case of war, placed their armies at the disposal of Prussia. The military solidarity of Germany having been thus achieved, peace could not long endure in Europe.

The Crimean War, the Italian Revolution, and the Austro-Prussian conflict were the major crises in which Redeemer Napoleon's ineptitude was revealed, but there were also minor crises and expeditions in which that ineptitude was no less obvious.

In 1860 the Emperor sent six thousand soldiers to Syria on account of a massacre of Christians in Damascus. The Sultan, protected by the Powers, had promised to protect the Christians, but he was unable to fulfill his contract. Napoleon undertook to help him to do so.

But Palmerston of England was not one to give Napoleon credit for pure nobility of intention; he suspected that the French intervention in Syria might go beyond the protection of Christians to the attainment of political and commercial advantages which England would prefer to have for herself. He secured the support of the other powers for the proposition that Napoleon's crusade should be short-lived. The French troops were withdrawn from Syria in 1861. After all, they had been sent to the defense of Catholics largely in order to diminish the Catholic hostility to the Emperor which had been aroused by his policy in Italy. The gain of this expedition, if any, was purely moral.

The rapid development of steam navigation permitted religious and commercial exploitation of formerly inaccessible quarters of the globe. England went to China and the United States went to Japan. France followed suit. French missionaries went to Indo-China which was composed of Siam, Annam, and, between them, the romantic little kingdom of Cambodia. In 1856 Siam made a commercial treaty with France, but Annam was less friendly.

The Annamites persecuted French missionaries. This gave Napoleon another opportunity to court Catholic favor. An expedition compelled the Emperor of Annam to cede Cochin-China to France, and the King of Cambodia was persuaded to place his country under French protection. Thus the foundation was laid for the development of French control in Indo-China.

There were French colonists and missionaries in Madagascar also. To them Napoleon did not give military support, but their enterprise led to subsequent possession by France of another important colony.

The most ridiculous of all Napoleon's blunders was his Mexican blunder. He believed that he could successfully disregard the Monroe Doctrine because of the Civil War in the United States. Mexico had become a republic in 1821. In 1858, Juarez, a leader of the liberals, was president. Miramon, a Catholic and conservative leader, had been president before Juarez; to him European loans had been made. Juarez suspended payment of the interest on these loans. That gave to France, England, and Spain an excuse for joint intervention. In

1861 they landed troops at Vera Cruz. In the following year England and Spain withdrew their troops, but Napoleon foolishly ordered his to proceed to Mexico City.

The Redeemer had decided to undertake the redemption of the Americas as well as of Europe. He believed that the Western Hemisphere would be greatly improved by the foundation of a Catholic empire which would be in a position to check the dangerously liberal influence of the United States, and, incidentally, give to France desirable economic opportunities. He thought he saw a chance in Mexico to gain favor both with the Pope and with the businessmen. To the general in command of his expedition he wrote, "It is not in our interest that the United States should become the mistress of Mexico and of Central America. It is our duty to establish a stable government in Mexico so that from there French influence may extend both north and south and great commercial advantages be gained thereby."

Thirty-five thousand soldiers were sent to fight and many of them to die in a hopeless effort to make a sick man's fantastic dream come true. Mexico City was occupied in 1863. The Pope and the businessmen were not the only ones whom Napoleon was trying to please. He wished also to please Francis-Joseph, whose friendship he had lost when France fought with Sardinia against Austria. He believed that he might regain that friendship by making an emperor out of Francis-Joseph's brother.

An unrepresentative "National Assembly" proclaimed the Archduke Maximilian of Austria to be the Emperor of Mexico. Maximilian, after some hesitation, made the fatal mistake of leaving his peaceful home in Trieste to become the most conspicuous victim of an imperial aberration.

Napoleon and Maximilian had counted upon solid support for the new regime by Mexican Catholics. A group of swarthy émigrés had told them that they could count on that. The émigrés had exaggerated. The French troops were shot at more than they were supported. Guerilla warfare made a nightmare out of their experience in Mexico.

When the Civil War was over, the United States gave Napoleon very definitely to understand that the presence of French soldiers in

Mexico was displeasing to the government at Washington. The Emperor had no choice but to sweep up the debris of his dream. The French soldiers sailed for home and Maximilian should have sailed with them. The liberals regained the upper hand. Maximilian, having refused to abdicate, was captured by them and shot. That was in June, 1867.

After Napoleon's expedition had sailed for Vera Cruz, it was found that the claim on Mexico which it had gone to support was extremely shady. A financial harpy, for a loan of less than a million dollars, had received fifteen million in Mexican bonds from a government that was about to fall. After it had fallen, its conscienceless creditor bribed certain influential gentlemen in order to secure the support of the French government for his preposterous claim. This enterprising harpy was not even French. He was Swiss.

The less the Emperor had to do with French efforts in foreign lands the more likely they were to be successful. After a brief visit to Algeria in 1863 he ordered a complete change of policy there, a change that ended in failure. Senegal, however, was so far away and so unhealthy that it was spared the handicap of an imperial visit. There Faidherbe, an army engineer, did a magnificent piece of work which, at the time, was almost unnoticed.

Faidherbe had only four companies of white soldiers, but, recruiting and training athletic natives, he developed that nucleus into a small army of efficient and devoted soldiers. He was a genius in colonial administration. There were marauders who had to be restrained. Having restrained them, he took the sons of their chiefs into custody as hostages. He established a school for these hostages and gradually transformed ignorant enemies into appreciative friends. In ten years he pacified the Senegalese and tripled their economic productivity.

Napoleon's plan for reform in Algeria was, like most of his other plans, grandiose and impracticable. He declared, "I am the Emperor of the Arabs as well as of the French. I shall use their courage rather than oppress their poverty." In order not to oppress Arab poverty, he stopped the flow of French colonists to Algeria, recalled the civil administrators, and re-established military control. Algeria was saved for the Algerians, but Arab courage proved inadequate for the task of economic development. In 1869 a government commission reported that, under Napoleon's plan, things had gone from bad to worse.

Napoleon's liberalism was tinged with expediency. He became liberal after he had lost the support of the illiberal, and his interest in the condition of the working classes synchronized with the political value of that interest.

The Emperor's intervention in Italy was disapproved by those who had previously supported him and applauded by those who had opposed him. His loss of Catholic support was counterbalanced by gain on the liberal side; he hoped, by means of a minimum of concessions, to increase and to solidify that gain. He had helped the people of Italy to gain their liberty; he was always more interested in liberty for other people than he was in liberty for the French. Jules Favre, one of the *Cinq* (the five republican *députés*), eloquently attacked the inconsistency of fighting for liberty in Italy and at the same time proscribing it in France.

Napoleon had found himself in a position which necessitated a little loosening of the reins. He made an additional play for popular support by reducing the tariff on foreign goods. In January, 1860, after secret negotiations with Richard Cobden, he signed a commercial treaty with England which favored the sale of British products in France; he proposed to adopt England's new policy of free trade. The abrupt announcement of this treaty was a great shock to French manufacturers; they had not been consulted about a measure which might require them to make a sharp cut in their prices. Napoleon at once became as unpopular with the manufacturers as he already was with the Catholics. From that time on he felt compelled to favor the liberals.

Amnesty was extended to all political prisoners and exiles. In November, 1860, a decree was issued which aroused the two legislative *Chambres* from their long torpor. It gave to them the right to discuss governmental policies and to have their speeches printed in the *Journal officiel*. The *députés* and the *sénateurs* had been kept gagged by Napoleon ever since his assassination of the Assembly

nine years before. Political life had become atrophied, but, with removal of the gag, it revived. An anti-government coalition called
l'Union liberale was formed. In the elections of 1863 this new group
gained thirty-two seats, making a clean sweep in Paris. Thiers, the
best-known man in political life, was a leader of this opposition party.

The Emperor's steps toward liberalism were slow, reluctant, and
vacillating. In 1863 he appointed the historian Victor Duruy minister of public instruction; the schools made admirable progress in
the six years that Duruy remained in office. In 1865 the right of
workers to organize and to strike was recognized. But all the reforms looked better on paper than they did in practice. Rouher continued to be the most influential of the ministers and he was no
friend of liberalism.

Napoleon gained little by the apparent softening of his heart; his
head seemed to soften with it. The failure of his efforts in Mexico,
in Poland, and in Germany lost for him both at home and abroad
most of the prestige that he had won in the Crimea and in Italy.
Chronically ill, he was aging rapidly, and Bismarck had proved that
he was the better man.

Another new party appeared, *le Tiers Parti*. Emile Ollivier, a be-
spectacled orator, became its leader. Ollivier, one of the five republican *députés* of 1858, had been an eloquent opponent of the Empire,
but, six years later, he became the Emperor's tutor in liberalism. "I
accept good," he said, "whatever the hand that gives it." He argued
that he could support a liberal monarchy without violation of his republican principles. His republican colleagues, being mentally less
elastic, did not agree with him; they read him out of their party.
When he took office under the government in 1864 he was compelled
to identify himself with the *Tiers Parti* (third party).

Between 1867 and 1870 Ollivier advised Napoleon to be liberal
and Rouher advised him to be autocratic. In trying to be both, the
Emperor made a success of neither. His reforms had strings tied to
them. They served only to intensify republican hostility. There was
a tendency toward revolution.

Young republicans, dissatisfied with the moderation of the republican *députés,* demanded action. A loosening of the censorship

in 1868 gave greater freedom of expression to the enemies of the Empire. The most effective writer was Henri Rochefort and the most eloquent speaker was a fiery young lawyer from the south named Gambetta.

Baudin was a republican *député* who had been killed on a barricade while resisting Napoleon's *coup d'état*. A liberal journal was prosecuted for attempting to make Baudin a popular hero. Gambetta pleaded for the defendant. Referring to December 2, 1851, "On that day," he said, "the usurper was surrounded by men of whom France had never heard, men who had neither talent, nor rank, nor honor. They were of the kind that is always attracted by illegality. . . . For seventeen years these men have been the masters of France. We do not ask what they have done with her treasure, her honor, her blood, or her glory. We have only to ask why this regime of force has not sought to have France honor the day of its birth. France is proud to honor all days which have been epochal in her progress, but there are two days which this government dares not ask France to honor." One of the days to which Gambetta referred was the day of Louis-Napoleon's *coup d'état;* the other was the day on which his uncle had, in like manner, assassinated a republic.

Gambetta had put into words what the people felt in their hearts. His speech gave Paris a new hero. The government dared not move against him. He was elected to the *Chambre des députés.* In 1869 the government lost the majority in the *Chambres* which it had held since 1852. Even without the Franco-Prussian War the Empire might have endured but little longer.

Henri Rochefort published a weekly pamphlet called *La Lanterne.* His ironic wit was delightful and pitiless. His ridicule of Napoleon was more effective than all the speeches. Proscription of *La Lanterne* increased its popularity. Rochefort, condemned to imprisonment, fled to Belgium and published his paper there. Smuggled across the border, it was more eagerly read than ever. From May, 1868, to November, 1869, its red covers could be seen in all the *cafés* of Paris.

The elections of 1869 made it clear that more concessions to liberalism were necessary. Napoleon dismissed Rouher, made Ollivier his chief minister, and gave new powers to the legislative bodies. In the few months of life that were left to it, the Empire was unhappily wedded to parliamentary government. That was the last flare-up of an illegitimate regime. Only when fearful for its life did that regime restore to France the liberties which it had stolen.

In January, 1870, revolution was narrowly avoided. Pierre Bonaparte, a cousin of the Emperor, shot Victor Noir, a republican journalist. Henri Rochefort, in a black-bordered edition of *La Lanterne,* declared that murder and treachery were traditional in the Corsican family named Bonaparte. There was a "terrible effervescence" and the government called out the troops.

In April the people were given an opportunity to vote yes or no upon a proposition so worded that approval of the liberal reforms implied approval of the government that had granted them. The rural population, still apathetic about politics, voted yes. In Paris and in other large cities the majority vote was no. This plebiscite was a defeat for the republicans, but a very astute gentleman in Berlin was planning to succeed where they had failed. The reign of the usurper was swiftly drawing to its close.

The Second Empire was co-existent with a period of prosperity which would have occurred whatever the government. It was Napoleon's good fortune that his *coup d'état* came at a time when new inventions caused rapid economic expansion. He did not create the prosperity which permitted his authority to survive. Had he come into power in a period of depression he might have been swept out, as the Bourbons were, long before the Prussians crossed the frontier.

Napoleon's policy about material improvements was like that which his uncle and other tyrants have made classic. They believed that material gain makes people forgetful of spiritual loss, and that in the presence of prosperity there is little regret for the absence of political liberty. The Emperor appeared to be sincerely interested in improvement of the condition of the workers, but he was also sincerely interested in keeping their minds off political questions.

Baron Haussman was the prefect of the *Département* of the Seine from 1853 to 1870. To him the Emperor assigned the task of enlarging and beautifying Paris. The Baron was delighted to do so. He was an energetic administrator who rode roughshod over all obstacles and made himself intensely unpopular. He destroyed acres of old buildings and built miles of new boulevards. His plans served a military as well as an esthetic objective. The breadth of the new boulevards made barricades difficult and cavalry charges easy; the Parisian proletariat was not enthusiastic about the improvements. Haussman modernized the water-works and the sewers. The *Opéra,* the *Halles Centrales,* and many new churches were built. The *Bois de Boulogne* was transformed into the world's most fashionable park.

The embellishment of Paris made it more than ever the social capital of Europe. It set styles that were imitated by all who had more wealth than wisdom. Life was very gay and glamorous on the *Grands Boulevards* and along the *Champs Elysées.* Prosperous pleasure-seekers came from all lands. The beauty, frivolity, music, and romance of the Second Empire became legendary.

The Expositions of 1855 and 1867 contributed greatly to the gaiety and prosperity of Paris. The first one attracted more than five million visitors and the second one doubled that number. The Czar, King William of Prussia, Bismarck, and Von Moltke were among the distinguished visitors who were lavishly entertained in 1867. The Second Empire's political failures were obscured in that year by the brilliance of its social success. The Emperor had spoken of "black spots on the horizon," but Paris, beguiled by Offenbach's music, delighted in the day and gave little thought to the morrow.

There was a great increase of railroads, of telegraph lines, and of speculation. The later days of the Empire were golden days for the Bourse. Thousands made unearned fortunes and tens of thousands were fleeced. There was an enormous expansion of credit. New banks financed new enterprises. Powerful companies gained control of the basic industries. Proudhon called attention to the rapid development of an "industrial feudalism." Four-ninths of the wealth that was produced each year went into the pockets of those who produced none of it.

The most notable engineering achievements were the Mont-Cenis tunnel through the Alps and the Suez Canal. It took twelve years to complete the eight-mile tunnel and ten to dig the hundred-mile canal. France furnished most of the money for the canal and Ferdinand de Lesseps built it. The Empress Eugénie represented the Emperor at its elaborate inauguration in November, 1869. Napoleon deserved credit for overcoming English opposition to this epoch-making project.

The Emperor's free-trade policy did not have the disastrous effect upon French manufacturers that had been predicted, nor did it appreciably reduce the cost of goods. The volume of production steadily increased. Between 1859 and 1869 France doubled her foreign business. When the government sought a loan of four hundred millions, fifteen billions were offered. The reserves of capital accumulated in this period enabled France to make prompt payment of the indemnity demanded by Prussia in 1870.

Until near its very end, the prosperity of the Second Empire was accompanied by little improvement in the condition of the workers. The enlargement of industry caused a flow of population cityward. Factory workers were paid more than farm workers, but they were compelled to live under more expensive and less healthful conditions. In 1851 only one-fourth of the people lived in towns of more than two thousand inhabitants; in 1866 that fraction had risen to three-sevenths. In the same period, the number of cities larger than one hundred thousand rose from five to eight.

Theoretically the workers were free, but practically they were held in servitude by their bourgeois employers as firmly as their ancestors had been held in serfdom by their feudal overlords. Prior to 1865, they were not allowed to organize or to strike, and they were required, like the soldiers, to carry with them a record of their service and status which was called a *livret*. Woe to the worker whose *livret* was not in good order!

Wages were whatever the employers saw fit to pay; there was no appeal; the civil code stipulated that, in the matter of wages, the word of an employer should be accepted as final. The Second Republic had decreed that the hours of work should not exceed ten or eleven per day, but this decree was not enforced. Wages were so closely adjusted to the cost of living that it was practically impossible for the workers to save. Unemployment meant misery and sometimes starvation.

Napoleon in his days of exile wrote an essay entitled *l'Extinction du Pauperisme*. That, as well as his need for their political support, contributed to his interest in the workers. His construction projects were preventive of unemployment. He permitted the organization of mutual-aid societies under the condition of an "approval" by the government which amounted to control. His police, however, showed no laxity in preventing the development of organizations which were disapproved. In 1858 a worker was arrested when it was discovered that he had been the director of a disapproved organization ten years before.

Charity was dispensed in the name of the Empress and of her young son, the *Prince impérial;* insurance and pensions for the aged were provided on liberal terms. The Emperor did what he could to soften the fetters of economic and political slavery, but he took care not to weaken them.

The workers were not deceived; the high hopes and the tragic disillusion of 1848 had not been forgotten. That disillusion had made them apathetic about the *coup d'état,* but that did not mean that they approved of it. A government official at Lyon wrote in 1853, "Many of the best workers are opposed to the government. They believe that society is unjustly organized to the detriment of the workers. They are familiar with philosophical theories of social organization."

The philosophy of socialism was first expounded in France by certain theorists of the upper classes, but, after 1848, its most eloquent exponents were found among the workers. Of these, Tolain, a metalworker, and Proudhon, a proofreader, were the most influential.

The quality of Tolain's reasoning is revealed in a manifesto of 1864 which was signed by sixty workers. "We have been wearied," that document stated, "by hearing so often that there are no classes, and that since 1789 all are equal before the law. But there is a property qualification. To those of us whose only property is our capacity to work, equality is denied. Many of us have been denied even the opportunity to learn to read. Our children, for whom there are no schools, are compelled to work under demoralizing and unhealthful conditions. Our wives are forced to neglect their homes and to work at tasks unfitted to their nature. Our family life is destroyed. We are not allowed to co-operate in peaceful efforts to improve our condition. We maintain, therefore, that the equality which the law prescribes exists in theory but not in fact. . . . We should not be accused of dreaming of a re-distribution of property. We entertain no such chimerical idea. Those who have accused us of entertaining it are our enemies who seek to discredit us by calumny. Only those who are ignorant can believe this malicious misrepresentation."

The government, soon after this manifesto was issued, granted to workers the right to organize and to strike. Victor Duruy, in the same year, secured approval for the establishment of ten thousand new elementary schools.

The international organization of workers began in 1864. With Napoleon's approval, Tolain and some of his colleagues conferred with English labor leaders in London. As a result of that conference, Tolain founded *l'Association Internationale des Travailleurs*. Its primary aim was education. Proudhon wrote a book entitled *De la Capacité Politique des Classes Ouvrières*. The Tolain group gave its support to the moderate and nonrevolutionary theories of Proudhon. They succeeded in having them endorsed by the delegates to the first assembly of the International. But after Tolain had returned to Paris, that assembly succumbed to the influence of a German refugee in London named Karl Marx. Governmental dissolution of the French section of the International strengthened the Marxian influence and weakened that of Proudhon.

The pioneer leaders of labor organization in France were absolutely opposed to communism and revolution. That opposition has preserved its strength. Communism still strives in vain to gain control of the workers of France.

Chapter Twenty-nine

THE FRANCO-PRUSSIAN WAR

PRUSSIA FOUGHT FRANCE IN ORDER TO GAIN CONTROL OF GERMANY. A
HOHENZOLLERN BECAME A CANDIDATE FOR THE THRONE OF SPAIN. MODI-
FICATION OF THE TENOR OF A TELEGRAM MADE WAR INEVITABLE. PRUSSIAN
VICTORY GAVE TO FRANCE HER THIRD REPUBLIC AND TO GERMANY HER
UNIFICATION. LEON GAMBETTA WAS THE MAN OF THE HOUR.

THE FRANCO-PRUSSIAN WAR was essential to the fulfillment of
Bismarck's ambition to create a united German nation under the
leadership of Prussia. The defeat of Austria permitted half-fulfillment
of his great objective. A defeat of France was necessary for attainment of the other half.

Domination by Prussia was unwelcome to the states of southern
Germany. Even after Berlin had humbled Vienna, they were in no
haste to bow down to the victor. They were jealous of their independence. The treaties that they made with Prussia called for co-
operation only in case of war. Bismarck believed that, if he provided
the war, military co-operation would lead to political solidarity. The
high command of the armies would be Prussian.

There were obvious reasons for making France the victim. She was
the only Power that might intervene to prevent Prussian control of
the southern states. She had reluctantly recognized Prussia's mastery
of all Germany north of the Main, but she might fight to prevent
southward extension of that mastery.

The danger to France of such extension was not difficult to perceive. Thiers was one of those who perceived it. In May, 1866, when
war between Austria and Prussia appeared to be inevitable, he became
prophetic. "If Prussia wins," he said, "she will have all Germany
under her authority, directly or indirectly. There will be a new organization of the German states into which Austria will be admitted
as a *protégé*. We may then witness a re-creation of the Germanic
Empire of Charles V with the difference that its capital will be Berlin
instead of Vienna and that Spain will be replaced by Italy. The peace

384

of Europe is contingent upon the independence of the German states. Their union will lead to war."

The first Napoleon's conquest and rule of Germany made France seem to the Germans to be their hereditary enemy. This feeling was most intense in Prussia. The Prussians did what they could to intensify it in the less militaristic and less ambitious south. Alsace and Lorraine had been joined to France for more than two centuries, but the German people were urged to believe that their honor required the winning of these provinces.

When wars are over and all the dead have been buried, some seek comfort in trying to believe that war is inevitable, that men are compelled from time to time to murder one another in order to fulfill an obscure but imperative mandate of nature. War, according to this theory, is, like cyclones, earthquakes, and unhappy marriages, one of the curses of the inescapable environment in which men must continue helplessly to struggle until, with the aid of their own contrivances, they shall so successfully annihilate one another that this good green earth will be rid forever of a species whose intelligence served to hasten its own extinction.

But that is not true! Wars are not unavoidable. More of them have been avoided than have been fought. The Franco-Prussian War was avoidable. Bismarck wanted it, but, had Napoleon been even a second-rate statesman, it might have been avoided. Prussia might have been restrained. It was the Emperor's blundering that brought victorious invaders into the heart of France and permitted the unification of the German states. Germany should be grateful to both of the Bonapartes. Both of them, in the long run, served Germany better than they served France.

Napoleon, a sick man, wavered between war and peace-at-almost-any-price. He solicited the co-operation of Austria and Italy in case of war, and he sought to appease Prussia in hope of peace. In secret negotiations he agreed not to oppose the union of north and south Germany in case territorial concessions were made to France in order to save his face. The only result of these negotiations was to strengthen Bismarck's hand.

Bismarck's certainty was in striking contrast to Napoleon's vacillation. The Iron Chancellor knew what he wanted. Untroubled by any conflict of ideas, he moved steadily and craftily forward toward the attainment of his great objective. Years later he wrote in his memoirs, "I was convinced that the abyss which separated north and south Germany could be closed by no better means than a war in which we would fight together against our historic enemy on the other side of the Rhine."

Napoleon realized that a storm was brewing, but he was at a loss about how to meet it or to avoid it. He took measures to strengthen the army and to secure allies, but all this was done without continuity, conviction, or conclusion. In 1868 there was much talk of army enlargement and of improved weapons. The *Garde Mobile* was expanded and a new rifle, the *chassepot,* was adopted. A primitive machine gun made its appearance. The people acquired the illusion that their army was invincible, but the military progress that was made in France was chiefly conversational. That made in Germany was real. While Bismarck constantly talked peace, Von Moltke and Roon labored incessantly to perfect the weapon that Germany would use when she was ready for war.

Diplomatic preparation for the conflict was no more adequate than the military preparation. Austria agreed to a defensive alliance, but she made no commitment to send troops to fight on French soil. The aid of Italy could be secured only by withdrawal of the French force that remained at Rome to protect the Pope. Napoleon, afraid to risk Catholic hostility, would not promise to withdraw that force. When the war began he was compelled to withdraw it. Had he done so sooner, Italian forces, instead of marching into Rome, might have marched to the aid of France.

Ollivier, who became prime minister in 1870, shared the Emperor's delusion that Austria and Italy could be relied upon to aid France. He believed that Prussia would not dare to attack. On the last day of June he asked the legislative bodies to authorize a reduction of ten thousand in the forces that were under arms. He declared that "the peace of Europe has never seemed to be more assured than it is today." Three days later an unexpected development put an abrupt end to that assurance. A cousin of King William of Prussia became a candidate for the throne of Spain. That upset the Emperor's and Ollivier's calculations. It was "like the bursting of a bomb."

Spain had been without a king since 1868. Her provisional government was in search of a suitable sovereign. Napoleon had attempted to form a coalition against Prussia; Bismarck's bold response was the proposal to put a Prussian on the throne of Spain. His candidate, Leopold von Hohenzollern, shared two grandmothers, a Murat and a Beauharnais, with Napoleon, but that could not lessen French opposition to the coronation of a Prussian at Madrid.

In March, 1869, there had been a Spanish suggestion of Leopold for king, but William of Prussia as well as Napoleon opposed that suggestion. It was believed that this matter had been definitely settled, but Bismarck did not share that belief. Perceiving the advantage that Prussia might gain by a revival of Leopold's candidacy, he secretly encouraged Spain to revive it. He pointed out to King William and to Prince Leopold that it would be vastly to their country's interest if Spain, on the other side of France, could be counted upon to sympathize with Germany. William and Leopold succumbed to Bismarck's argument. It was planned that the Spanish *Cortes* (parliamentary body) should declare Leopold to be King of Spain before France knew what was going on. But somebody gave the secret away. A Madrid newspaper published the story on the second of July, 1870, and a Paris paper had it on the third.

Revival of Leopold's candidacy was a challenge to France, and its secrecy made it more than a challenge. In the opinion of the Parisian public, it was an insult which no apology could efface; it was clear evidence of Prussia's hostile intentions.

The Duke of Gramont, minister of foreign affairs, addressed the legislative bodies and said, "We maintain that respect for the rights of a neighboring nation does not oblige us to permit another power to place one of its princes upon the throne of Charles V, thus destroying the political equilibrium of Europe and imperiling the interests and the honor of France. We have the firm hope that this will not happen, but, if it does, we shall know how to fulfill our duty." The declaration of the Duke was loudly applauded. The only dissent came from the republican benches on the left.

Benedetti, France's ambassador to Prussia, was directed to ask King William for a formal disavowal of Prince Leopold's candidacy. William, then seventy-three, was taking the cure at Ems. Benedetti went there and secured the King's promise that Leopold's candidacy would be withdrawn if Leopold made no objection. Withdrawal of the Prussian candidacy was announced on the twelfth of July. Guizot called this a superb diplomatic victory and Bismarck, disgusted, thought of resigning.

Napoleon, unfortunately, was unable to leave well enough alone. He yielded to the influence of a group that desired war. Confident of victory, that group believed that war would repair the damage that concessions had done to autocracy. The most important member of this group was the Empress Eugénie. Almost as blind to reality as Marie-Antoinette, she wished for war as a means of restoring the dignity and authority of the crown. Her group maintained that it would be disgraceful for France to be content with the merely verbal assurances of King William and Prince Leopold; they should be compelled to give guarantees that no Hohenzollern should ever become a candidate for the throne of Spain. The wish to goad Prussia into war was obvious.

On the night of July 12 Napoleon made his most calamitous blunder. He authorized a telegram to Benedetti instructing him to ask King William for permanent renunciation by Prussia of interest in the throne of Spain. On the morning of the thirteenth, the ambassador accosted King William while he was walking on the promenade at Ems. Venerable William was visibly annoyed by this unpleasant interruption of his constitutional. He wished to hear no more about a troublesome question which he had considered settled. He declined to discuss it. Later in the day he sent word to Benedetti that his approval of Leopold's withdrawal remained unmodified, but that he would make no further commitment.

Bismarck was biting his nails in Berlin. His well-laid plan seemed doomed to failure. His King was too much inclined to be a gentleman and his own hands were tied. Etiquette demanded that the Chancellor should not be intrusive about the affairs of the royal family; the question about Leopold was, despite its political implications, a private affair of the Hohenzollerns. Bismarck had already said all that he could say.

On the afternoon of the thirteenth a dispatch from Ems was eagerly awaited in Berlin. The generals Von Moltke and Roon sat with the Chancellor and shared his faint hope that a way to war would yet be found. The army was ready. All that was needed was for the King to be impolite to France's ambassador. But the King was not impolite. His response to Benedetti stated that he maintained "his entire approval without reserve" to Prince Leopold's withdrawal. It would be difficult for France to feel herself insulted by a reply like that, even though it did not contain a pledge for all future time. Napoleon, less bellicose on the morning of the thirteenth than he had been on the night of the twelfth, had agreed with his ministers that a response like that would be acceptable.

Late in the afternoon of that historic day a royal dispatch went from Ems to Berlin. It was delivered while Bismarck, Von Moltke, and Roon were together at dinner. There had been progress from beer to champagne. A brighter outlook had been achieved, but the royal dispatch was a wet blanket. It dashed the fond hopes of the diners. It did not report discourtesy to France. It did not make war certain.

Bismarck carefully adjusted his glasses and re-read the dispatch more slowly. It contained no command for privacy. It even suggested publicity. The alert mind of the reader saw an opening. Publicity might warrant condensation, and condensation might permit modification. A little verbal change here and there might bring swift death to tens of thousands. Hope revived.

The Chancellor turned to Von Moltke. "If we fight," he asked, "are you sure we can win?" "We are ready," was the soldierly answer. "Very well," said Bismarck, "enjoy your dinner. The dispatch from Ems shall not sound the retreat. It shall sound the attack."

On the following morning the papers announced that France had demanded permanent renunciation of Hohenzollern candidacy for the throne of Spain, that His Majesty had declined to receive the French Ambassador and had notified him that he had nothing to say. King William's "entire approval of the Prince's withdrawal" was deleted. The King's warrant of peace had been transformed into an assurance of war.

Publication of Bismarck's *communiqué* unleashed fury on both sides of the Rhine. The Prussians were led to believe that France had sought to humiliate their sovereign, and the French believed that King William had insulted their ambassador. Both were eager to fight. Bismarck had predicted that his alteration of the dispatch would "make the French bull see red." It did.

The featured item from Berlin which the Paris papers printed on the morning of the fourteenth had the effect of a slap in the face. The *cafés* were in an uproar that evening. On the fifteenth there was a tumultuous meeting of the legislative bodies. Prime Minister Ollivier declared that "the government, having done all that is honorably possible to avoid war, accepts with light heart the responsibility that has been thrust upon it." (Later he had reason bitterly to regret his expression of lightness of heart; it was not forgotten.) Ollivier's speech was thunderously applauded. Thiers urged in vain that the exact facts be ascertained before an irretrievable step was taken. The only opposition to the government's attitude came from the "unpatriotic" minority of the left. The "true patriots" of the center and the right were all for rushing the young men forward to the field of slaughter. On the seventeeenth of July, 1870, France declared war.

Europe had been sympathetic with France's opposition to the placing of a Hohenzollern on the throne of Spain. But France lost that sympathy when she insisted upon guarantees after Leopold's candidacy had been withdrawn. It was felt that her declaration of war was unjustified. Bismarck was entirely successful in obscuring the fact that he was the true artisan of this war. He completed France's isolation by publishing Napoleon's secret proposal of 1866 to annex Belgium; that destroyed English sympathy for France.

Napoleon counted upon the dislike of the southern German states for Prussia, but he himself helped them to overcome that dislike and to join the Germans of the north in an all-German crusade against France. Too late, negotiations with Austria and Italy were speeded up. At Vienna, late in July, it was planned that Austria and Italy should act jointly as mediators between Prussia and France. Failure of this mediation was to bring the mediators into action on the side of France. But, when Italy called for the withdrawal of the French force from Rome, the Duke of Gramont declared that "France could not defend her honor on the Rhine and sacrifice it on the Tiber." Thus all hope for outside help was lost. France, unaided materially or morally, entered upon a war for which the ineptitude of her own government was largely responsible.

The fighting began on the second of August, 1870, and continued for six months. The first month sufficed to reveal the grave error of those who had believed that victory was certain. But the military disasters of that month did France one good turn; they relieved her forever of the curse of Bonapartism. September 4, 1870, is one of the great dates in French history. On that day the Second Empire ended and the Third Republic began.

The imperial armies collapsed in the first few weeks, but the people of France fought valiantly on for five more months. Famished Paris, besieged for four months, did not surrender until the end of January.

Prussia had been planning her campaign for more than two years; France had talked much, but had definitely planned nothing. Half a million excellently equipped German soldiers were concentrated on the northern frontiers of Alsace and Lorraine. They were organized into three armies and Von Moltke was the general-in-chief.

Napoleon attempted to be his own general-in-chief. That alone made confusion certain. It had been believed that 350,000 men could be mobilized in fifteen days. The right figure turned out to be 265,000. To save time, troops were advanced toward the front before the mobilization was complete. The only thing that was complete was the confusion. Soldiers could not find their regiments and there were generals who could not find their brigades. Orders and counter-orders succeeded each other so swiftly that fulfillment of them was impossible.

The first fighting was at the northern end of narrow Alsace. The French were defeated at Wissemburg and at Froeschwiller. Having conquered Alsace with ease, the Germans took their time about advancing into Lorraine. That gave the French a breathing spell, but Napoleon did not know how to take advantage of it. He fluttered, unable to decide which of four or five plans to adopt. Finally he decided to retreat and to turn the command over to General Bazaine.

Bazaine was a brave soldier, but a poor general. Lacking imagination, he failed to take advantage of his opportunities. His one idea was to establish his forces in a strong position and then wait for the enemy to attack. Metz was the position he chose, and near Metz the greatest battle of the war was fought. On the eighteenth of August, between the villages of Saint-Privat and Gravelotte, 200,000 Germans fought 140,000 French. The German losses were greater than those of the French, but the end of the day found France's strongest army blockaded in Metz.

Napoleon had retreated to the Camp of Châlons, headquarters of the reserve army commanded by MacMahon. The Emperor had seen enough of the fighting and wished to return to Paris, but the Empress wired that if he returned without a victory he would have to face a revolution. So he turned eastward again, believing that he had less to fear from the Prussians than from the Parisians.

MacMahon made an effort to join his forces to those of Bazaine. It became necessary to make a detour by way of the city of Sedan. There, on the first of September, MacMahon's army was surrounded by the enemy. Seven hundred of the new Krupp guns were brought into action. Napoleon gave the order to raise the white flag. At Sedan the Prussians took more than 100,000 prisoners and the Emperor was one of them.

The surrender at Sedan made Napoleon an ex-Emperor. It occurred on a Friday. On the following Sunday, the historic fourth of September, the *Corps Legislatif* declared the throne vacant. Léon Gambetta and Jules Favre were directed to organize a provisional government. In accordance with tradition, these founders of the new regime proceeded at once to the Hôtel de Ville. There the rebirth of the republic was proclaimed. Not a hand was raised in defense of the fallen empire. For the first time in her long experience with revolutions, Paris witnessed one which was not accompanied by civil strife. The Prussians, by defeating the armies of France, had enabled her people to regain their liberty without striking a blow.

The provisional government called itself the *Gouvernement de la Défense nationale*. It named General Trochu president. It proclaimed that it would not yield an inch of territory. It offered an indemnity as the price of peace, but Bismarck insisted upon the cession of Alsace and a part of Lorraine. So the war went on.

Moving at their ease and meeting no opposition, Prussian forces closed in on Paris. On the nineteenth of September the siege began. Half a million men were available for the defense of the capital, but only a small fraction of them were trained soldiers. Even Trochu, who commanded, considered the defense of Paris "an heroic folly." There was one, however, who did not consider it folly, one who would not give up, one who gave all the fire and passion of his intense nature to the cause of the defense of France. That was Gambetta.

No hero of France has had more streets and public squares named in his honor than Léon Gambetta; no patriot is more loved by her people. Son of a grocer of Cahors, he became a *député* in 1869. He was the leader of the revolution of September 4 when he was only thirty-two. No one contributed more than he to the difficult establishment of the Third Republic. His accidental death at the age of forty-four was an inestimable loss to the nation.

Before the siege began the government decided to remain in Paris, but it sent a delegation to Tours. The primary purpose of that delegation was to raise an army, but it made little progress in doing so until Gambetta joined it. To get out of Paris he used a balloon. The ninth of October found him in Tours. There he became the spark plug of the provincial effort. Von Moltke said that the rapidity with which Gambetta organized new armies was "incredible." Aided by a few military experts, by the time the war was over he had completed the organization and equipment of 600,000 men. There were many foreign volunteers who came to fight in France for the cause of liberty. Garibaldi was one of them.

Early in November the hastily formed Army of the Loire moved toward the enemy. It defeated Germans at Coulmiers and compelled their withdrawal from Orléans. At that moment the prospect of relieving Paris seemed excellent, but the brightness of this prospect quickly faded. There came bad news from Metz. Bazaine had surrendered.

Since the eighteenth of August Bazaine had not moved. He had the best army of France under his command and his forces outnumbered the divisions that blockaded him, but he had made no effort to fight his way out. A partial explanation of Bazaine's inaction lies in the fact that he disliked the republic. Remaining a Bonapartist, he negotiated both with the Empress and with Bismarck; it is said that his ambition was to establish Eugénie as regent and himself as her lieutenant-general. Eugénie balked, however, at acceptance of Bismarck's demand for Alsace and Lorraine.

The surrender at Metz occurred on the twenty-seventh of October. Bazaine's army of 173,000 became prisoners. It was a worse catastrophe than the surrender at Sedan. More than a hundred thousand Prussians had been held at Metz on blockade duty. Relieved of that duty, they marched southwestward, drove the French out of Orléans, and put the first Army of the Loire to rout. There was a German admission that if Metz had held out only one day longer they would have been compelled to abandon their siege of Paris.

At the end of November a force of 100,000 tried to break through the German encirclement of Paris, but, after three days of continuous fighting in bitter weather, it was forced to retreat with a loss of ten thousand. Gambetta refused to be discouraged. With unflagging zeal he stimulated the organization of new armies. He placed Chanzy in command of a second Army of the Loire, and Faidherbe commanded the Army of the North; both of these officers had been generals in Algeria at the outbreak of the war and both were ignored by the imperial government, but they were the only French generals who showed real military ability. Their small armies harassed the Germans incessantly, but they were not strong enough to break the siege of Paris.

A force of 130,000 was called the Army of the East. Commanded by General Bourbaki, it advanced on Belfort where Denfert-Rochereau directed a valiant resistance of the enemy. It was hoped that, after Belfort had been relieved, the German lines of communication could be cut and the enemy compelled to withdraw into Alsace. The success of this maneuver depended upon its speed; it was an imitation of the strategy of Napoleon I in 1814. He knew how to manage such a maneuver, but Bourbaki did not. He gave the Germans ample time to move against him and to compel his retreat across the frontier into Switzerland. That put the Army of the East out of action for the duration of the war.

Early in January, 1871, the Germans grew impatient and began to bombard unhappy Paris where the threat of a new and a violent revolution had been added to the threat of starvation. The thousands of Prussian shells that came crashing in each day supplemented the misery of a severe winter. Long queues of women shivered in icy rain, watching the bursting of the shells while they waited outside the municipal butcher shops for their daily ration of less than two ounces of horse meat. Rats sold at two francs apiece. For long weeks and months the Parisians accepted suffering without complaint. There was joking and laughter about the change of diet. But, toward the end of January, the joking and laughter ceased. There was an insurrection that had to be suppressed by force of arms.

The government realized that further resistance could serve no useful purpose. It had become clear that the provincial armies were unable to save the capital. Bismarck was installed at Versailles. Jules Favre was sent there to discuss the conditions of surrender. On January 28, 1871, an armistice of three weeks' duration was declared. In that period France was to elect a National Assembly which would have the power to negotiate the final conditions of peace. With the signing of this armistice, the war ended.

Directly after the Third Republic was declared, the Empress Eugénie left Paris for England. There, after a brief confinement in Germany, Napoleon joined her, and there, on January 9, 1873, he died.

CHAPTER THIRTY

THE FEEBLE INFANCY OF THE THIRD REPUBLIC

CREATION OF THE GERMAN EMPIRE AT VERSAILLES. BISMARCK'S ONE
GREAT BLUNDER WAS ABOUT ALSACE-LORRAINE. THIERS BECAME EXECU-
TIVE CHIEF OF FRANCE. THE TRAGEDY OF THE COMMUNE. THE NATION'S
SURPRISINGLY SWIFT RECOVERY. THE NARROW VICTORY OF THE REPUB-
LICANS OVER THE ROYALISTS.

THE major result of the Franco-Prussian War was the unification of
Germany. While Von Moltke concentrated on defeating the French,
Bismarck concentrated on overcoming German prejudice against
Prussia. Von Moltke's victories facilitated Bismarck's task. Even
the traditional hostility of Bavaria was diminished by the inescapable
fact of Germany's debt to Prussia. Bavaria and Wurtemberg had
strong dislike for the idea of taking orders from Berlin, but they
could not deny that Germany had Berlin to thank for the defeat of
France. The southern Germans were caught between love of independence and a vision of a powerful and united nation. Finally they
sacrificed their independence in order to ally themselves with power
That is, their princes made this sacrifice. The people were not con
sulted. No plebiscites were held. The unification of Italy was essen
tially a democratic process, but the unification of Germany was
definitely not that. Germany was unified by the force of arms, and,
once unified, the glorification of force became fundamental in the
creed which the people were taught to believe.

Bismarck handled his diplomatic problem with consummate skill.
His finishing touch was to persuade the King of Bavaria to be the
one who proposed to King William of Prussia that he should become
the Emperor of Germany. William felt that it was his patriotic duty
to concur in Bavaria's proposal.

The German Empire was born on the eighteenth of January, 1871,
ten days before the surrender of Paris. King William and the other
German princes came to the château of Versailles. They came to

witness both the birth of an empire and its baptism in battle. The sound of the guns that were shelling Paris could be heard in the Hall of Mirrors. There old William stood erect before an altar that was half-hidden by the flags of the besieging regiments. There he was declared to be the hereditary emperor of a united Germany, a new Germany whose godfather was fittingly symbolized by the massed battle-flags and the distant roar of the Krupp cannon.

Preliminary terms of peace were agreed upon on the 26th of February, and the final treaty was signed at Frankfort on the tenth of May, 1871. France was compelled to cede Alsace and the northern part of Lorraine, to pay an indemnity of five billion francs within three years, and to be host to a German army of occupation until the indemnity was paid. Thiers conducted the negotiations for France. The only concession he obtained from the Iron Chancellor was the retention of Belfort, and that was granted only upon the condition that German troops should enter Paris and remain there until the treaty was ratified.

The cession of Alsace and Lorraine was the one feature of the Treaty of Frankfort which the French people bitterly resented. Even before the surrender of Paris, the representatives of these provinces made a vigorous formal protest against their prospective separation from France; they declared that "the indissoluble pact which has attached Alsace and Lorraine to France for more than two centuries has been sealed with blood. . . . We proclaim the inviolable right of our people to remain French and to resist all who would disregard that right." Bismarck insisted, however, that possession of Strasbourg and of Metz was necessary in order to make Germany secure against attack by France.

Seen in retrospect, Bismarck's insistence upon the cession of Alsace and Lorraine stands out clearly as his one great mistake. In 1866 he successfully opposed King William's desire to enlarge the Prussian domain at the expense of Austria; had he shown similar wisdom and foresight in 1871, modern civilization might have been spared its greatest catastrophe. But he allowed his generals to convince him that, for military reasons, it was important to hold Strasbourg and Metz even against the will of their people; there were many German residents of Strasbourg, but Metz was wholly French. Presumably he believed that the security and the economic interests of Germany warranted this usurpation, but the gain in security and economic advantage was far outweighed by the hatred and mistrust which that usurpation engendered. That hatred and mistrust were largely accountable for the formation in later years of the Franco-Russian alliance, and that alliance, in turn, was largely accountable for another and a far greater war, a war in which Germany was defeated. The brutal annexation of Alsace-Lorraine destroyed all chance for the development of Franco-German amity and mutual appreciation.

The people of the martyred provinces were given a limited period in which to choose between German and French nationality, but, if they chose the latter, they were required to leave their old homes and migrate beyond the new frontier. Sixty thousand did so. Many of them moved to Paris. *L'Ecole d'Alsace et de Lorraine* is a distinguished monument of that migration. The London *Times* wrote, "We know of no historic example of an equally great devotion to the fatherland."

Bismarck's tragic mistake ushered in an era marked by so much of mistrust, ill-feeling, and desire for revenge that the only peace Europe has known since 1870 has been an armed peace. The German seizure of Alsace-Lorraine has proved to be a major factor in the incalculable retardation of human progress.

The armistice agreement of January 28, 1871, called for the immediate election of a national assembly. The question at issue in that election was whether to continue the war or to surrender. Gambetta was passionately in favor of continuance, but the election went against him. The great majority of those elected wished to see the hopeless struggle ended. There were 400,000 French prisoners of war in Germany, 100,000 were interned in Switzerland, and about 140,000 had been killed.

The Assembly met in Bordeaux on the twelfth of February. Thiers was chosen "executive chief of the French Republic," but the fact that a large majority in the Assembly were royalists suggested that the Republic might be short-lived. Thiers, posing the question of his duty, described his conception of it as follows: "Loyalty, not to one, but to all the groups. What we owe to all is to deceive no one. Our task is the reorganization of the country. When that has been accomplished, we may return to the question of what form its permanent government shall take. Now France lies bleeding, covered with wounds, barely alive. I pledge to you the word of an honest man that, in the effort to bind up those wounds, nothing political shall be done. The great decision to be made later shall not be prejudiced by any infidelity on our part."

On the first of March the Assembly ratified the peace preliminaries which Thiers had negotiated on February 26. After that, it moved from Paris to Versailles, intentionally avoiding the dangers of revolutionary Paris. Royalists dominated the Assembly, but republican extremists controlled the capital. Co-operation between these two groups was impossible. The result was a small but bloody civil war with the Germans as interested spectators. The French, having been crushingly defeated by a foreign foe, proceeded to fly at one anothers' throats. There is no more lamentable chapter in French history than the mercifully brief chapter of the *Commune*. The spring months of 1869 had seen Paris at its bedizened best; those of 1871 saw it at its worst.

The long siege played havoc with the morale of the Parisians. That was especially true of the workers; upon them the burden of misery rested most heavily. There had been a larger supply of alcohol than of food. Commercial employment had practically ceased. A pittance of a franc and a half per day was paid for military service; that was nearly all the workers had on which to live. The Assembly curtailed payment of this pittance and ordered cessation of the moratorium that had existed during the siege. Thereby 150,000 workers were deprived of legal right to occupy their lodgings unless they paid rent which they were unable to pay. Thus their heroic defense of Paris was punished rather than rewarded. The cup of their bitter indignation overflowed when the Assembly settled itself in Versailles rather than in Paris. They knew that the royalists possessed a majority. Louis Blanc, Victor Hugo, Gambetta, Garibaldi, Edgar Quinet, and Henri Rochefort were among the liberals whom the Parisians had elected, but the liberals were outnumbered by the reactionaries returned by the provinces. Paris had no more love for the Versailles

Assembly of 1871 than she had had for the nobles who lived there in 1789.

The workers were armed and organized. The National Guard had not surrendered its guns. When German troops occupied the west side of Paris, the Guard removed two hundred cannon to the east side, to Montmartre and to Belleville which were strongholds of the workers. Early in March a *Comité central* was formed to direct what was called the *Fédération Républicaine de la Garde Nationale.* The authority of the Assembly was defied by a force that had seized the arsenals and was in possession of more than 400,000 rifles. This force held Paris at its mercy in the spring months of 1871. The brief period of its illegal control is called the *Commune.*

No statesman has ever been confronted by a more difficult situation than the one which confronted Thiers after he was chosen to be the executive chief of the new Republic. Then seventy-four, this dynamic little gentleman and scholar, a native of Marseille, had already had an extraordinary career. He was one of the promoters of the revolution of 1830, a minister in Louis-Philippe's government, the leader of the Party of Order in the Second Republic, and one of the leaders of the opposition to Napoleon III. He was the only man of political influence who steadfastly opposed the declaration of war with Prussia. When subsequent events proved how right he had been, he became the trusted leader of a great majority of the people.

Thiers was no theorist. He was a realist whose liberalism was strongly flavored by his bourgeois respect for order and property. Alert and tireless, his passion was for what could be realized rather than for what might be more desirable; for what would work rather than for what one might wish. He was an incarnation of middle-class common sense. Once a monarchist, he had come to realize that monarchy, however liberal, could not be made acceptable to a majority of his fellow countrymen. He supported the Republic because, in his own words, "republicanism divides us least." But the kind of republic Thiers favored was one that would maintain order, respect established rights, and manage its social reforms with a minimum of economic disturbance.

When he returned from Bordeaux, the Chief Executive found Paris in the possession of a "republican federation" whose leaders proposed to rule France in the name of the *Commune* of Paris. These extremists had little in common except their passionate opposition to the legally constituted government. In an unsuccessful effort to secure support outside of Paris, they proposed that all the *communes* should become autonomous, national solidarity to be assured only by an inter-communal contract.

The *Commune,* as a name, does not mean communism; the name is a word whose nearest English equivalent is "community." The proposed autonomy of the *communes* did not necessarily mean communism, but a redistribution of property was implied in the proposal that "the land should belong to the peasant and the tools should belong to the workers."

The first need of the nation was to pay the war indemnity and thereby put an end to the German occupation which cost the government more than a million francs per day. But this could not be done while Paris was held by a group that defied the government. No loan could be floated so long as the cannon of the *Commune* controlled the capital.

Thiers did not hesitate. When he returned from Bordeaux he ordered regular troops to recover the cannon that the *Commune* had seized. An unsuccessful attempt to fulfill this order was made on the eighteenth of March. The troops that were sent were sympathetic with the insurrectionists. They refused to obey orders and arrested their own general. Later, he and another general were shot.

Thiers then ordered the withdrawal of the troops and left the *Commune* in undisputed possession of Paris. The *députés* and the municipal officials of Paris did their utmost to quell the insurrection by pacific means, but these efforts failed. Louis Blanc and other socialistic Parisian leaders had no sympathy with the *Commune,* but their former followers would no longer listen to them. Finally, even Blanc denounced a movement which amounted to "a revolt by the populace of Paris against the rest of France in the presence of the enemy."

This intolerable situation endured for many weeks. May came before the regular army, re-inforced by prisoners of war who returned from Germany, was strong enough to justify an offensive. A force of one hundred thousand commanded by MacMahon then began a second siege of Paris. In April an expedition of the Federation had marched out to attack Versailles. They had been defeated. Reprisal executions on both sides had made a peaceful outcome impossible. The *Fédérés* of the *Commune* were determined to resist to the bitter end.

The "Bloody Week" began on May 21. On that day the government's army entered Paris with instructions to put an end to all resistance. It was then that the *Fédérés* burned the Tuileries, the Hôtel de Ville, and part of the Louvre. They massacred prisoners whom they had arrested as hostages. Madness seized both sides. More than twenty thousand were killed. The *Commune* ended in carnage.

There were fifty thousand arrests after the fighting ceased. Six thousand were deported. The trial of prisoners dragged on for four years. The *Commune* is the most pitiful chapter in French history. Some have blamed Thiers for the holocaust that marked its suppression. Others have maintained that there was no other practicable way to get forward in the work of reconstruction. Bloody Week proved again the readiness of the French, when aroused, to fight and to die in defense of what they believe to be their rights. They are not a submissive people.

Its difficulty in suppressing the *Commune* endangered the Republic. Many believed that the prolonged and bloody struggle with the *Fédérés* would make the people favor a return to royal government. But the elections of July indicated the contrary. They were favorable to the republicans. One of the younger *députés* was jubilant over the result. "All is saved!" he exclaimed. "The country has not lost its courage." He was a young man from the Vendée who had turned from his medical studies in Paris to enter politics and had been elected *maire* of the 18th *arrondissement*. Although an ardent republican, he had been one of those who did their utmost to prevent the conflict of the *Commune* with the government. His name was Georges Clemenceau.

The royalists continued to hold a majority in the Assembly, but Thiers was more than a match for them. In August, 1871, he secured the legalization of a provisional constitution which gave him the title of President of the Republic without diminution of his executive power. The older he grew, the more forceful this dauntless and diligent little man became. His expert and vigilant nursing saved the life of the frail infant republic. He preserved political liberty for France, and at the same time relieved her of the crushing burden of German occupation.

Bismarck had believed that it would take France much longer than the specified three years to pay the five-billion-franc indemnity. Thiers paid it in a year and a half. On September 16, 1873, the German army was withdrawn, and the Assembly rendered to Thiers the highest tribute France can confer, a tribute that has been rendered to but very few of her statesmen; it decreed that he had *"bien merité de la patrie."*

Interest on the loan which was floated in order to pay the indemnity, plus the other costs of the final Napoleonic catastrophe, increased the budget by seven hundred and thirty millions. This necessitated a heavy increase in the taxes, both direct and indirect. There was little complaint and the new taxes produced the revenue needed to balance the budget. The economic health of the country was demonstrated as well as its loyalty to republicanism.

In 1872 a new military law was enacted whose object was to make the standing army equal in strength to that of Germany. Reluctantly France assumed what seemed to her the necessary burden of obligatory military service, a burden which subsequent years have not lightened. The armed-camp aspect of western Europe dates from the Franco-Prussian War. The youth of France and her economic life continue to pay dearly for the illusion that created the Second Empire.

No sooner had the Germans left than the royalists began a campaign against Thiers. While he was engaged in liberating the country and in restoring order, they had been inactive, but, once the country was on its feet again, they sought to regain control of it. As a first step in that direction, they formed a coalition with the Bonapartists and thus secured a majority in the Assembly.

Thiers, true to his promise, invited the Assembly to determine the future form of government. He favored continuance of the Republic because he believed that a return to monarchy would cause a new revolution, but he held for an extremely conservative republic. Liberalism, for him, spelled disorder and the breakdown of authority.

In March, 1873, the royalist group succeeded in passing a law which curtailed the President's right to intervene in legislative procedure. In May the Assembly, by a small majority, defeated the government on a question of confidence. Thiers at once resigned.

The Duke of Broglie was the leader of the royalists. Their cause was handicapped by a fundamental difference of opinion. They agreed in wishing to impose a king upon the people of France, but they did not agree about who that king should be. Some of them favored the Count of Paris, Louis-Philippe's grandson; others were for the Count of Chambord who was a grandson of Charles X. The best plan appeared to be to allow some figurehead to serve as president while the royalists were making up their minds about the kingship. The figurehead chosen for this ignoble role was General Mac-Mahon, a soldier who had had no political experience. The Assembly elected him to succeed Thiers.

In August of that same year, 1873, the royalists finally came to an agreement about who should be their candidate. The corpulent and heavily-whiskered Count of Chambord was living in Austria. His name was Henri and he was a direct descendant of the great Henri IV. It was decided to make a Henri V out of him. So the Count of Paris went to Austria and saluted his middle-aged cousin as "head of the House of France." Paris could wait his turn; he was only in his thirties. Chambord was in his fifties and childless. He was the last prince in the direct line of the Bourbons. Paris, who was of the Orléans branch, would succeed him.

Since the royalists were in control of the government, it appeared that all that remained to be done was to select the date on which the Republic should die and a new king be crowned. Fortunately for the Republic, an unexpected complication arose.

The whiskery Chambord was a very obstinate man who had inherited full measure of the Bourbon inability to learn. Louis-Philippe had accepted the tricolor and Louis-Napoleon had no objection to it, but the tricolor was not good enough for Chambord. He bluntly refused to become Henri V unless the white flag of his illustrious ancestor became again the flag of France. He said that no one could persuade him to become "a king legitimized by the Revolution." He admitted that he was "the necessary pilot, the only one capable of steering the ship of state safely into port," but he made it clear that the ship would have to fly a white flag before he would consent to take the helm.

Even the most ardent of the royalists realized that the people would never consent to the sacrifice of their beloved tricolor. MacMahon said that "the guns would go off of themselves." Some have maintained that Chambord still had implicit faith in the divine right of kings. Others have suggested that he used the flag question as an excuse for avoiding an extremely dangerous responsibility. In any case, he put himself so definitely out of the running that his disappointed backers had no choice but to extend the tenure of the figurehead they had elected president.

Grand plans had been made for the royal entry into Paris. Great gilded carriages that bear the monogram of Henri V still wait patiently in the château of Chambord, and the regal draperies that noble ladies embroidered grow moldier each year above the sculptured bed in which he never slept.

The royalists did not give up hope. If Chambord should pass away, then they could make a king out of his Orléans cousin; they could count upon him not to let the color of a flag stand between him and a crown. Meanwhile they sustained their figurehead. A law passed in November, 1873, prolonged the presidential term to seven years. MacMahon, ennobled by the title of Duke of Magenta, remained the titular head of the government, but it was Broglie who controlled it.

The Broglie ministry did all it could to break down the opposition to a return to royalty. It had the aid of the clergy in a vigorous anti-republican campaign. It sought to dignify the end in view by describing it as "the restoration of moral order." Taking its cue from the encyclical of Pius IX, the Broglie ministry tried to identify republicanism with immorality. Republican insignia were removed from the town halls. France, legally a republic, was governed by a group whose primary object was to destroy republicanism.

Constant effort was made to nullify the influence of the republican press; in a single year nearly two hundred editors were brought to trial and convicted. The commission which had been appointed to draft a constitution deliberately neglected its duty; more than a year passed before the matter of constitutional laws was brought up again in the Assembly.

Despite all the efforts of the government to the contrary, there was a steady increase in the political strength of the republican party. This was largely due to the tireless efforts of that fiery orator, Léon Gambetta. His opponents sought to ridicule him by calling him the "traveling salesman of democracy." He responded that he was proud to deserve that title. Accused of stirring up class hatred, he turned that charge against his accusers. "Class," he said, "is a bad word. I never employ it. What France needs is not a republic controlled by a ruling group, but a truly national republic representative of all groups. I advocate the extension of political power to the workers because I believe that their abuse of it would be less than that of those who now monopolize it. Their leaders have proved that in political sagacity they have little to learn from those who have heretofore been their masters. Our country has imperative need of the strength which national solidarity would give. That solidarity can never be attained so long as the workers are excluded from political life."

The municipal elections of 1874 provided indisputable proof that a large majority of the people were opposed to a return to monarchy. The royalist coalition in the Assembly began to break up. Some of those who had favored the Orléans succession, perceiving that their cause was lost, came to an understanding with the conservative republicans. In January, 1875, the Third Republic finally escaped from the threat of swift extinction which had menaced it from the day of its birth. When discussion of the "constitutional laws" at last became the order of the day, a motion to strike out the word "republic" was carried by a small majority. But on the following day, Wallon, one of the royalists, came over to the republican side and proposed an amendment concerning the method of election of the president. This amendment began with the words, "The President of the *Republic.*" It was carried by a vote of 353 to 352. Republicanism, although desired by a large majority of the people, won in the Assembly only by an eyelash. France again came perilously near to having an authoritarian regime imposed upon her.

In that same year, 1875, the Assembly enacted a series of constitutional laws which still form the basis of French government. Those laws established a parliamentary regime modeled after that of England. They clearly indicated a parallelism in social and political development. France, in 1875, moved a long step forward toward that inevitable alliance whose inevitability was to be more clearly revealed by future developments then unforeseen.

Summary of Chapters Twenty-one to Thirty

In the fifty years between 1825 and 1875 France knew five different forms of government. The reactionary reign of Charles X ended in 1830; the conservatively-liberal monarchy of Louis-Philippe ran from 1830 to 1848; the Second Republic, 1848-51; the Second Empire, 1851-70; in 1871 the Third Republic began.

Charles X attempted a return to the hopelessly outmoded *ancien régime.* The people soon had their fill of this second of the Bourbons imposed upon them by foreign powers. On a July day of 1830 the Parisians swept their streets clean of royal troops that had been sent against them. The King fled to England.

Those who had fought to overthrow King Charles wished to be rid of royalty forever. But to certain level-headed gentlemen it was clear that the Powers which had restored the Bourbons would intervene again unless France maintained at least a semblance of respect for royal authority. Swift and dramatic action enabled Louis-Philippe, a cousin of Charles X, to become king, but his was a restricted monarchy; it was called "the Government of July"; it survived for eighteen years. On February 23, 1848, a demonstration in favor of enlargement of the electorate led to violence. Louis-Philippe abdicated and left for England.

This time the popular will prevailed. The Second Republic was attempted. A principal cause of its failure was that the bourgeois-controlled government suppressed by force an insurrection of the starving workers; in June, 1848, occurred the most murderous street-fighting Paris has ever seen. The Republic, established in February, was controlled in June by those who had not favored its establishment. The workers, disillusioned, turned against the government which they had helped to create. In December they helped to elect as president Louis-Napoleon Bonaparte. There was a popular feeling that the Second Republic was a failure, and that a Bonaparte, even as emperor, would be better than a bourgeois government that was not truly representative. Louis-Napoleon did all he could to foster the growth of this feeling.

On December 2, 1851, occurred the *coup d'état* whereby the Second Republic was destroyed and the Second Empire began. Louis-Napoleon Bonaparte, a nephew of Napoleon I, became Napoleon III, not because France desired a return of autocracy, but chiefly because she was rebellious against the injustices of a false democracy.

In 1854 Napoleon III fought as an ally of England in the Crimean war against Russia. In 1858, in a secret agreement with Cavour, he agreed to help Sardinia fight Austria. In 1859 the Austrians were defeated in the battles of Magenta and Solferino, but Napoleon withdrew before he had advanced to Venice as he had agreed, and thereby he lost favor with the Italians. In 1860 he agreed to support the enlargement of Sardinia in Italy if plebiscites were held in Savoy and Nice on the question of annexation to France; the plebiscites were held and Savoy and Nice were annexed.

Victor-Emmanuel of Sardinia became King of Italy, March 14, 1861. In that same year Napoleon made his unsuccessful attempt to transform Mexico into an empire. In 1866 he encouraged Victor-Emmanuel to fight as an ally of Prussia against Austria. Prussia defeated Austria. Austria defeated the Italians, but, to secure Napoleon's neutrality, she had to cede Venice to Italy. When the Franco-Prussian War began in 1870, French troops were still in Rome to protect the Pope; their withdrawal enabled Victor-Emmanuel to make Rome his capital.

The underlying cause of the Franco-Prussian War was Bismarck's belief that it was essential for the achievement of Prussia's control of Germany. The immediate cause was his issuance of a *communiqué* to the press which made it appear that France had been insulted by Prussia's King William. Napoleon surrendered at Sedan, September 1, 1870, and, three days later, France became a republic. Gambetta was the most active leader in the new regime. Resistance of the invaders continued until Paris surrendered, January 28, 1871. Ten days before that, at Versailles, William Hohenzollern of Prussia had been declared Emperor of Germany.

By the Treaty of Frankfort of 1871 France was compelled to cede Alsace and part of Lorraine to Germany. This territorial seizure was Bismarck's great mistake; it was an underlying cause of the war of 1914-1918.

Thiers became "executive chief" of the Third Republic. He made a splendid record, both in paying the war indemnity to the Germans and in averting a return to monarchy. It was imperative to put an end to the insurrectionary *Commune* of Paris; unfortunately that necessitated cruel procedure.

In August, 1871, a provisional constitution was adopted and Thiers was named President of the Republic. In 1873 the strong royalist group forced Thiers out of office and replaced him by MacMahon. In the same year they attempted to re-establish a monarchy with the Count of Chambord for king as Henri V. They might have succeeded except that Chambord disqualified himself by refusing to accept the tricolor.

Constitutional laws which were enacted in 1875 are still in effect. France, like England, does not have a specific constitution. The statutes of 1875 constitute the legal basis of her form of government; they maintain the spirit of her earlier democratic constitutions, re-establishing those "rights of man" so dearly won nearly a century before, only to be lost again for many years. The realistic Third Republic has prevailed over the forces of reaction and has dispelled the dreams of glory that once misled the people. It has given to France a form of government that her people can control.

CHAPTER THIRTY-ONE

THIRTY-EIGHT YEARS OF POLITICAL HISTORY

FRANCE ADOPTED ENGLAND'S SYSTEM OF GOVERNMENT. THE VIRTUE OF
POLITICAL ELASTICITY. THE REPUBLICANS FORCED THE RESIGNATION OF
THE ROYALIST PRESIDENT. GRÉVY ESTABLISHED THE NONPOLITICAL
NATURE OF THE PRESIDENCY. LIBERALISM PERMITTED INCREASE OF RADI-
CALISM. THE MINISTRIES OF JULES FERRY. THE BOULANGER MOVEMENT.
THE DREYFUS AFFAIR.

THE constitutional laws of 1875 created the *Sénat* and the *Chambre
des députés* as legislative bodies. The *députés* were to be elected by
"universal suffrage" every four years. One-fourth of the *sénateurs*
were to be elected for life by the *Sénat* itself, and three-fourths by a
limited electorate for nine-year terms. The President was to be chosen
by the two legislative bodies meeting in joint session; his term of
office was to be seven years. The executive power was vested in a
ministry appointed by the President, but responsible to the legislative
bodies; it could retain office only so long as it was supported by a
majority of the lawmakers.

This system, with minor modifications, is still in effect. In its
original form it represented a compromise between the liberal royalists and the conservative republicans. The royalists accepted it because it was a plan which would require a minimum of change if the
president were supplanted by a king; their willingness to accept the
English system was largely due to the fact that democratic England
retained the form if not the reality of monarchy. The republicans
accepted it because, at that time, the adoption of anything more democratic could not be secured. However, as their political strength increased, the liberal republicans steadily modified this elastic plan in
the direction of greater democracy. Since 1875 the political system
of France has been progressively republicanized.

The definite organization of the Republic did not end its difficulties.
It could not have survived had not the enlargement of the electorate

permitted the people of France to indicate their determination to oppose any return to autocracy. It was constantly menaced, either by a royalist group on the right, or, later, by a party of the extreme left that favored social and economic revolution. The fact that republicanism in France has surmounted many difficult crises without departure from an essentially moderate middle course is a true index of the spirit of her people. After the elimination of Bonapartism, they quickly regained their political sanity.

The strong individualism of the French made it inevitable that there would be many rather than few political parties. Ministries could survive only by virtue of commanding a majority in the legislative bodies, but only rarely has one party had such a majority. The majorities that have sustained or reversed ministries have usually been coalitions of various groups. The instabilities of such coalitions have caused frequent changes of ministries. There were as many as fifty such changes between 1875 and 1914.

Executive power resides in a cabinet or *conseil* which is composed of ministers whose number is not fixed by law. Cabinets vary in size; there may be "ministers without portfolio." The chief of the cabinet is called the *président du conseil;* his authority corresponds almost precisely to that of the British prime minister. The instability of the executive power is more apparent than real. A personnel that is permanent assures the continuity of executive routine. Changes of government are far less momentous in France than they are in the United States, and the disadvantage of their frequency is largely counterbalanced by the gain in freedom and speed of action.

When disaccord exists between a majority of the American Congress and the President, legislation suffers and deadlocks may ensue. In France, however, when a majority in either of the legislative bodies votes against the executive power on a question of confidence, that particular executive power ceases to exist. The cabinet submits its resignation to the President. The President then calls in the leader who appears to be most likely to gain the support of a majority of the lawmakers, and invites him to form a new cabinet. The new one may be identical with the old one except for one or two ministers in whom the legislators had lost confidence. The prime minister may even succeed himself as president of the new cabinet. Thus a French ministry may fall and another one replace it within a day or two, and the functioning of the governmental machinery be improved rather than impaired thereby. Theoretically, this is suggestive of the changing of a spark plug that has ceased to fire.

Party ties are less binding in France than in America. There is more political independence. Many of France's most influential statesmen have passed through a succession of political affiliations without loss of prestige. New parties and new coalitions appear when new conditions call for them. There is a rapidity in readjustment which cannot be equaled under the more rigid American plan. The flexibility of the system has permitted the surmounting of crises which might otherwise have brought disaster.

In France no party is strong enough effectively to control the electorate by the use of patronage. The absence of formidable political machines gives to political honesty a better chance for its life. There is an opportunity for individual independence which the two-party system tends to thwart. The French plan gives less encouragement to that kind of political subservience upon which the American system thrives. Despite its weaknesses of operation, it does retain fertility for the growth of idealism, whereas the American two-party system is built upon a hard foundation of practical political experience in which idealism finds few crevices wherein to thrust its roots.

In the political history of the Third Republic from 1876 until 1914, there were four phases. The first of these was marked by a crisis in 1877 and by the resignation of President MacMahon in 1879. He was succeeded by Jules Grévy. The second, 1879 to 1885, was a peaceful period of liberal reforms. In the third, 1885 to 1899, there were several crises which led to socialistic demands and to a tightening up of the liberalism of the republicans. In the fourth, 1899 to 1914, there was a steady growth of the political power of the left, a growth that was arrested only when the threat of war suddenly thrust political differences into the background.

The elections of 1876 gave to the republicans a large majority in the *Chambre;* Gambetta, Grévy, and Ferry were the leaders of this majority. The *Sénat,* however, was about equally divided in its sympathies; there, with the support of President MacMahon, the royalists hoped to prevail. Their most powerful ally was the Catholic clergy. The Church was unceasing in its efforts to undermine confidence in republicanism and to secure French intervention in Italy in order to win back for the Pope the temporal rights of which he had been deprived.

Gambetta, with undiminished vigor, ceaselessly insisted that the Church should keep out of politics. In a memorable speech before the *Chambre* he declared, "I speak for the deep and sincere sentiment of the people of France when I say that political domination by the clergy is no less repugnant to them than the *ancien régime* itself. I declare that at this moment clericalism is the Republic's most formidable enemy."

The conflict of ideas between the republicans and those who controlled the President led to the crisis of May 16, 1877. On that day President MacMahon, persuaded by his royalist bosses that he had a legal right to do so, caused the resignation of the republican ministry and replaced it by a royalist one which was inacceptable to a majority of the *députés*. The *Sénat* supported the government in ordering the dissolution of the *Chambre,* and the question was carried to the country.

In the campaign that followed, Gambetta's fearless attack upon the government's position cost him a fine of two thousand francs and a sentence to three months' imprisonment. But, despite desperate efforts by the reactionaries, the liberals won the election; the new *Chambre* was made up of 327 republicans and 208 monarchists. MacMahon was compelled to appoint a ministry that the majority would support. Two years later, in 1879, the republicans gained control of the *Sénat.* MacMahon then resigned and Jules Grévy was elected to succeed him.

Grévy made a new definition of the function of the presidency which has had the force of law ever since. He declared that the President of the Republic should take no action prejudicial to the parliamentary form of government. That meant that the President, despite his appointive power, should never seek to maintain in office any ministry or minister inacceptable to a majority of the lawmakers. It also meant that the President should keep aloof from politics. Herein lies a striking dissimilarity between the French and the American systems. Some Americans believe that, in this matter, the advantage is on the side of the French.

Control of Paris by the *Commune* in 1871 had made it expedient for the legislative bodies to convene in Versailles. They continued to convene there until Grévy's presidency marked the escape of the Republic from control by the royalists. Then they moved to Paris, declared the fourteenth of July to be the *fête nationale* in honor of the Republic, and extended amnesty to all who had been condemned on account of participation in the *Commune*. There was no longer any question about republican control of the political life of the nation, but leaders in industry and finance, many magistrates and generals, and practically all of the clergy, remained unshaken in their belief that the salvation of France depended upon a return to monarchy.

Differences of opinion soon developed among the republicans. Those who had had more political experience favored solving the nation's problems one at a time rather than all at once; they had learned the importance of awaiting "the opportune moment"; they were called the opportunists. Those who had had less experience were in greater haste for reform; they were called radicals.

Gambetta was one whose experience had transformed him from a radical into an opportunist. His place as a leader of the radical minority had been taken by Clemenceau. Later it became Clemenceau's turn to move as Gambetta had from radicalism toward conservatism, from a position on the extreme left to one that approached the center; in both cases, experience and responsibility induced growth in political wisdom.

Gambetta's ambition was to organize all republicans into a single party. He would have been the logical chief of such a party. But the qualities which had made him an idol of the people did not recommend him to the conservative republicans. As an inspiring orator and as a fearless patriot, Gambetta was in a class by himself, but there was reason to believe that he would be less successful as an administrator. President Grévy was one of the influential men who believed that Gambetta was better on the rostrum than he would be in an office. His great popularity made him seem dangerous.

The republicans, instead of becoming more united, became more fragmented. Four rival groups appeared. The President appointed as executives those who were more conservative and less popular than either Gambetta or Clemenceau. Gambetta did not become a minister until 1881. His untimely death came in 1882.

Grévy and Ferry became the wheel-horses of the Republic that owed its life to Thiers and Gambetta. Grévy, in 1848, had been a leader of the opposition to that enlargement of the electorate which led to France's second martyrdom under a Bonaparte. The excellent foresight he had shown upon that occasion recommended him highly to the more thoughtful republicans of the 1870's. He presided over the National Assembly of 1871-1873, and over the *Chambre* from 1876 to 1879. He was the aristocrat of the republicans, possessing a dignity and a reserve that were more characteristic of the royalists. He spoke but little, but, when he did speak, he had the effect of an oracle. He was seventy-two when they elected him President of the Republic.

Jules Ferry, born in 1832, died in 1893. Twice prime minister, he rendered extremely valuable service to the state in many ways, but he is best remembered for what he did for the schools. From the time that he became minister of public instruction in 1879, he worked unceasingly at the enlargement of free educational opportunity. Ferry, more than any one, is responsible for the creation of the public school system of France. But he was appreciated for his great worth only after his death. His frosty manner compelled misunderstanding and unpopularity. Gambetta once said to him, "You are the best man in the world, but you are like a rosebush that bears only thorns." "That is my curse," Ferry answered. "My roses all grow within."

The Catholic Church continued to be the most formidable opponent of republicanism. The republicans felt compelled to curtail the educational influence of the clergy. Ferry stated the government's position as follows: "To maintain the rights of the state, not against religious Catholicism, but against political Catholicism. To diminish neither the spiritual heritage nor the financial resources of the Church, but to require cessation of its opposition to the form of government which the people have seen fit to establish."

Ferry proposed a law which would give the state exclusive control of the universities. The *Chambre* passed it, but the *Sénat* rejected it. Dispersal of the Jesuits was then ordered by governmental decree. Instead of dispersing, the Jesuits barricaded themselves in their colleges. The government deemed it unwise to resort to force.

Ferry was convinced that the future health of the Republic depended upon breaking the grip of the Catholic clergy on the schools. He favored requirement of attendance at public elementary schools in which there should be no charge for instruction nor any control by religious organizations. In 1881 he secured remission of the school fees, but he had great difficulty in making school attendance obligatory and in removing religious control. Ultimately a compromise was reached whereby on one week day the schools were to be closed in order to give opportunity for such religious instruction as parents might wish their children to have. The right of supervision previously enjoyed by the clergy was withdrawn, and after 1886 all priests were disbarred from teaching in the public schools.

Passage of the *lois scolaires* was followed by the erection of thousands of new school buildings. Normal schools were established in every *département* for the training of elementary teachers. In the last days of Napoleon III only twelve million francs were expended each year on primary education. In 1888 that figure had risen to a hundred million, and in 1908 it was half a billion.

Educational reform was not the only progressive step taken in 1881. In that year laws were passed which removed previous restrictions on the press and on freedom of assembly. Beginning in 1882, new liberties were extended to the *communes;* they were given the right to elect their own *maires*. The *grande loi municipale* of 1884 established local governments upon their present basis; it defined in detail the functions and powers of mayors and of municipal councils. Also in 1884, *syndicats professionnels* were the subject of a new statute that gave to the workers' organizations a better status than they had previously enjoyed; their political and their economic power were greatly increased thereby.

A revision of the constitutional laws occurred in 1884. The provision for a life term for one-third of the senators was abolished and the method of their indirect election was made more equitable. The *loi militaire* of 1889 set the period of obligatory military service at three years, with diminution of that term under certain conditions, such as the necessity to support a family.

In the later 1880's the royalists and the radicals combined in an unsuccessful attempt to change the form of government. The unpopularity of Ferry led to the defeat of his ministry in 1885. The election of that year produced a *Chambre* so divided into political factions that a stable ministry could not be established. To the parliamentary disorder, economic and foreign difficulties were added. The confidence of the people in their Republic was shaken.

A "man on horseback" appeared. Boulanger, minister of war in 1886, was a handsome and dashing general whose clever criticisms of a government in difficulty gained for him with the less thoughtful an easy and ill-founded popularity. On his spirited black horse, he made a fine figure at the military reviews. He posed as the soldiers' best friend, talking glibly of making their service less arduous and of winning back Alsace-Lorraine. He became the hero of popular songs that everybody sang at the *café-concerts*. It occurred to some of the royalists that this new favorite of the boulevards and of the army might be the very man they were looking for.

The ministry of which the handsome General was a member had a short life. The one that succeeded it assigned him to a provincial post. The Paris crowd did not care to lose their darling. Thousands showed their disapproval of the government's order by going to the railroad station and preventing the departure of the trains. In order to escape from his admirers, the General had to ride on a locomotive.

An untimely scandal added to the embarrassment of the government. It was discovered that President Grévy's son-in-law had been doing a flourishing business in the selling of decorations. That compelled Grévy's resignation in December, 1887. He was succeeded by Sadi-Carnot, an honest man of modest ability who was a grandson of the great Carnot of the Revolution. But the illustrious name of the new president was not enough to restore confidence.

Boulanger became the head of a motley combination of extreme rightists and extreme leftists. They demanded a new national assembly that would make a new constitution. They maintained that the "constitution" of 1875 was more oligarchical than democratic. They charged the government with "disorder, corruption, and sterility." They demanded that ministers should have no seat in the legislative bodies and that the *Sénat* should be either suppressed or elected by universal suffrage. There was much in their program that recalled the successful demagoguery of President Louis-Napoleon.

Boulanger retired from the army and certain royalists contributed millions to his anti-governmental campaign. That campaign was so successful that, in January, 1889, his supporters urged him to attempt a *coup d'état*. But the General was not quite brave enough to take that risk.

The government, finally realizing that Boulanger's hold on the people was more apparent than real, planned to bring him to trial on a charge of plotting against the state. Boulanger did not wait to be brought to trial. In April he fled to Belgium. His flight was a fatal blow to his popularity. In the fall elections of that year, 1889, the moderate republicans regained control of the *Chambre*. Boulanger, condemned to deportation in his absence, committed suicide in 1891.

After the collapse of the Boulanger movement, the stability of the established form of government seemed assured. Another thing which contributed to that stability was a change in the papal attitude toward republicanism. Pius IX had been its irreconcilable enemy, but Leo XIII, who succeeded Pius in 1878, believed that all good Catholics should cease to oppose the governments under which they lived. In an encyclical of 1892, addressed to the Catholics of France, he declared, "When new governments are established, acceptance of them is not only permitted, it is requisite. . . . Insurrection is contrary to social good. . . . All French citizens should be loyal to the Republic in their civil relations to it." The Pope advised that legislation unfavorable to the Church should be vigorously opposed, but only by "honest and legal procedure." The conciliatory attitude of Leo XIII led to a rapid diminution of Catholic opposition to the Republic.

While opposition to the government diminished on the right, it increased on the left. Socialism gained ground. The amnesty of 1880 permitted the return to France of many who had been associated with the *Commune*. They added strength to the Marxian demand for collective ownership. In 1886 and 1891 there were strikes and riots. Millerand and Jean Jaurès, influential republican *députés,* moved leftward, giving their support to socialistic doctrines. In 1893 the Socialist party won fifty seats in the *Chambre* and became for the first time a party that had to be reckoned with.

Millerand stated that the primary objective of the Socialists was state control of production and distribution, with attainment of this objective gradually and only when supported by a majority of the electorate. The party endorsed the international organization of workers, but qualified that endorsement by insistence upon the primary importance of patriotism. The acceptance of Marxian principles was only partial. The socialists placed law, order, and patriotism in the forefront of their plan and denounced all revolutionary effort.

The Panama scandal occurred in the early 1890's. Ferdinand de Lesseps, who had built the Suez canal, organized a company to construct a similar one across the isthmus of Panama. A law was passed which permitted his company to sell shares without proper control. The project failed and those who had invested in it found that they had been badly fleeced. They also found that some politicians had been well paid for securing passage of the law which permitted the fleecing. The exposure put a sudden end to a number of political careers, but, since those who had been most deeply involved were already out of office, the government survived.

The wave of assassination which the spread of Marxism brought in its wake did not spare France. Anarchists, exceeding Marxism, exploded many bombs in Paris. One of them burst in the *Chambre des députés.* In 1894 President Sadi-Carnot was assassinated at Lyon by an Italian. He was succeeded by Jean Casimir-Perier.

The disorders, since they appeared to be a by-product of liberalism, led to a political shift. The moderate republicans, alarmed by the dangers discernible on the left, became conciliatory toward the right. The anti-clerical laws were not rigidly enforced. Catholic schools were allowed to reopen. The moderates and the reactionaries made common cause in defense of order. The government denied the charge of persecution of the Church and solicited its co-operation. In the later 1890's there was a brief period of political peace which was to be rudely shattered by a dramatic miscarriage of justice that stirred the nation to its very depths.

A group of high-ranking army officers shared a prevalent prejudice against the Jews. Military secrets had been sold to Germany. Captain Dreyfus, a Jew, was charged with this crime, found guilty, and condemned to a life sentence on Devil's Island. That was in 1894. Some years later, Colonel Picquart, a staff officer, became convinced that Dreyfus was innocent and attempted to secure a reopening of the case. When that proved to be impossible, Emile Zola, the literary champion of justice, was persuaded to intervene.

Georges Clemenceau was editor of a newspaper called *l'Aurore*. In January, 1898, he published an open letter to the President of the Republic written by Zola. That letter covered the front page of the paper. Its screaming headline was, "I ACCUSE . . ."

Zola violently attacked the government for its failure to require a rehearing of the Dreyfus case. His passionate plea for justice aroused the nation. *L'Affaire Dreyfus* became far more than a question of injustice to an obscure officer; it became a question of the attitude of the nation toward justice itself. Zola obtained more than a retrial of Dreyfus; he obtained a moral retrial of the French people.

Many believed that the "honor" of the army, and even the safety of the nation, required that the case be not reopened; the discrediting of the General Staff could not be risked. Others demanded that the truth should be laid bare whatever the cost. The clergy and the royalists supported the army; the intellectuals and the socialists supported Zola. There was a profound cleavage in public opinion. Families as well as political parties became divided. Feeling rose to fever heat. Street manifestations ended in brawls and arguments led to duels.

Zola became the incarnation of the demand for justice. He was brought to trial on the charge of defamation of the government. The General Staff produced convincing documentary evidence of the guilt of Dreyfus. Zola was fined and condemned to prison, but that only added strength to the general feeling that justice had not been done. His sentence was annulled before it was enforced.

Some time later it was discovered that the documentary evidence produced at Zola's trial was a forgery. The colonel who had forged it committed suicide. Esterhazy, an officer of Polish origin, had been the real criminal. In 1906 Dreyfus was brought back from his tropical prison and restored to his rightful rank in the army. In that same year, the memory of Zola, who had died four years before, was honored by his burial in the *Panthéon* among "the great men of the fatherland." For years the Dreyfus case had aroused religious passions, disrupted political groups, and divided the country into two camps.

In 1899 a coalition ministry was formed with Waldeck-Rousseau, a moderate republican, as its chief, and with the Socialist Millerand one of its members. Thanks to its support by a *bloc républicain,* this ministry survived for nearly three years. Jean Jaurès, scholar, Socialist, and magnificent orator, was one of those who supported it. Jaurès was another, and in intellectual power a greater, Gambetta. These two sons of the *Midi* came from the vineyard country, Gambetta from Cahors, Jaurès from Castres in old Languedoc. Their lyric eloquence reflected the warmth, the generosity, the tolerant philosophy, and the ardent love of life that grow with the grape in the sunny south.

The political power of the left steadily increased. The repercussions of the Dreyfus affair had much to do with that; they tended to discredit the moderate republicans. The Radicals and the Radical-Socialists became the most powerful groups. Two Radical ministries were those of Combes from 1902 to 1905 and of Clemenceau from 1906 to 1909. But the *bloc* which sustained these ministries was unstable. A split among the Socialists led to the formation of the United Socialists, a party that proposed to socialize all production and distribution, to oppose colonial expansion, and to vote against appropriations for the army. The Millerand group could not follow their colleagues so far. They became "independent socialists," not allowing socialism to prevent co-operation with the bourgeois moderates.

Jean Jaurès, however, stood by his party. Thanks to his eloquent leadership, the anti-bourgeois Socialists won 74 seats in 1910 and 104 in 1914. When the war broke out, there was a belief that Jaurès' outspoken opposition might interfere with mobilization. As he sat one evening with friends in a boulevard *café,* he was shot. Today France does great honor to his memory.

Renewal of restraints put upon the Church led, in 1904, to a severance of diplomatic relations with the Vatican. Pius X, who became Pope in 1903, was less conciliatory than Leo XIII had been. Napoleon's *Concordat* of 1801 had given the Church a privileged status, but this contract, already violated in practice, was definitely nullified by a law passed in 1905. That law was presented and defended by Aristide Briand, a *deputé* from Brittany who, ten times prime minister, was to become the world's most eloquent advocate of peace.

The new law denied to the Catholic Church any privileges not equally enjoyed by other cults. All church edifices were declared to be state property, but the congregations and clergy were not to be dispossessed. The Pope issued an encyclical in which he forbade Catholics to form the "associations" called for by the new law. The breach between the French government and the Vatican continued from that time until after the war.

A president of France, no matter how active he may previously have been in politics, must strive to be absolutely neutral while he is president. He becomes the head, almost the figurehead, of the whole nation and ceases to be allied with any political group. Nonetheless, it is possible for him, like the King of England, to exercise great and beneficent influence. The prime ministers, *présidents du conseil,* whom he appoints are the responsible heads of the government; usually, during his seven-year term, he has a good many of them to appoint. They, in turn, appoint the ministers who serve in their cabinets.

The only presidents who have been re-elected were the second and the third, MacMahon and Grévy, and Lebrun in 1939. The election is made in a joint meeting of the *sénateurs* and the *deputés* which is held at Versailles.

After the assassination of Sadi-Carnot in 1894, Casimir-Perier was elected. He had made a brilliant record in the Franco-Prussian War. His grandfather had been Louis-Philippe's most efficient minister and his father had been a minister of the interior. He himself became *président du conseil* in 1893. Casimir-Perier was unable to be content for long with the neutrality which the presidency required. Seven months after he was elected, he resigned on the ground that he was not kept sufficiently informed about what the government was doing. He retired to private life and died in 1907.

Félix Faure, originally a businessman of Havre, succeeded Casimir-Perier. He had become a *député* in 1881 and a member of various cabinets after 1882. The Franco-Russian alliance was made in 1897 under his presidency. Faure was tactful and very popular. After four years in office, he died suddenly in 1899.

Emile Loubet was president from 1899 to 1906. He was from the south, a lawyer from the sunny and sycamore-shaded little town of Marsanne in the Drôme. *Député* in 1876, he became a *sénateur* in 1885. In 1902 President Loubet returned the visit the Czar had made to France in the previous year. In 1903 he exchanged visits with Edward VII of England; the *entente cordiale* was strengthened thereby; King Edward, familiar to Parisians as the Prince of Wales, was a great friend of France.

Clement-Armand Fallières, Loubet's successor, was also a lawyer from the *Midi,* from Mézin, a small town in the Lot-et-Garonne. *Député* in 1876, he was a colleague of Faure and Loubet in various governments after 1880. His presidency, 1906 to 1913, was marked by the separation of the Church from the State, by the final phases of the Dreyfus case, and by the difficulties with Germany about Morocco.

Raymond Poincaré, a lawyer from Bar-le-Duc in Lorraine, was president from 1913 to 1920. Eloquent, indefatigable, and scholarly, he achieved great success both in politics and in law. He became a *député* in 1887 and a cabinet member in 1893. In 1909 he had the rare honor for a politician of election to the French Academy, the "Forty Immortals." He was prime minister when elected to the presidency. His record as war president was admirable. After his retirement he was twice summoned to serve as prime minister in times of crisis. He died in 1934.

From 1871 to 1914 Europe lived through a period of armed peace, a peace that hovered more than once upon the very brink of war. Thinly veiled by the forms of international courtesy, intense economic and colonial rivalries produced a tension which made an appeal to force inevitable, inevitable because men had not outgrown belief in the justification of force.

The people of Europe played a minor role in the evolution of international politics. The governments, by secret treaties, made offensive and defensive alliances whose predication of war was not realized by the public. Continuously the governments proclaimed their hope for peace, but their continuous increase of armament indicated the emptiness of that hope.

Formation of the Triple Entente between England, France, and Russia in 1907 caused German fear of "encirclement." By this time the French people had ceased to think of a war to win back Alsace-Lorraine, the *revanchists* were but a small minority, but that old difficulty still prevented true friendship between France and Germany. Material progress only added to the threat of war through increase of economic rivalry and national ambition.

Bismarck, after the defeat of France in 1871, strengthened Germany's position by alliances with Russia, Austria, and Italy. France was isolated. In 1882 Germany, Austria, and Italy formed the Triple Alliance.

Until 1888 Bismarck dominated the development of international relationships in Europe. But in that year, Czar Alexander III, vexed by the progress of German control in the Balkans, began to show friendship for France, a friendship which the French Government ardently cultivated.

William II, who became Emperor of Germany in 1888, did not see eye to eye with Bismarck, either about foreign relations or about certain domestic policies. He took offense at the Iron Chancellor's autocratic manner. In 1890 he dismissed the venerable pilot who had so successfully steered the German Ship of State for more than a generation.

After the fall of Bismarck, France was able gradually to escape from her isolation. She made an alliance with Russia in 1891, became reconciled with Italy, and, in 1904, the *entente cordiale* with England became a reality rather than a theory. After that date, *Entente Cordiale* began to be written with capitals.

Many obstacles had to be overcome in achievement of the "inevitable alliance" between France and England. Prior to the Boer War, England showed more political sympathy for Germany than for France with whom she had come into sharp conflict over colonial questions. However, the great development of industry in Germany and the rapid increase of her fleet made England realize that she had more to fear from Germany as a rival than from France.

The Anglo-French agreements of 1904 were largely due to Edward VII, who succeeded his mother Victoria in 1901, and to Théophile Delcassé who was the French foreign minister from 1898 to 1905. Germany brought pressure upon the French Government that compelled Delcassé's resignation.

In 1907, thanks again to the pacific influence of Edward VII, England concluded an "accord" with her old rival Russia, the "Bear" that had for so long threatened her frontiers in northern India. This accord permitted the formation in the same year of the Triple Entente, composed of France, England, and Russia. Berlin, crying out against "encirclement," responded by renewing the Triple Alliance for six years. Thus was the alignment formed of the great powers which, seven years later, were to engage in the most murderous and destructive war the world has ever known.

CHAPTER THIRTY-TWO

SOCIAL, ECONOMIC, AND POLITICAL DEVELOPMENTS

IMPROVEMENT IN THE STATUS OF THE WORKERS. THE POPULATION PROB-
LEM. COLONIAL DEVELOPMENT. FAIDHERBE, GALLIENI, AND LYAUTEY. THE
RISE OF SCIENCE. THE REALISTS IN PHILOSOPHY AND LITERATURE. NIETZSCHE
AND KARL MARX. VICTOR HUGO AND LOUIS PASTEUR.

THE French people have astonishing ability to recover quickly from
disaster. They showed this ability after the Hundred Years' War,
after the religious wars of the Sixteenth Century, and after Waterloo.
But never have they shown it more clearly than in the years that followed Prussia's triumph. Between 1871 and 1914, despite frequent
political and social crises, the economic life of France made steady
progress. As early as 1873, even with the loss of two of her most
productive provinces and of more than a million and a half of her
inhabitants, France's volume of business surpassed that of the pre-
war years.

In 1878 an *Exposition universelle* attracted sixteen million visitors
to Paris. The world's interest in France was undiminished. Her defeat by Germany did not lessen her social and intellectual prestige.
There appeared to be more of sympathy for the vanquished than of
admiration for the victor. It was evident that the world, as a whole,
was not prepared to worship at the shrine of force.

In the last decades of the Nineteenth Century, Germany, England,
the United States, and France were all busily occupied with the building of factories and the laying of railroads. In those years the
foundations were laid upon which a new economic order was to be
established, an order that would lead to profound social and political
changes. France, always conservative about material progress because
she is more interested in other things, was a laggard in this development. The number of her factory workers rose from five million in
1870 to eight million in 1914, but, nonetheless, the country remained

primarily agricultural. Between the factories and the farms an equilibrium of production was maintained. Both in England and in Germany industry in this period outstripped agriculture and those countries became increasingly dependent upon others for their food supply.

In one item of major importance French agriculture suffered a grievous blow. The production of wine in 1889 was only one-third of what it had been in 1875. This was due to an outbreak of phylloxera, a grapevine disease that came from America. Its ravages were arrested only by the use of phylloxera-resistant stocks, also imported from America. The wine grapes of France are produced from shoots that are still grafted upon hardy roots and stems of American lineage.

The competition of foreign manufactured goods led to abandonment of the free-trade policy which had been introduced by Napoleon III. The erection of tariff barriers began in 1892. France was not alone in erecting them, but, despite the tariffs, international trade increased. The value of France's imports rose from four to eight billion francs per annum between 1892 and 1905.

The railroad mileage increased from about eleven thousand in 1870 to about thirty-two thousand in 1914. The early efforts of the radicals to obtain national owership of the railroads were unsuccessful. Later, however, the state acquired ownership of some of the more important lines and control of the others. The telegraph system was a part of the post office from the beginning. The telephone lines were purchased by the state in 1889. Since that time there has been a united governmental administration of the postal, telegraphic, and telephonic services.

The rapid increase of the national wealth was not accompanied by equity in its distribution. France, in proportion to her population, has had a larger and more prosperous middle class than any other European country, but the statistics of 1900 showed that two-thirds of the property inherited that year went to no more than two per cent of all the heirs. It could not be expected that the French people would be permanently submissive to such economic maladjustment as these figures represented.

Large concentrations of capital became controlled by corporations.

There was a steady diminution of personal relations between employers and employees. An inevitable result was to increase the strength of the workers' organizations and to enlarge their interest in politics. The workers perceived that their only chance to resist the tyranny of concentrated capital lay in increase of their own political power.

The formation of unions was encouraged by political leaders who believed that unionization would diminish the danger of revolution; the workers would learn through experience to negotiate rather than to fight. The *loi Waldeck-Rousseau* of 1884 removed all restraints upon the formation of unions; by 1913 there were more than five thousand of them with a total membership in excess of a million. Today the *Confédération générale du Travail* is the parent organization of the syndicated workers of France. Popularly known as the "C.G.T.," it is one of the major factors in the political and economic life of the nation.*

Increase of their political influence led to gradual improvement of the material situation of the workers. The abolition of the *livret* in 1890 freed them from their previous semi-military servitude; they ceased to be a class rigidly set apart from the rest of society. Increase of pay and decrease in the hours of work were more difficult to obtain. The *loi Millerand* of 1900 called for progressive reduction of the working day so that, after four years, it should be ten hours long instead of twelve. But this law applied only to factories in which women and children were employed. The twelve-hour day remained the standard. Even the six-day week was not legally required until 1906.

---

* The C.G.T. has important political influence, but it is not a political party. A majority of the workers are socialists. Some belong to the Communist party, but few of them advocate complete communism; no idea is more foreign to the common mind of France than the idea of sacrifice of individual ownership. The French workers ask for social justice, but they retain their traditional devotion to individualism.

The republican belief that the organization of labor would lead to less rather than to more of violence has been, on the whole, justified. There have been many strikes, but they have been accompanied by less violence than has been witnessed in some other countries. The "sit-down" strikes of 1936 were remarkable for their orderliness. There was no loss of life and the damage to property was negligible. Factories and stores were returned to the control of their owners in even better condition than when the strikes began. The Socialist program stressed the education of the workers and increased their respect for property. They protected the property of their employers as though it had been their own. They had acquired a feeling of moral if not actual partnership in ownership of the factories, public utilities, and stores that they operated.

The average daily wage of the workers rose from forty-five cents in 1853 to ninety cents in 1921, but the increase in cost of living was not much less than the increase in wages. The workers were able to eat meat more frequently and to wear better clothes, but there was little improvement in the condition of their homes. Education, enlargement of production, and the expansion of luxury all contributed to increase of the wants of the workers. Thus, despite better material conditions, there was little diminution of discontent. The workers of 1921 were no better satisfied with their lot than their grandfathers had been. The economic gap between them and their employers had not been lessened; the lion's share of the profits still went to the schemers rather than to the workers. There had been an increase in pay, but there had been no increase in equity of distribution.

Between 1871 and 1914 there developed a situation which, more than any other, threatened, and continues to threaten, the future of France. In 1870 her population was about the same as that of England and the United States, thirty-eight million. In all Europe only Russia exceeded France in man power. But, in 1913, Germany had sixty-seven million, Austro-Hungary fifty-three, and England forty-six. France, remaining stationary, fell to fifth place. She had to let in foreigners to help do her work in fields and factories; in 1913 more than a million of them were resident in France. The population pressures from hungrier countries that had led to invasions in the early centuries became evident again. There began to be talk of French "decadence" and of "race suicide." Even in the 1880's it was said that "the five hungry sons of a German family will easily prevail over the one son of a French family."

In later years arrest of increase in population has also occurred in England and the United States. Education and improved economic conditions have brought small families in their train. As civilization has become more urban, large families have become a liability rather than an asset. In a world controlled by reason, this might be well. But if force is to prevail, the result will be obviously unfortunate for those states whose populations remain stationary or diminish.

When the Third Republic began, France's colonies, compared with those of England, were almost negligible. There were less than five million inhabitants in the regions she controlled in Africa and in Indo-China. But by 1914 her colonial possessions had increased tenfold both in population and in area. The volume of her colonial trade rose from six hundred million francs per annum to three thousand million.

Jules Ferry inaugurated in 1880 the policy which led to this enormous expansion. His policy was vigorously opposed by many who believed that it would make France less able to defend herself. Ferry was accused of playing into the hands of Bismarck. In 1885 he was compelled to resign as prime minister because a majority voted against him on a question that involved his colonial policy. Succeeding governments, however, continued the work that he had begun. The success of it gradually silenced even the opposition of the radicals.

The most important developments were in northern Africa. From Algeria, French control was extended to Tunisia on the east, to Morocco on the west, and southward into the Sahara. In Morocco the principal difficulty was with a hard-fighting native population. In Tunisia the chief complication was the presence there of Italian colonists.

Tunisia, prior to 1881, was a vassal state of Turkey. In that year its sovereign *bey* signed a treaty which made it a protectorate of France. Colonization began at once, but the French colonists were outnumbered by Italians who showed little inclination to become French citizens. The status of Tunisia has continued to trouble Franco-Italian relations.

Morocco was an independent empire, mountainous and rich in natural resources. The continuity of its shoreline on the Atlantic and on the Mediterranean gave it great strategic importance. Nonetheless, it retained its medieval isolation until the end of the Nineteenth Century. Tangiers was the only port in which Europeans had gained a foothold. Spain, having found Morocco too tough a nut to crack, contented herself with a few fortified posts on the coast.

France realized that control of Morocco by another power would endanger her whole position in Africa. But it required unremitting effort from 1902 to 1912 for her to gain control for herself. Diplomatic as well as military difficulties had to be overcome. Agadir is a

Moroccan port on the Atlantic. In 1911, while French forces were operating in the interior, Germany, by sending a warship to Agadir, indicated that she would dispute the enlargement of French influence in that region. England made it clear that she would oppose German interference. There was a threat of war. However, when France made concessions to Germany in the Congo, Germany agreed to recognize French control of Morocco. By the Convention of Fez of 1911, Morocco became a protectorate of France.

The *Maréchal* Lyautey was the civil as well as the military hero of France in Morocco. His pacification and administration of that difficult area is one of the bright chapters in colonial history. France has modernized northern Africa from the Libyan desert to the Atlantic. Her development of that region has been one of the most significant achievements of the Twentieth Century. The wise policies which Lyautey inaugurated have resulted in a true loyalty to France on the part of the natives, and fulfillment of his economic plans has completely changed the face of the country. Northern Africa has become a part rather than a colony of France, a part upon which she is increasingly dependent.

The word Sudan comes from an Arabic expression which means "country of the blacks." It names a wide belt of territory that stretches across the African continent, south of the desert of Sahara, from the Atlantic Ocean to the Red Sea. The eastern part of it is the Anglo-Egyptian Sudan. The western part, traversed by the Niger river and lying north of the great Gulf of Guinea, is partly French and partly English; before the war it was also partly German.

The French colonies in the western Sudan constitute *Afrique occidentale française*. Colonies that lie farther to the south and east form *Afrique équatoriale française*. These separately administered regions are referred to as "A.O.F." and "A.E.F." Each has its own governor general.

Before 1871, Senegal on the western coast was the only important French colony in tropical Africa. It was developed by Faidherbe, as described in a previous chapter. After 1875, explorations of the interior led to vast increases of the French domain. Savorgnan de Brazza was the most notable of the explorers. He won the western part of the lower Congo valley without having to fight for it. His chief competitor in exploration of this difficult region was the American, Henry M. Stanley. The eastern side of the Congo valley and all its upper reaches were claimed by Stanley for Leopold II of Belgium.

French expeditions into the upper valley of the Niger and into Dahomey met with great difficulties, both on account of native resistance and on account of the rival claims of England. Ultimately, however, the territory which now forms "A.O.F." was extended westward to Lake Tchad, following the northern boundary of England's Nigeria.

The A.O.F. has become a very valuable possession. Its climate is favorable to the development of its natural resources, and its native Senegalese and Soudanese have proved their worth as soldiers in fighting for France. They helped to save Verdun.

The economic development of the A.E.F. has been difficult. There the natives are more primitive and the climate far less healthful than in the A.O.F. This equatorial region is, however, rich in possibilities, especially for the production of rubber and for the exploitation of its forest resources.

France's effort to gain a foothold in the upper part of the valley of the Nile was repulsed by England. Her control on the east side of Africa is limited to a strip of territory in the Somali country. In 1880 she founded the port of Djibouti on the coast, and began the construction of a railroad into Abyssinia. (Italy's possession of Abyssinia makes her covetous of Djibouti and of the railroad.)

In the days of Richelieu a French fort was built on the southern tip of the great island of Madagascar. Established in 1642, it was abandoned a few years later, but the shadowy claim which it symbolized was not forgotten. In the middle of the Nineteenth Century, England and France competed for control of the Malay princes, themselves invaders, who ruled at Tananarive, the populous capital of the island. France, despite expeditions that met with disaster, finally prevailed over the Malays. Madagascar became a French colony in 1896. It took years, however, to perfect the administration of this rich territory and to pacify its people. That was done by Gallieni, a master in colonial diplomacy and a superb administrator, the same Gallieni who, in 1914, led the "taxicab army" from Paris to the first battle of the Marne.

Cochin-China and Cambodia were won for France in the time of the Second Empire. To these colonies in Indo-China the Third Republic added Annam, Tonkin, and Laos. China opposed the French in Tonkin. In March, 1885, it was inaccurately reported in Paris that a French force had been disastrously defeated. On that ground Clemenceau bitterly attacked Ferry and obtained a vote of the *Chambre* that compelled his resignation as prime minister. Ferry, when he was attacked, knew that peace was about to be concluded with the Chinese, but, since he had given his word not to speak of the negotiations that were in progress, he accepted in silence a political defeat which he might have turned into victory.

The prosperity of French Indo-China depends largely upon its large production and exportation of rice. In late years the agitations for political independence in India have been reflected in Annam and Tonkin. French control is not so firmly established in Indo-China as it is in Algeria and Morocco, but the policy of "education, collaboration, and friendship" has prevented insurrections which might otherwise have occurred. Voluntary service in the French army is popular with the Annamites; they rendered important service behind the front in the Great War.

Faidherbe, Gallieni, and Lyautey were three great artisans of colonial policy and practice. Their methods are suggested in the following extract from Gallieni's instructions to his subordinates in Madagascar. "Force should be used only when absolutely unavoidable. . . . In case the destruction of a village cannot be avoided, reconstruction should follow immediately. A market place should be created and a school established. . . . The use of tact is always to be preferred to the use of force." Whatever the theoretical criticisms of colonial procedures may be, it is a fact that the native populations which have accepted French administration have, in general, greatly benefited thereby. There has been a minimum of interference with traditional customs and religions, and services rendered to France have been quickly honored by official recognition.

The peace of Europe from 1871 to 1914 was an armed peace. There was constant threat of a new Franco-Prussian war. England strove to prevent the outbreak of hostilities, as well as to serve her own interests, by continuance of her traditional "balance-of-power" policy, but her own economic and political development made it increasingly difficult for her to make this policy successful. Socially, economically, historically, and racially she had more in common with Germany than with France, but, when it comes to war, things more fundamental than social, economic, and historic considerations may determine a nation's attitude. With respect to freedom, individualism and social responsibility there was in France and England a similar evolution of ideas that inevitably brought them together despite the intensity of their antagonisms in other fields. About these matters there was a convergence of French and English thought, whereas German thought took another and less democratic direction.

Despite the international tension which existed, material and intellectual progress was not arrested. Fascinated by the evidences of that progress, the world forgot the precariousness of its peace. It seemed incredible that this happy and well-nigh universal enrichment of human life should be arrested again by war, that the nations which had produced Pasteur, Darwin, and Tolstoy could not find a way to avoid a return to the horrors of savagery. Men seemed to have grown too intelligent to permit that to happen. Progressive betterment of the world seemed to be assured at last. But the philosopher who had the most influence upon German thought was Nietzsche, and his philosophy was not an endorsement either of democracy or of peace.

Toward the end of the Nineteenth Century science began to exert a preponderant influence, an influence that extended far beyond its original subject matter. The scientific method affected the technique of philosophy, art, and literature. Its only rival in intellectual influence was the principle of democracy. Acceptance of the validity of this principle by the democratic countries rested on faith rather than on evidence.

Enlargements of the electorate were made on the basis of an optimism about human nature which the facts may not have justified. In the belief that democracy could be perfected by education, educational opportunity was greatly extended. The effect of public education upon the quality of citizenship was debatable, but its effect upon literacy was undeniable. The circulation of books and newspapers increased enormously, and so did popular interest in music and the drama. Superficial culture became widespread. The new intellectual demand increased intellectual production, in quantity and diversity if not in quality. The new and rapid means of communication so facilitated the spread of ideas that culture began to become cosmopolitan rather than national. There was a world interchange of thought.

Taine and Renan were the leaders of philosophical thought in France. They were both devotees of the scientific approach. More conservative thinkers questioned the complete validity of the inductive method when applied to philosophy and religion, but, to Taine and Renan, conclusions reached by any other method were unacceptable. The work of Darwin and Spencer added such prestige to the scientific method that, in the last years of the century, the anti-scientists were definitely on the defensive.

In 1906 the mathematician Jules-Henri Poincaré, a cousin of President Raymond Poincaré, published a book entitled *Valeur de la Science*. Poincaré was a pioneer among the scientists of distinction who have acknowledged the limitations of the method of science as an instrument for the discernment of truth. He admitted his belief in things which are not scientifically demonstrable. The American William James and the Frenchman Bergson made further contributions to arguments and to evidence which tended to limit science to what they believed to be its proper domain.

Nietzsche also escaped the restraints of science. His genius ended in hopeless insanity, but that did not lessen the popularity in Germany of his "will-to-power" philosophy. He found virtue in "supermen" who dared to live dangerously and to free themselves from the moral restraints of ordinary mortals.

The danger of the scientific method when too rigorously applied to the solution of human problems is exemplified in the work of the man who has had the greatest influence upon the thought of the workers. Karl Marx maintained that man's social behavior is determined by economic factors. Since philanthropy is negligible as compared with acquisitiveness, capitalism is necessarily less interested in social justice than in its own increase. Therefore, class warfare is inevitable, and social justice can be achieved only after capitalism is destroyed. All who believe that the economic urge is the major determinant of human behavior thereby accept the premise upon which Karl Marx built up his impressively logical argument. If capitalism is to be saved, it appears that there must be a diminution of interest in the accumulation and conservation of capital. There must be a new realization that acquisitiveness defeats its own ends, and that security is permanently attainable only when material values are subordinated to spiritual values.

In literature, science contributed to the reaction from romanticism and to the movement toward realism. Young writers, witnessing the dazzling results of progress in science and industry, lost their faith in idealism; they saw materialism dominant in the new and more luxurious world; Mammon was the god that the Second Empire worshiped. Their vision of life became like that of scientists who accept as truth only that which can be demonstrated. Many of the new writers were "realists." They portrayed the obvious and usually the more sordid aspects of life. They ignored its idealism and its spiritual qualities; because these may not be weighed or measured, their actuality is questionable.

The novelists Flaubert and the Goncourt brothers were leaders of the realists. Flaubert, despite his realism, remained faithful to classic forms, but Edmond and Jules de Goncourt wrote about the lives of the underprivileged in a style that was all their own; their esteem of science did not lessen their unscientific devotion to democracy. Zola carried realism beyond the limits of common decency; his obscenity was super-realistic, but his passion for justice betrayed him as a romantic at heart.

Toward the end of the century the novel was used for the presentation of all sorts of ideas. Pierre Loti used it as a medium for the presentation of fantastic descriptions, Maurice Barrés used it as a camouflage for cynical commentary, and Anatole France used it as a foundation for brilliant philosophical banter. In 1897 Edmond Rostand's *Cyrano de Bergerac* marked a definite revival of romanticism.

Both in prose and in poetry, both before the Second Empire and after it, both as realist and as romanticist, there was one great literary figure in France with which no other could compare. The fall of Louis-Napoleon permitted Victor Hugo to return from exile. His ardent devotion to republican and humanitarian ideals had made him beloved by the people. His funeral in 1885 was a national event. His body lay in state under the *Arc de Triomphe* and was followed by thousands to its final resting place in the Pantheon.

In 1822, at Dôle which lies between Dijon and Besançon, there was born one whose life and work, more than that of any other man, symbolizes and summarizes the modern French idealism. Louis Pasteur is the nation's most popular hero. He had naught to do with war nor with political strife. He worked obscurely in a dingy laboratory, devoting his life to a search for truth that mankind might benefit thereby. He was a hero of peace.

When he was twenty Pasteur came to Paris to study at the *Ecole normale supérieure.* Afterward he became a professor of chemistry at Dijon and at Strasbourg. In 1857 he returned to Paris as director of science in the school from which he had graduated. There he did the work which revolutionized man's conception of the nature and prevention of disease. He died at Marnes-la-Coquette, near Paris, in 1895.

There was violent opposition to the acceptance of Pasteur's new ideas. His "germ theory" called for a revolution in medical procedure. His presentation of that theory before the Academy of Medicine was met with derision. Many influential men sought to discredit him. But the truth presently prevailed. The old idea of "spontaneous generation" went into the discard. Pasteur's research had revealed the existence of disease-producing bacteria. Procedure to destroy them, antisepsis, became basic in medical practice; the art of healing multiplied its efficiency. The Pasteurization of milk has become familiar to all. Pasteur's studies of fermentation led to fundamental changes in the manufacture of beer and wine.

By constant and patient research he enlarged the practical applications of his discoveries. His study of animal diseases saved the sheep from a plague which threatened their extermination. He prepared a virus whose injection into the blood stream might counteract the effect of a mad dog's bite; poison to be overcome by poison. His whole career hung in the balance when he first applied this treatment, but a child's life was saved and the great labor of a courageous scientist was vindicated.

If the French were a nation of glory lovers, they might not so greatly honor the memory of Pasteur. He typifies neither glory nor power nor conquest. He typifies rather that element in man which may enable him to rise to things which are superior to glory, power, or conquest. Dimly we perceive today that the preservation of human opportunity depends upon the spread of the spirit which animated Louis Pasteur. He neglected materialism and devoted himself to an indomitable search for truth in the service of his fellow men. It is because of his spirit even more than because of his achievements that France believes Pasteur to have been the greatest of her great men.

In material force France may have become a "second-rate power," but the turning of her hero-worship from Napoleon to Pasteur suggests that her spiritual force has not diminished. The significance of modern France to the world depends upon the world. It depends upon man's ability to discern that those things which concern his spirit are even more important than those things which concern his body.

POSTSCRIPTUM

HISTORY is a record of courage and of frailty, of construction and of destruction, a record in which valiant struggles to enlarge man's opportunity alternate with pathetic failures to fulfill opportunities that were won. History makes it clear that the success of any system whereby men seek to improve their status depends far less upon the system than upon the spirit of those who compose it. The great problems reduce themselves to the problem of the individual, a problem whose magnitude has multiplied as freedom has increased. The hope that remains for a good society can be no other than hope for greater goodness of the individual. Democracy has done little to fulfill that hope, but autocracy has done less. Under autocracy man's body may be fed, but his spirit is starved. His growth in social-mindedness is stultified.

Democracy blunders along and pays dearly for its slow learning, but it does not deprive its people of opportunity to learn, of their opportunity to learn now, if they will, that they are living in a world so interlocked that international co-operation has become imperative. The citizens of the democracies are permitted to perceive, if they will, that the ideal of human brotherhood has become more than an ideal. It has become a necessity. But modern autocracies have deprived their submissive subjects of opportunity to learn the truth, the truth that shall make men free, the truth that, if man is to be saved from himself, his brotherhood must now run beyond its old frontiers.

He who has stripped the scales of prejudice from his eyes sees clearly that man has so transformed the modern world that, if liberty is to survive, we must break out of the strait jacket of old boundaries, boundaries of the mind as well as of the nations.

When freedom dies, human opportunity dies with it. Without freedom man may not see the truth; his vision becomes distorted. France has fought to preserve freedom of vision and of opportunity. Modern autocratic states have sought to destroy that opportunity. They have darkened the windows through which their people might

see the world as it is and their fellow men as they are. They have
made it impossible for their people to realize that the only hope for
peace lies in the enlargement of tolerance, of co-operation, of charity,
and of brotherhood.

In the history of France we are impressed by two things which are
antithetic. One is the reasonableness of old demands for greater pol-
litical freedom, for less economic inequality, for justice. The other is
the justification of those who, in the interest of order, resisted these
demands. Those who fought for greater freedom hoped that their
victory would bring justice in its wake. Repeatedly that hope was
disappointed. More than once a dearly-won freedom opened the
door to abuses no less than those which had been destroyed. The
common man often proved to be no less rapacious than the tyrant,
and, through his own misdeeds, permitted the restoration of tyranny.
Only the Third Republic, and it by the narrowest of margins, has
survived despite disorder, malfeasance, economic distress, and mis-
carriages of justice. Only since 1871 has France been able to resist
those powerful forces which would push her back again into autocracy. The threat of those forces has not ceased. Their victory would
be disastrous to the cause of human opportunity throughout the
world.

The history of France gives support both to the optimism of the
liberals and to the pessimism of the conservatives. If it be true that
"human nature never changes," pessimism is justified. The optimism
of humanists and liberals rests upon the belief that education and
experience may lead men to realize the folly of unsocial behavior.
Man's nature may not change, but its manifestations may be modified.
He may yet justify his freedom. History, despite its many dark pages,
supports the latter view rather than the former. It does not prove
the case of the pessimists. If it did, France's Third Republic would
have long since gone the way of its first one.

Nonetheless, faith in the achievement of justice through freedom
is almost outweighed by evidence of the inability of free men to be
just. Having valiantly gained new liberties, men have hastened to
abuse them. Thiers was more than once a witness of his countrymen's
inability to achieve justice without injustice. His record portrays the
realism which has tempered the idealism of the French mind since

his time. A leader of revolution in 1830, he became a leader of conservatism in 1848. He achieved that mental balance in the face of conflicting claims which is essential to successful statesmanship. He saved France from a return to autocracy, but he firmly applied the brakes of conservatism to the republic which he guided through its most precarious years. He believed in justice, but not at the price of disorder. He knew that the health of the nation required prudent control of the growth of liberty.

With all her faults and shortcomings, France has preserved what, in the interest of humanity, has been most precious to preserve. She has preserved freedom of opportunity for the human spirit. She has fought, and she continues to fight, upon a frontier of freedom where attack has been incessant. Her case is not like ours. The United States has inherited the most fortunate situation in the world in which to put to the proof man's ability to be just when he is free. No autocracies have pressed upon our borders, invaded us, threatened our very existence. No royalists have constantly striven to restore an *ancien régime*. No Napoleonic legend has dazzled our people with dreams of glory. If anti-democratic forces have arisen in our midst, we have ourselves to blame.

It has not been like that with France. Constantly she has felt compelled to drain her strength, not for conquest, but for the defense of her existence as a free people. She has defended a frontier of liberty whose loss would be our loss as well as hers. We are only beginning to realize the importance to us of her defense of that frontier.

Would that the isolationists were right! Would that we could foresee the day when America's aloofness would be justified, the day when there would be a better world because America took no part in the defense of freedom! But that day will not come. The isolationists are wrong. The world is not what they presume it to be. They do not lead us away from war. For war can be avoided and liberty preserved only through the co-operative effort of nations that still are free, nations whose people are able to perceive that man's only chance for a better future lies in the betterment of his spirit. Material loss he can repair, but the loss of those immaterial values which France defends would be irreparable. Will it require another Armageddon to make us see where our greater interest lies?

INDEX

INDEX

445